# Macroeconomics

## A Modern Approach

**Robert J. Barro**

Harvard University

THOMSON

SOUTH-WESTERN

Australia · Brazil · Canada · Mexico · Singapore · Spain · United Kingdom · United States

**THOMSON**

**SOUTH-WESTERN**

Macroeconomics: A Modern Approach
Robert J. Barro

**VP/Editorial Director:**
Jack W. Calhoun

**Editor-in-Chief:**
Alex von Rosenberg

**Sr. Acquisitions Editor:**
Michael Worls

**Sr. Developmental Editor:**
Jennifer Baker

**Sr. Marketing Manager:**
John Carey

**Content Project Manager:**
Robert Dreas

**Marketing Communications Manager:**
Sarah Greber

**Technology Project Manager:**
Dana Cowden

**Sr. 1st Print Buyer:**
Sandee Milewski

**Production House:**
ICC Macmillan Inc.

**Printer:**
R.R. Donnelley
Willard, Ohio

**Art Director:**
Michelle Kunkler

**Internal Designer:**
Michael Stratton Design

**Cover Designer:**
Michael Stratton Design

**Cover Images:**
© Getty Image

**Illustration:**
LaFleur Studio

Library of Congress Control Number:
2006908079

For more information about our products, contact us at:

Thomson Learning Academic Resource Center

1-800-423-0563

**Thomson Higher Education**
5191 Natorp Boulevard
Mason, OH 45040
USA

*To Rachel, Zac, and Wiggles.*

# Barro – An Integrated, Modern Approach

Offering a uniquely modern presentation of macroeconomics, leading economist and proven author Robert J. Barro makes it easy for you to use solid microfoundations for macroeconomic analyses. These tools are applied to an equilibrium business-cycle model and to alternatives, including new Keyensian analysis. *Macroeconomics: A Modern Approach* begins with theoretical and empirical analysis of economic growth, and then continues to studies of economic fluctuations, monetary models, the government sector, and international macroeconomics. The consistent use of microfoundations and equilibrium analysis creates a groundbreaking new macroeconomics textbook resonating with real-world applications. Accessibly written and student friendly, the book is packed with current policy and data examples, reflecting Barro's extensive research in the field. He has also included challenging exercises, innovative online resources like *ThomsonNOW™*, and captivating boxed features that are sure to grab your attention and bring home to readers the real impact of contemporary macroeconomics.

**Four different boxed features support the story of fully modern and accessible macro theory.**

## (1) *Back To Reality*

- *Back to Reality* situates theory in the real world with historical and policy examples. A feature in chapter 2 discusses controversy with the consumer price index and its ramifications (with entitlement programs such as social security tied to CPI) and chapter 5 discusses the author's meeting with U2's Bono, and the rock star's perspective on debt relief and foreign aid. An example in chapter 10 also asks, "Where is all the currency?"

### Back To Reality

**Where is all the currency?**

As mentioned, in March 2006, the amount of U.S. currency held by the public was about $2,500 per person in the United States. To understand this surprisingly large number, start with the observation that, at the end of 2005, 72% of currency in circulation by value, including coins, was in $100 bills. (The data on currency by denomination are in the *Treasury Bulletin*.) Thus, much of the currency is likely not used for ordinary transactions. Because currency is anonymous, it is attractive for illegal activities, such as the drug trade. Currency transactions also facilitate tax evasion. However, the amount of U.S. currency held for these purposes is unknown.

More is known about the amounts of U.S. currency held abroad, mostly in the form of $100 bills. Foreigners like U.S. money as a store of value and a medium of exchange because the money has a reasonably stable value and

can readily be exchanged for goods or other assets. In addition, transactions carried out in currency can usually be hidden from local governments, and this secrecy is particularly attractive when the government is oppressive. The foreign demand for U.S. currency is especially high in countries experiencing economic and political turmoil. A recent joint study by the Federal Reserve and the U.S. Treasury estimated that 55–60% of the total U.S. currency in circulation in 2002 was held abroad. The geographical division was estimated to be 25% in Latin America (with Argentina the highest demander), 20% in the Middle East and Africa, 15% in Asia, and 40% in Europe (with Russia and other former Soviet republics as particularly high users). For additional discussion, see Richard Porter and Ruth Judson (2001) and Board of Governors of the Federal Reserve System (2003).

## *Extending The Model*

9038.0
18.860
7.7577
61.851

**Demand and supply curves are functions**

The market demand for coffee can be written as a function:

$$Q_c^d = D(P_c, Y, P_T)$$

The function $D(\cdot)$ determines the quantity of coffee demanded, $Q_c^d$, for any specified values of the three demand determinants: $P_c$, Y, and $P_T$. We assume that the function $D(\cdot)$ has the properties that $Q_c^d$ decreases with the price of coffee, $P_c$, rises with income, Y, and rises with ... f tea, $P_T$. Figure 1.7 graphs $Q_c^d$ against ... of the other demand deter-

between quantity demanded and price, $D(\cdot)$, whereas the quantity demanded, $Q_c^d$, refers to one of the points along the curve.

The market supply of coffee is also a function, which can be written as

$$Q_c^s = S(P_c, weather)$$

We assume that the function $S(\cdot)$ has the properties that the quantity supplied, $Q_c^s$, rises with $P_c$ and with better weather in coffee-producing areas. Figure 1.8 graphs the quantity supplied, $Q_c^s$, against $P_c$, for given weather conditions. It is important to remember that the supply curve, $S(\cdot)$, refers to the whole functional relationship between quantity supplied and price, $Q_c^s$, refers to the quantity supplied, ... along the curve.

## (2) *Extending The Model*

- *Extending the Model* helps to clarify and build on chapter concepts, such as showing how supply and demand curves are functions (chapter 1), and exploring endogenous population growth (chapter 4).

### By The Numbers

- *By the Numbers* shows empirical data, and how it is used by macro-economists. For example, one box shows an overview of Gross State Products for the U.S., examining how each state contributes to GDP (chapter 2), while another looks at empirical evidence for the response of consumption to anticipated income changes (chapter 7).

9038.0
18.860
7.7577
61.851

## By The Numbers

**Empirical evidence on intertemporal substitution of consumption**

The intertemporal-substitution effect predicts that a higher interest rate motivates households to reduce current consumption compared to future consumption. A study by David Runkle (1991) isolated the effect of interest rates on consumption by examining food outlays for 1100 U.S. households from 1973 to 1982. (The data are from the *Panel Study of Income Dynamics*, or PSID, conducted at the University of Michigan.) Runkle found that an increase in the annual interest rate by one percentage point raises the typical family's growth rate of consumption by about one-half percentage point per year.

The isolation of intertemporal-substitution effects in aggregate consumption data has proven to be more difficult, as discussed by Robert Hall (1989). However, a study of U.S. non-durable consumption by Joon-Ho Hahm (1998) estimated that a rise in the annual interest rate by one percentage point increases the growth rate of aggregate consumption by around one-third percentage point per year. Thus, the intertemporal-substitution effect does apply to aggregate consumption data.

## Do The Math

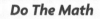

We can determine the steady-state capital per worker, $k^*$, algebraically from the steady-state condition given in equation (3.19). We repeat this result here:

(4.4)        $A \cdot f(k^*)/k^* = \delta + n/s$

An increase in $s$ lowers the right-hand side. Hence, the left-hand side must be lower, and this reduction can occur only through a decrease in the average product of capital, $A \cdot f(k^*)/k^*$. We know from Figure 3.8 that, if $A$ is fixed, a decrease in the average product of capital requires an increase in capital per worker, $k$. Therefore, an increase in $s$ raises $k^*$.

### Do The Math

- *Do the Math* helps lead readers through the algebra used in careful steps. For example, as chapter 4 explores working with the Solow Growth Model, numerous *Do the Math* boxes help students grasp concepts and work through the model as the theory is explained.

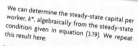

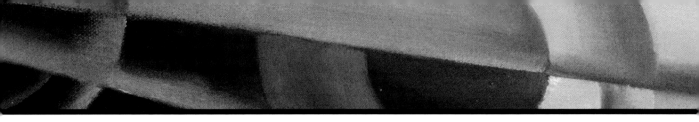

# *ThomsonNOW™* and BCRC for Barro

## *ThomsonNOW™*

Designed by instructors for instructors, *ThomsonNOW* is the most reliable, flexible, and easy-to-use online suite of services and resources. *ThomsonNOW* for Economics takes the best of current technology tools including online homework management; a fully customizable test bank; and course materials such as a customized learning path, videos, and tutorials to support your course goals and save you significant preparation and grading time!

This powerful, fully integrated online teaching and learning system provides you with the ultimate in flexibility, ease of use, and efficient paths to success to deliver the results you want—NOW!

- **Plan** student assignments with easy online homework management.
- **Manage** your grade book with ease.
- **Teach** today's student using valuable course support materials.
- **Reinforce** student comprehension with personalized study plans.
- **Test** with a customizable test bank.
- **Grade** automatically for seamless, immediate results.

## Business and Company Resource Center (BCRC)

Barro keeps you and your students up-to-date and continually interacting with the business world by offering students an opportunity to search articles located in our BCRC. Reading business and economic articles encourages students to apply their knowledge of concepts discussed in the text to the ideas in the articles. The BCRC opens up an entire database in which they can research company histories, articles, industry data, company financials and more!

**Business & Company**
RESEARCH CENTER
PL: 91 1/8  DIS: 27 7/8  K
THOMSON GALE

# New! Tomlinson Economics Videos!

**TOMLINSON ECONOMICS VIDEOS**

Thomson South-Western is excited to announce our new **Economic JumpStart®
Videos**! Featuring award-winning teacher and professional communicator, Steven
Tomlinson (Ph.D, Stanford), these web-based lecture videos are sure to engage
your students, while reviewing and reinforcing the foundational economic concepts they need to know

## Economic JumpStart® Videos

*Great resources to accompany any Economics text, these segments are designed
to make sure that your students are on a firm foundation before moving on to
more advanced topics in the course.*

Save valuable class time by eliminating the need to review fundamental economic concepts. The **Economic JumpStart** web-based video package contains all of
the introductory "building block" topics from the ***Economics with Steven
Tomlinson*** video text with approximately 5 hours of video lecture and demon-
stration (more than 45 segments). This package is ideal when used at the beginning of an intermediate course to ensure that students have a review of the
building block topics that they covered in their principles course and that they

will need to ensure success
in the intermediate course.
When used with a Thomson
South-Western economics
book, your students can take
advantage of a significant
cost savings.

***Economics with Steven
Tomlinson*** is a complete online
course that presents and develops
the fundamentals of economics.
This online text offers comprehen-
sive coverage of economic principles with more than 40 hours of
video lecture.

For more information on these videos, please visit
**www.thomsonedu.com/economics/tomlinson/videos**

# Preface

## Sound Theory and a Unified Approach

Macroeconomics and microeconomics are the two pillars of economics. Yet, there is a wide gulf between the two pillars in the undergraduate curriculum. Micro courses teach material that is easier but basically consistent with the content taught to graduate students and used by economists in their research. In contrast, macro courses often bear little resemblance to graduate courses or academic research. Undergraduate macro textbooks and courses seem frequently to compromise good economics for presentations that are breezy, closely linked to arguments found in the popular press, and not very intellectually challenging. But sacrificing solid economics to capture student interest is not necessary—sound theory can be clearly written with vivid examples to reinforce it.

My dissatisfaction with the textbook environment motivated me to write my first intermediate macro textbook in 1984. That book appeared in five editions, and I like to think it had a positive impact—directly and also indirectly—in terms of influencing the subject matter and approaches of competitor works. Yet there have been tremendous advances in macroeconomic theory and evidence over the last 20 years, and much of this research was left out of my earlier books. I also think I have progressed over time in my ability to convey serious macroeconomics in an accessible, engaging way. Hence, I decided to put my energies into this new book, *Macroeconomics: A Modern Approach*.

In addition to providing a more accurate presentation of the current state of macroeconomic thought, this text provides a unified approach that most macro textbooks lack. Rather than presenting a completely new model when shifting from a discussion of long-run theory to short-run theory, this book develops short-run and long-run models that build on one another in a natural, comprehensible, and elegant way. And all this is done *without* ignoring the important differences between the economy in the long run and the short run. Similarly, I bring in the Keynesian idea of sticky prices as a new idea but one that builds coherently on the structure of the basic equilibrium model.

## Organizational Structure

### Long-Term Growth

I now begin with long-run macroeconomics—that is, with the determinants of long-term economic growth. Great advances in theory and empirical analysis took place in this area since the late 1980s. Fortunately, it is possible to convey these important findings to undergraduates in a manageable and interesting way. In fact, students can understand the exciting results (in Chapters 3–5) without having to first master the details of the underlying microeconomic foundations (which come in Chapters 6 and 7). This early consideration of results with important policy implications helps to drive home the impact and relevance of macroeconomics.

### The Equilibrium Business-Cycle Model

A complete microeconomic framework is more important for satisfactory analyses of economic fluctuations. Therefore, I apply the micro foundations from Chapters 6 and 7 to the development of an equilibrium business-cycle model in Chapters 8 and 9. This model generalizes the real business-cycle model, which has become a centerpiece of macroeconomic research since the mid 1980s. The modeling is, I believe, more transparent and more empirically anchored than the treatments in my earlier books. Chapters 10–14 extend the equilibrium model to allow for money and inflation and for the government sector (expenditure, taxes, transfers, and public debt). These chapters on government were always viewed as strengths of my textbooks, and I believe that characterization still applies.

## Incomplete Information and Sticky Prices

The next part focuses on interactions between money and the real economy. Chapter 15 extends the equilibrium business-cycle model to allow for incomplete information about prices in a setting of rational expectations. The exposition of this model is far superior to that in my previous books. Chapter 16 introduces the Keynesian idea of sticky prices and wages, with a focus on the new Keynesian model, another major development since the mid-1980s. This model recognizes that, rather than being perfect competitors, producers typically set prices, which represent markups on costs of production. Most importantly, these prices adjust only infrequently to changed circumstances. Chapters 15 and 16 together usefully supplement the equilibrium business-cycle model to allow for significant real effects from monetary policy.

## The Open Economy

Finally, Chapters 17 and 18 extend the equilibrium model to an open economy. I deal first with a purely real setting in which the home and foreign countries share a common currency. One significant topic is the current-account deficit, a great concern for the United States in recent years. The next chapter introduces different moneys and allows for the determination of exchange rates. An important issue here—relevant today to debates about China's currency—concerns the relative merits of fixed versus flexible exchange rates.

# Acknowledgements

Throughout the writing and development of this book, many dedicated professors have generously contributed their time and comments to help improve its presentation. I am grateful for their consideration and assistance.

James Ahiakpor
  *California State University, Hayward*
Francis Ahking
  *University of Connecticut*
David Aschauer
  *Bates College*
Javed Ashraf
  *University of West Florida*
Scott Baier
  *Clemson University*
J. Ulysses Balderas
  *Sam Houston State University*
Christopher Baum
  *Boston College*

James Butkiewicz
  *University of Delaware*
Marco Cagetti
  *University of Virginia*
Rob Catlett
  *Emporia State University*
Byron Chapman
  *University of Georgia*
Amaresh Das
  *Tulane University*
A. Edward Day
  *University of Texas, Dallas*
Dennis Debrecht
  *Carroll College*

Larry Fu
*Illinois College*
Michael Goode
*University of North Carolina, Charlotte*
David B. Gordon
*Clemson University*
John Grether
*Northwood University*
David Hakes
*University of Northern Iowa*
David Hammes
*University of Hawaii, Hilo*
Joe Haslag
*University of Missouri*
Peter Hess
*Davidson College*
Jeanne Hey
*Lebanon Valley College*
William Horace
*Syracuse University*
Dennis Jansen
*Texas A&M University*
Bryce Kanago
*University of Northern Iowa*
Manfred Keil
*Claremont McKenna College*
Doug Kinnear
*Colorado State University*
Todd Knoop
*Cornell College*
Robert Krol
*California State University, Northridge*
Paul Lau
*University of Hong Kong*
Joshua Lewer
*West Texas A&M University*
Tony Lima
*California State University, Hayward*
Ming Lo
*St. Cloud State University*
Prakash Loungani
*Georgetown University*
Paul Mason
*University of North Florida*
B. Starr McMullen
*Oregon State University*
Stephen O. Morrell
*Barry University*
John J. Nader
*Grand Valley State University*

Nick Noble
*Miami University of Ohio*
Farrokh Nourzad
*Marquette University*
Salvador Ortigueira
*Cornell University*
Christopher Otruk
*University of Virginia*
Stephen Parente
*University of Illinois, Champaign*
Peter Pedroni
*Williams College*
Jaishankar Raman
*Valparaiso University*
Robert Reed
*University of Kentucky*
William R. Reed
*University of Oklahoma*
Bernard Rose
*Rocky Mountain College*
Esteban Rossi-Hansberg
*Princeton University*
William Seyfried
*Winthrop University*
Mohamad Shaaf
*University of Central Oklahoma*
Nicole Simpson
*Colgate University*
Rodney Smith
*University of Minnesota*
John Stiver
*University of Connecticut*
Jack Strauss
*St. Louis University*
Mark Strazicich
*Appalachian State University*
James Swofford
*University of South Alabama*
Mark Toma
*University of Kentucky*
David Torgerson
*USDA Economics Research Service*
Dosse Toulaboe
*Fort Hays State University*
Fred Tyler
*Marist College*
Bijan Vasigh
*Embry-Riddle Aeronautical University*
Christian Zimmerman
*University of Connecticut*

# Brief Contents

# Contents

# Author

**Robert J. Barro**

I was born in New York City, then moved to Los Angeles, where I attended high school. After studying physics at Caltech, including classes from Richard Feynman, I switched to economics for graduate school at Harvard. The change to economics was a great move for me! After jobs at Brown, Chicago, and Rochester, I returned to Harvard as a professor in 1987. I am presently a senior fellow of Stanford's Hoover Institution and a research associate of the National Bureau of Economic Research. I co-edit Harvard's *Quarterly Journal of Economics* and was recently president of the Western Economic Association and vice president of the American Economic Association. I have been visiting China a lot recently and am now honorary dean of the China Economics & Management Academy of the Central University of Beijing. My research has focused on macroeconomics and economic growth but includes recent work with my wife, Rachel, on the economics of religion. I am also studying the economic effects of rare disasters, such as depressions, world wars, epidemics, and natural disasters. Aside from academic research, I enjoy more popular writing, including work as a viewpoint columnist for *Business Week* from 1998 to 2006 and as a contributing editor of *The Wall Street Journal* from 1991 to 1998. My recent books include *Economic Growth* (2nd edition, with Xavier Sala-i-Martin, who astoundingly served for a time as acting president of the famous soccer team F.C. Barcelona), *Nothing Is Sacred: Economic Ideas for the New Millennium, Determinants of Economic Growth,* and *Getting It Right: Markets and Choices in a Free Society,* all from MIT Press.

Introduction **Part 1**

# C h a p t e r    1
## Thinking About Macroeconomics

Macroeconomics deals with the overall, or aggregate, performance of an economy. We study the determination of the economy's total production of goods and services, as measured by the real **gross domestic product (GDP)**. We analyze the breakdown of GDP into its major components: consumption, gross investment (purchases of new capital goods—equipment and structures—by the private sector), government purchases of goods and services, and net exports of goods and services. We also examine the aggregates of **employment** (persons with jobs) and **unemployment** (persons without jobs who are seeking work).

These terms refer to quantities of goods or labor. We are also interested in the prices that correspond to these quantities. For example, we consider the dollar prices of the goods and services produced in an economy. When we look at the price of the typical or average item, we refer to the **general price level**. We also study the **wage rate**, which is the dollar price of labor; the **rental price**, which is the dollar price paid to use capital goods; and the **interest rate**, which determines the cost of borrowing and the return to lending. When we consider more than one economy, we can study the **exchange rate**, which is the rate at which one form of money (e.g., the euro) exchanges for another form of money (e.g., the U.S. dollar).

We will set up an economic model, which will allow us to study how the various quantities and prices are determined. We can use the model to see how the quantities and prices respond to technological advances, government policies, and other variables. For example, we will consider monetary policy, which involves the determination of the quantity of money and the setting of interest rates. We will also study fiscal policy, which describes the government's expenditures, taxes, and fiscal deficits.

The performance of the overall economy matters for everyone because it influences incomes, job prospects, and prices. Thus, it is important for us—and even more important for government policymakers—to understand how the macroeconomy operates. Unfortunately, as is obvious from reading the newspapers, macroeconomics is not a settled scientific field. Although there is consensus on many issues—such as some of the determinants of long-run economic growth—there is also controversy about many topics, such as the sources of economic fluctuations and the short-run effects of monetary policy. The main objective of this book is to convey the macroeconomic knowledge that has been attained, as well as to point out areas in which a full understanding has yet to be achieved.

## Output, Unemployment, and Prices in U.S. History

To get an overview of the subject, we can look at the historical record of some of the major macroeconomic variables in the United States. Figure 1.1 shows the total output or production of goods and services from 1869 to 2005. (The starting date is determined by the available data.) Our measure of aggregate output is the **real gross domestic product** (GDP).[1] This concept expresses quantities in terms of a base year—in our case, 2000. Chapter 2 considers **national-income accounting** and thereby provides the conceptual details for measuring **real GDP**.

The general upward trend of real GDP in Figure 1.1 reflects the long-term growth of the U.S. economy. Figure 1.2 on the next page plots the growth rate of real GDP for each year, from 1870 to 2005. A simple way to compute the growth rate for year $t$ is to take the difference between the levels of real GDP in years $t$ and $t-1$, $Y_t - Y_{t-1}$, divide by year $t-1$'s level of real GDP, $Y_{t-1}$, and then subtract one:

$$\text{growth rate of real GDP for year } t = (Y_t - Y_{t-1})/Y_{t-1} - 1$$

If we then multiply by 100, we get the growth rate of real GDP in percent per year.

**F i g u r e   1 . 1** | U.S. Real GDP, 1869–2005

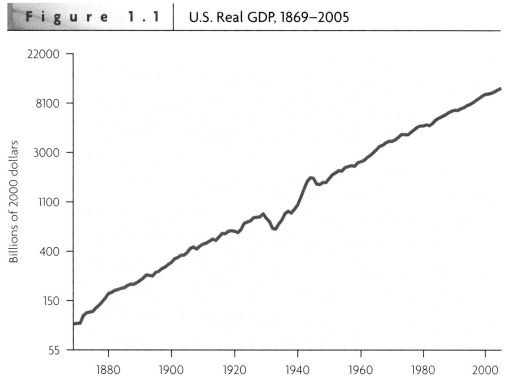

The graph shows the real gross domestic product (GDP) on a proportionate (logarithmic) scale. Data before 1929 are for real gross national product (GNP). The numbers are in billions of 2000 U.S. dollars.

**Sources:** Data since 1929 are from Bureau of Economic Analysis (http://www.bea.gov). Values from 1869 to 1928 are based on data from Christina Romer (1988, 1989).

---

[1] The graph uses a proportionate scale, so that each unit on the vertical axis corresponds to the same percentage change in real GDP. Because of data availability, the numbers before 1929 refer to real gross national product (GNP). We discuss the relation between GDP and GNP in Chapter 2.

**Figure 1.2** | Growth Rate of U.S. Real GDP, 1870–2005

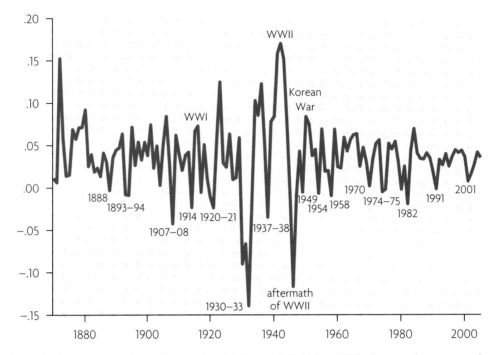

The graph shows the annual growth rate of real GDP (real GNP before 1929). The growth rates are calculated from the values of real GDP (or real GNP) shown in Figure 1.1. Aside from the years of major war, the years marked are recession periods. These periods have low (typically negative) rates of economic growth.

The mean growth rate of real GDP from 1870 to 2005 was 3.5% per year. This growth rate meant that the level of real GDP, shown in Figure 1.1, expanded 121-fold from 1869 to 2005. If we divide through by population to determine real per capita GDP, it turns out that the mean per capita growth rate was 2.0% per year. This rate equals the 3.5%-per-year growth rate of real GDP less the 1.5% per-year growth rate of population. The growth rate of real per capita GDP by 2.0% per year meant that real GDP per capita increased 16-fold from 1869 to 2005.

Figure 1.2 shows that the year-to-year growth rates of real GDP varied substantially around their mean of 3.5%. These variations are called **economic fluctuations** or, sometimes, the **business cycle**.[2] When real GDP falls toward a low point or trough, the economy is in a **recession**, or an economic contraction. When real GDP expands toward a high point or peak, the economy is in a **boom**, or an economic expansion.

The dates marked in Figure 1.2 correspond to the major U.S. recessions since 1870. There are many ways to classify periods of recession. In this graph, we mark as years of recession the years of low economic growth. In Chapter 8, we use a more sophisticated method to classify recessions. However, most of the classifications are the same as those shown in Figure 1.2.

Note in Figure 1.2 the **Great Depression** from 1930 to 1933, during which real GDP declined at 8% per year for four years. Other major recessions before World War II

---

[2] The term "business cycle" can be misleading because it suggests a more regular pattern of ups and downs in economic activity than actually appears in the data.

| **F i g u r e    1 . 3** | U.S. Unemployment Rate, 1890–2005 |

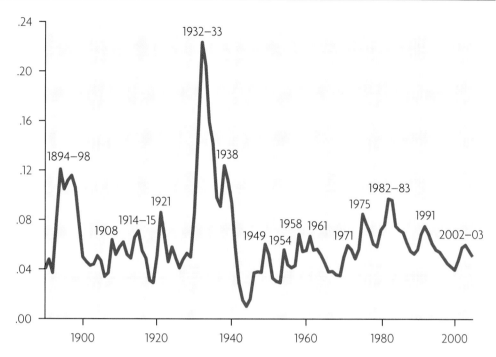

The graph shows the U.S. unemployment rate.

**Sources:** Data since 1929 are from Bureau of Labor Statistics (http://www.bls.gov). Values from 1890 to 1928 are based on data from Christina Romer (1986, Table 9). Values for 1933 to 1943 were adjusted to classify federal emergency workers as employed, as discussed in Michael Darby (1976).

occurred in 1893–94, 1907–8, 1914, 1920–21, and 1937–38. In the post-World War II period, the main recessions occurred in 1958, 1974–75, and 1980–82.

For economic booms, note first in Figure 1.2 the high rates of economic growth during World Wars I and II and the Korean War. Peacetime periods of sustained high economic growth before World War II were 1875–80, 1896–1906, much of the 1920s, and the recovery from the Great Depression from 1933 to 1940 (except for the 1937–38 recession). After World War II, periods of sustained high economic growth occurred in 1961–1973 (except for the brief recession in 1970), 1983–89, and 1992–2000.

Another way to gauge recessions and booms is to consider the **unemployment rate**—the fraction of persons seeking work who have no job. Figure 1.3 shows the unemployment rate for each year from 1890 to 2005. The mean unemployment rate was 6.3%, and the median was lower—5.5%. During recessions, the unemployment rate typically rises above its median. The extreme example is the Great Depression, during which the unemployment rate reached 22% in 1932. Also noteworthy in the pre-World War II period are the average unemployment rates of 18% for 1931–35, 12% for 1938–39, 11% for 1894–98, and 8% for 1921–22. In the post-World War II period, the highest unemployment rate was 10% in 1982–83. Other periods of high unemployment rates included 1975–76 (8%) and 1958, 1961, and 1991–93 (7%).

Figures 1.2 and 1.3 show the turbulence of the U.S. economy during the two world wars and the 1930s. But suppose that we abstract from these extreme episodes and compare the post-World War II period with the period before World War I. Then the major

**Figure 1.4** | U.S. Price Level, 1869–2005

The graph shows the price deflator for the GDP (GNP before 1929). The numbers are on a proportionate (logarithmic) scale, with the value for the year 2000 set at 100. The sources are those indicated for GDP in Figure 1.1.

message from the data is the similarity between the post–World War II and pre–World War I periods.

The mean growth rate of real GDP was 3.4% per year from 1948 to 2005, compared with 3.8% from 1870 to 1914 and 3.4% from 1890 to 1914. The mean unemployment rates were 5.6% from 1948 to 2005 and 6.4% from 1890 to 1914. The extent of economic fluctuations—in the sense of the variability of growth rates of real GDP or of unemployment rates—was only moderately larger in the pre–World War I period than in the post–World War II period.[3] The economy has, of course, changed greatly over the 136 years from 1869 to 2005—including a larger role for government, a diminished share of agriculture in the GDP, and dramatic changes in the monetary system. Nevertheless, the U.S. data do not reveal major changes in the intensity of economic fluctuations or in the average rate of economic growth.

Figure 1.4 shows the evolution of the U.S. price level from 1869 to 2005. This graph measures the price level as the deflator for the GDP (we discuss the details of this price index in Chapter 2). For present purposes, the important point is that the GDP deflator is a broad index, corresponding to the prices of all the items that enter into the gross domestic product.

One striking observation is the persistent rise in the price level since World War II, contrasted with the up and down movements before World War II. There are long periods in the earlier history—1869 to 1892 and 1920 to 1933—during which the price level fell persistently.

---

[3] For a detailed comparison of real GDP and unemployment rates for the two periods, see Christina Romer (1986, 1988, 1989).

| Figure 1.5 | U.S. Inflation Rate, 1870–2005 |

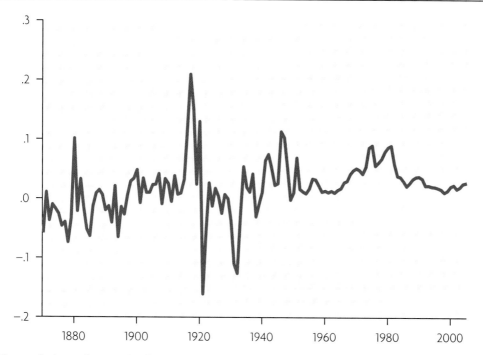

The graph shows the annual inflation rate based on the GDP deflator (GNP deflator before 1929). The inflation rate is the annual growth rate of the price level shown in Figure 1.4.

Figure 1.5 shows the annual **inflation rate** from 1870 to 2005. Each year's inflation rate is calculated as the growth rate in percent per year of the price level shown in Figure 1.4. A simple way to compute the inflation rate for year $t$ is to take the difference between the price levels in years $t$ and $t-1$, $P_t - P_{t-1}$, divide by year $t-1$'s price level, $P_{t-1}$, and then subtract one:

$$\text{inflation rate for year } t = (P_t - P_{t-1})/P_{t-1} - 1$$

If we then multiply by 100, we get the inflation rate in percent per year.

Notice from Figure 1.5 that the inflation rates after World War II were all greater than zero, except for 1949. In contrast, many of the inflation rates before World War II were less than zero. Note also in the post-World War II period that the inflation rate fell sharply from a peak of 8.8% in 1980–81 to means of 2.5% from 1983 to 2005 and only 2.0% from 1992 to 2005.

In subsequent chapters, we will relate the changing behavior of the inflation rate to the changing character of monetary institutions and monetary policy. A key element of the pre-World War II period was the **gold standard**, a system in which the dollar price of gold was nearly constant. The United States adhered to this system from 1879 until World War I and, to some extent, from World War I until 1933. A key element of the post-World War II period was the changing monetary policy of the U.S. Federal Reserve. Notably, since the mid-1980s, the Federal Reserve and other major central banks have successfully pursued a policy of low and stable inflation.

# Economic Models

As mentioned, we want to understand the determinants of major macroeconomic variables, such as real GDP and the general price level. To carry out this mission, we will construct a macroeconomic model. A model can be a group of equations or graphs, or a set of conceptual ideas. We will use all of these tools in this book—some equations but, more often, graphs and ideas.

An economic model deals with two kinds of variables: endogenous variables and exogenous variables. The **endogenous variables** are the ones that we want the model to explain. For example, the endogenous variables in our macroeconomic model include real GDP, investment, employment, the general price level, the wage rate, and the interest rate.

The **exogenous variables** are the ones that a model takes as given and does not attempt to explain. A simple example of an exogenous variable is the weather (at least in models that do not allow the economy to affect the climate). In many cases, the available technologies will be exogenous. For a single country's economy, the exogenous variables include the world prices of commodities such as oil and wheat, as well as levels of income in the rest of the world. In many cases, we will treat government policies as exogenous—for example, choices about monetary policy and the government's spending and taxes. We also treat as exogenous war and peace, which have important macroeconomic consequences.

The central idea of a model is that it tells us how to go from the exogenous variables to the endogenous variables; Figure 1.6 illustrates this process. We take as given the group of exogenous variables shown in the left box in the diagram. The model tells us how to go from these exogenous variables to the group of endogenous variables, shown in the right box the diagram. Therefore, we can use the model to predict how changes in the exogenous variables affect the endogenous variables.

In macroeconomics, we are interested in the determination of macroeconomic—that is, economy-wide aggregate—variables, such as real GDP. However, to construct a useful macroeconomic model, we will find it helpful to build on a microeconomic approach to

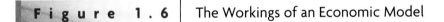

**F i g u r e   1 . 6**   |   The Workings of an Economic Model

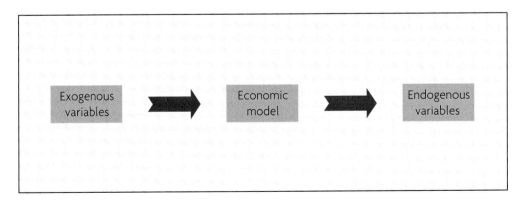

A model is a theory that tells us how to go from a group of exogenous variables to a group of endogenous variables. The model may be a list of equations or graphs or a set of conceptual ideas. The exogenous variables come from outside the model and are therefore not explained by the model. The endogenous variables are the ones that the model seeks to explain. With the help of the model, we can predict how changes in the exogenous variables affect the endogenous variables.

the actions of individual households and businesses. This microeconomic approach investigates individual decisions about how much to consume and save, how much to work, and so on. Then we can add up, or aggregate, the choices of individuals to construct a macroeconomic model. This underlying microeconomic analysis is called **microeconomic foundations**.

## A Simple Example—The Coffee Market

To illustrate general ideas about models and markets, we can examine the market for a single product, such as coffee. Our analysis will focus on three key tools used by economists: demand curves, supply curves, and market-clearing conditions (quantity demanded equals quantity supplied).

Individuals decide how much coffee to buy—that is, the quantity of coffee to demand. Influences on this demand include the individual's income, the price of coffee, $P_c$, and the price of a substitute good, say, $P_T$, the price of tea. Since each individual is a negligible part of the coffee and tea markets, it makes sense that each individual would neglect the effect of his or her coffee and tea consumption on $P_c$ and $P_T$. That is, each individual is a **price taker**; he or she simply decides how much coffee and tea to buy at given prices, $P_c$ and $P_T$. Economists use the term **perfect competition** to describe a market in which there are so many buyers and sellers that no individual can noticeably affect the price.

Reasonable behavior for an individual household dictates that each household's quantity of coffee demanded would rise with income, fall with the coffee price, $P_c$, and rise with the price of the substitute good, $P_T$. These results for individual households are examples of microeconomic analysis. When we add up across all households, we determine the aggregate quantity of coffee demanded as a function of aggregate income, denoted by $Y$, and the prices $P_c$ and $P_T$. We can isolate the effect of the coffee price, $P_c$, on the total quantity of coffee demanded by drawing a market **demand curve**. This curve shows the total quantity of coffee demanded, $Q_c^d$, as a function of $P_c$.

Figure 1.7 on the next page shows the market demand curve for coffee. As already noted, a decrease in $P_c$ increases $Q_c^d$. Recall, however, that the demand curve applies for given values of aggregate income, $Y$, and the price of tea, $P_T$. If $Y$ rises, the quantity of coffee demanded, $Q_c^d$, increases for a given price, $P_c$. Therefore, the demand curve shown in Figure 1.7 shifts to the right. If $P_T$ falls, the quantity of coffee demanded, $Q_c^d$, decreases for a given price, $P_c$. Therefore, the demand curve shifts to the left.

We also have to consider how individual producers of coffee decide how much to offer for sale on the market—that is, how much coffee to supply. Influences on this supply include the price of coffee, $P_c$, and the cost of producing additional coffee. We assume, as in our analysis of demand, that the suppliers of coffee are price takers with respect to $P_c$. This assumption could be questioned because some producers of coffee are large and might consider the effects of their actions on $P_c$. However, an extension to allow for this effect would not change our basic analysis of the market for coffee.

Reasonable behavior by an individual producer dictates that the quantity of coffee supplied would rise with the price of coffee, $P_c$, and fall with an increase in the cost of producing additional coffee. For example, bad weather that destroys part of the coffee crop in Brazil would raise the cost of producing coffee and, thereby, reduce the coffee supplied by Brazilians. These results for individual producers are examples of microeconomic analysis.

When we add up across all producers, we determine the aggregate quantity of coffee supplied. One result is that a rise in $P_c$ increases the aggregate quantity of coffee supplied, $Q_c^s$. The total quantity supplied also depends on weather conditions in coffee-producing areas, such as Brazil and Colombia.

9038.0
18.860
7.7577
61.851

# Extending The Model

## Demand and supply curves are functions

The market demand for coffee can be written as a function:

$$Q_c^d = D(P_c, Y, P_T)$$

The function $D(\cdot)$ determines the quantity of coffee demanded, $Q_c^d$, for any specified values of the three demand determinants: $P_c$, $Y$, and $P_T$. We assume that the function $D(\cdot)$ has the properties that $Q_c^d$ decreases with the price of coffee, $P_c$, rises with income, $Y$, and rises with the price of tea, $P_T$. Figure 1.7 graphs $Q_c^d$ against $P_c$ for given values of the other demand determinants, $Y$ and $P_T$. It is important to distinguish the demand curve, $D(\cdot)$, shown in Figure 1.7, from the quantity demanded, $Q_c^d$, at a given price, $P_c$ (and for given $Y$ and $P_T$). The demand curve refers to the whole functional relationship between quantity demanded and price, $D(\cdot)$, whereas the quantity demanded, $Q_c^d$, refers to one of the points along the curve.

The market supply of coffee is also a function, which can be written as

$$Q_c^s = S(P_c, \textit{weather})$$

We assume that the function $S(\cdot)$ has the properties that the quantity supplied, $Q_c^s$, rises with $P_c$ and with better weather in coffee-producing areas. Figure 1.8 graphs the quantity supplied, $Q_c^s$, against $P_c$, for given weather conditions. It is important to remember that the supply curve, $S(\cdot)$, refers to the whole functional relationship between quantity supplied and price, whereas the quantity supplied, $Q_c^s$, refers to one of the points along the curve.

---

**F i g u r e    1 . 7**  |  Demand Curve for Coffee

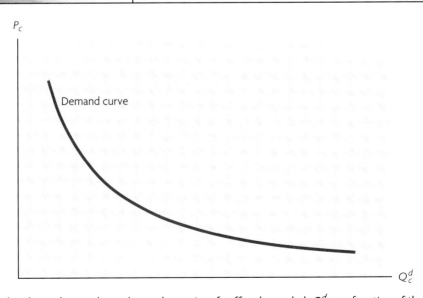

The market demand curve shows the total quantity of coffee demanded, $Q_c^d$, as a function of the price of coffee, $P_c$. A decrease in $P_c$ raises $Q_c^d$. The demand curve applies for given aggregate income, $Y$, and the price of tea, $P_T$. If $Y$ rises, the quantity of coffee demanded, $Q_c^d$, increases for a given $P_c$. Therefore, the demand curve in the diagram shifts to the right. If $P_T$ falls, the quantity of coffee demanded, $Q_c^d$, decreases for a given $P_c$. Therefore, the demand curve shifts to the left.

## Figure 1.8 | Supply Curve for Coffee

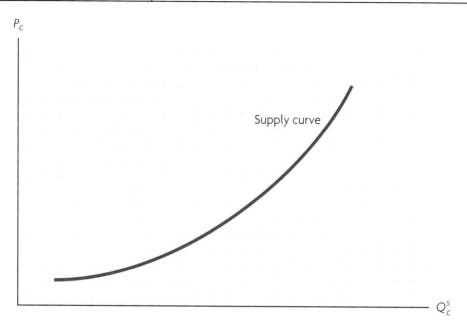

The market supply curve shows the total quantity of coffee supplied, $Q_c^s$, as a function of the price of coffee, $P_c$. An increase in $P_c$ raises $Q_c^s$. The supply curve applies for given conditions that affect the cost of producing coffee. For example, a harvest failure in Brazil would decrease the total quantity of coffee supplied, $Q_c^s$, for a given price, $P_c$. Therefore, the supply curve shifts to the left.

As in our analysis of demand, we can isolate the effect of the coffee price, $P_c$, on the total quantity of coffee supplied by drawing a market **supply curve**. This curve, shown in Figure 1.8, gives the total quantity of coffee supplied, $Q_c^s$, as a function of $P_c$. As already noted, an increase in $P_c$ raises $Q_c^s$. This supply curve applies for given cost conditions for producing coffee and, in particular, for given weather in coffee-producing areas. If bad weather destroys part of Brazil's coffee crop, the market quantity of coffee supplied, $Q_c^s$, decreases for a given price, $P_c$. Therefore, the supply curve shown in Figure 1.8 shifts to the left.

Figure 1.9 on the next page shows the clearing of the market for coffee. The price of coffee, $P_c$, is assumed to adjust to equate the quantity supplied, $Q_c^s$, to the quantity demanded, $Q_c^d$. This market-clearing price is the value $(P_c)^*$ shown in the figure. The corresponding market-clearing quantity of coffee is $(Q_c)^*$.

Why do we assume that the coffee price, $P_c$, adjusts to the market-clearing value, $(P_c)^*$? For any other price, the quantities supplied and demanded would be unequal. For example, at point 1 in Figure 1.9, where $P_c$ is less than $(P_c)^*$, the quantity demanded, $Q_c^d$, would be greater than the quantity supplied, $Q_c^s$. In that case, some coffee drinkers must be unsatisfied; they would not be able to buy the quantity of coffee that they want at the price $P_c$. That is, suppliers would be unwilling to provide enough coffee to satisfy all of the desired purchases at this low price. In this circumstance, we would think that competition among the eager demanders of coffee would raise the market price, $P_c$, toward $(P_c)^*$.

Conversely, at point 2 in Figure 1.9, where $P_c$ is higher than $(P_c)^*$, the quantity demanded, $Q_c^d$, would be less than the quantity supplied, $Q_c^s$. In this case, some coffee producers must be unsatisfied; they would not be able to sell the full quantity of coffee that they want to sell at the price $P_c$. That is, coffee drinkers would be unwilling to buy all the coffee that the producers offer at this high price. In this situation, we would expect that competition among the eager suppliers of coffee would reduce the market price, $P_c$, toward $(P_c)^*$.

## Figure 1.9 | Clearing of the Market for Coffee

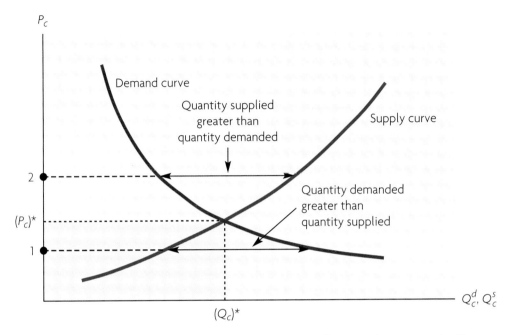

The coffee market clears at the price $(P_c)^*$ and quantity $(Q_c)^*$. At this point, the quantity of coffee supplied equals the quantity demanded.

The market-clearing price, $P_c = (P_c)^*$, is special because only at this price is there no pressure for the coffee price to rise or fall. In this sense, the market-clearing price is an **equilibrium** price. This price tends to remain the same unless there are shifts to the demand curve or the supply curve.

We can think of our market-clearing analysis of the coffee market as a model of how the coffee market operates. The two endogenous variables in the model are the price, $P_c$, and quantity, $Q_c$, of coffee. We can use the market-clearing analysis from Figure 1.9 to see how changes in exogenous variables affect the endogenous variables in the model. The exogenous variables are the outside forces that shift the demand and supply curves for coffee. For demand, we referred to two exogenous variables: income, $Y$, and the price of tea, $P_T$.[4] For supply, we mentioned as exogenous variables the weather conditions in coffee-producing areas, such as Brazil.

Figure 1.10 shows how an increase in demand affects the coffee market. The rise in demand could reflect an increase in income, $Y$, or the price of tea, $P_T$. We represent the increase in demand by a rightward shift of the demand curve. That is, consumers want to buy more coffee at any given price, $P_c$. We see from the diagram that the market-clearing price rises from $(P_c)^*$ to $(P_c)^{*\prime}$, and the market-clearing quantity increases from $(Q_c)^*$ to $(Q_c)^{*\prime}$. Thus, our model of the coffee market predicts that increases in $Y$ or $P_T$ raise $P_c$ and $Q_c$. As in the diagram in Figure 1.6, the model tells us how changes in the exogenous variables affect the endogenous variables.

---

[4] From a broader perspective that encompasses the tea market and the overall economy, the price of tea, $P_T$, and incomes would also be endogenous variables. This broader analysis is called general-equilibrium theory—that is, it considers the conditions for the clearing of all markets simultaneously. The limitation to a single market, such as the one for coffee, is an example of partial-equilibrium analysis. In this case, we assess the clearing of the coffee market while taking as given the outcomes in the other markets.

| Figure 1.10 | Effect of an Increase in Demand on the Coffee Market |
| --- | --- |

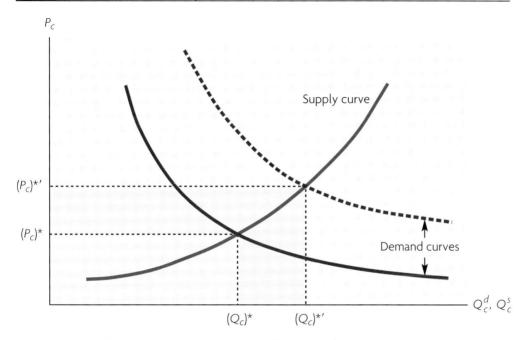

In Figure 1.9, the coffee market cleared at the price $(P_c)^*$ and quantity $(Q_c)^*$. An increase in income, $Y$, or in the price of tea, $P_T$, raises the demand for coffee. Therefore, the demand curve shifts rightward from the solid red curve to the dashed red curve. The market-clearing price of coffee rises to $(P_c)^{*'}$, and the market-clearing quantity of coffee rises to $(Q_c)^{*'}$.

Figure 1.11 on the next page shows how a decrease in supply affects the coffee market. The reduction in supply could reflect poor weather conditions in coffee-producing areas, such as Brazil and Colombia. We represent the decrease in supply by a leftward shift of the supply curve. That is, producers want to sell less coffee at any given price, $P_c$. We see from the diagram that the market-clearing price rises from $(P_c)^*$ to $(P_c)^{*'}$, and the market-clearing quantity decreases from $(Q_c)^*$ to $(Q_c)^{*'}$. Thus, our model of the coffee market predicts that a poor coffee harvest raises $P_c$ and lowers $Q_c$.

Table 1.1 summarizes the results from the market-clearing model of the coffee market. As in Figure 1.6, the model tells us how changes in the exogenous variables affect the endogenous variables.

Our macroeconomic model will use this kind of market-clearing analysis to predict how changes in exogenous variables affect the endogenous macroeconomic variables.

| Table 1.1 | Effects of Changes in Exogenous Variables on the Endogenous Variables in the Coffee Market |
| --- | --- |

| Change in Exogenous Variable | Effect on $P_c$ | Effect on $Q_c$ |
| --- | --- | --- |
| Increase in income, $Y$ | rises | rises |
| Increase in price of tea, $P_T$ | rises | rises |
| Poor coffee harvest | rises | falls |

| **Figure 1.11** | Effect of a Decrease in Supply on the Coffee Market |

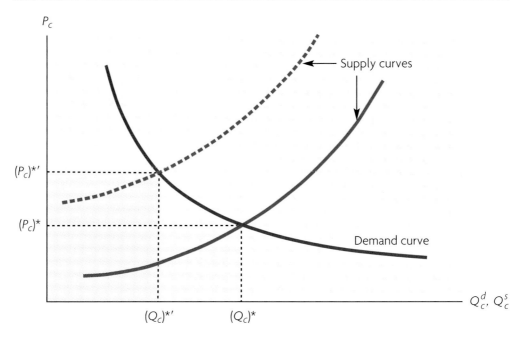

In Figure 1.9, the coffee market cleared at the price $(P_c)^*$ and quantity $(Q_c)^*$. A harvest failure in Brazil reduces the supply of coffee. Therefore, the supply curve shifts leftward from the solid blue curve to the dashed blue curve. The market-clearing price of coffee rises to $(P_c)^{*\prime}$, and the market-clearing quantity of coffee falls to $(Q_c)^{*\prime}$.

However, we will not study an array of goods, such as coffee, tea, and so on. Rather, we will consider the aggregate demand for and supply of a composite good that corresponds to the economy's overall output, the real GDP. We will also analyze the demand for and supply of factors of production—labor and capital services.

## Flexible Versus Sticky Prices

When we studied the market for coffee, we focused on market-clearing conditions. Therefore, when an exogenous variable changed, we based our predictions on how this change altered the market-clearing price and quantity. The assumption that underlies this analysis is that the price of coffee adjusts rapidly to clear the market for coffee—that is, to equate the quantity demanded to the quantity supplied. We observed that, if the price differed from its market-clearing value, either demanders or suppliers of coffee could not be satisfied in their offers to buy or sell at the established price. Consequently, there was always pressure for the coffee price to adjust toward its market-clearing value—the market-clearing price was the only equilibrium price.

   Although most economists accept the focus on market-clearing prices when analyzing coffee or similar products, there is less agreement on whether macroeconomics should focus on market-clearing conditions. In particular, not all economists agree that we should consider only situations of market clearing in the market for the composite good that represents real GDP or in the market for labor. For long-run analysis, there is a consensus that the market-clearing framework provides the best guide to how an economy operates. Therefore, in our study of long-run economic growth in Chapters 3–5, we use a market-clearing, equilibrium approach. However, for analyses of short-run macroeconomic fluctuations, there is a sharp divide among economists as to whether a market-clearing model provides useful insights.

The famous economist John Maynard Keynes, writing in the wake of the Great Depression in the 1930s, argued that the labor market typically did not clear—he thought that the labor market was usually in a state of **disequilibrium**, by which he meant a discrepancy between the quantities of labor demanded and supplied. In particular, he argued that wage rates were sticky and adjusted only slowly to generate equality between the quantities of labor demanded and supplied. More recently, some macroeconomists have emphasized instead the tendency of some goods markets to be in disequilibrium. This approach, called the **new Keynesian model**, argues that some prices are sticky and move only slowly to equate the quantities of goods demanded and supplied.

Other economists argue that an equilibrium approach, which relies on market-clearing conditions, gives us the best insights into short-run economic fluctuations. This approach applies the same methodology to short-run fluctuations that most economists apply to long-run economic growth. Wages and prices are viewed as sufficiently flexible in the short run so that a useful macroeconomic analysis can concentrate on market-clearing situations. As in our analysis of the coffee market (summarized in Table 1.1), we can then focus on how changes in exogenous variables affect market-clearing quantities and prices.

One point that seems clear is that we cannot understand or evaluate sticky-price models unless we have the flexible-price, market-clearing model as a benchmark. After all, macroeconomists agree that the economy is always approaching the market-clearing position—that is why this setting is the one typically used to study long-run economic growth. A reasonable inference is that, whatever the ultimate verdict on the significance of sticky prices in the short run, it is best to begin macroeconomic analysis with a market-clearing model.

We set out the basic market-clearing model of economic fluctuations in Chapters 6–10. We call this model an equilibrium business-cycle model (a broader term than real business-cycle model, which often appears in the economics literature). We extend the model to allow for inflation in Chapter 11 and for government spending, taxes, and fiscal deficits in Chapters 12–14. Chapter 15 allows for misperceptions about prices and wages but continues to assume a market-clearing framework. Only in Chapter 16 are we ready to assess the sticky wages and prices that are the hallmarks of Keynesian and new Keynesian models.

## Key Terms and Concepts

| | |
|---|---|
| boom | interest rate |
| business cycle | microeconomic foundations |
| demand curve | national-income accounting |
| disequilibrium | new Keynesian model |
| economic fluctuations | perfect competition |
| employment | price taker |
| endogenous variables | real GDP |
| equilibrium | real gross domestic product |
| exchange rate | recession |
| exogenous variables | rental price |
| general price level | supply curve |
| gold standard | unemployment |
| Great Depression | unemployment rate |
| gross domestic product (GDP) | wage rate |
| inflation rate | |

# Chapter 2

## National-Income Accounting: Gross Domestic Product and the Price Level

In Chapter 1, we used terms such as *gross domestic product (GDP)* and the *price level* without defining them precisely. Now, by looking at national-income accounting, we develop the meanings of these terms. Many challenging issues arise in the construction of the national-income accounts. However, for our purposes, we will deal only with the basic concepts.

### Nominal and Real GDP

We begin with the gross domestic product, or GDP. **Nominal GDP** measures the dollar (or euro, etc.) value of all the goods and services that an economy produces during a specified period, such as a year. For example, in 2005, the U.S. nominal GDP was 12.5 trillion U.S. dollars. The nominal GDP is a **flow variable**: it measures the dollar amount of goods produced per unit of time, such as a year.

Consider the definition of nominal GDP one step at a time. The word "nominal" means that the goods produced during a year are measured as values in dollars (or in units of another currency, such as euros). For most goods and services—pencils, automobiles, haircuts, and so on—the dollar value is determined by the price at which these items sell in the marketplace.

Some goods and services, including many produced by governments, are not exchanged on markets. For example, the government does not sell its services for national defense, the justice system, and police. These items enter into nominal GDP at their nominal (dollar) cost of production. This treatment is problematic because it amounts to assuming that government employees experience no changes over time in their productivity. However, in the absence of market prices, it is unclear what alternative approach would be more accurate.

Another item, owner-occupied housing, enters into GDP as an estimate of what this housing would fetch on the market if the owner rented the property to another person. This amount is called the **imputed rental income** on owner-occupied housing. Conceptually, the same approach ought to apply to consumer durables, such as households' automobiles, furniture, and appliances. However, this treatment has not been followed; that

Table   2.1  |   The Calculation of Nominal and Real GDP: A Simple Example

| | 2006a | 2006b | 2007a | 2007b |
|---|---|---|---|---|
| **Prices** | | | | |
| butter | $2.00 per pound | $2.00 per pound | $3.00 per pound | $1.50 per pound |
| golf balls | $1.00 per ball | $1.00 per ball | $1.10 per ball | $0.89 per ball |
| **Quantities** | | | | |
| butter | 50 pounds | 50 pounds | 40 pounds | 70 pounds |
| golf balls | 400 balls | 400 balls | 391 balls | 500 balls |
| **Nominal Market Values** | | | | |
| butter | 100 | 100 | 120 | 105 |
| golf balls | 400 | 400 | 430 | 445 |
| nominal GDP | 500 | 500 | 550 | 550 |
| **2006–07 Average Price** | | | | |
| butter | $2.50 per pound | $1.75 per pound | $2.50 per pound | $1.75 per pound |
| golf balls | $1.05 per ball | $0.945 per ball | $1.05 per ball | $0.945 per ball |
| **Market Values at 2006–07 Average Prices** | | | | |
| butter | 125.0 | 87.5 | 100.0 | 122.5 |
| golf balls | 420.0 | 378.0 | 410.6 | 472.5 |
| total | 545.0 | 465.5 | 510.6 | 595.0 |
| ratio to 2005 | 1.0 | 1.0 | 0.937 | 1.278 |
| **Chained Real GDP, 2006 Base** | 500.0 | 500.0 | 468.5 | 639.0 |
| **Implicit GDP Deflator, 2006 Base** | 100 | 100 | 117 | 86 |

is, the GDP does not include the estimated rental income on consumer durables.[1] For government-owned property, the assumption in the national accounts is that the imputed rental income equals the estimated depreciation. This assumption is troublesome but, again, a preferred alternative method is not obvious.

It is important to understand that the nominal GDP includes the value of the goods and services produced during a specified time interval, such as a year. That is, GDP measures current production. For example, if an automaker manufactures and sells a new car in 2007, the full value of the car counts in the GDP for 2007. However, if someone sells in 2007 a used car that was built in 2006, this sale does not count in the GDP for 2007.

The nominal GDP can be misleading because it depends on the overall level of prices, as well as on the physical quantity of goods produced. Table 2.1 illustrates this problem.

---

[1] The capital owned by businesses (such as factories and machinery) contributes to the goods and services produced by the businesses. Therefore, the market value of output already includes the rental income on business capital. For this reason, it is unnecessary for measures of GDP to include an imputed rental income on business capital.

Think about a simple economy that produces only butter and golf balls. The table shows the hypothetical quantities and prices of these goods in 2006 and 2007. In 2006, the economy produces 50 pounds of butter, which sell at $2.00 per pound. Thus, the dollar value of 2006's butter output is $100. In 2006, the economy also produces 400 golf balls, priced at $1.00 per ball, for a golf-ball output of $400. The nominal GDP for 2006 is the sum of the dollar values of butter and golf-ball output: $100 + $400 = $500.

The columns labeled 2007a and 2007b show two possibilities for prices and quantities in 2007. In case *a*, the prices of both goods rise—to $3.00 per pound of butter and $1.10 per golf ball. In case *b*, the prices of both goods decline—to $1.50 per pound of butter and $0.89 per golf ball. In case *a*, the quantities of both goods decline—to 40 pounds of butter and 391 golf balls. In case *b*, the quantities of both goods rise—to 70 pounds of butter and 500 golf balls.

We have assumed numbers so that the nominal GDP in 2007 is the same in both cases. In case *a*, the nominal GDP is $120 for butter plus $430 for golf balls, for a total of $550. In case *b*, the nominal GDP is $105 for butter plus $445 for golf balls, for a total again of $550. However, the quantities of both goods are higher in case *b* than case *a*. Thus, any sensible measure of real GDP in 2007 would show a higher value in case *b* than case *a*. Thus, the equality of the nominal GDPs is misleading. Identical figures on nominal GDP can conceal very different underlying differences in levels of production.

## Calculating Real GDP

Economists solve the problem of changing price levels by constructing measures of real GDP. Until recently, the most common way to compute real GDP was to multiply each year's quantity of output of each good by the price of the good in a base year, such as 2000. Then all of these multiples were added to get the economy's aggregate real GDP. The resulting aggregate is called "GDP in 2000 dollars" (if 2000 is the base year). Or, sometimes, the result is called **GDP in constant dollars**, because we use prices (for the base year, 2000) that do not vary over time. In contrast, the nominal GDP is sometimes called **GDP in current dollars**, because this calculation of GDP uses each good's price in the current year.

Since the prices from the base year (say, 2000) do not vary over time, the method just described provides a reasonable measure of changes over time in the overall level of production. That is, it provides a sensible measure of real GDP. However, a shortcoming of this approach is that it weights the outputs of the various goods by their prices in the base year, which happened to be 2000. For example, suppose that a personal computer costs more than a couch in 2000. In this case, each computer produced in 2007 (of the same quality as ones produced in 2000) would count more than each couch for 2007's real GDP, even though computers were then cheaper than couches. More generally, the base-year weights become less relevant over time as relative prices of goods change. The response of the Bureau of Economic Analysis (the BEA, a part of the U.S. Commerce Department) had been to make frequent shifts in the base year. However, a more accurate solution, called the chain-weighted method, was adopted in the mid 1990s to get a better measure of real GDP. The resulting variable is called **chain-weighted real GDP**. This chain-weighted measure is the one publicized in the media, and it is the one we shall use in this book to measure real GDP.

To illustrate how chain-weighting works, we can again use our hypothetical data for a simple economy from Table 2.1. The method starts by computing the average price of each good for two adjacent years—2006 and 2007 in the table. For example, in scenario *a*, the average price of butter for 2006 and 2007 is $2.50 per pound. In scenario *b*, it is $1.75 per pound.

In each year—2006 and 2007 in the table—the quantities produced of each good are multiplied by the average prices for the two adjacent years. For example, in case *a*, the value of the butter produced in 2006 is $125 when calculated at the average price for 2006 and 2007, compared to $100 when the (lower) price for 2006 is used. For 2007, in case *a*, the value of the butter is $100 when computed at the average price, compared to $120 when the (higher) price for 2007 is used.

Using these average-price numbers, we sum the values of the goods produced in each year to get the totals shown in Table 2.1. For example, for 2006, in case *a*, the total dollar value is $545, compared to $500 when we used prices for 2006. For 2007, in case *a*, the total dollar value is $510.60, compared to $550 when we used prices for 2007.

Next we compute the ratios of each of these totals to the totals for 2006. Thus, the ratios are 1.0 for the two cases (*a* and *b*) that apply to 2006. For 2007, the ratio is 0.937 in case *a* and 1.278 in case *b*.

To get chained real GDP on a 2006 base, we multiply the ratios just calculated by the nominal GDP ($500) for 2006. Thus, chained real GDP for 2006 on a 2006 base is the same as nominal GDP—$500 (for cases *a* and *b*). For 2007, chained real GDP on a 2006 base is $468.5 in case *a* and $639.0 in case *b*. Thus, although the nominal GDPs for 2007 are the same, the chained real GDP is substantially higher in case *b*. This result makes sense because the quantities of butter and golf balls are both higher in case *b* than in case *a*.

We can proceed the same way for other years. For example, when we get data for 2008, we can calculate the ratio of the value of output in 2008 to that for 2007. These ratios are analogous to those calculated for 2007 compared to 2006 in Table 2.1. We then want to express the results for 2008 on a 2006 base, so that all the chained values apply to the same base year. To do this, we multiply the ratio for 2008 compared to 2007 by the ratio for 2007 compared to 2006. This gives us the ratio of 2008 values to 2006 values. Finally, we multiply the last ratio by nominal GDP for 2006 to get the chain-weighted GDP for 2008 on a 2006 base. This procedure is called *chain-linking*. If we carry out this procedure from one year to the next, we end up with a time series for chain-weighted real GDP expressed in terms of a single base year.

In Table 2.1, the base year for chain-weighted real GDP is 2006. However, the actual base year used by the Bureau of Economic Analysis in the early 2000s was 2000. With the chain method, the choice of which year to use for the base is not important. We use a single base year only to ensure that the real GDPs for each year are comparable. (The ratio of chain-weighted real GDPs for two years, such as 2006 and 2007, is the same for any choice of base year.)

We can use the results on real GDP to construct an index for the overall level of prices. In Table 2.1, where 2006 is the base year, we can think of the overall price level for 2006 as "100." This number is arbitrary; it just serves as a comparative position that can be related to price levels in other years.

For case *a* in 2007, the nominal GDP is $550, and the chain-weighted real GDP on a 2006 base is $468.50. We can think of an implicit price level used to convert a dollar value—the nominal GDP of $550—into a real value—the real GDP of $468.50:

$$(\text{nominal GDP})/(\text{implicit price level}) = \text{real GDP}$$

If we rearrange the terms in the equation, we have

$$\text{implicit price level} = (\text{nominal GDP})/(\text{real GDP})$$

For example, for 2007 in case *a*, in Table 2.1, we have

$$implicit\ price\ level = (550/468.50) = 1.17$$

In contrast, for 2007 in case *b*, we have

$$implicit\ price\ level = (550/639.0) = 0.86$$

The numbers 1.17 and 0.86 do not mean anything as absolute magnitudes. However, they have meaning when compared with similarly calculated price levels for other years. As mentioned, the usual convention is to think of a price index that takes on the value 100 for the base year, which is 2006 in our example. When compared to this base, the price level for 2007 in case *a* is 1.17*100 − 117, whereas in case *b* it is 0.86*100 = 86. These values are shown in Table 2.1. The usual name for these price indexes is the **implicit GDP deflator** (on a 2006 base). That is, these values are the ones implicitly used to convert from nominal GDP to real GDP (on a 2006 base).

### Real GDP as a Measure of Welfare

Although real GDP reveals a lot about an economy's overall performance, it is not a perfect measure of welfare. Some of the shortcomings of real GDP from a welfare standpoint include:

- The aggregate real GDP does not consider changes in the distribution of income.
- The calculated real GDP excludes most nonmarket goods. The exclusions include legal and illegal transactions in the "underground economy," as well as services that people perform in their homes. For example, if a person cares for his or her child at home, the real GDP excludes this service. But if the person hires someone to care for the child at home or at a day-care center, the real GDP includes the service.
- Real GDP assigns no value to leisure time.
- Measured real GDP does not consider environmental damage, such as air and water quality, except to the extent that this pollution affects the market value of output.

Despite these shortcomings, the real GDP tells us a lot about how an economy's standard of living changes over time. It also allows us to compare standards of living across countries. Measured real GDP helps us to understand short-run economic fluctuations as well as long-term economic development.

## Alternative Views of GDP—Expenditure, Income, and Production

We can think about the gross domestic product, or GDP, in three different ways. First, we can consider expenditure on goods and services produced domestically by households, businesses, government, and foreigners. Second, we can calculate the incomes earned domestically in the production of goods and services—compensation of employees, rental income, corporate profits, and so on. Finally, we can measure the domestic production of goods and services by industry—agriculture, manufacturing, wholesale and retail trade, and so on. An important point is that all three approaches will end up with the same totals for nominal and real GDP. To see this, we take up each approach in turn, beginning with the breakdown by type of expenditure.

## Measuring GDP by Expenditure

The national accounts divide GDP into four parts, depending on who or what buys the goods or services. The four sectors are households, businesses, all levels of government, and foreigners. Table 2.2 shows the details of this breakdown for 2005. The first column lists values in current (2005) dollars, and the second column expresses each amount as a percentage of nominal GDP. The third column shows each value as chained real dollars in terms of the base year, 2000. The nominal GDP for 2005 of $12.49 trillion corresponds to $11.13 trillion in 2000 dollars. If we make these calculations for other years, we can compare across years to see how real GDP has changed over time.

    1. **Personal consumption expenditure.** The purchases of goods and services by households for consumption purposes are called **personal consumption expenditure**. This variable, like GDP, is a flow concept. Thus, nominal personal consumption expenditure has units of dollars per year. This spending typically accounts for more than half of GDP. For example, Table 2.2 shows that, in 2005, the nominal personal consumption expenditure of $8.75 trillion was 70% of the nominal GDP of $12.49 trillion.

**Table 2.2** | Expenditure Components of U.S. Gross Domestic Product in 2005

| Category of Expenditure | Trillions of dollars | % of Nominal GDP | Trillions of Chained 2000 dollars |
|---|---|---|---|
| **Gross domestic product** | **12.49** | **100.0** | **11.13** |
| **Personal consumption expenditure** | **8.75** | **70.0** | **7.86** |
| durable goods | 1.03 | 8.2 | 1.14 |
| nondurable goods | 2.56 | 20.5 | 2.30 |
| services | 5.15 | 41.3 | 4.44 |
| **Gross private domestic investment** | **2.10** | **16.9** | **1.92** |
| fixed investment | 2.09 | 16.7 | 1.90 |
| nonresidential | 1.33 | 10.7 | 1.29 |
| residential | 0.76 | 6.1 | 0.60 |
| change in business inventories | 0.02 | 0.0 | 0.02 |
| **Government purchases*** | **2.36** | **18.9** | **1.99** |
| federal | 0.88 | 7.0 | 0.74 |
| state and local | 1.49 | 11.9 | 1.25 |
| **Net exports of goods and services** | **−0.73** | **−5.8** | **−0.63** |
| exports | 1.30 | 10.4 | 1.20 |
| imports | 2.03 | 16.2 | 1.83 |

**Source:** Bureau of Economic Analysis (http://www.bea.gov).

* This category corresponds in the national accounts to government consumption and investment. The national-accounts category includes depreciation of government capital stocks.

The national accounts distinguish purchases of consumer goods that are used up quickly, such as toothpaste and various services, from those that last for a substantial time, such as automobiles and furniture. The first group is called **consumer nondurables and services**, and the second is called **consumer durables**. An important point is that consumer durables yield a flow of services for an extended period. An automobile, for instance, can be used by the owner for many years or can be sold or rented to another driver. Therefore, purchases of consumer durables can be viewed as a type of investment. Table 2.2 shows the division of personal consumption expenditure among durable goods, nondurable goods, and services. In 2005, the nominal spending on durables of $1.03 trillion constituted 12% of total nominal personal consumption expenditure.

The third column of Table 2.2 reports the components of GDP in chained 2000 dollars. For example, the nominal personal consumption expenditure of $8.75 trillion in 2005 corresponds to $7.86 trillion in 2000 dollars. If we apply this calculation to other years, we can compute the changes over time in real personal consumption expenditure or in the other real components of GDP. However, there are difficulties in comparing the level of real personal consumption expenditure in a given year with the level of real GDP in the same year. As already mentioned, the nominal personal consumption expenditure for 2005 was 70% of nominal GDP. However, a comparison of real personal consumption expenditure with real GDP depends on which base year one happens to use. The reason is that the comparison of real consumer expenditure with real GDP depends on the changes in relative prices that occurred between the base year (say, 2000) and the comparison year (say, 2005). In particular, the results depend on how prices of items contained in personal consumption expenditure changed compared to the prices of the other items that entered into GDP.

2. **Gross private domestic investment.** The second major category of GDP is **gross private domestic investment**. Investment, like personal consumption expenditure, is a flow variable, measured in dollars per year. The "fixed" part of gross private domestic investment comprises purchases by domestic businesses of new capital goods, such as factories and machinery. These capital goods are durables, which serve as inputs to production for many years. Thus, these goods are analogous to the consumer durables that we already mentioned. In fact, in the national accounts, an individual's purchase of a new home—which might be considered the ultimate consumer durable—is counted as part of fixed business investment, rather than personal consumption expenditure.

Gross private domestic investment is the sum of fixed investment and the net change in businesses' **inventories** of goods. In 2005, this net inventory change was a comparatively small amount, $0.02 trillion. The total nominal gross private domestic investment was $2.10 trillion, which constituted 17% of nominal GDP.

One common error about national-income accounting arises because the spending on new physical capital is called "investment." This terminology differs from the concept of investment used in normal conversation, where investment refers to the allocation of financial assets among stocks, bonds, real estate, and so on. When economists refer to a business's investment, they mean the business's purchases of newly produced goods, such as a factory or machine.

Another point about investment concerns **depreciation**. The stock of capital goods is the outstanding quantity of goods in the form of factories, machinery, and so on. Thus, the capital stock is a **stock variable**, measured as a quantity of goods. Since capital goods wear out or depreciate over time, a part of gross investment merely replaces the old capital that has depreciated. Depreciation is a flow variable—the dollar value of the goods that wear out per year. Depreciation is comparable in units to GDP and gross private domestic investment.

The difference between gross private domestic investment and depreciation—called **net private domestic investment**—is the net change in the value of the stock of physical capital goods. The GDP includes gross private domestic investment. If we replace this gross investment by net investment (by subtracting depreciation), we also subtract depreciation from GDP. The difference between GDP and depreciation is called **net domestic product (NDP)**. The NDP is a useful concept because it measures GDP net of the spending needed to replace worn-out or depreciated capital goods.

**3. Government purchases of goods and services.** The third component of GDP is government purchases of goods and services.[2] This category includes consumption outlays (such as salaries of military personnel and public-school teachers), as well as public investment (such as purchases of new buildings). One important point is that the government sector includes all levels of government, whether federal, state, or local. Another point is that government purchases of goods and services exclude transfers, such as payments to Social Security retirees and welfare recipients. These transfers do not represent payments for currently produced goods and services. Therefore, these outlays do not appear in GDP. In 2005, nominal government purchases of goods and services totaled $2.36 trillion, or 19% of nominal GDP.

**4. Exports and imports.** Some of the goods and services produced domestically are exported to foreign users. These **exports** of goods and services must be added to domestic purchases to compute the economy's total domestic production (GDP). Foreigners also produce goods and services that are imported into the home country—for use by households, businesses, and government. These **imports** of goods and services must be subtracted from domestic purchases to calculate the economy's total production (GDP). The foreign component therefore appears in GDP as **net exports**: the difference between spending of foreigners on domestic production (exports) and spending by domestic residents on foreign production (imports). Net exports may be greater than zero or less than zero. Table 2.2 shows that, in 2005, net nominal exports were −$0.73 trillion, or −5.8% of nominal GDP. The net export component breaks down into $1.30 trillion of exports (10.4% of GDP) less $2.03 trillion of imports (16.2% of GDP).

Economists often use a theoretical model that omits net exports. Then the model applies to a **closed economy**, which has no trade linkages to the rest of the world. In contrast, an economy that is linked through trade to the rest of the world is called an **open economy**. Reasons for using a closed-economy model include the following:

- It simplifies the analysis.
- At least for the United States, exports and imports have been small compared to GDP, so that not too much error arises from ignoring international trade. This point was reasonably persuasive in 1950, when exports and imports were each only 4% of GDP. However, the point is less convincing for 2005, when exports were 10% of GDP and imports were 16% of GDP.
- The world as a whole really is a closed economy, so we have to carry out a closed-economy analysis to assess the world economy.

We follow the closed-economy tradition of macroeconomics until Chapter 17, which allows for international trade.

---

[2] The national accounts refer to this category as "government consumption and investment." Government consumption includes an estimate of rental income on existing government capital. However, as already mentioned, the assumption is that this rental income coincides with the estimated depreciation of government capital stocks. Therefore, "government consumption and investment" in the national accounts adds depreciation of government capital to the category "government purchases of goods and services."

T a b l e   2 . 3   |   Hypothetical Data for Calculation of National Income

| Type of Revenue | Amount | Type of Cost or Profit | Amount |
|---|---|---|---|
| **Bakery (produces final good)** | | | |
| Sale of bread | $600 | Labor | $200 |
| | | Flour | 350 |
| | | Profit | 50 |
| | | Total cost & profit | $600 |
| **Mill (produces intermediate good)** | | | |
| Sale of flour | $350 | Labor | $250 |
| | | Profit | 100 |
| | | Total cost & profit | $350 |

## Measuring GDP by Income

Another way to look at GDP is in terms of the income earned by various factors of production. This concept is called **national income**. To make clear the relation between production and income, we can think of a simple closed economy that has only two businesses. One, a mill, uses only labor to produce flour. The second, a bakery, uses flour and labor to produce bread. Bread is the only final product. Flour is the only intermediate product—it is used up entirely in the production of the final good, bread. Notice that, to simplify matters, we are ignoring capital inputs, such as factories and machines.

Income statements for the two businesses appear in Table 2.3. The nominal GDP for this economy is the value of the final product, bread, of $600. This amount is also the revenue of the bakery. The income statement shows that the costs and profit for the bakery break down into $350 for flour, $200 for labor (for workers in the bakery), and $50 for profit (of the bakery). For the mill, the $350 of revenue goes for $250 of labor (for workers at the mill) and $100 for profit (of the mill). The national income equals the total labor income of $450 plus the total profit of $150, or $600. Thus, in this simple economy, national income equals GDP.

Notice that the GDP counts the value of the final product, bread, of $600, but does not count separately the value of the flour, $350. The flour is used up in the production of bread—that is, the $600 in bread sales already takes into account the $350 cost of the intermediate good, flour. If we added the $350 in sales of flour to the $600 in sales of bread, we would *double-count* the contribution of the intermediate good, flour. To put it another way, the **value added** by the bakery is only $250—sales of $600 less payments for flour of $350. The value added by the mill is the full $350, because we assumed that the mill uses no intermediate goods. Therefore, if we combine the value added of $350 for the mill with the value added of $250 for the bakery, we get the GDP of $600. Hence, GDP equals the sum of value added from all sectors. The national income in this simple economy equals the GDP and, therefore, also equals the sum of value added from all sectors.

Table 2.4 shows the breakdown of U.S. national income in 2005. The total nominal national income was $10.90 trillion. Although the method for computing national income is conceptually the same as that in Table 2.3, the U.S. economy includes additional forms of income. The largest part of U.S. national income was compensation of employees— $7.13 trillion, or 65% of the total. This component is analogous to the labor income shown in Table 2.3.

Table 2 . 4 | U.S. National Income by Type in 2005

| Type of Income | Trillions of dollars | % of National Income |
|---|---|---|
| **National income** | **10.90** | **100.0** |
| Compensation of employees | 7.13 | 65.3 |
| Proprietors' income | 0.94 | 8.6 |
| Rental income of persons | 0.07 | 0.7 |
| Corporate profits | 1.35 | 12.4 |
| Net interest | 0.50 | 4.6 |
| Taxes on production | 0.90 | 8.3 |
| Less: subsidies | (0.06) | (0.5) |
| Business transfers | 0.08 | 0.7 |
| Surplus of government enterprises | (0.01) | 0.0 |

**Source:** Bureau of Economic Analysis (http://www.bea.gov).

Several parts of the U.S. national income in Table 2.4 represent income that accrues to capital. These amounts did not appear in Table 2.3 because we did not consider that the bakery and mill each have capital equipment, such as machinery, that contributes to the production of goods. In the U.S. national accounts, the categories of income from capital comprise rental income of persons, corporate profits, and net interest. The total of $1.92 trillion represented 18% of national income.

The U.S. national income for 2005 also includes proprietors' income of $0.94 trillion (9% of the total). This income represents payments to self-employed persons, including unincorporated businesses. This income represents a mix of payments to labor and capital. The breakdown into labor and capital is unknown, although economists have made estimates.

Taxes on production—sales, excise, and value-added (or VAT)[3]—are included in market prices of goods. Therefore, these taxes on production appear in GDP, which is calculated from market values of output. The tax revenues are also part of government revenue—therefore, these revenues enter into national income as income of the government sector. Subsidies paid to producers by government amount to negative production taxes. Therefore, subsidies enter with a negative sign in national income. In 2005, the total of taxes on production less subsidies was $0.85 trillion, or 8% of national income.[4]

**1. Differences between GDP and national income.** In the simplified economy of Table 2.3, GDP and national income were equal. In practice, divergences between GDP and national income reflect two main items: income receipts and payments involving the rest of the world, and depreciation of capital stocks. We take up these two items in turn.

The U.S. GDP is the value of goods and services produced within the United States. The U.S. national income is the income received by all sectors residing in the United States. One

---

[3] The value-added tax is important in many countries but does not exist in the United States.

[4] The U.S. national income for 2005 also includes two minor components. business's net transfers to households and government ($0.08 trillion, or 1% of national income) and the surplus of government enterprises (which was close to zero).

T a b l e   2 . 5   |   Relations Between U.S. GDP and Income in 2005

| Category of Product or Income | Trillions of dollars |
| --- | --- |
| **Gross domestic product (GDP)** | **12.49** |
| Plus: income receipts from rest of world | 0.51 |
| Less: income payments to rest of world | (0.47) |
| **Equals: Gross national product (GNP)** | **12.52** |
| Less: depreciation of capital stock | (1.57) |
| **Equals: Net national product (NNP)** | **10.95** |
| Less: statistical discrepancy | (0.04) |
| **Equals: National income** | **10.90** |
| Less: corporate profits, taxes on production, contributions for social insurance, net interest, business transfers, surplus of government enterprises | (3.64) |
| Plus: personal income receipts on assets, personal transfer payments | 2.98 |
| **Equals: Personal income** | **10.25** |
| Less: personal taxes | (1.21) |
| **Equals: Disposable personal income** | **9.04** |

**Source:** Bureau of Economic Analysis (http://www.bea.gov).

source of divergence between GDP and national income is that residents of the United States receive income from the rest of the world. The main item is the income on capital (assets) owned by U.S. residents but located abroad. A secondary part is labor income of U.S. residents working abroad. The total of this "factor income from abroad" in 2005 was $0.51 trillion, as shown in Table 2.5. The counterpart to the U.S. factor income from abroad is the U.S. payments to factors located abroad. These payments are to capital (assets) located in the United States but owned by foreigners and to foreigners working in the United States. The total of these payments to the rest of the world in 2005 was $0.47 trillion. The **net factor income from abroad** is the difference between U.S. income receipts from the rest of the world and U.S. income payments to the rest of the world: $0.51 trillion less $0.47 trillion, or $0.04 trillion. The addition of this amount to the GDP of $12.49 trillion yields the **gross national product (GNP)** of $12.52 trillion, as shown in Table 2.5. The GNP gives the total gross income to U.S. factors of production, whether located in the United States or abroad.

One part of U.S. GDP covers the depreciation of the fixed capital stock located in the United States. This depreciation does not show up as income for factors of production. In particular, depreciation is subtracted from gross business revenue to calculate corporate profits or proprietors' income. If we subtract from GNP the estimated depreciation of $1.57 trillion, we get the net national product (NNP) for 2005 of $10.95 trillion. Aside from a statistical discrepancy (−$0.04 trillion in 2005), the NNP corresponds to national income. Thus, Table 2.5 shows how we get to the national income of $10.90 trillion, the number that we saw before in Table 2.4.

**2. Personal income and personal disposable income.** We can also calculate the income that households receive directly, a concept called **personal income**. The route from national income to personal income involves a number of adjustments. First, only a portion of corporate profits are paid out as dividends to households. The other part is called *retained earnings*. Second, personal income excludes contributions for government social-insurance programs, because individuals do not receive these contributions directly as income. Other adjustments involve transfer payments and the surplus of government enterprises. Table 2.5 lists the various items. The personal income for 2005 of $10.25 trillion turned out to be $0.65 trillion less than national income.

We can also compute the income that households have left after paying personal taxes, which include individual income taxes and property taxes. (Some other levies—production taxes and contributions for social insurance—were already deducted to calculate personal income.) Personal income after taxes is called **disposable personal income**. In 2005, personal taxes were $1.21 trillion. Deducting this amount from the personal income of $10.25 trillion leads to the disposable personal income of $9.04 trillion, as shown in Table 2.5.

## Measuring GDP by Production

We can also break down national income in accordance with the sectors of production that generate the income. Table 2.6 on the next page shows this breakdown for the United States in 2005.

The total national income of $10.89 trillion[5] in 2005 breaks down into $10.86 trillion from domestic industries and $0.03 trillion from the rest of the world. The last item is the net factor income from abroad. For the domestic industries, $9.56 trillion, or 88% of national income, comes from the private sector, and $1.30 trillion, or 12%, comes from government (federal, state, and local).

Table 2.6 shows how the $9.56 trillion of income from private industries divides into 14 sectors. The largest shares are 19% in finance, insurance, and real estate; 16% in professional and business services; 14% in manufacturing; 10% in education, health care, and social assistance; 9% in retail trade; 7% in wholesale trade; 6% in construction; 4% in arts, entertainment, recreation, accommodation, and food services; 4% in information; and 3% in transportation. Note that agriculture and mining together constitute only 2.5% of the total.

## Seasonal Adjustment

Data on GDP and its components are available for the United States and most other countries on a quarterly basis. These data allow us to study economic fluctuations at a quarterly frequency. However, one problem with the raw data is that they include sizeable systematic variations due to seasonal factors. The typical pattern is that U.S. real GDP rises during a calendar year and reaches a peak in the fourth quarter (October–December). Then real GDP usually falls sharply in the first quarter of the next year (January–March) before rebounding from the second to the fourth quarters.

The seasonal fluctuations in real GDP and other macroeconomic variables reflect the influences of weather and holidays (notably the Christmas period and summer vacations). For most purposes, we want to use the national-accounts data to study economic fluctuations that reflect factors other than normal seasonal patterns. For this reason, the BEA

---

[5] This total differs slightly from the national income of $10.90 trillion shown in Tables 2.4 and 2.5 because of a differing treatment of depreciation.

Table 2.6 | U.S. National Income by Sector in 2005

| Sector of Production | Trillions of dollars | % of National Income |
|---|---|---|
| **National income** | 10.89 | 100.0 |
| Net factor income from abroad | 0.03 | 0.3 |
| Domestic industries | 10.86 | 99.7 |
| Government | 1.30 | 12.0 |
| Private industries | 9.56 | 87.7 |

| | | % of Private National Income |
|---|---|---|
| Agriculture, forestry, fishing, hunting | 0.08 | 0.8 |
| Mining | 0.16 | 1.7 |
| Utilities | 0.18 | 1.9 |
| Construction | 0.61 | 6.4 |
| Manufacturing | 1.34 | 14.0 |
| Wholesale trade | 0.68 | 7.2 |
| Retail trade | 0.84 | 8.8 |
| Transportation, warehousing | 0.32 | 3.3 |
| Information | 0.39 | 4.1 |
| Finance, insurance, real estate, rental, leasing | 1.86 | 19.4 |
| Professional and business services | 1.48 | 15.5 |
| Education, health care, social assistance | 0.95 | 9.9 |
| Arts, entertainment, recreation, accommodation, food services | 0.40 | 4.2 |
| Other private services | 0.26 | 2.9 |

**Source:** Bureau of Economic Analysis (http://www.bea.gov).

adjusts real GDP and its components to filter out the typical seasonal variation. Variables adjusted this way are called **seasonally adjusted data**. The national-accounts information reported in the news media and used for most macroeconomic analyses comes in this seasonally adjusted form. We use seasonally adjusted quarterly data in this book to analyze economic fluctuations.

Seasonal adjustments apply also to many of the monthly variables reported in the news media and used for macroeconomic analyses. These variables include employment and unemployment, labor earnings, industrial production, retail sales, and the consumer price index.[6] When we discuss these monthly variables in this book, we refer to seasonally-adjusted data.

---

[6] The seasonal variation in the consumer price index turns out to be minor but is substantial in the other variables. Seasonal variation is not detectable in various interest rates, and these variables are not seasonally adjusted.

9038.0
18.860
7.7577
61.851 | # By The Numbers

## Gross state product for U.S. states

We have focused on the overall U.S. GDP. It is also possible to break down GDP into amounts produced within each of the 50 U.S. states plus the District of Columbia. The value of the gross output produced in a state is called **gross state product (GSP)**. Table 2.7 on the next page shows how the total nominal U.S. GDP of $11.7 trillion in 2004 broke down by state.[7] California contributed 13.3% of U.S. GDP, New York 7.7%, Texas 7.6%, and Florida 5.1%. At the low end, Vermont, North Dakota, Wyoming, Montana, and South Dakota each had only 0.2% of U.S. GDP.

## Prices

We already discussed how the computation of chained real GDP generates an implicit price deflator for the GDP. The resulting series gives us a good measure of an overall price index. That is, we get a price index that matches up with the overall market basket of goods and services produced domestically. We can also use this approach to get implicit price deflators for the components of GDP. For example, we have a deflator for personal consumption expenditure, one for gross private domestic investment, and so on.[8]

In addition to these implicit price deflators, we have broad price indexes that the Bureau of Labor Statistics (BLS) computes directly. The most important examples are the **consumer price index (CPI)** and the **producer price index (PPI)**, which is also called the **wholesale price index**.

The main CPI series comes from monthly and bi-monthly surveys of prices of goods and services in 87 urban areas. Data are collected on roughly 80,000 items from 23,000 retail and service establishments. The CPI also includes data on rents, which come from a survey of 50,000 landlords or tenants. The index that receives the most attention applies to urban consumers, estimated to cover 87% of the overall U.S. population. The CPI is a weighted average of individual prices, where the current weights reflect expenditure shares found in the Consumer Expenditure Survey of over 30,000 individuals and families in 1993–95. These weights remain fixed from month to month, until a new survey is taken.[9]

The CPI computed in 2006 was defined to equal 100 for the average of months in 1982–84. Thus, the CPI for March 2006 of 199.8 meant that the price of the average item rose by 99.8% from mid-1983 to March 2006. This cumulative increase in the price level

---

[7] The total of gross state product for the states, $11.67 trillion, is slightly less than the U.S. GDP for 2004, $11.73 trillion, because GDP includes compensation of government employees and depreciation of military capital stocks located abroad (and, therefore, not within any state)

[8] However, the deflator for government purchases of goods and services is not very useful. Since most of the government output is not sold on markets, this price deflator reflects arbitrary assumptions about costs of providing public services. The main assumption is that the productivity of government employees does not vary over time.

[9] The CPI, which weights individual prices by the importance of goods in a prior year (such as 1993–95), is called a Laspeyres index of prices. In contrast, a price index that weights prices by the importance of goods in the current year is called a Paasche index. The old-style implicit GDP deflator, which weighted current expenditure in accordance with prices from a prior base year, turns out to be a Paasche index of prices. However, the modern version of the implicit GDP deflator is a chain-linked index, where the weights effectively change with each observation. The PPI is another example of a Laspeyres index of prices.

T a b l e   2 . 7   |   Gross State Product by U.S. State in 2004

| State | Gross State Product ($ billion) | % of U.S. Total | State | Gross State Product ($ billion) | % of U.S. Total |
|---|---|---|---|---|---|
| U.S. | 11,666* | 100.0 | Missouri | 203 | 1.7 |
| Alabama | 140 | 1.2 | Montana | 27 | 0.2 |
| Alaska | 34 | 0.3 | Nebraska | 68 | 0.6 |
| Arizona | 200 | 1.7 | Nevada | 100 | 0.9 |
| Arkansas | 81 | 0.7 | New Hampshire | 52 | 0.4 |
| California | 1551 | 13.3 | New Jersey | 416 | 3.6 |
| Colorado | 200 | 1.7 | New Mexico | 61 | 0.5 |
| Connecticut | 186 | 1.6 | New York | 897 | 7.7 |
| Delaware | 54 | 0.5 | North Carolina | 336 | 2.9 |
| D.C. | 77 | 0.6 | North Dakota | 23 | 0.2 |
| Florida | 599 | 5.1 | Ohio | 420 | 3.6 |
| Georgia | 343 | 2.9 | Oklahoma | 108 | 0.9 |
| Hawaii | 50 | 0.4 | Oregon | 128 | 1.1 |
| Idaho | 44 | 0.4 | Pennsylvania | 468 | 4.0 |
| Illinois | 522 | 4.5 | Rhode Island | 42 | 0.4 |
| Indiana | 228 | 2.0 | South Carolina | 136 | 1.2 |
| Iowa | 111 | 1.0 | South Dakota | 29 | 0.2 |
| Kansas | 99 | 0.8 | Tennessee | 218 | 1.9 |
| Kentucky | 136 | 1.2 | Texas | 884 | 7.6 |
| Louisiana | 153 | 1.3 | Utah | 83 | 0.7 |
| Maine | 43 | 0.4 | Vermont | 22 | 0.2 |
| Maryland | 228 | 2.0 | Virginia | 329 | 2.8 |
| Massachusetts | 318 | 2.7 | Washington | 262 | 2.2 |
| Michigan | 372 | 3.2 | West Virginia | 49 | 0.4 |
| Minnesota | 224 | 1.9 | Wisconsin | 212 | 1.8 |
| Mississippi | 76 | 0.7 | Wyoming | 24 | 0.2 |

**Source:** Bureau of Economic Analysis (http://www.bea.gov).

*Total is less than the 2004 GDP of $11,734 because GDP includes compensation of government employees and depreciation of military capital stocks located abroad.

corresponded to an average growth rate of the price level by 3.1% per year over the 23 years since mid-1983. That is, the inflation rate measured by the CPI was 3.1% per year. In contrast, the inflation rate computed from the implicit GDP deflator over the same period was 2.5% per year. As discussed in the nearby box, the higher CPI inflation rate—by 0.6% per year—probably reflects an upward bias created by the maintenance of fixed weights for long periods in the CPI market basket.

# Back To Reality

## Problems with the consumer price index

The CPI receives a lot of attention because it provides monthly information on the prices of a broad market basket of goods and services bought by households. Part of the attention arises because some public and private contracts index nominal payments to the CPI. For example, benefits paid under Social Security, payments made on the U.S. Treasury's inflation-protected securities, and bracket limits in the U.S. individual income tax adjust automatically for changes in the CPI.

Many economists think that the reported increases in the CPI overstate inflation and, hence, that the automatic adjustments of Social Security benefits and some other payments have been too large to keep the outlays fixed in real terms. Naturally, this assessment is controversial, because any repairs would have significant consequences for real transfer payments, real tax collections, and so on. The idea that changes in the CPI seriously overstate inflation was expressed in 1996 by the President's Commission on the Consumer Price Index (see Michael Boskin et al. [1996]). The Commission's conclusion was that the growth rate of the CPI exaggerated inflation on average by over one percentage point per year.

One reason for the overstatement of inflation is called *substitution bias*. The idea is that changes in supply conditions shift the relative prices of various goods and services, and households respond by shifting expenditure toward the goods and services that have become relatively cheaper. However, because the weights in the CPI are fixed for long intervals, the formula for computing the CPI responds only with a substantial lag to changes in the pattern of purchases. In particular, the CPI fails to give increasing weight to the cheaper items that tend to become more important in the typical household's expenditures. This problem is conceptually easy to fix by shifting to the chain-weighting approach described before for the calculation of the implicit GDP deflator. This

deflator is free of substitution bias because the weights change nearly continuously over time.

The BLS has constructed a chain-weighted measure of the CPI since December 1999. This series showed an annual inflation rate of 2.45% per year from December 1999 to April 2006, compared to 2.84% per year for the standard CPI over the same period. The inflation rate from the implicit GDP deflator (a chain-weighted index) over the same period was 2.41% per year—close to the chain-weighted CPI. These comparisons suggest that the substitution bias in the standard CPI led to an overstatement of inflation by around 0.4% per year.

Another, more challenging problem—which applies to the implicit GDP deflator as well as the CPI—involves quality change. Despite attempts to measure improvements in quality, these changes tend to be underestimated. Therefore, some of the price increases that are recorded as inflation should actually be viewed as increases in money spent to get better quality products. A full accounting for quality improvements would therefore lower the inflation rate. Some improved measurement has been made for goods such as automobiles, computers, houses, and television sets. Interesting proposals for measuring quality change have also been offered in the medical area, where technical advances that save lives or improve the quality of life tend to be labeled as inflation.

A different kind of quality improvement involves the retail revolution associated with the rise of Wal-Mart and other big-box stores. Because of improved efficiencies in distribution and sales, customers get merchandise at lower prices than those offered by traditional outlets. However, BLS procedures do not count the substitution of low-priced Wal-Mart goods for high-priced alternative products as decreases in prices.

Another problem is that the various price indexes do not consider the effective reductions in the price level due to the introduction of new products. For example, when personal computers or DVD players became available, households were made better off for a given dollar income—even if the new goods were initially "expensive." The same idea applies to the invention of new prescription drugs, even if the prices of these drugs are "high" at the outset. The creation of useful new products tends to raise households' real income or, equivalently, lower the effective price level. Thus, a proper accounting for new products would lower the average inflation rate. The economy's real economic growth would also look stronger if the effects of new products were properly considered.

The PPI is computed in a manner conceptually similar to that of the CPI. However, the PPI does not cover services and primarily includes goods that are raw materials and semi-finished products. Each month the PPI survey collects about 100,000 prices from about 30,000 businesses. One shortcoming of the PPI is that it is too narrow a concept to reflect the general level of prices in an economy.

## Key Terms and Concepts

chain-weighted real GDP
closed economy
consumer durables
consumer nondurables and services
consumer price index (CPI)
depreciation
disposable personal income
exports
flow variable
GDP in constant dollars
GDP in current dollars
gross national product (GNP)
gross private domestic investment
gross state product (GSP)
implicit GDP deflator
imports

imputed rental income
inventories
national income
net domestic product (NDP)
net exports
net factor income from abroad
net private domestic investment
nominal GDP
open economy
personal consumption expenditure
personal income
producer price index (PPI)
seasonally adjusted data
stock variable
value added
wholesale price index

## Questions and Problems

**A.** Review questions

1. Define nominal and real GDP. Are these flow or stock concepts? Explain why the differences between nominal and real GDP are important.

2. Define the implicit price deflator. Where does this concept come from? How does it relate to nominal and real GDP? How does the implicit price deflator differ from the consumer price index (CPI)?

3. We discussed alternative views of GDP from the perspectives of expenditure, income, and production. What are the basic differences in these approaches? Why do they add to the same total for GDP?

**B.** Problems for discussion

4. What are some of the shortcomings of real GDP from a welfare perspective? Do you have any practical suggestions for revising the computation of GDP to achieve a better measure of welfare?

5. Table 2.5 shows the relation between GDP and income for the United States in 2005. Replicate this table for any European country.

# Economic Growth

## Part 2

# C h a p t e r 3

## Introduction to Economic Growth

In 2000, the real gross domestic product, or real GDP, per person in the United States was $34,800 (valued in U.S. dollars for the year 2000). This high output per person meant that the typical U.S. resident had a high **standard of living**, which refers to the quantity and quality of the goods and services consumed. Most families had their own home, at least one car, several television sets, education at least through high school and often college, and a level of health that translated into a life expectancy at birth of nearly 80 years. Nearly as high standards of living applied to most Western European countries—including the United Kingdom, Germany, France, and Italy—and a few other places, such as Canada, Australia, New Zealand, Japan, Singapore, and Hong Kong.

The residents of most other countries were not nearly as well off in 2000. For example, the real GDP per person was $9,100 in Mexico, $3,900 in China, $2,600 in India, and $740 in Nigeria, the most populous country in Africa.[1] Lower real GDPs per person meant lower standards of living. The typical resident of Mexico could afford food, shelter, and basic health care but could not attain the range and quality of consumer goods available to most Americans. Even more seriously, the typical Nigerian had concerns about nutrition and housing, and faced a life expectancy at birth of less than 50 years.

How can countries with low real GDP per person catch up to the high levels enjoyed by the United States and other rich countries? The only answer is to have a high **rate of economic growth**— the rate at which real GDP per person increases—over long periods, such as 20 or 40 years. To illustrate, Table 3.1 shows the level of real GDP per person that China would attain in 2020, based on its growth rate of real GDP per person from 2000 to 2020. It would take a growth rate of 10% per year— an unprecedented accomplishment for 20 years—for China's real GDP per person in 2020 to approach $30,000, nearly the U.S. level in 2000. Moreover, since the U.S. real GDP per person will likely be growing, even a 10% growth rate would leave China's real GDP per person in 2020 far short of the U.S. level. Worse yet, if China's real GDP per person grew at only 2% per year, its level of real GDP per

---

[1] These GDP numbers adjust for purchasing-power differences across countries. The data are from Alan Heston, Robert Summers, and Bettina Aten (2002).

| Table 3.1 | Economic Growth and China's Real GDP per Person in 2020* |
|---|---|

| Growth Rate of Real GDP per Person from 2000 to 2020 | Real GDP per Person in 2020 (in 2000 dollars) |
|---|---|
| 2% per year | 5,820 |
| 5% per year | 10,600 |
| 10% per year | 28,800 |

*China starts with real per capita GDP of $3,900 in 2000. We calculate the level of real GDP per person in 2020 as follows. Start with the natural logarithm of real GDP per person in 2000: ln (3,900) = 8.269. Then multiply the number of years, 20, by the growth rate—for example, 0.02 if the growth rate is 2% per year: $20 \times 0.02 = 0.40$. Add this to 8.269 to get 8.669. Then take the exponential of 8.669 to get the answer, 5,820.

person in 2020 would be only $5,800, 17% of the U.S. level in 2000. Thus, differences in rates of economic growth, when sustained for 20 years or more, make an enormous difference in standards of living, measured by levels of real GDP per person.

The benefits of sustained economic growth apply to all nations, not just China. Thus, the universal question is, what can we—or our governments—do to increase the rate of economic growth? The importance of this question inspired economist Robert Lucas (1988) to ask: "Is there some action a government of India could take that would lead the Indian economy to grow like Indonesia's or Egypt's? If so, what, exactly? If not, what is it about the 'nature of India' that makes it so? The consequences for human welfare involved in questions like these are simply staggering: once one starts to think about them, it is hard to think about anything else" (p. 5).[2] Questions like these underline the challenge of developing policies that promote economic growth. This challenge motivates the study that we begin in this chapter and continue in the following two chapters.

We start by presenting key facts about economic growth, first for a large number of countries since 1960 and, second, for the United States and other rich countries for over a century. These observations bring out patterns that we need to understand to design policies to promote economic growth. As a way to gain this understanding, we construct a model of economic growth, called the Solow model. In Chapters 4 and 5, we extend this model and see how these extensions relate to patterns of economic growth and to Lucas's policy challenge.

---

[2] When Lucas wrote these words in the mid 1980s, India had been growing more slowly than Egypt and Indonesia for some time. The growth rates of real GDP per person from 1960 to 1980 were 2.5% per year in Egypt, 3.5% in Indonesia, and 1.6% in India. However, India did manage to surpass the other two countries in terms of growth rates from 1980 to 2000: the growth rates of real GDP per person were 2.7% per year for Egypt, 3.3% for Indonesia, and 3.8% for India. Thus, the Indian government may have met Lucas's challenge.

# Facts About Economic Growth

## Economic Growth Around the World, 1960 to 2000

We start our study of economic growth by comparing living standards—gauged by real GDP per person—for a large number of countries. This comparison will allow us to see at a glance which countries are rich and which are poor. In Figure 3.1, the horizontal axis plots real GDP per person (in U.S. dollars for the year 2000), and the vertical axis shows the number of countries with each real GDP per person in 2000. The graph applies to 151 countries with data, and representative countries are labeled for each bar.

The United States, with a real GDP per person of $34,800, was only the second richest country in 2000—the number one spot went to Luxembourg, a very small country, with $45,900. More generally, the top positions were dominated by the long-term members of the rich countries' club, which is known as the Organization for Economic Cooperation and Development (OECD). This elite group includes most of Western Europe, the United States, Canada, Australia, New Zealand, and Japan. Overall, 20 of the richest 25 economies in 2000 were OECD members. The other five were Singapore (ranked 3rd), Hong Kong (6th), Macao (14th), Cyprus (23rd), and Taiwan (25th). (Hong Kong and Macao are parts of China, and Taiwan's status is in dispute.)

The poorest country in Figure 3.1 is Congo (Kinshasa), a sub-Saharan African country, with a real GDP per person of $238, again in 2000 U.S. dollars. Therefore, in 2000, the richest country (Luxembourg) had a real GDP per person that was 193 times that of the

**Figure  3 . 1  |  World Distribution of Real GDP per Person in 2000**

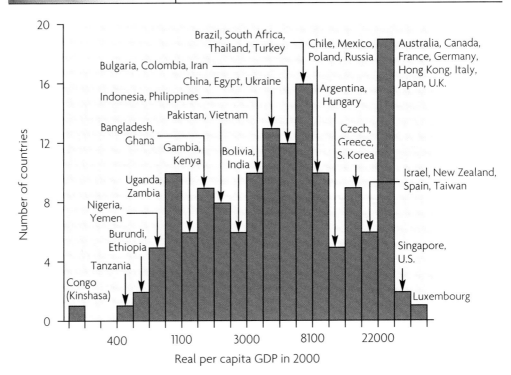

The graph shows the distribution of real gross domestic product (GDP) per person for 151 countries in 2000. The horizontal axis is in 2000 U.S. dollars and uses a proportionate scale. Representative countries are indicated for the ranges of real GDP per person.

poorest country. If we exclude Luxembourg because of its small size and compare instead with the United States, we find that the United States had a real GDP per person that was 146 times as large as Congo's.

Economists use the term **poverty** to describe low standards of living. A person or family living in poverty has difficulty affording the basic necessities of life—food, clothing, shelter, and health—and can only dream about automobiles and television sets. Poverty reflects low real incomes of individuals and families. According to one definition used by international organizations such as the United Nations and the World Bank, an individual was living in poverty in 2000 if his or her annual income was less than $570 per year in 1996 prices. The value of $570 per year is a modification of a well-known standard established in the 1980s that viewed the poverty line as an income of $1 per person per day. Therefore, we can refer to $570 per year as the $1-per-day poverty standard.

The number of persons living in poverty in a country depends on two things. One is the way that the country's income is distributed among persons; for example, the total income might be distributed nearly evenly, or a small fraction of the population might have most of the income. The second is the country's average real income, which can be approximated by real GDP per person. If this average is very low, the typical resident will be living in poverty even if income is distributed evenly.

In practice, the second factor—a country's real GDP per person—is the most important determinant of the number of people living in poverty. Countries with very low real GDP per person are the ones in which a large fraction of the population lives in poverty. Therefore, the data plotted in Figure 3.1 tell us that world poverty in 2000 was dominated by sub-Saharan Africa—an amazing 23 of the lowest 25 real GDPs per person were in this region. The two other countries in this poorest group were Yemen (9th from the bottom) and Tajikistan (25th).

Real GDP per person in 2000 gives us a snapshot of the standard of living at a point in time. The rich countries, such as the OECD members, were rich in 2000 because their levels of real GDP per person rose for a long period. Similarly, the levels of real GDP per person in poor countries in 2000—especially in sub-Saharan Africa—had not been growing. In fact, as we shall see, many of these growth rates were negative, so that real GDP per person fell over time.

To measure economic growth, we have to compare the levels of real GDP per person in 2000 with those from earlier years. Figure 3.2 on the next page begins this comparison by showing a graph of real GDP per person 40 years earlier, in 1960. This graph is similar to the one in Figure 3.1. The horizontal axis again shows real GDP per person, still using U.S. dollars in the year 2000. The vertical axis shows the number of countries with each real GDP per person in 1960. The total number of countries is only 113, given the availability of data for 1960.

In 1960, Switzerland was at the top with a real GDP per person of $15,600, and the United States was again second, at $12,800. The top 25 was dominated by the long-term members of the OECD—again, 20 of the richest 25 countries were OECD members. One difference from 2000 was that no Asian countries were in the top 25 in 1960. Several Latin American countries (Argentina, Uruguay, and Venezuela) were in the top group, but none remained in 2000. Israel and South Africa were also in this group in 1960 but not in 2000 (at which point Israel was ranked 27th, and South Africa 55th).

The low end for real GDP per person was dominated somewhat less by sub-Saharan Africa in 1960 than in 2000. The poorest country in 1960 was Tanzania, at $400, but "only" 19 of the 25 countries with the lowest real GDPs per person were in sub-Saharan Africa. Five of the poorest 25 in 1960 were in Asia—Pakistan, China, Nepal, India, and Indonesia. The other member of the lowest 25 was Romania (25th from the bottom). The six non-African countries grew rapidly enough over the next 40 years to escape the lowest category. In fact, the high growth in Asia and the low growth in sub-Saharan Africa from

| Figure 3.2 | World Distribution of Real GDP per Person in 1960 |

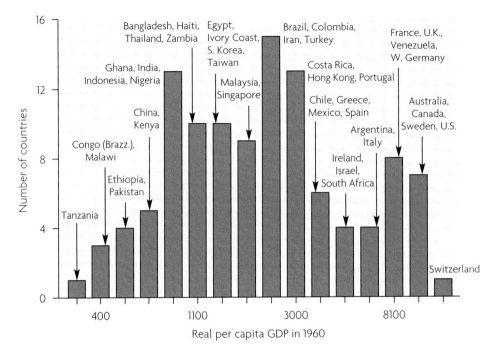

The graph shows the distribution of real gross domestic product (GDP) per person for 113 countries in 1960. The horizontal axis is in 2000 U.S. dollars and uses a proportionate scale. Representative countries are indicated for the ranges of real GDP per person.

1960 to 2000 were major parts of the story about world standards of living in 2000. In the next section, we discuss how these developments affected world poverty.

In 1960, the richest country (Switzerland) had a real GDP per person that was 39 times that of the poorest country (Tanzania). This spread was lower than the one in 2000, where the U.S. real GDP per person was 146 times that of Congo (Kinshasa).

If we compare the levels of real GDP per person in 2000 and 1960 for each country, we can compute the country's growth rate of real GDP per person over the 40 years.[3] Figure 3.3 shows the distribution of these growth rates for the 112 countries with the necessary data. The construction of this graph is similar to those in Figures 3.1 and 3.2. The horizontal axis now shows the growth rate of real GDP per person from 1960 to 2000, and the vertical axis shows the number of countries with each growth rate.

The average growth rate of real GDP per person from 1960 to 2000 for 112 countries was 1.8% per year. The fastest-growing country was Taiwan, with a rate of 6.4%. More generally, many of the fast growers from 1960 to 2000—8 of the top 12—came from East Asia. Aside from Taiwan, the East Asian countries in the top 20 were Singapore, South Korea, Hong Kong, Thailand, China, Japan (which grew rapidly mainly up to the early 1970s), Malaysia, and Indonesia. Some long-term OECD countries were among the top 20 for economic growth: Ireland, Portugal, Spain, and Luxembourg. The other members of the top 20 were Botswana (the star performer of sub-Saharan Africa), Cyprus, Barbados, Mauritius, Romania, Cape Verde, and Congo (Brazzaville).

---

[3] The easiest way to compute the growth rate of real GDP per person from 1960 to 2000 is to calculate (1/40) * log (real GDP per person in 2000/real GDP per person in 1960), where log is the natural logarithm.

| Figure 3.3 | World Distribution of Growth Rates of Real GDP per Person, 1960–2000 |

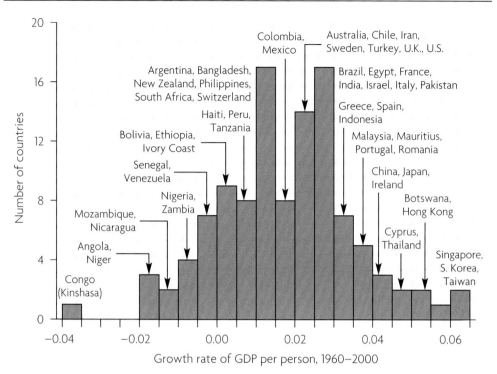

The graph shows the distribution of the growth rate of real GDP per person for 112 countries from 1960 to 2000. Representative countries are indicated for the ranges of growth rates. The unweighted average growth rate was 1.8% per year.

At the bottom end, 18 of the 20 worst performers for economic growth from 1960 to 2000 were in sub-Saharan Africa. The two non-African slow growers were Nicaragua (−1.2% per year) and Venezuela (−0.5%). Among the 18 African countries, 15 experienced negative growth of real GDP per person, with Congo (Kinshasa) the worst at −3.6% per year. Thus, the reason for low levels of real GDP per person in 2000 is partly that countries in this region started off badly in 1960 (around the time of independence for most of the countries) and, even more so, that they performed so poorly in terms of the growth of real GDP per person from 1960 to 2000. The poorest countries in 2000—especially in sub-Saharan Africa—were poor mainly because they had grown at low or negative rates since 1960. Thus, to go further, we have to understand why these countries failed to grow at higher rates.

We have also learned that a group of countries in East Asia grew at high rates from 1960 to 2000. This strong growth enabled these countries to move from low levels of real GDP per person in 1960 to much higher levels in 2000. To understand this change, we have to understand why these countries grew at high rates.

To appreciate the high levels of real GDP per person in the OECD countries in 2000, we have to look at data before 1960. That is, these countries were rich in 2000 partly because they grew from 1960 to 2000 but, even more so, because they were already rich in 1960. To get a feel for these longer-term developments in currently rich countries, we will look at historical data for the United States and other OECD countries in Section C of this chapter.

## World Poverty and Income Inequality

We noted that poverty refers to a minimally acceptable level of real income, such as the World Bank's $1-per-day standard (which actually corresponds to $570 per year in 1996 dollars). The term **inequality** is often used interchangeably with poverty but is actually different in meaning. Inequality describes an unequal distribution of income across individuals at a point in time within a country or around the world. One common measure of inequality is the fraction of a nation's income received by persons in the lowest fifth of the distribution. If income were equally distributed, this number would be 20%. The greater the shortfall of this share from 20%, the higher the income inequality. Similarly, we can look at the fraction of income received by persons in the upper fifth of the distribution. The greater the excess of this share above 20%, the higher the income inequality.

In practice, the distribution of income is far from equal—for 73 countries with data around 1990, the average amount of the income received by the lowest fifth was 6.6%, whereas the average for the highest fifth was 45%. These income shares were 6.5% and 39% for the United States (about average inequality based on the lowest fifth, and lower than average inequality based on the highest fifth), 7.8% and 41% for the United Kingdom (less unequal than the U.S. at the bottom but slightly more unequal at the top), 9.4% and 28% for Canada (a country with relatively little inequality), and 4.4% and 60% for Brazil (a country with a lot of inequality).

For a given average income per person, the degree of inequality determines the fraction of the population that falls below the $1-per-day poverty line. Unless average real income is extremely low, more inequality means that a higher fraction of the population falls below the poverty line. However, when average real income changes—for example, when real GDP per person rises—inequality and poverty behave differently.

To understand why, suppose that everyone's real income were to double. In this case, inequality would not change—for example, if the lowest fifth of the distribution started with 6% of total income, the lowest fifth would still have 6% after everyone's income doubled. In contrast, poverty would fall sharply if everyone's real income doubled—because more people's real incomes would exceed the $1-per-day standard. If we think that a person's welfare depends on his or her real income, rather than income measured relative to that of other persons, then poverty is more meaningful than inequality as a measure of welfare.

Xavier Sala-i-Martin (2006) showed that economic growth led to a dramatic fall in world poverty from 1970 to 2000. The estimated number of people below the $1-per-day poverty line ($570 per year in 1996 prices) fell from 700 million, or 20% of the world's population in 1970, to 398 million, or 7% of the population in 2000.[4]

Figure 3.4 shows how these changes occurred. Part (a) describes the distribution of income for the world's people in 1970. The horizontal axis plots real income on a proportionate scale, and the vertical axis shows the number of people with each level of income. The vertical lines marked $1 show the income levels that correspond to the $1-per-day poverty line. Consider the area below the upper curve and to the left of the $1 line. To find the fraction of the world's population with incomes below $1 per day, we take the ratio of this area to the total area under the upper curve. The result is 20%.

World economic growth from 1970 to 2000 led to a shift from Figure 3.4a to Figure 3.4b. Notice that the whole distribution of income shifted to the right, because larger proportions of the world's people had higher real incomes. Hence, the fraction of the

---

[4] The fraction of the population living in poverty is called the *poverty rate*, whereas the number of people living in poverty is called the *poverty headcount*. The decrease in the poverty rate from 1970 to 2000 was so sharp that the world poverty headcount decreased, despite the substantial rise in world population.

| Figure 3.4 | (a) World Income Distribution in 1970; (b) World Income Distribution in 2000 |

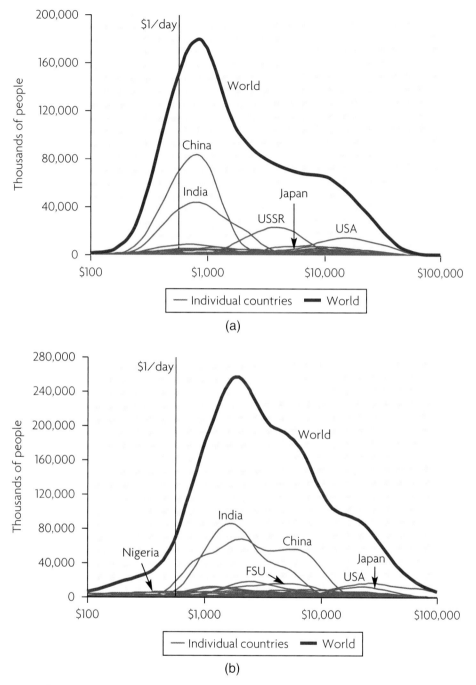

(a)

(b)

Figure 3.4a is for 1970 and Figure 3.4b is for 2000. In each case, the horizontal axis plots real income in 1985 U.S. dollars on a proportionate scale. For the upper curves in the two figures, the vertical axis shows the number of people in the world with each level of income. The vertical lines marked $1 show the annual real incomes that correspond to the standard poverty line of $1 per day ($570 per year in 1996 prices). The income distributions for a few large countries are shown separately. FSU is the former Soviet Union. (Nigeria is hidden beneath the Asian countries in Figure 3.4a.) The values shown on the upper curves for numbers of people in the world are the vertical sums of the numbers of people in all of the individual countries. However, only a few of the countries can be discerned in these graphs.

**Source:** These graphs come from Xavier Sala-i-Martin (2006).

world's population with incomes below the $1-per-day poverty line was much smaller in 2000 than in 1970. The percentage for 2000 was 7%, compared to 20% in 1970. This sharp decline in poverty rates shows the dramatic progress over three decades as a result of economic growth.

The graphs also show how some of the world's largest countries fared from 1970 to 2000. For poverty, the biggest changes occurred in China and India, which accounted for nearly 40% of world population in 2000. In 1970, many residents of China and India and other Asian countries were below the $1-per-day poverty line—Asia accounted for 80% overall of persons living in poverty. However, Figures 3.4a and 3.4b show that the income distribution curves for China and India (and also Indonesia, another large Asian country) shifted dramatically to the right from 1970 to 2000. This change reflected the strong economic growth in Asia, particularly since the late 1970s for China and the mid-1980s for India. Consequently, by 2000, Asia accounted for only 19% of persons living in poverty.

We also know that recent decades saw very low economic growth in sub-Saharan Africa. Consequently, the poverty numbers soared. In 1970, sub-Saharan Africa accounted for only 13% of persons living in poverty. However, in 2000, this region accounted for 74% of persons in poverty. Thus, poverty shifted from primarily an Asian problem to mainly an African problem.

The results are more complicated for world inequality. We can think of the changes in two parts: the first is within countries and the second is across countries. Inequality rose from 1970 to 2000 within several large countries, including the United States, the United Kingdom, and China. However, Sala-i-Martin showed that these changes within countries had only minor effects on inequality across persons in the entire world.

The second factor is the dispersion of average incomes across countries. We know from Figures 3.1 and 3.2 that the ratio of the highest real GDPs per person (concentrated in the OECD countries) to the lowest (primarily in sub-Saharan Africa) rose from 1960 to 2000. However, since world inequality involves numbers of people, rather than numbers of countries, we have to give more weight to the larger countries. The income changes in the larger countries, especially China and India, matter a lot more than the changes in the smaller countries. Since China and India had very low average real incomes in 1970, their strong economic growth from 1970 to 2000 contributed heavily to a reduction of world income inequality. It turns out that this force dominated the others and led to a decrease in standard measures of world income inequality from 1970 to 2000.

## Long-Term Growth in the United States and Other Rich Countries

We mentioned that, for the United States and other OECD countries, the main reason for high real GDP per person in recent years is that these countries already had high real GDP per person in 1960. Therefore, to understand U.S. prosperity, we have to take a long-term view that starts well before 1960.

If we go back more than a century, we find that U.S. real GDP per person in 1869 (the first year for which reliable annual data are available) was $2,311, measured in 2000 U.S. dollars. Therefore, the real GDP per person of $37,600 in 2005 was 16 times that of 1869. An increase in real GDP per person and, hence, in the typical person's real income by a factor of 16, makes an enormous difference in the standard of living. In 2005, unlike in 1869, the typical U.S. family not only owned a comfortable home and had ample food and clothing but also possessed many things not even imagined in 1869: automobiles, television sets, telephones, personal computers, and a connection to the Internet. Also, compared with 136 years earlier, education levels were much higher, life expectancy was substantially longer, and a much larger fraction of the population lived in cities.

The average growth rate of real GDP per person in the United States from 1869 to 2005 was 2.0% per year. This growth rate does not seem all that impressive—it is only slightly higher than the average rate of 1.8% for year from 1960 to 2000 for the 112 countries shown in Figure 3.3. Moreover, the long-term U.S. growth rate is much less than the 6% per year achieved by some East Asian countries from 1960 to 2000. Nevertheless, the U.S. growth rate of 2.0% per year—when sustained for such a long time—was enough to make the United States the world's second richest country in 2005.

Living standards in the United States in 2005 would have been very different if the average growth rate of real GDP per person since 1869 had been much lower or higher than 2.0%. If the growth rate had been 1.0% per year, real GDP per person in 2005 would have been $9,004, only four times the value in 1869. In this case, the typical American family would have possessed reasonable food and health care but would lack a comfortable home and a fine automobile, would be missing an array of pleasant consumer products, and would have lower levels of education. Alternatively, if the growth rate had been 3.0%, the level of real GDP per person in 2005 would have been $136,700, 59 times the level in 1869. A real GDP per person of $136,700 means that the typical family would have had a grand home, a couple of nice cars, no problems with expensive private schooling and health care, and so on.

Similar calculations apply to other OECD countries, many of which are now nearly as rich as the United States. These countries also came to be rich because their real GDP per person grew for a long time at the unspectacular rate of around 2% per year.

Although average growth rates of real GDP per person over a century or more were around 2% per year, the growth rates were not constant over time. To see this, consider Table 3.2, which shows growth rates for 17 OECD countries, including the United States. The table shows unweighted averages for the 17 countries of the growth rates of real GDP per person over 20-year periods from 1820 to 2000. The average growth rate over the full

**T a b l e  3 . 2  |  Long-Term Economic Growth in OECD Countries**

| Period | Growth Rate of Real GDP per Person (percent per year) | Number of Countries |
|---|---|---|
| 1820–1840 | 1.2 | 10 |
| 1840–1860 | 2.1 | 10 |
| 1860–1880 | 1.3 | 14 |
| 1880–1900 | 1.4 | 17 |
| 1900–1920 | 0.8 | 17 |
| 1920–1940 | 1.8 | 17 |
| 1940–1960 | 2.4 | 17 |
| 1960–1980 | 3.1 | 17 |
| 1980–2000 | 1.8 | 17 |

**Note:** The data are from Angus Maddison (2003). The 17 countries included are Australia, Austria, Belgium, Canada, Denmark, Finland, France, Germany, Italy, Japan, Netherlands, New Zealand, Norway, Sweden, Switzerland, the United Kingdom, and the United States. The growth rates are unweighted averages for the countries with available data. Fewer countries have data for the earlier periods.

180 years was 1.8% per year, with no clear trend. However, the average growth rates since 1940 were somewhat higher: 2.4% per year.

The decline in the growth rate of real GDP per person from 3.1% per year for 1960–1980 to 1.8% per year for 1980–2000 is sometimes called the **productivity slow-down**. Measures of productivity—such as output per person and per worker—did not grow as fast from 1980 to 2000 as in the previous 20 years. However, the growth rate of 1.8% per year for 1980–2000 equaled the average growth rate since 1820. Thus, the high growth rate for 1960–1980 (and, it turns out, for 1950–1960) may have been the outlier. A reasonable guess from the numbers in Table 3.2 is that future growth rates of real GDP per person will average something close to 2% per year.

## Patterns of World Economic Growth

In looking at the data, we observed some important patterns in economic growth. First, some countries, such as those in East Asia, grew rapidly from 1960 to 2000 and thereby raised their levels of real GDP per person substantially over 40 years. Second, over the same period, other countries—especially in sub-Saharan Africa—grew at low or negative rates and therefore ended up with low levels of real GDP per person in 2000. Third, the United States and other OECD countries had high levels of real GDP per person in 2000 mostly because they grew at moderate rates—around 2% per year—for a century or more.

These observations suggest questions that we would like to answer about economic growth:

- What factors caused some countries to grow fast and others to grow slow over periods such as 1960 to 2000? In particular, why did the East Asian countries do so much better than the sub-Saharan African countries?
- How did countries such as the United States and other OECD members sustain growth rates of real GDP per person of around 2% per year for a century or more?
- What can policymakers do to increase growth rates of real GDP per person?

The answers to these questions could contribute a great deal to the living standards of future generations. The theories about economic growth that we turn to next bring us closer to finding these answers.

# Theory of Economic Growth

Now we will build a model of economic growth to help understand the patterns found in the international data. We start by considering the *production function,* which tells us how goods and services are produced.

## The Production Function

We begin our theoretical study of economic growth by considering how a country's technology and factors of production—or factor inputs—determine its output of goods and services, measured by real GDP. The relation of output to the technology and the quantities of factor inputs is called a **production function**.

We will build a simplified model that has two factor inputs: **capital stock**, $K$, and labor, $L$. In this model, capital takes a physical form, such as machines and buildings used by businesses. A more complete model would include **human capital**, which embodies the effects of education and training on workers' skills, and the effects of medical care, nutrition, and sanitation on workers' health. In our simplified model, the amount of labor input, $L$, is the quantity of work-hours per year for labor of a standard quality and effort. That is, we imagine that, at a point in time, each worker has the same skill. For convenience, we often refer to $L$ as the **labor force** or the number of workers—these interpretations are satisfactory if we think of each laborer as working a fixed number of hours per year.

We use the symbol $A$ to represent the **technology level**. For given quantities of the factor inputs, $K$ and $L$, an increase in $A$ raises output. That is, a more technologically advanced economy has a higher level of overall **productivity**. Higher productivity means that output is higher for given quantities of the factor inputs.

Mathematically, we write the production function as

---

Key equation (production function):

(3.1) $$Y = A \cdot F(K, L)$$

---

One way to see how output, $Y$, responds to the variables in the production function—the technology level, $A$, and the quantities of capital and labor, $K$ and $L$—is to change one of the three variables while holding the other two fixed. Looking at the equation, we see that $Y$ is proportional to $A$. Hence, if $A$ doubles, while $K$ and $L$ do not change, $Y$ doubles.

For a given technology level, $A$, the function $F(K, L)$ determines how additional units of capital and labor, $K$ and $L$, affect output, $Y$. We assume that each factor is productive at the margin. Hence, for given $A$ and $L$, an increase in $K$—that is, a rise in $K$ at the margin—raises $Y$. Similarly, for given $A$ and $K$, an increase in $L$ raises $Y$.

The change in $Y$ from a small increase in $K$ is called the **marginal product of capital**, which we abbreviate as **MPK**. The MPK tells us how much $Y$ rises when $K$ increases by one unit, while $A$ and $L$ do not change. The corresponding change in $Y$ from a small increase in $L$ is called the **marginal product of labor**, or **MPL**. The MPL tells us how much $Y$ rises when $L$ increases by one unit, while $A$ and $K$ do not change. We assume that the two marginal products, MPK and MPL, are greater than zero.

Figure 3.5 on the next page shows how output, $Y$, responds to an increase in capital input, $K$. This figure is a graph of the production function, $A \cdot F(K, L)$, from equation (3.1). The special feature of this graph is that we are holding constant the values of $A$ and $L$. Therefore, the graph shows how increases in $K$ affect $Y$ when $A$ and $L$ do not change.

The curve in Figure 3.5 goes through the origin, because we assume that output, $Y$, is zero if the amount of capital stock, $K$, is zero. The slope of the curve at any point is the marginal product of capital—that is, the change in $Y$ from a small increase in $K$. Since we have assumed that this marginal product, MPK, is always greater than zero, the slope of the curve is positive throughout. We also assume that the slope flattens as $K$ rises. The curve has this shape because we assume that the MPK declines as $K$ rises, for given $A$ and $L$. This property is known as **diminishing marginal product of capital**. As an example, at a low $K$, such as point $a$ in the graph, an increase in $K$ by one unit might raise $Y$ by 0.1 units per year. However, at a high $K$, such as point $b$, an increase in $K$ by one unit might raise $Y$ by only 0.05 units per year.

Figure 3.6 on the next page shows the corresponding graph for output, $Y$, as a function of labor input, $L$. This figure is again a graph of the production function, $A \cdot F(K, L)$, from equation (3.1). The special feature now is that we are holding constant the values of $A$ and $K$. This graph shows how increases in $L$ affect $Y$ when $A$ and $K$ do not change. Again, the curve goes through the origin, because we assume that $Y$ is zero if $L$ is zero. The

## Figure 3.5 | The Production Function in Terms of Capital Input

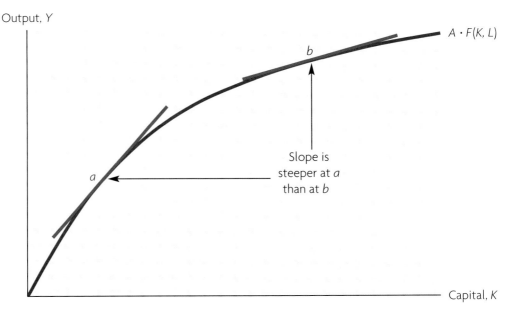

The curve shows the effect of capital input, $K$, on output, $Y$. We hold fixed the technology level, $A$, and the quantity of labor input, $L$. Therefore, the slope of the curve at any point is the marginal product of capital, MPK. This slope gets less steep as $K$ rises because of diminishing marginal product of capital. Therefore, the slope at point $a$ is greater than that at point $b$.

## Figure 3.6 | The Production Function in Terms of Labor Input

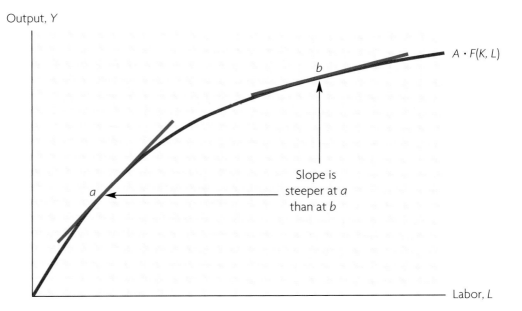

The curve shows the effect of labor input, $L$, on output, $Y$. We hold fixed the technology level, $A$, and the quantity of capital input, $K$. Therefore, the slope of the curve at any point is the marginal product of labor, MPL. This slope gets less steep as $L$ rises because of diminishing marginal product of labor. Therefore, the slope at point $a$ is greater than that at point $b$.

positive slope of the curve at any point is the marginal product of labor, MPL. The flattening of the curve as $L$ rises indicates that the MPL falls as $L$ increases, for given $A$ and $K$. Hence, we are assuming **diminishing marginal product of labor**. As an example, at a low $L$, such as point $a$ in the graph, an increase in $L$ by one unit might raise $Y$ by 0.1 units per year. However, at a high $K$, such as point $b$, an increase in $L$ by one unit might raise $Y$ by only 0.05 units per year.

Another assumption is that the production function in equation (3.1) exhibits **constant returns to scale** in the two factor inputs, $K$ and $L$. The idea is that if we double the scale of inputs—double $K$ and $L$—the output, $Y$, doubles. As an example, assume that a business starts with 5 machines, $K = 5$, and 5 workers, $L = 5$. The business has a given technology level, $A$, and is able to produce an output, $Y$, of, say, 100 widgets per year. Now, suppose that $K$ and $L$ double, so that the business has $K = 10$ machines and $L = 10$ workers. The technology level, $A$, is the same as before. Our assumption is that, with twice as many machines and workers and the same technology level, the business can produce twice as much output. That is, $Y$ is now 200 widgets per year.

More generally, if the production function exhibits constant returns to scale, a multiplication of the two factor inputs, $K$ and $L$, by any positive number leads to a multiplication of output, $Y$, by the same number. Therefore, if we multiply $K$ and $L$ by the quantity $1/L$ in equation (3.1), we also multiply $Y$ by $1/L$ to get

$$Y/L = A \cdot F(K/L, L/L)$$

The value $L/L$ on the right-hand side equals one (a constant) and can, therefore, be ignored. By writing the production function this way, we see that output per worker, $Y/L$, depends only on the technology level, $A$, and the quantity of capital per worker, $K/L$. We can show this property more clearly by defining $y \equiv Y/L$ to be output per worker and $k \equiv K/L$ to be capital per worker, and then defining a new function, $f$, that relates $y$ to $k$:

(3.2) $$y = A \cdot f(k)$$

Figure 3.7 on the next page shows the graph of output per worker, $y$, versus capital per worker, $k$, for a given technology level, $A$. This graph looks the same as the one in Figure 3.5. The slope of the curve in Figure 3.7 again tells us the effect of more capital on output; that is, it measures the marginal product of capital, MPK. Note that the marginal product of capital diminishes as capital per worker, $k$, rises.

## Growth Accounting

The production function in equation (3.1) determines the level of output or real GDP, $Y$, at a point in time for given values of its three determinants: the technology level, $A$, and the quantities of capital and labor, $K$ and $L$. However, the production function is also the starting point for our investigation of economic *growth*. To use the production function to study growth, we use a method called **growth accounting** to consider how growth in $Y$ depends on growth in $A$, $K$, and $L$. Whereas *the production function is a relation between the level of Y and the levels of A, K, and L, growth accounting is a relation between the growth rate of Y and the growth rates of A, K, and L.*

To begin the analysis of growth accounting, let $\Delta Y$ represent the change in $Y$ over an interval of time—say, a year. (The symbol $\Delta$, the Greek letter capital delta, represents the change in a variable.) The growth rate of $Y$ over the year is given by $\Delta Y/Y$. For example, if $Y = 100$ and $\Delta Y = 1$ over a year, the growth rate is $\Delta Y/Y = 1\%$ per year. Similarly, if we use $\Delta A$, $\Delta K$, and $\Delta L$ to represent the changes in technology, capital, and labor, the growth rates of each are $\Delta A/A$, $\Delta K/K$, and $\Delta L/L$, respectively.

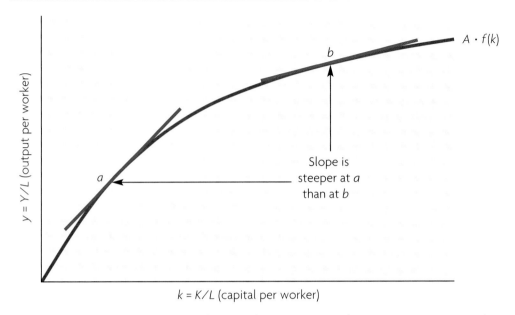

**Figure 3.7** | Output per Worker Versus Capital per Worker

This method for showing the production function plots output per worker, $y = Y/L$, against capital per worker, $k = K/L$. We hold fixed the technology level, $A$. The slope of the curve at any point is the marginal product of capital, MPK. This slope gets less steep as $k$ rises because of diminishing marginal product of capital. Therefore, the slope at point $a$ is greater than that at point $b$.

Our next task is to explain precisely how $\Delta A/A$, $\Delta K/K$, and $\Delta L/L$ contribute to the growth rate of real GDP, $\Delta Y/Y$. Start with the contribution of technology. We see from the production function

$$(3.1) \qquad Y = A \cdot F(K, L)$$

that $Y$ would grow at the same rate as $A$ if $K$ and $L$ were unchanged. For example, if $\Delta A/A = 1\%$ per year and $K$ and $L$ are constant, then $\Delta Y/Y = 1\%$ per year. Even if $K$ and $L$ are changing, equation (3.1) tells us that a higher growth rate of $A$ would contribute to a higher growth rate of $Y$. If $\Delta A/A$ is higher by 1% per year, $\Delta Y/Y$ is higher by 1% per year, for given growth rates of capital and labor, $\Delta K/K$ and $\Delta L/L$.

Now consider the contributions to the growth of real GDP from growth in capital and labor. We know that $\Delta Y/Y$ increases when $\Delta K/K$ and $\Delta L/L$ increase. To be more precise, suppose that the contribution of growth in capital to the growth of real GDP is given by $\alpha \cdot \Delta K/K$, where $\alpha$ (the Greek letter alpha) is greater than zero. Similarly, suppose that the contribution of growth in labor to the growth of real GDP is given by $\beta \cdot \Delta L/L$, where $\beta$ (the Greek letter beta) is also greater than zero. In this case, we can write that the growth rate of real GDP is given by

$$(3.3) \qquad \Delta Y/Y = \Delta A/A + \alpha \cdot (\Delta K/K) + \beta \cdot (\Delta L/L)$$

That is, the growth rate of real GDP, $\Delta Y/Y$, equals the growth rate of technology, $\Delta A/A$, plus the contributions from the growth of capital, $\alpha \cdot (\Delta K/K)$, and labor, $\beta \cdot (\Delta L/L)$.

Notice that, since $Y$ is proportional to $A$ in the production function, equation (3.1), the coefficient on $\Delta A/A$ in equation (3.3) is one.

To think about the effects from the growth rates of capital, $\Delta K/K$, and labor, $\Delta L/L$, let's simplify for the moment by neglecting growth of technology, so that $\Delta A/A = 0$. If $\Delta K/K$ and $\Delta L/L$ were the same, say, 1% per year, the condition of constant returns to scale tells us that the growth rate of real GDP, $\Delta Y/Y$, would also be 1% per year. But we see from equation (3.3) that, if $\Delta K/K$ and $\Delta L/L$ each equal one, $\Delta Y/Y$ must equal $\alpha + \beta$. Therefore, we must have

$$\alpha + \beta = 1$$

The condition of constant returns to scale implies that $\alpha$ and $\beta$ add up to one.

Since the coefficients $\alpha$ and $\beta$ add up to one, and each coefficient is greater than zero, we know that $\alpha$ and $\beta$ are each less than one. That is, the coefficients satisfy

$$0 < \alpha < 1$$

and

$$0 < \beta < 1$$

Notice that, if $\Delta K/K = 1\%$ per year and $\Delta L/L = 0$, the effect on $\Delta Y/Y$ is given by $\alpha$ in equation (3.3). Thus, if $K$ grows while $L$ stays fixed, $Y$ grows at a rate slower than the growth rate of $K$ (because $\alpha < 1$). Similarly, if $\Delta L/L = 1\%$ per year and $\Delta K/K = 0$, the effect on $\Delta Y/Y$ is given by $\beta$ in equation (3.3). Thus, if $L$ grows while $K$ stays fixed, $Y$ grows at a rate slower than the growth rate of $L$ (because $\beta < 1$).

We know from Chapter 2 that—if we neglect net flows of income from the rest of the world—the economy's total real income equals real GDP, $Y$, less depreciation of capital stocks. If the depreciation of capital is small, Appendix A to this chapter shows that the coefficient $\alpha$ approximates the share of capital income in the economy's total real income. For example, if $\alpha = 1/3$—a commonly assumed value for the share of capital income—then a growth rate of capital, $\Delta K/K$, of 1% a year would contribute $(1/3)\%$ per year to the growth rate of real GDP, $\Delta Y/Y$.

Similarly, under the conditions explored in Appendix A to this chapter, $\beta$ approximates the share of labor income in the economy's total real income. For example, if $\beta = 2/3$—a commonly assumed value for the share of labor income—a growth rate of labor, $\Delta L/L$, of 1% a year would contribute $(2/3)\%$ per year to $\Delta Y/Y$.

The interpretations of $\alpha$ and $\beta$ as shares of capital and labor in total real income fit with our result that $\alpha + \beta = 1$. That is, we have

$$share\ of\ capital\ income + share\ of\ labor\ income = 1$$
$$\alpha + \beta = 1$$

Thus, payments to capital and labor exhaust all of the real income in the economy.

We can rearrange the condition $\alpha + \beta = 1$ to substitute $1 - \alpha$ for $\beta$ on the right-hand side of equation (3.3) to get

Key equation (growth-accounting formula):

(3.4) $\Delta Y/Y = \Delta A/A + \alpha \cdot (\Delta K/K) + (1-\alpha) \cdot (\Delta L/L)$

Equation (3.4) says that we can break down the growth rate of real GDP, $\Delta Y / Y$, into the growth rate of technology, $\Delta A / A$, and a weighted average of the growth rates of capital and labor, $\alpha \cdot \Delta K / K$ and $(1 - \alpha) \cdot \Delta L / L$. The growth rate of capital gets the weight $\alpha$ (corresponding to capital's share of income), and the growth rate of labor gets the weight $1 - \alpha$ (corresponding to labor's share of income).

We now simplify by assuming that the coefficient $\alpha$, which we interpret as capital's share of income, is fixed. That is, we assume that this coefficient does not change as the economy grows. The constancy of income shares does not always apply in the real world, but it does work as a reasonable approximation for the United States and many other countries. In Appendix C to this chapter, we show that the constancy of $\alpha$ holds for a commonly assumed form of the production function, $A \cdot F(K, L)$.

## The Solow Growth Model

We learned from growth accounting in equation (3.4) that the growth rate of real GDP, $\Delta Y / Y$, depends on the growth rate of technology, $\Delta A / A$, and a weighted average of the growth rates of capital and labor, $\Delta K / K$ and $\Delta L / L$. To go from growth accounting to a theory of economic growth, we have to explain the growth rates of technology, capital, and labor. We begin this explanation by constructing the **Solow growth model**.

The Solow model makes several simplifying assumptions. First, labor input, $L$, equals the labor force, which is the number of persons seeking work. That is, the model does not allow for unemployment—labor input equals the labor force, all of which is employed. However, the important assumption is that the unemployment rate is constant, not necessarily zero. For example, if 96% of the labor force is always employed, labor input would always be a fixed multiple of the labor force and would grow at the same rate as the labor force.

The relation between the labor force, $L$, and population is given by

*labor force, L = (labor force/population) · population*

The ratio of labor force to population is the **labor-force participation rate**. In the United States, in recent years, the labor-force participation rate has been close to one-half. For example, in March 2006, the sum of the civilian labor force (150.6 million) and active-duty military (1.4 million) was 51% of the total population.[5] The second assumption in the Solow model is that this participation rate does not change over time. In this case, the equation tells us that the growth rate of labor input, $L$, equals the growth rate of population.

Third, the model ignores a role for government, so that there are no taxes, public expenditures, government debt, or money. Fourth, the model assumes a closed economy; that is, there is no international trade in goods and services or in financial assets.

To begin our analysis of the Solow model, consider again the growth-accounting equation:

**(3.4)** $$\Delta Y / Y = \Delta A / A + \alpha \cdot (\Delta K / K) + (1 - \alpha) \cdot (\Delta L / L)$$

We focus initially on growth of the two inputs, $K$ and $L$, and ignore changes in the technology level, $A$. That is, we assume $\Delta A / A = 0$. In this case, the growth-accounting equation simplifies to

**(3.5)** $$\Delta Y / Y = \alpha \cdot (\Delta K / K) + (1 - \alpha) \cdot (\Delta L / L)$$

---

[5] The Bureau of Labor Statistics (BLS) computes a different measure of the labor-force participation rate—the ratio of the civilian labor force to the civilian noninstitutional population, which is the population (aged 16 and over) not on active military duty and not in institutions such as prisons. Defined this way, the labor-force participation rate in March 2006 was (150.6/228.0) = 66%.

# Back To Reality

**Intellectual origin of the Solow growth model**

The Solow model was created during the 1950s by the MIT economist Robert Solow. This research led eventually to a Nobel Prize in 1987 for "contributions to the theory of economic growth." The Solow model was extended during the 1960s, especially by David Cass (1965) and Tjalling Koopmans (1965), and became known as the **neoclassical growth model**. The Solow model and the 1960's extensions were actually anticipated in theoretical work done by the mathematician Frank Ramsey in the 1920s. Hence, this growth model is often called the **Ramsey model**. Unfortunately, Ramsey's brilliant career was cut short by his death in 1930 at age 26.

Hence, in this version of the Solow model, the growth rate of real GDP, $\Delta Y/Y$, is a weighted average of the growth rates of capital, $\Delta K/K$, and labor, $\Delta L/L$.

We will find it useful to focus on real GDP per worker, $y = Y/L$, rather than the level of real GDP, $Y$. If $Y$ were fixed, growth in $L$ means that $y$ would decline over time. For example, with a fixed $Y$, growth in workers at 1% per year implies that $y$ falls by 1% per year. More generally, we have the formula:

(3.6)
$$\Delta y/y = \Delta Y/Y - \Delta L/L$$

*growth rate of real GDP per worker = growth rate of real GDP − growth rate of labor*

Using the same reasoning, the growth rate of capital per worker, $\Delta k/k$, falls short of the growth rate of capital, $\Delta K/K$, by the growth rate of the number of workers:

(3.7)
$$\Delta k/k = \Delta K/K - \Delta L/L$$

*growth rate of capital per worker = growth rate of capital − growth rate of labor*

Hence, for a given $\Delta K/K$, a higher $\Delta L/L$ means that, over time, each worker has less capital to work with.

If we rearrange the terms on the right-hand side of equation (3.5), we get

$$\Delta Y/Y = \alpha \cdot (\Delta K/K) - \alpha \cdot (\Delta L/L) + \Delta L/L$$

Then, if we move $\Delta L/L$ from the right side to the left side and combine the two terms on the right side that involve $\alpha$, we get

$$\Delta Y/Y - \Delta L/L = \alpha \cdot (\Delta K/K - \Delta L/L)$$

We see from equation (3.6) that the left-hand side is the growth rate of real GDP per worker, $\Delta y/y$, and from equation (3.7) that the term in parentheses on the right-hand side is the growth rate of capital per worker, $\Delta k/k$. Therefore, the key result is that the growth rate of real GDP per worker depends only on the growth rate of capital per worker:

(3.8)
$$\Delta y/y = \alpha \cdot (\Delta k/k)$$

We see from equation (3.8) that, to analyze the growth rate of real GDP per worker, $\Delta y/y$, we need only determine the growth rate of capital per worker, $\Delta k/k$. Moreover, we know from equation (3.7) that $\Delta k/k$ is the difference between the growth rate of capital, $\Delta K/K$, and the growth rate of labor, $\Delta L/L$. We first assess $\Delta K/K$ and then turn to $\Delta L/L$.

**The growth rate of the capital stock**     The change in the stock of capital, $\Delta K$, will depend on the economy's **saving**, which is the income that is not consumed. In our analysis in Chapter 7, we analyze saving behavior by considering the optimal choices of individual households. However, we simplify here by using Solow's assumption that each household divides up its real income in a fixed proportion $s$ to saving and $1 - s$ to consumption, $C$.

For the economy as a whole, we know from our study of national-income accounting in Chapter 2 that national income equals net domestic product (NDP), which equals GDP less depreciation of capital stocks. In our model, some of the national income is labor income, which goes to workers, and some is capital income, which goes to owners of capital. However, all income must flow eventually to households, partly in their role as workers and partly in their role as owners of capital (or owners of businesses). We assume that saving depends only on households' total income, not on how this income divides up between labor income and capital income.

Depreciation arises because capital stocks wear out over time. Buildings need repairs, machines deteriorate, and vehicles require new parts. We capture depreciation in a simple way by assuming that all forms of capital depreciate at the same constant rate, $\delta$ (the Greek letter delta). Therefore, the flow quantity $\delta K$ is the amount of capital that depreciates or disappears each year. In practice, the value of $\delta$ depends on the type of building or machine, but a reasonable average number is 5% per year. For example, if the stock of capital, $K$, is 100 machines, and $\delta$ is 5% per year, depreciation equals 5 machines per year.

The economy's real national income equals real NDP, which equals real GDP, $Y$, less depreciation, $\delta K$. From now on, we shorten the term national income to income. If households save the fraction $s$ of all income, the economy's total real saving is

$$real\ saving = s \cdot (Y - \delta K)$$
$$real\ saving = (saving\ rate) \cdot (real\ income)$$

Since household real income, $Y - \delta K$, goes either to consumption, $C$, or real saving, $s \cdot (Y - \delta K)$, we can also write

(3.9)
$$Y - \delta K = C + s \cdot (Y - \delta K)$$
$$real\ income = consumption + real\ saving$$

In a closed economy with no government sector, real GDP, $Y$, must be either consumed or invested. That is, the goods and services produced are used for only two purposes: consumption and outlays on capital goods or **gross investment**, $I$. Therefore, we have

$$Y = C + I$$
$$real\ GDP = consumption + gross\ investment$$

If we subtract depreciation, $\delta K$, from both sides, we get

(3.10)
$$Y - \delta K = C + (I - \delta K)$$
$$real\ NDP = consumption + net\ investment$$

Notice on the right-hand side that we have defined **net investment** as gross investment, $I$, less the part of that investment, $\delta K$, needed to make up for the depreciation of existing capital.

Equations (3.9) and (3.10) have the same variable on the left-hand side (because real national income equals real NDP). Consequently, the right-hand sides must be equal:

$$C + s \cdot (Y - \delta K) = C + I - \delta K$$

If we cancel out the variable $C$ on the two sides of the equation, we get a key equality between real saving and net investment:

(3.11)
$$s \cdot (Y - \delta K) = I - \delta K$$

*real saving = net investment*

The change in the capital stock equals gross investment, $I$—the purchases of new capital goods—less the depreciation of existing capital:

$$\Delta K = I - \delta K$$

*change in capital stock = gross investment − depreciation*

*change in capital stock = net investment*

Since net investment equals real saving from equation (3.11), we also have

(3.12)
$$\Delta K = s \cdot (Y - \delta K)$$

*change in capital stock = real saving*

If we divide through each side of equation (3.12) by $K$, we get the formula we are seeking for the growth rate of the capital stock:

(3.13)
$$\Delta K / K = s \cdot Y / K - s\delta$$

This result for $\Delta K / K$ is one of the two pieces needed to determine the growth rate of capital per worker:

(3.7)
$$\Delta k / k = \Delta K / K - \Delta L / L$$

We now turn to the second piece—the growth rate of labor, $\Delta L / L$.

**The growth rate of labor**   Given our previous assumptions (a constant labor-force participation rate and a constant unemployment rate), the growth rate of labor, $\Delta L / L$, equals the growth rate of population. Thus, we now consider **population growth**.

Population growth rates vary across countries and over time. In the United States, the population growth rate has been about 1% per year for several decades. In many Western European countries, population growth rates fell from around 1% per year in the 1960s to roughly zero in 2000. In China and India, population growth rates declined from over 2% per year in the 1960s to recent values between 1 and 1 1/2% per year. Many low-income countries still have population growth rates above 2% per year. However, there has been a worldwide tendency for population growth rates to decline over time.

In the model, we assume that population grows at a constant rate, denoted by $n$, where $n$ is a positive number ($n > 0$). At this point, we do not attempt to explain the

## Figure 3.8 | Time Path of Labor Input

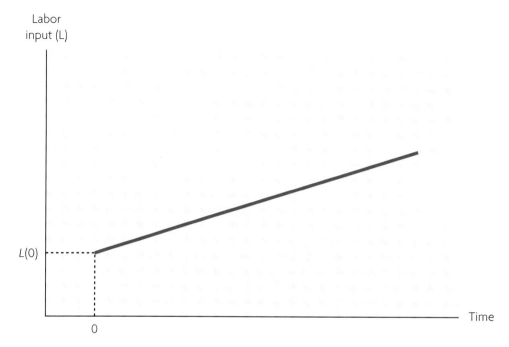

Labor
input (L)

$L(0)$

0        Time

Labor input, $L$, starts at time 0 at $L(0)$. Labor input then grows with population at the constant rate $n$. On a proportionate scale, $L$ follows a straight line, as shown in the figure.

population growth rate within the model; that is, we take $n$ to be exogenous. We assume that labor, $L$, begins at an initial year, denoted by year 0, at the quantity $L(0)$, as shown in Figure 3.7. Thereafter, the growth rate of $L$, $\Delta L/L$, equals the exogenous population growth rate, $n$:

(3.14) $$\Delta L / L = n$$

Since $n$ is constant, Figure 3.8 shows the time path of $L$ as a straight line (using a proportionate scale on the vertical axis).

**The growth rate of capital and real GDP per worker**   We can substitute our result for the growth rate of capital, $\Delta K/K$, from equation (3.13) and for the growth rate of labor, $\Delta L/L$, from equation (3.14) into equation (3.7) to determine the growth rate of capital per worker, $\Delta k/k$. We get

(3.15)
$$\Delta k/k = \Delta K / K - \Delta L / L$$
$$\Delta k/k = s \cdot (Y/K) - s\delta - n$$

Equation (3.15) is a key result in the Solow growth model. Because of the importance of this equation, we will examine the various terms. On the left-hand side, the growth rate of capital per worker has units of per year. For example, a value for $\Delta k/k$ of 0.02 per year means that capital per worker is growing at 2% per year.

The terms on the right-hand side of equation (3.15) are determinants of the growth rate of capital per worker. Hence, each of these terms must also have units of per year. Consider the term $s \cdot (Y/K)$, which is the product of the saving rate, $s$, and $Y/K$. The saving rate, $s$, is a pure number—that is, a number without units of time or goods. For example, if $s = 0.2$, households save 20% of their income. The term $Y/K$—output per unit of capital—is called the **average product of capital**. The units for $Y$—a flow variable—are goods per year and those for $K$—a stock variable—are goods. Therefore, the average product of capital has units of

$$(goods\ per\ year)\,/\,goods = per\ year$$

Since $s$ is a pure number, the units of $s \cdot (Y/K)$ are the same as the units of $Y/K$, which are per year, just like $\Delta k/k$.

The other terms on the right-hand side of equation (3.15) also have units of per year. The term $s\delta$ is the product of a pure number, $s$, and $\delta$, which has units of per year. The population growth rate, $n$, also has units of per year.

We will find it useful to express the average product of capital, $Y/K$, in terms of real GDP per worker, $y$, and capital per worker, $k$. The relation is

$$Y/K = \frac{Y/L}{K/L} \quad \text{or}$$

$$Y/K = \frac{y}{k}$$

If we substitute this result for $Y/K$ into equation (3.15), we get the central relation of the Solow model:

---

Key equation (Solow growth model):

(3.16) $$\Delta k/k = s \cdot (y/k) - s\delta - n$$

---

Finally, once we know the growth rate of capital per worker from equation (3.16), we can use equation (3.8) to determine the growth rate of real GDP per worker:

(3.17)
$$\Delta y/y = \alpha \cdot (\Delta k/k)$$

$$\Delta y/y = \alpha \cdot [s \cdot (y/k) - s\delta - n]$$

If the capital-share coefficient, $\alpha$, is fixed, we can go readily from the growth rate of capital per worker, $\Delta k/k$, in equation (3.16) to the growth rate of real GDP per worker, $\Delta y/y$, in equation (3.17). Since the number of workers grows at the same rate, $n$, as population, $\Delta y/y$ also equals the growth rate of real GDP per person.

**The transition and the steady state**    The key to the Solow growth model is equation (3.16), which determines the growth rate of capital per worker, $\Delta k/k$. The equation shows that $\Delta k/k$ depends on the saving rate, $s$, the depreciation rate, $\delta$, the population growth rate, $n$, and the average product of capital, $y/k$. We have assumed that $s$, $\delta$, and $n$ are constants. Therefore, the only reason that $\Delta k/k$ varies over time is that the average product of capital, $y/k$, varies. We will now consider how this average product depends on capital per worker, $k$. In this way, we will find that changes over time in $k$ lead to changes in $y/k$ and, thereby, to changes in $\Delta k/k$.

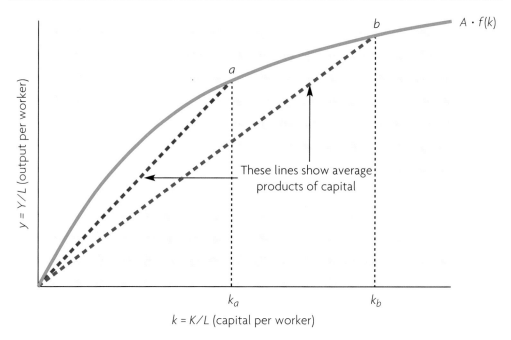

### Figure 3.9 | The Average Product of Capital

The graph shows the production function for output per worker, $y = Y/L$, versus capital per worker, $k = K/L$, as in Figure 3.7. The slope of a straight line from the origin to the production function gives the average product of capital, $y/k$, at the associated value of $k$. As $k$ rises, for a given technology level, $A$, the average product of capital falls. For example, the slope of the dashed red line, from the origin to point $a$, is greater than that of the dashed blue line, from the origin to point $b$. Therefore, the production function exhibits diminishing average product of capital.

We considered before the marginal product of capital, MPK, which is the ratio of a change in real GDP, $\Delta Y$, to a change in capital, $\Delta K$. Geometrically, the marginal product was given by the slope of the production function, shown in Figure 3.7. We reproduce this construction in Figure 3.9. In this new graph, we compute the average product of capital, $y/k$, as the ratio of $y$ (the variable on the vertical axis) to $k$ (the variable on the horizontal axis). This ratio equals the slope of a straight line from the origin to the production function. The graph shows two such lines, one from the origin to point $a$ and another from the origin to point $b$. The first line corresponds to capital per worker $k_a$ and the second to the larger capital per worker $k_b$. The graph shows that the average product of capital, $y/k$, declines as capital per worker, $k$, rises, for example, from $k_a$ to $k_b$. This **diminishing average product of capital** is analogous to the diminishing marginal product of capital, which we discussed before.

We can show diagrammatically how equation (3.16) determines the growth rate of capital per worker, $\Delta k/k$, by graphing the terms on the right-hand side of the equation versus capital per worker, $k$. In the first term, $s \cdot (y/k)$, the crucial property is the one just derived: the average product of capital, $y/k$, diminishes as $k$ rises. Hence, the curve for $s \cdot (y/k)$ slopes downward versus $k$, as shown in Figure 3.10.

The remaining terms on the right-hand side of equation (3.16) can be written as $-(s\delta + n)$. The term $s\delta + n$ is described by the horizontal line in Figure 3.10. Since $s\delta + n$ enters with a minus sign in equation (3.16), we have to subtract the position along the horizontal line from that of the curve (which gives $s \cdot [y/k]$) to determine $\Delta k/k$.

To study how the growth rate of capital per worker, $\Delta k/k$, changes over time, we have to know the capital per worker that the economy has initially—that is, at year 0. The economy begins with an accumulated stock of capital in the forms of machines and buildings. We represent this starting stock by $K(0)$. Since the initial labor is $L(0)$, the initial capital per worker is

$$k(0) = K(0)/L(0)$$

Recall that the production function in per-worker form is

(3.2)     $$y = A \cdot f(k)$$

Therefore, the initial level of real GDP per worker is given by

$$y(0) = Y(0)/L(0)$$
$$y(0) = A \cdot f[k(0)]$$

In Figure 3.10, the growth rate of capital per worker, $\Delta k/k$, is the vertical distance between the $s \cdot (y/k)$ curve and the horizontal line, $s\delta + n$ (see equation [3.16].) We assume that, when $k = k(0)$, the curve lies above the line. In this case, capital per worker grows

| **F i g u r e   3 . 1 0** | Determination of the Growth Rate of Capital per Worker in the Solow Model |

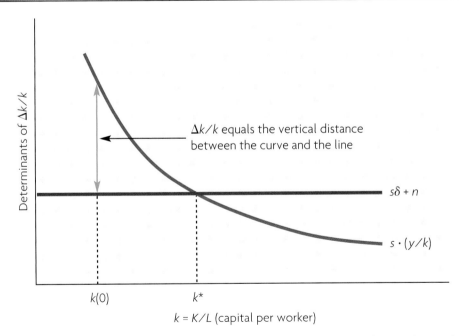

The technology level, $A$, is fixed. The vertical axis plots the two determinants of the growth rate of capital per worker, $\Delta k/k$, from the right-hand side of equation (3.16). $\Delta k/k$ equals the vertical distance between the negatively-sloped $s \cdot (y/k)$ curve (in blue) and the horizontal line at $s\delta + n$ (in red). At the steady state, where $k = k^*$, the curve and line intersect, and $\Delta k/k = 0$. The initial capital per worker, $k(0)$, is assumed to be less than $k^*$. Therefore, when $k = k(0)$, $\Delta k/k$ is greater than zero and equal to the vertical distance shown by the green arrows.

initially. That is, $\Delta k/k$ is greater than zero and is given by the distance marked by the green arrows. This positive growth rate means that capital per worker, $k$, increases over time—that is, $k$ moves rightward in Figure 3.10. Notice that the distance between the curve and the horizontal line diminishes over time. Since this distance equals $\Delta k/k$, we have shown that the growth rate of capital per worker slows down over time. This result is an important property of the Solow model.

Eventually, the increase in capital per worker, $k$, eliminates the gap between the $s \cdot (y/k)$ curve and the $s\delta + n$ line in Figure 3.10. The gap gets close to zero when $k$ approaches the value $k^*$ on the horizontal axis. When $k = k^*$, $\Delta k/k$ equals zero. Therefore, $k$ no longer moves to the right—with $\Delta k/k = 0$, $k$ stays fixed at the value $k^*$. For this reason, we call $k^*$ the capital per worker in the **steady state**. The corresponding real GDP per worker in the steady state is given from the production function in per-worker form in equation (3.2) by

$$y^* = f(k^*)$$

The results tell us that capital per worker, $k$, follows a **transition path** from its initial value, $k(0)$, to its steady-state value, $k^*$. Figure 3.11 shows this transition path as the red curve. Note that $k$ starts at $k(0)$, rises over time, and eventually gets close to $k^*$, shown as the dashed blue line.

Recall that the formula for the growth rate of capital per worker is

(3.16)                    $\Delta k/k = s \cdot (y/k) - s\delta - n$

**F i g u r e   3 . 1 1** | The Transition Path for Capital per Worker

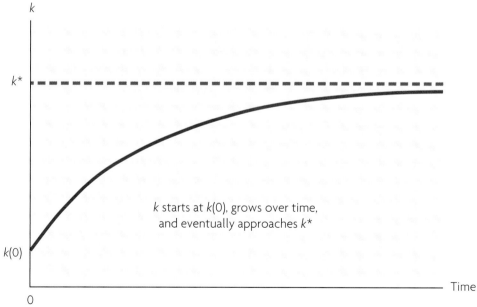

In the Solow model, described by Figure 3.10, capital per worker, $k$, starts at $k(0)$ and then rises over time. The growth rate of $k$ slows down over time, and $k$ gradually approaches its steady-state value, $k^*$. The transition path from $k(0)$ to $k^*$ is shown by the red curve. The dashed blue line shows the steady-state value, $k^*$.

# Do The Math

We have seen how Figure 3.10 determines the steady-state capital per worker, $k^*$. We can also determine $k^*$ algebraically. If we set $\Delta k/k = 0$ in equation (3.16), the right-hand side of the equation must be zero, so that

$$s \cdot (y^*/k^*) - s\delta - n = 0$$

If we rearrange the terms in this equation and divide by $s$, we find that the average product of capital in the steady state is

(3.18)    $$y^*/k^* = \delta + n/s$$

If we use equation (3.2) to substitute $A \cdot f(k^*)$ for $y^*$, we find that the steady-state capital per worker, $k^*$, must satisfy

(3.19)    $$A \cdot f(k^*)/k^* = \delta + n/s$$

This algebraic result for $k^*$ will be helpful in the next chapter, when we work further with the Solow model.

In the steady state, $\Delta k/k$ equals zero. Therefore, the right-hand side of equation (3.16) must also be zero in the steady state:

$$s \cdot (y^*/k^*) - s\delta - n = 0$$

If we move $n$ to the right-hand side, combine the terms involving $s$ on the left-hand side, and multiply through by $k^*$, we get

(3.17)    $$s \cdot (y^* - \delta k^*) = nk^*$$

*steady-state saving per worker = steady-state capital provided for each new worker*

The left-hand side is saving per worker in the steady state. The right-hand side is the capital provided to each new worker in the steady state. Recall that $k^*$ is the steady-state quantity of capital for each worker. The investment per worker needed to generate the necessary new capital is $k^*$ multiplied by the growth rate, $n$, of the labor force. Therefore, the steady-state investment per worker, $nk^*$, on the right-hand side of equation (3.17) equals the steady-state saving per worker on the left-hand side of the equation.

Our analysis allows us to think of the process of economic growth in the Solow model as having two phases. In the first phase, there is a transition from an initial capital per worker, $k(0)$, to its steady-state value, $k^*$. This transition is shown by the red curve in Figure 3.11. During this transition, the growth rate of capital per worker, $\Delta k/k$, is greater than zero but declining gradually toward zero. In the second phase, the economy is in (or near) the steady state, represented by the dashed blue line in Figure 3.11. In this phase, $\Delta k/k = 0$.

Our goal was to determine how the growth rate of real GDP per worker (and per person), $\Delta y/y$, varies over time. We can now reach this goal, because $\Delta y/y$ equals the growth rate of capital per worker, $\Delta k/k$, multiplied by $\alpha$, which we assume to be constant (with $0 < \alpha < 1$):

(3.8)    $$\Delta y/y = \alpha \cdot (\Delta k/k)$$

Therefore, everything that we said about $\Delta k/k$ applies also to $\Delta y/y$, once we multiply by $\alpha$. In particular, starting at the initial capital per worker $k(0)$ shown in Figure 3.10, we have that $\Delta y / y$ starts out positive, then declines as capital per worker, $k$, and real GDP per worker, $y$, rise. Eventually, when $k$ reaches its steady-state value, $k^*$, $\Delta y / y$ falls to zero (because equation [3.8] implies $\Delta y / y = 0$ when $\Delta k / k = 0$). In the steady state, real GDP per worker, $y$, equals its steady-state value, $y^*$.

In Figure 3.11, we can view the transition as applying to real GDP per worker, $y$, as well as to capital per worker, $k$. That is, the red curve also describes the transition from the initial real GDP per worker, $y(0)$, to its steady-state value, $y^*$.

## Summing Up

We began our study of economic growth with observations about the importance of growth for standards of living. Now we have constructed the Solow growth model and are ready to work with it to understand how economic variables influence growth. We will begin to put the model to use in the next chapter.

## Key Terms and Concepts

average product of capital
capital stock
constant returns to scale
diminishing average product of capital
diminishing marginal product of capital
diminishing marginal product of labor
gross investment
growth accounting
human capital
inequality
labor force
labor-force participation rate
marginal product of capital (MPK)
marginal product of labor (MPL)
neoclassical growth model

net investment
population growth
poverty
production function
productivity
productivity slowdown
Ramsey model
rate of economic growth
saving
Solow growth model
standard of living
steady state
technology level
transition path

## Questions and Problems

**A.** Review questions

1. What is a production function? In what way does it represent a relation between factor inputs and the level of output?

2. Explain the concepts of marginal and average products of capital. What is the difference between the two? Is the average product always greater than the marginal product?

3. Does a positive saving rate, $s > 0$, mean that capital per worker, $k$, rises over time? Explain by referring to equation (3.16).

4. Does a positive saving rate, $s > 0$, mean that output per worker, $y$, and capital per worker, $k$, grow in the long run? Explain.

5. Explain why an increase in capital per worker, $k$, reduces the growth rate of capital per worker, $\Delta k/k$. How does this result depend on diminishing productivity of capital?

**B.** Problems for discussion

6. Constant returns to scale

We have assumed that the production function, $A \cdot F(K, L)$, exhibits constant returns to scale. That is, if we multiply the inputs, $K$ and $L$, by any positive number, we multiply output, $Y$, by the same number. Show that this condition implies that we can write the production function as in equation (3.2):

$$y = A \cdot f(k)$$

where $y = Y/L$ and $k = K/L$.

7. Cobb-Douglas production function

The Cobb-Douglas production function, discussed in the appendix to this chapter, is given by

$$Y = AK^\alpha L^{1-\alpha}$$

where $0 < \alpha < 1$

a. Define $A$, $K$, and $L$.
b. What does it mean that $Y$ is proportional to $A$?
c. What does it mean that the marginal product of capital (or labor), MPK (or MPL), is greater than zero? Show that the marginal products are positive in the Cobb-Douglas case.
d. What does it mean that the marginal product of capital (or labor), MPK (or MPL), is decreasing? Show that the marginal products are diminishing in the Cobb-Douglas case.
e. Does the Cobb-Douglas production function satisfy the property of constant returns to scale, discussed in Problem 6? Explain your answer.

8. Determination of steady-state capital per worker

Consider the steady-state capital per worker, $k^*$, determined in Figure 3.10. How is $k^*$ affected by the following?

a. An increase in the saving rate, $s$.
b. An increase in the technology level, $A$.
c. An increase in the depreciation rate, $\delta$.
d. An increase in the population growth rate, $n$.

9. Growth with a Cobb-Douglas production function

Suppose that the production function takes the Cobb-Douglas form, discussed in Problem 7: $Y = A \cdot F(K, L) = AK^\alpha L^{1-\alpha}$, where $0 < \alpha < 1$.

a. In the steady state, $\Delta k/k$, given by equation (3.16), equals zero. Use this condition, along with the form of the production function, to get a formula for the steady-state capital and output per worker, $k^*$ and $y^*$.
b. Let $c = C/L$ be consumption per worker. What is steady-state consumption per worker, $c^*$?
c. Use equation (3.16) to work out a formula for the growth rate of capital per worker, $\Delta k/k$. Can you show that $\Delta k/k$ falls during the transition as $k$ rises? What happens during the transition to the growth rate of output per worker, $\Delta y/y$?

10. Growth without diminishing productivity of capital

Suppose that the production function is $Y = AK$ (the so-called AK model).

a. What is the condition for the growth rate of capital per worker, $\Delta k/k$, in equation (3.16)? What does the $s \cdot (y/k)$ curve look like in Figure 3.10?

b. What are the growth rates of capital and output per worker, $\Delta k/k$ and $\Delta y/y$? Are these growth rates greater than zero? Do these growth rates decline during a transition?

c. Discuss how your results relate to diminishing productivity of capital. Is it plausible that diminishing productivity would not apply?

# Appendix

This appendix has three parts. Part A provides a formal derivation of the growth-accounting equation, given in equation (3.4). Part B shows how to use the growth-accounting equation to analyze productivity growth. Part C discusses a common form of the production function, known as the Cobb-Douglas production function.

## Part A: The growth-Accounting Equation

The growth-accounting equation is

(3.4)     $$\Delta Y/Y = \Delta A/A + \alpha \cdot (\Delta K/K) + (1 - \alpha) \cdot (\Delta L/L)$$

We derive this equation more formally here and work out a formula for the coefficient $\alpha$.

The production function is

(3.1)     $$Y = A \cdot F(K, L)$$

The form of this equation tells us that, for given $K$ and $L$, an increase in the growth rate of technology, $\Delta A/A$, by 1% per year raises the growth rate of real GDP, $\Delta Y/Y$, by 1% per year. This reasoning explains why the term $\Delta A/A$ appears as it does in equation (3.4).

Consider now the effect from changes in $K$, when $A$ and $L$ are held fixed. If $K$ increases by the amount $\Delta K$, while $A$ and $L$ do not change, the increase in real GDP equals $\Delta K$ multiplied by the marginal product of capital, MPK:

$$\Delta Y = MPK \cdot \Delta K$$

To get the growth rate of $Y$, divide each side by $Y$:

$$\Delta Y/Y = (MPK/Y) \cdot \Delta K$$

Then, if we multiply and divide by $K$ on the right-hand side, we get

$$\Delta Y/Y = \left( \frac{MPK \cdot K}{Y} \right) \cdot (\Delta K/K).$$

This result determines $\Delta Y/Y$ when $K$ is growing but $A$ and $L$ are held fixed. More generally, it tells us the contribution of $\Delta K/K$ to $\Delta Y/Y$, even when $A$ and $L$ are changing. That is, to get the contribution of $\Delta K/K$ to $\Delta Y/Y$, multiply $\Delta K/K$ by the term $(MPK \cdot K)/Y$. Therefore, in equation (3.4), we must have that the coefficient $\alpha$ is given by

(3.20)
$$\alpha = (MPK \cdot K)/Y$$

In a competitive economy, capital's marginal product, MPK, equals the real rental price paid per unit of capital. (We work out this result in Chapter 6.) In that case, the term $MPK \cdot K$ equals the amount paid per unit of capital, MPK, multiplied by the quantity of capital, $K$, and therefore equals the total real rental payments to capital. Therefore, $\alpha$ is given by

$$\alpha = (MPK \cdot K)/Y$$
$$\alpha = (real\ rental\ payments\ to\ capital)/(real\ GDP)$$

If depreciation of capital stocks were zero, the real rental payments would equal the real income on capital and real GDP would equal the economy's total real income (that is, real national income). In this case, equation (3.20) implies that $\alpha$ equals the *capital share of income*. More generally, depreciation of capital stocks has to be subtracted from real rental payments and real GDP to compute real incomes. In this case, the capital share of income will be less than $\alpha$. In any event, since the real rental payments to capital have to be smaller than real GDP, we have $0 < \alpha < 1$.

Now we consider the contribution to the growth of real GDP from growth in labor input. If $L$ increases by the amount $\Delta L$, while $A$ and $K$ are held fixed, the increase in real GDP equals $\Delta L$ multiplied by the marginal product of labor:

$$\Delta Y = MPL \cdot \Delta L$$

If we divide through by $Y$, we get

$$\Delta Y/Y = (MPL/Y) \cdot \Delta L$$

Then, if we multiply and divide by $L$ on the right-hand side, we get

$$\Delta Y/Y = \left(\frac{MPL \cdot L}{Y}\right) \cdot (\Delta L/L).$$

Therefore, to get the contribution of $\Delta L/L$ to $\Delta Y/Y$, we have to multiply $\Delta L/L$ by the term $(MPL \cdot L)/Y$. Hence, in equation (3.4), we must have

(3.21)
$$1 - \alpha = (MPL \cdot L)/Y$$

In a competitive economy, labor's marginal product, MPL, equals the real wage rate. (We work out this result in Chapter 6.) Therefore, the term $MPL \cdot L$ equals the amount paid per unit of labor, MPL, multiplied by the quantity of labor, $L$, and therefore equals the total real wage payments to labor. If depreciation of capital stocks were zero, real GDP, $Y$, would equal total real income. In this case, equation (3.21) implies that $1 - \alpha$ equals the *labor share of income*. More generally, since total real income is less than $Y$, the labor share of income will be greater than $1 - \alpha$.

## Part B: The Solow Residual

We know that the growth rate of technology, $\Delta A/A$, contributes to the growth rate of real GDP, $\Delta Y/Y$. Since the technology level, $A$, is not directly observable, we need some way to measure it from national-accounts data. A common approach is to rearrange the growth-accounting formula, equation (3.4), to get

(3.22)
$$\Delta A/A = \Delta Y/Y - \alpha \cdot (\Delta K/K) - (1 - \alpha) \cdot (\Delta L/L)$$

*growth rate of A = growth rate of real GDP − contribution of capital and labor*

The terms on the right-hand side can be measured from national-accounts data. Therefore, we can use this equation to measure the left-hand side, which equals the growth rate of technology, $\Delta A/A$.

The term $\Delta A/A$ in equations (3.4) and (3.22) is often called **total factor productivity growth**, or **TFP growth**. This concept comes from Robert Solow (1957) and is also often called the **Solow residual**. This terminology arises because equation (3.22) shows that we can compute $\Delta A/A$ as the *residual* after we take the growth rate of real GDP, $\Delta Y/Y$, and subtract out the contributions to growth from the changing factor inputs, $\alpha \cdot (\Delta K/K)$ for capital and $(1 - \alpha) \cdot (\Delta L/L)$ for labor. Economists have calculated these Solow residuals for various countries and time periods.

## Part C: The Cobb-Douglas Production Function

We assumed in our analysis of the Solow model that $\alpha$ (which equals the capital share of income if depreciation can be neglected) was constant. That is, $\alpha$ did not change as capital per worker, $k$, varied. We can show that this assumption is valid for a particular form of the production function:

(3.23)
$$Y = A \cdot F(K, L)$$
$$Y = AK^\alpha L^{1-\alpha}$$

In this form, the constant $\alpha$ appears as the exponent on capital, $K$, whereas $1 - \alpha$ appears as the exponent on labor, $L$. We assume that $\alpha$ is a fraction, so that $0 < \alpha < 1$. This form of the production function has been used by economists in many theoretical and empirical studies.

The function in equation (3.23) is called the **Cobb-Douglas production function**, named after the economist and U.S. Senator Paul Douglas, who apparently teamed up with a mathematician named Cobb. It is easy to show that the Cobb-Douglas production function satisfies constant returns to scale. (Multiply $K$ and $L$ each by two and see what happens to $Y$.) In terms of real GDP and capital per worker, $y$ and $k$, the Cobb-Douglas production function is

(3.24)
$$\begin{aligned}
y &= Y/L \\
&= AK^\alpha L^{1-\alpha} \cdot (1/L) \\
&= AK^\alpha L^{1-\alpha} \cdot L^{-1} \\
&= AK^\alpha L^{-\alpha} \\
&= A \cdot (K/L)^\alpha \\
y &= Ak^\alpha
\end{aligned}$$

We can show using calculus that the exponent $\alpha$ that appears in the Cobb-Douglas production function in equation (3.23) satisfies equation (3.20):

**(3.20)**
$$\alpha = (MPK \cdot K) / Y$$

To verify this result, recall that MPK is the effect on $Y$ from a change in $K$, while holding fixed $A$ and $L$. If we take the derivative of $Y = AK^{\alpha}L^{1-\alpha}$ with respect to $K$, for given $A$ and $L$, we get

$$MPK = dY/dK$$
$$= \alpha A K^{\alpha-1} L^{1-\alpha}$$
$$= \alpha A K^{\alpha} K^{-1} L^{1-\alpha}$$
$$= \alpha A K^{\alpha} L^{1-\alpha} \cdot (1/K)$$
$$= \alpha \cdot (Y/K)$$

Therefore, we have

$$(MPK \cdot K) / Y = [\alpha \cdot (Y/K) \cdot K] / Y$$
$$= \alpha$$

as in equation (3.20).

# Chapter 4

## Working with the Solow Growth Model

Now that we have constructed the Solow growth model, we can put it into action by seeing how various economic changes affect growth in the short and long run. We begin by studying variations in the saving rate, the technology level, the level of labor input, and the population growth rate. Then we explore convergence, or a tendency for poor countries to catch up to rich ones.

We found in the Solow model that the growth rate of capital per worker, $\Delta k/k$, was given from equation (3.16). We repeat this key equation here:

$$(4.1) \qquad \Delta k/k = s \cdot (y/k) - s\delta - n$$

where $k$ is capital per worker, $y$ is real gross domestic product (real GDP) per worker, $y/k$ is the average product of capital, $s$ is the saving rate, $\delta$ is the depreciation rate, and $n$ is the population growth rate. We assumed that everything on the right-hand side was constant except for $y/k$. We found that, in the transition to the steady state, the rise in $k$ led to a fall in $y/k$ and, hence, to a fall in $\Delta k/k$. In the steady state, $k$ was constant and, therefore, $y/k$ was constant. Hence, $\Delta k/k$ was constant and equal to zero.

The production function in per-worker form was given in equation (3.2). We repeat this equation here:

$$(4.2) \qquad y = A \cdot f(k)$$

If we substitute for $y$ from equation (4.2) into equation (4.1), we get a revised version of the basic Solow equation:

$$(4.3) \qquad \Delta k/k = sA \cdot f(k)/k - s\delta - n$$

Up to now, we assumed that the saving rate, $s$, the technology level, $A$, and the population growth rate, $n$, were fixed. Now we allow for changes in $s$, $A$, and $n$. We also consider changes in the level of labor input, $L$. We analyze the effects of these changes on the two phases of the Solow model. What are the effects on the transition to the steady state, and what are the effects on the steady state? We can think of the first part as representing the short-run effects and the second part as representing the long-run effects.

# A Change in the Saving Rate

How do differences in the saving rate, $s$, affect economic growth? As an example of differences in saving rates, we can compare nations in which the residents regularly save at a high rate—such as Singapore and South Korea, or some other East Asian countries—with places in which the residents typically save at a low rate—such as most countries in sub-Saharan Africa or Latin America. Some of the differences in saving rates result from government policies and some may stem from cultural differences. The important point is that saving rates differ across societies and over time.

Figure 4.1 extends the Solow model from Figure 3.9 to consider two saving rates, $s_1$ and $s_2$, where $s_2$ is greater than $s_1$. Each saving rate determines a different curve for $s \cdot (y/k)$—the one with $s_2$ lies above that for $s_1$. Recall that the growth rate of capital per worker, $\Delta k/k$, equals the vertical distance between the $s \cdot (y/k)$ curve and the horizontal line, $s\delta + n$. There are also two positions for this horizontal line, one for $s_1$ and the other for $s_2$. However, this shift in the horizontal line turns out to be minor. Therefore, we can see from the Figure 4.1 that $\Delta k/k$ is higher at any capital per worker, $k$, when the saving rate is $s_2$ rather than $s_1$.[1] Specifically, at $k(0)$, $\Delta k/k$ is higher when the saving

| **Figure 4.1** | Effect of an Increase in the Saving Rate in the Solow Model |
|---|---|

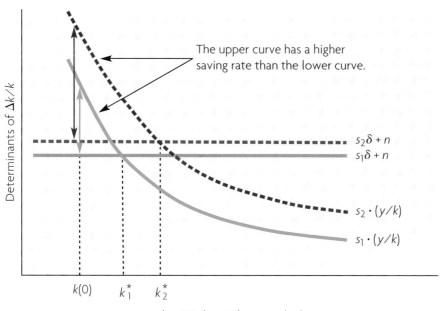

$k = K/L$ (capital per worker)

This graph comes from Figure 3.9. The curves for $s \cdot (y/k)$ are for the saving rates $s_1$ and $s_2$, where $s_2$ is greater than $s_1$. Similarly, the horizontal lines for $s\delta + n$ are for the saving rates $s_1$ and $s_2$. The growth rate of capital per worker, $\Delta k/k$, is higher at any $k$ when the saving rate is higher. For example, at $k(0)$, when the saving rate is $s_1$, $\Delta k/k$ equals the vertical distance shown by the green arrows. When the saving rate is $s_2$, $\Delta k/k$ equals the vertical distance shown by the red arrows. In the steady state, $\Delta k/k$ is zero, regardless of the saving rate. The higher saving rate yields a higher steady-state capital per worker; that is, $k_2^*$ is greater than $k_1^*$.

---

[1] The rise in the $s \cdot (y/k)$ curve is greater than the increase in the $s\delta + n$ line as long as $y/k > \delta$; that is, as long as real GDP per worker, $y$, is greater than depreciation per worker, $\delta k$. Thus, we need only to be sure that the net domestic product is greater than zero, as is surely the case.

# Do The Math

We can determine the steady-state capital per worker, $k^*$, algebraically from the steady-state condition given in equation (3.19). We repeat this result here:

(4.4)     $A \cdot f(k^*)/k^* = \delta + n/s$

An increase in $s$ lowers the right-hand side. Hence, the left-hand side must be lower, and this reduction can occur only through a decrease in the average product of capital, $A \cdot f(k^*)/k^*$. We know from Figure 3.8 that, if $A$ is fixed, a decrease in the average product of capital requires an increase in capital per worker, $k$. Therefore, an increase in $s$ raises $k^*$.

rate is $s_2$, rather than $s_1$. (We have assumed that $\Delta k/k$ is greater than zero for both saving rates.)

For either saving rate, the growth rate of capital per worker, $\Delta k/k$, declines as capital per worker, $k$, rises above $k(0)$. When the saving rate is $s_1$, $\Delta k/k$ reaches zero when $k$ attains the steady-state value $k_1^*$ in Figure 4.1. However, at $k_1^*$, $\Delta k/k$ would still be greater than zero if the saving rate were higher—for example, if it equaled $s_2$. If the saving rate is $s_2$, capital per worker, $k$, rises beyond $k_1^*$ until it reaches the higher steady-state value, $k_2^*$. Since capital per worker is higher, we also know that real GDP per worker is greater when the saving rate is $s_2$—that is, $y_2^* > y_1^*$.

To summarize, in the short run, an increase in the saving rate raises the growth rate of capital per worker. This growth rate remains higher during the transition to the steady state. In the long run, the growth rate of capital per worker is the same—zero—for any saving rate. In this long-run or steady-state situation, a higher saving rate leads to higher steady-state capital per worker, $k^*$, not to a change in the growth rate (which remains at zero).

One important extension of the Solow model—carried out in the mid-1960s by David Cass (1965) and Tjalling Koopmans (1965)—allowed households to choose the saving rate, $s$. To study this choice, we need the microeconomic analysis of how households determine consumption at different points in time. We defer this analysis to Chapter 7.

## A Change in the Technology Level

We have assumed, thus far, that the technology level, $A$, was fixed. In reality, technology varies over time and across locations. For examples of improvements in technology over time, we can think of the introductions of electric power, automobiles, computers, and the Internet. For differences across locations, we can think of businesses in advanced economies, such as the United States and Western Europe, as having better access to leading technologies than their counterparts in poor countries. To assess the influences from differences in technologies, we begin by considering the effects in the Solow model from a change in the technology level, $A$.

The formula for the growth rate of capital per worker is again

(4.3)                          $\Delta k/k = sA \cdot f(k)/k - s\delta - n$

9038.0
18.860
7.7577
61.851

# Extending The Model

## Consumption in the Solow model

Recall that real income equals real net domestic product, $Y - \delta K$, which equals consumption, $C$, plus saving, $s \cdot (Y - \delta K)$. Therefore, in terms of quantities per worker, we have

$$y - \delta k = c + s \cdot (y - \delta k)$$

where $c$ is consumption per worker. An increase in the saving rate, $s$, means that $c$ must fall for given $y - \delta k$. However, since higher saving leads in the long run to higher real GDP, consumption may increase in the long run. Here, we consider what the Solow model says about the effect of saving on consumption in the long run.

We found that an increase in the saving rate, $s$, raises the steady-state capital and real GDP per worker, $k^*$ and $y^*$. The rise in real GDP per worker leads to an increase in the typical person's real income. However, people care about their consumption, not their income, *per se*. Thus, we want to know how a rise in the saving rate affects steady-state consumption per person.

Consumption per person is given by

consumption per person
= (consumption per worker)
× (workers/population)

The ratio of workers to population is the labor-force participation rate, which we have assumed to be constant. Therefore, consumption per person always moves along with consumption per worker, $c$. This result means that we can focus on $c$ to see what happens to consumption per person.

Since consumption equals the real income not saved, and saving per worker in the steady state is $s \cdot (y^* - \delta k^*)$, we have

$$(4.5) \quad c^* = y^* - \delta k^* - s \cdot (y^* - \delta k^*)$$

where $c^*$ is the steady-state value of $c$. We also know from Chapter 3 that steady-state saving

per worker is just enough to provide new workers with capital to work with:

$$(3.17) \qquad s \cdot (y^* - \delta k^*) = nk^*$$

Therefore, we can substitute $nk^*$ for $s \cdot (y^* - \delta k^*)$ on the right-hand side of equation (4.5) to get

$$(4.6) \qquad c^* = y^* - \delta k^* - nk^*$$

We know that a rise in the saving rate, $s$, raises $k^*$, say, by the amount $\Delta k^*$. The change in $c^*$ follows from equation (4.6) as

$$\Delta c^* = \Delta y^* - (\delta + n) \cdot \Delta k^*$$

We can compute $\Delta y^*$ by noting that it must equal $\Delta k^*$ multiplied by the marginal product of capital, MPK:

$$\Delta y^* = MPK \cdot \Delta k^*$$

Therefore, if we substitute $MPK \cdot \Delta k^*$ for $\Delta y^*$, we get that the change in $c^*$ is given by

$$\Delta c^* = MPK \cdot \Delta k^* - (\delta + n) \cdot \Delta k^*$$
$$(4.7) \quad \Delta c^* = (MPK - \delta - n) \cdot \Delta k^*$$

We see from equation (4.7) that $\Delta c^*$ is greater than zero if MPK is greater than $\delta + n$. The part $MPK - \delta$ is the net marginal product of capital—that is, the MPK net of depreciation. This term gives the rate of return on additional capital. Hence, equation (4.7) says that an increase in steady-state capital per worker, $k^*$, raises steady-state consumption per worker, $c^*$, as long as the rate of return on capital, $MPK - \delta$, is greater than the population growth rate, $n$. Typical estimates of rates of return on capital are around 10%, whereas population growth rates are around 0–2%. Therefore, in normal circumstances, $\Delta c^*$ is greater than zero.

The positive effect of the saving rate, $s$, on steady-state consumption per worker, $c^*$, and, therefore, on steady-state consumption per person, does not necessarily mean that the typical person is better off by saving more. In order to achieve the higher steady-state capital per worker, $k^*$, households have to save more during the transition to the steady state. Hence, levels of consumption per person during part of the transition have to be reduced. Thus, there is a trade-off—less consumption per person in the short run and more consumption per person in the long run. Whether the typical person is better or worse off depends on, first, how much consumption is gained in the long run in comparison with how much is lost in the short run and, second, on how patient people are about deferring consumption.

where $A \cdot f(k)/k$ is the average product of capital, $y/k$. Note that a higher $A$ means that $y/k$ is higher at a given $k$.

Figure 4.2 compares two levels of technology, $A_1$ and $A_2$, where $A_2$ is greater than $A_1$. Each technology level corresponds to a different curve for $s \cdot (y/k) = s A \cdot f(k)/k$. The curve with the higher technology level, $A_2$, lies above the other one. Notice that the positions of the two curves are similar to those in Figure 4.1, which considered two values of the saving rate, $s$. Hence, our analysis of effects from a change in $A$ is similar to that for a change in $s$.

| Figure 4.2 | Effect of an Increase in the Technology Level in the Solow Model |

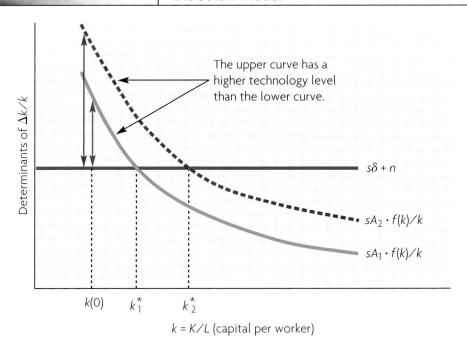

This graph comes from Figure 3.9. The two curves for $s \cdot (y/k) = s A \cdot f(k)/k$ are for the technology levels $A_1$ and $A_2$, where $A_2$ is greater than $A_1$. The growth rate of capital per worker, $\Delta k/k$, is higher at any $k$ when the technology level is higher. For example, at $k(0)$, when the technology level is $A_1$, $\Delta k/k$ equals the vertical distance shown by the blue arrows. When the technology level is $A_2$, $\Delta k/k$ equals the vertical distance shown by the red arrows. In the steady state, $\Delta k/k$ is zero, regardless of the technology level. The higher technology level yields a higher steady-state capital per worker; that is, $k_2^*$ is greater than $k_1^*$.

# Do The Math

We can derive the effect of $A$ on $k^*$ algebraically from the condition we used before:

(4.4)    $A \cdot (k^*)/k^* = \delta + n/s$

An increase in $A$ does not affect the right-hand side. Therefore, the steady-state capital per worker, $k^*$, must adjust on the left-hand side to keep the steady-state average product of capital, $A \cdot f(k^*)/k^*$, the same. Since the increase in $A$ raises this average product, $k^*$ must change in a way that reduces the average product. As we know from Figure 3.8, a reduction in the average product of capital requires a rise in $k^*$. Therefore, an increase in $A$ raises $k^*$.

At the initial capital per worker, $k(0)$, in Figure 4.2, the growth rate of capital per worker, $\Delta k/k$, is higher with the higher technology level, $A_2$, than with the lower one, $A_1$. In both cases, $\Delta k/k$ declines over time. For the lower technology level, $\Delta k/k$ falls to zero when capital per worker, $k$, attains the steady-state value $k_1^*$. For the higher technology level, $k$ rises beyond $k_1^*$ to reach the higher steady-state value $k_2^*$. Thus, an increase in $A$ results in a higher $\Delta k/k$ over the transition period. In the long run, $\Delta k/k$ still falls to zero, but the steady-state capital per worker, $k^*$, is higher. That is, $k_2^*$ is greater than $k_1^*$.

An increase in the technology level, $A$, raises the steady-state real GDP per worker, $y^* = A \cdot f(k^*)$, for two reasons. First, an increase in $A$ raises real GDP per worker, $y$, for given capital per worker, $k$. Second, the steady-state capital per worker, $k^*$, is higher when $A$ is higher. On both counts, an increase in $A$ raises $y^*$.

To summarize, in the short run, an increase in the technology level, $A$, raises the growth rates of capital and real GDP per worker. These growth rates remain higher during the transition to the steady state. In the long run, the growth rates of capital and real GDP per worker are the same—zero—for any technology level. In this long-run or steady-state situation, a higher technology level leads to higher steady-state capital and real GDP per worker, $k^*$ and $y^*$, not to changes in the growth rates (which remain at zero).

## Changes in Labor Input and the Population Growth Rate

We can consider two types of changes in labor input, $L$. First, $L$ could change at a point in time because of a sudden shift in the size of the labor force. Second, a change in the population growth rate could affect the long-term time path of labor input. We begin with a one-time change in $L$.

### A Change in Labor Input

Changes in labor input, $L$, can result from shifts in the labor force. For example, the labor force could decline precipitously due to an epidemic of disease. An extreme case from the mid-1300s is the bubonic plague, or Black Death, which is estimated to have killed about 20% of the European population. The potential loss of life due to the ongoing AIDS epidemic in Africa may be analogous, and there is also a lot of concern about avian flu. In these examples, physical capital does not change initially, and the starting capital per worker, $k(0) = K(0)/L(0)$, rises because of the drop in $L(0)$.

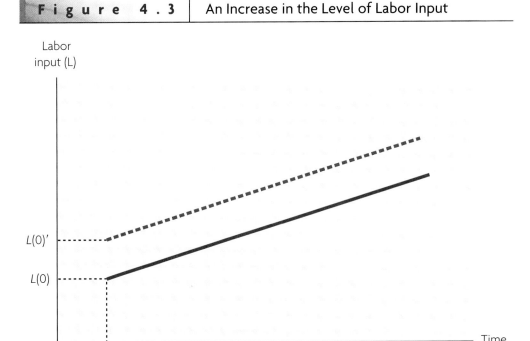

**Figure 4.3** | An Increase in the Level of Labor Input

In year 0, labor input jumps upward from $L(0)$ to $L(0)'$. The population growth rate, $n$, does not change.

Wartime casualties are another source of decrease in the labor force. However, since wartime tends also to destroy physical capital, the effect on capital per worker depends on the circumstances. Migration can also change the labor force. One example is the Mariel boatlift of over 100,000 Cuban refugees, mostly to Miami, in 1980. Another case is the large in-migration to Portugal in the mid-1970s by its citizens who had been residing in African colonies. When these colonies became independent, many residents returned to Portugal, and this inflow raised the domestic Portuguese population by about 10%. Finally, in Israel in the 1990s, the roughly 1,000,000 Russian Jewish immigrants constituted about 20% of Israel's 1990 population.

Figure 3.8 showed the path of labor input, $L$, starting at $L(0)$ and then growing at the constant rate $n$. In Figure 4.3, we assume that the initial level of labor input rises from $L(0)$ to $L(0)'$, while $n$ does not change. Thus, we are considering a proportionate increase in the level of labor input, $L$, in each year. Since the initial stock of capital, $K(0)$, does not change, the increase in $L(0)$ decreases the initial capital per worker, $k(0) = K(0)/L(0)$.

Figure 4.4 considers the effects of an increase in the level of labor input. The rise in initial labor from $L(0)$ to $L(0)'$ reduces the initial capital per worker from $k(0)$ to $k(0)'$. However, a key point is that the curve for $s \cdot (y/k)$ and the horizontal line at $s\delta + n$ do not change. The reduction in $k(0)$ raises the initial average product of capital, $y/k$ (see Figure 3.9) and leads, thereby, to a higher $s \cdot (y/k)$ along the unchanged curve. Consequently, the growth rate of capital per worker, $\Delta k/k$, rises initially. We can see this result in Figure 4.3 because the vertical distance between the $s \cdot (y/k)$ curve and the $s\delta + n$ line is greater at $k(0)'$ (the red arrows) than at $k(0)$ (the blue arrows). The growth rate $\Delta k/k$ remains higher during the transition to the steady state. However, $\Delta k/k$ still declines toward its long-run value of zero. Moreover, the steady-state capital per worker, $k^*$, is the same whether labor input starts at $L(0)'$ or $L(0)$. Thus, if $L(0)'$ is twice as large as $L(0)$, the long-run level of capital, $K$, is also twice as large (so that capital per worker remains the same). Since $k^*$ is

# Do The Math

We can again work out the steady-state results algebraically from the condition

(4.4)     $A \cdot f(k^*)/k^* = \delta + n/s$

Note that $A$, $s$, $n$, and $\delta$ are constant, and the level of labor input, $L$, does not enter into the equation. Therefore, the steady-state capital per worker, $k^*$, does not change when $L$ changes.

| **F i g u r e   4 . 4** | Effect of an Increase in Labor Input in the Solow Model |

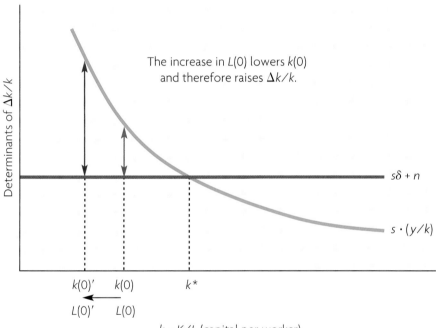

This graph comes from Figure 3.10. If the initial level of labor input rises from $L(0)$ to $L(0)'$, the initial capital per worker declines from $k(0) = K(0)/L(0)$ to $k(0)' = K(0)/L(0)'$. Therefore, the growth rate of capital per worker, $\Delta k/k$, rises initially. Note that the vertical distance shown by the red arrows is larger than that shown by the blue arrows. The steady-state capital per worker, $k^*$, is the same for the two values of $L(0)$.

unchanged, we also have that real GDP per worker, $y^*$, does not change. In the long run, an economy with twice as much labor has twice as much real GDP, $Y$.

To summarize, in the short run, an increase in labor input, $L(0)$, raises the growth rates of capital and real GDP per worker. These growth rates remain higher during the transition to the steady state. In the long run, the growth rates of capital and real GDP per worker are the same—zero—for any level of labor input, $L(0)$. Moreover, the steady-state capital and real GDP per worker, $k^*$ and $y^*$, are the same for any $L$. Thus, in the long run, an economy with twice as much labor input has twice as much capital and real GDP.

## A Change in the Population Growth Rate

Figure 4.5 shows an increase in the population growth rate from $n$ to $n'$. We assume now that the initial population and, hence, level of labor input, $L(0)$, do not change. Thus, the initial capital per worker, $k(0)$, does not change.

In Figure 4.6, the higher population growth rate corresponds to a higher horizontal line for $s\delta + n$. Recall that the growth rate of capital per worker, $\Delta k/k$, equals the vertical distance between the $s \cdot (y/k)$ curve and the $s\delta + n$ line. Therefore, $\Delta k/k$ is lower at any capital per worker, $k$, when the population growth rate is $n'$ rather than $n$. We can also see this result from the formula for the growth rate of capital per worker:

**(4.3)**                        $\Delta k/k = sA \cdot f(k)/k - s\delta - n$

A higher $n$—the yellow shaded term—lowers $\Delta k/k$ for given $k$. The reason that $\Delta k/k$ is lower when $n$ is higher is that a larger portion of saving goes to providing the growing labor force, $L$, with capital to work with.

For either population growth rate in Figure 4.6, the growth rate of capital per worker, $\Delta k/k$, declines as capital per worker rises above $k(0)$. When the population growth rate is $n'$, $\Delta k/k$ reaches zero when $k$ attains the steady-state value $(k^*)'$. However, at $(k^*)'$, $\Delta k/k$ would still be greater than zero if the population growth rate were lower—in particular, if it equaled $n$. Thus, if the population growth rate is $n$, capital per worker rises beyond $(k^*)'$—$k$ increases until it reaches the steady-state value $k^*$, which is greater than $(k^*)'$.

Figure 4.6 shows that, at the initial capital per worker, $k(0)$, an increase in the population growth rate from $n$ to $n'$ lowers the growth rate of capital per worker, $\Delta k/k$. The growth rate

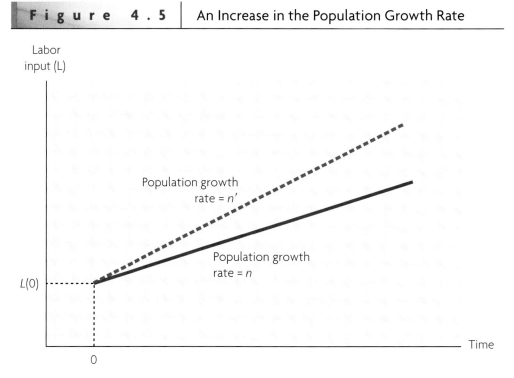

| **F i g u r e   4 . 5** | An Increase in the Population Growth Rate |

The population growth rate rises in year 0 from $n$ to $n'$. The initial level of labor input, $L(0)$, does not change.

# Do The Math

As usual, we can find the effect of $n$ on $k^*$ algebraically from the condition

(4.4)     $A \cdot f(k^*)/k^* = \delta + n/s$

An increase in $n$ raises the right-hand side of the equation. Hence, the steady-state average

product of capital, $A \cdot f(k^*)/k^* = y^*/k^*$, has to rise on the left-hand side. Because of diminishing average product of capital (Figure 3.9), this change requires a decrease in $k^*$. Therefore, as we already found, an increase in $n$ reduces $k^*$.

of real GDP per worker, $\Delta y/y$, falls correspondingly. Thus, in the short run, a higher $n$ lowers $\Delta k/k$ and $\Delta y/y$. These growth rates remain lower during the transition to the steady state. However, in the steady state, $\Delta k/k$ and $\Delta y/y$ are zero for any $n$. That is, a higher $n$ leads to lower steady-state capital and real GDP per worker, $k^*$ and $y^*$, not to changes in the growth

| **F i g u r e   4 . 6** | Effect of an Increase in the Population Growth Rate in the Solow Model |

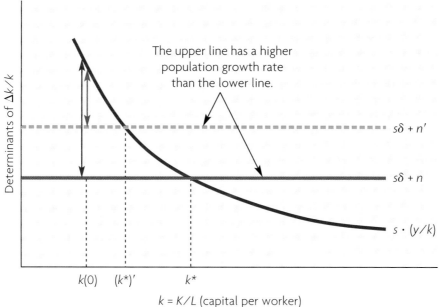

This graph comes from Figure 3.10. An increase in the population growth rate from $n$ to $n'$ raises the horizontal line from $s\delta + n$ to $s\delta + n'$. The growth rate of capital per worker, $\Delta k/k$, is lower at any $k$ when the population growth rate is higher. For example, at $k(0)$, when the population growth rate is $n$, $\Delta k/k$ equals the vertical distance given by the red arrows. When the population growth rate is $n'$, $\Delta k/k$ equals the vertical distance given by the blue arrows. In the steady state, $\Delta k/k$ is zero, regardless of the population growth rate. A higher population growth rate yields a lower steady-state capital per worker; that is, $(k^*)'$ is less than $k^*$.

rates, $\Delta k/k$ and $\Delta y/y$ (which remain at zero). A change in $n$ does affect the steady-state growth rates of the levels of capital and real GDP, $\Delta K/K$ and $\Delta Y/Y$. An increase in $n$ by 1% per year raises the steady-state values of $\Delta K/K$ and $\Delta Y/Y$ by 1% per year.

We can see from Figure 4.6 that an increase in the depreciation rate, $\delta$, affects the steady-state capital per worker in the same way as an increase in the population growth rate, $n$. This result follows because equation (4.3) involves the term $s\delta + n$, which can rise either from an increase in $n$ or an increase in $\delta$. The kind of analysis that we carried out for an increase in $n$ tells us that an increase in $\delta$ lowers the growth rates of capital and real GDP per worker, $\Delta k/k$ and $\Delta y/y$, in the short run. In the steady state, an increase in $\delta$ leads to lower capital and real GDP per worker, $k^*$ and $y^*$, not to changes in $\Delta k/k$ and $\Delta y/y$, which remain at zero.[2]

# Convergence

One of the most important questions about economic growth is whether poor countries tend to converge or catch up to rich countries. Is there a systematic tendency for low-income countries like those in Africa to catch up to the rich OECD countries? We will start our answer to this question by seeing what the Solow model says about **convergence**. Then we will look at how the facts on convergence match up with the Solow model.

## Convergence in the Solow Model

To study convergence, we focus on the transition for capital per worker, $k$, as it rises from its initial value, $k(0)$, to its steady-state value, $k^*$. In Figure 3.11, we see that $k^*$ works like a target or magnet for $k$ during the transition. Therefore, an important part of our analysis of convergence concerns the determination of $k^*$. We have studied how $k^*$ depends on the saving rate, $s$, the technology level, $A$, the population growth rate, $n$, the depreciation rate, $\delta$, and the initial level of labor input, $L(0)$. We can summarize these results in the form of a function for $k^*$:

**(4.7)**
$$k^* = k^*[s, A, n, \delta, L(0)]$$
$$(+)(+)(-)(-)(0)$$

The sign below each variable indicates the effect on $k^*$. Thus, equation (4.7) shows that $k^*$ rises with $s$ and $A$, falls with $n$ and $\delta$, and does not depend on the level of labor input, represented by $L(0)$. Table 4.1 summarizes these results.

To apply the Solow model to convergence, we have to allow for more than one economy. In making this extension, we assume that the economies are independent of each other. Specifically, they do not engage in international trade in goods and services or in financial assets. In other words, we still think of each economy as closed.

Think now of two economies, 1 and 2, and suppose that they start with capital per worker of $k(0)_1$ and $k(0)_2$, respectively, where $k(0)_1$ is less than $k(0)_2$. Each economy is assumed to have the same production function, $y = A \cdot f(k)$. Thus, economy 2 is initially more advanced in the sense of having higher capital and real GDP per worker, $k(0)$ and

---

[2] One difference is that an increase in n raises the steady-state growth rates of the levels of capital and real GDP, $(\Delta K/K)^*$ and $(\Delta Y/Y)^*$, whereas an increase in ffl does not affect these steady-state growth rates.

9038.0
18.860
7.7577
61.851

# Extending The Model

## Endogenous population growth

Our analysis treated the population growth rate, *n*, as exogenous—determined outside of the model. However, since the writings of Thomas Malthus (1798), economists have argued that population growth responds to economic variables. Malthus was a British economist and minister who wrote his *Essay on Population* in 1798. He argued that an increase in real income per person raised population growth by improving life expectancy, mainly through better nutrition but also through improved sanitation and medical care. Another influence, Malthus believed, was that higher income encouraged greater fertility. He thought that birth rates would rise as long as real income per person exceeded a **subsistence level**, which is the amount needed to pay for the basic necessities of life.

We can incorporate Malthus's ideas about population growth into the Solow model. In Figure 3.10, for a given population growth rate, *n*, the economy approaches a steady-state capital per worker, $k^*$, and a corresponding real NDP per worker, $y^* = A \cdot f(k^*) - \delta k^*$, which equals real national income per worker. The real income per person is then

$$\text{real income per person}$$
$$= (\text{real NDP per worker})$$
$$\times (\text{workers/population})$$

The last term on the right-hand side is the labor-force participation rate, which we assume to be fixed.

When household real income per person rose above the subsistence level, Malthus believed that the population growth rate would rise. Figure 4.6 showed the effect from a rise in the population growth rate; this change lowered the steady-state capital and real GDP per worker. According to Malthus, this process would continue until the steady-state real income per person fell to the subsistence level.

Malthus's view on the relation between real income per person and life expectancy is reasonable. Data across countries show that higher real GDP per person matches up closely with higher life expectancy at birth.[3] However, Malthus's idea about fertility seems unreasonable. At least in the cross-country data since 1960, higher real GDP per person matches up with lower fertility.[4] In fact, this relation is so strong that higher real GDP per person matches up with a lower population growth rate, even though countries with higher real GDP per person have higher life expectancy.

We can modify the Solow model to include Malthus's idea that population growth is endogenous. However, contrary to Malthus, we should assume a negative effect of real GDP per person—and, hence, of capital per worker, *k*—on the population growth rate, *n*.

The condition for the growth rate of capital per worker is again

(4.3)     $\Delta k / k = sA \cdot f(k) / k - s\delta - n$

During the transition to the steady state, a rise in *k* reduced the average product of capital, $y/k$, and thereby decreased the growth rate of capital per worker, $\Delta k / k$. Now we have that a rise in *k* also lowers *n*. This change raises $\Delta k / k$ and, thus, offsets the effect from a reduced average product of capital. Hence, a declining population growth rate is one reason why rich societies can sustain growing capital and real GDP per worker for a long time.

---

[3] Although this relation is suggestive, it does not prove that the causation is from higher real income per person to greater life expectancy, rather than the reverse. In fact, both directions of causation seem to be important.

[4] This relation does not prove that the causation is from higher real income per person to lower fertility, rather than the reverse. In fact, the reverse effect is predicted by the Solow model. If a society chooses, perhaps for cultural reasons, to have higher fertility and population growth, the model predicts lower steady-state real GDP per worker. In practice, both directions of causation seem to be important.

### Table 4.1 | Effects on Steady-State Capital per Worker, $k^*$

| Increase in this Variable | Effect on $k^*$ |
| --- | --- |
| saving rate, $s$ | increase |
| technology level, $A$ | increase |
| depreciation rate, $\delta$ | decrease |
| population growth rate, $n$ | decrease |
| level of labor force, $L(0)$ | no effect |

**Note:** The right-hand column shows the effect of an increase in the variable in the left-hand column on the steady-state ratio of capital to labor, $k^*$. These results come from equation (4.7).

### Figure 4.7 | Convergence in the Solow Model

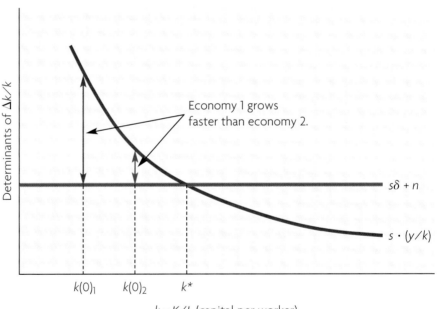

This graph comes from Figure 3.10. Economy 1 starts with lower capital per worker than economy 2—$k(0)_1$ is less than $k(0)_2$. Economy 1 grows faster initially because the vertical distance between the $s \cdot (y/k)$ curve and the $s\delta + n$ line is greater at $k(0)_1$ than at $k(0)_2$. That is, the distance marked by the red arrows is greater than that marked by the blue arrows. Therefore, capital per worker in economy 1, $k_1$, converges over time toward that in economy 2, $k_2$.

$y(0)$. Imagine that each economy has the same values for the determinants of $k^*$ listed in Table 4.1, so that they have the same steady-state capital per worker, $k^*$.

We show this situation in Figure 4.7, which has been adapted from Figure 3.10. The only difference between the two economies is that one starts at $k(0)_1$ and the other at $k(0)_2$. Therefore, the differences in the transition paths of $k$ depend only on the differences in these starting values. The graph in Figure 4.7 shows that the vertical distance between the $s \cdot (y/k)$ curve and the $s\delta + n$ line is greater at $k(0)_1$ than at $k(0)_2$. That is, the distance

| Figure 4.8 | Convergence and Transition Paths for Two Economies |

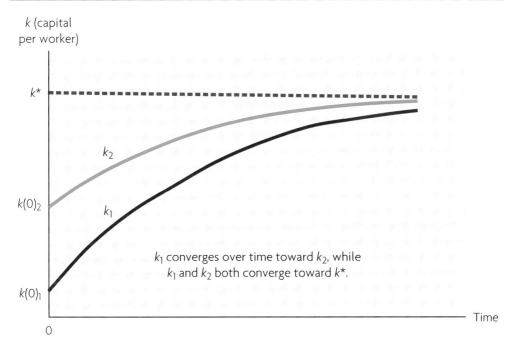

Economy 1 starts at capital per worker $k(0)_1$ and economy 2 starts at $k(0)_2$, where $k(0)_1$ is less than $k(0)_2$. The two economies have the same steady-state capital per worker, $k^*$, shown by the dashed blue line. In each economy, $k$ rises over time toward $k^*$. However, $k$ grows faster in economy 1 because $k(0)_1$ is less than $k(0)_2$. (See Figure 4.7.) Therefore, $k_1$ converges over time toward $k_2$.

marked with red arrows is greater than that marked with blue arrows. Therefore, the growth rate of capital per worker, $\Delta k/k$, is higher initially for economy 1 than economy 2. Because $k$ grows at a faster rate in economy 1, its level of $k$ converges over time toward economy 2's level.

Figure 4.8 shows the transition paths of capital per worker, $k$, for economies 1 and 2. Note that $k(0)_1$ is less than $k(0)_2$, but $k_1$ gradually approaches $k_2$. (At the same time, $k_1$ and $k_2$ both gradually approach $k^*$.) Thus, economy 1 converges toward economy 2 in terms of the levels of $k$.

We can express the results in terms of real GDP per worker, $y$. The capital per worker, $k$, determines $y$ from the production function:

(4.2) $$y = A \cdot f(k)$$

Since economy 1 starts with lower capital per worker, $k(0)$, it must also start with lower real GDP per worker—$y(0)_1$ is less than $y(0)_2$. The growth rate of real GDP per worker relates to the growth rate of capital per worker from equation (3.8), which we repeat:

(4.8) $$\Delta y/y = \alpha \cdot (\Delta k/k)$$

where $\alpha$ is the capital-share coefficient. (We assume that $\alpha$ is the same in the two economies.) We showed in Figure 4.7 that $\Delta k/k$ was higher initially in economy 1 than in economy 2.

Therefore, $\Delta y/y$ is also higher initially in economy 1. Hence, economy 1's real GDP per worker, $y$, converges over time toward economy 2's real GDP per worker. The transition paths for $y$ in the two economies look like those shown for $k$ in Figure 4.8.

To summarize, the Solow model says that a poor economy—with low capital and real GDP per worker—grows faster than a rich one. The reason is the diminishing average product of capital, $y/k$. A poor economy, such as economy 1 in Figure 4.7, has the advantage of having a high average product of capital, $y/k$. This high average product explains why the growth rates of capital and real GDP per worker are higher than in the initially more advanced economy, economy 2. Thus, the Solow model predicts that poorer economies tend to converge over time toward richer ones in terms of the levels of capital and real GDP per worker.

## Facts About Convergence

The main problem with these predictions about convergence is that they conflict with the evidence for a broad group of countries. We already looked, in Figure 3.3, at growth rates of real GDP per person from 1960 to 2000. To apply the Solow model to these data, we have to translate from amounts per worker to amounts per person. The formula for real GDP per person is again

*real GDP per person = (real GDP per worker) · (workers/population)*

The ratio of workers to population is the labor-force participation rate, which we have assumed to be constant. For example, if the ratio is around one-half, as in recent U.S. experience, real GDP per person is about one-half of real GDP per worker.

With this translation, we find that the Solow model predicts convergence for real GDP per person. Specifically, the model predicts that a lower level of real GDP per person would match up with a higher subsequent growth rate of real GDP per person.

Figure 4.9 uses the data for countries from Figure 3.3 to plot growth rates of real GDP per person from 1960 to 2000 against levels of real GDP per person in 1960. If the convergence predictions from the Solow model were correct, we should find low levels of real GDP per person matched with high growth rates, and high levels of real GDP per person matched with low growth rates. Instead, it is difficult to discern any pattern in the data— if anything, there is a slight tendency for the growth rate to rise with the level of real GDP per person.

The sample of countries included in Figure 4.9 is very broad; it includes the richest and poorest economies in the world. The convergence prediction of the Solow model accords better with the data if we limit the observations to economies that have more similar economic and social characteristics. Figure 4.10 on page 84 is the same as Figure 4.9, except that the sample is limited to 18 advanced OECD countries. For this limited sample, lower levels of real GDP per person in 1960 do match up, on average, with higher growth rates from 1960 to 2000. This pattern reflects especially the catching up of some of the initially poorer OECD countries—Greece, Ireland, Portugal, and Spain—to the richer ones.

Figure 4.11 on page 85 shows an even clearer pattern of convergence for a still more homogenous group of economies—the states of the United States. The figure plots the average growth rate of personal income per person from 1880 to 2000 against the level of personal income per person in 1880.[5] This graph shows a dramatic tendency for the

---

[5] We use personal income because data on gross state product are unavailable for the U.S. states for the period since 1880.

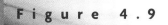

**F i g u r e   4 . 9** | Growth Rate Versus Level of Real GDP per Person for a Broad Group of Countries

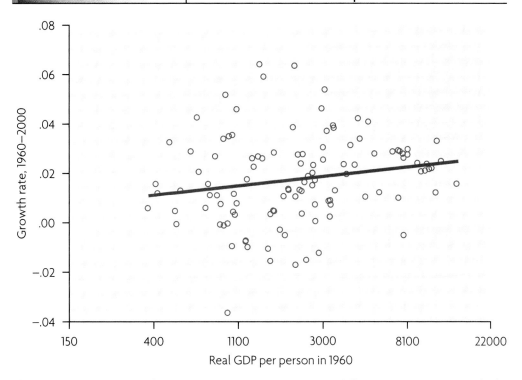

The horizontal axis shows real GDP per person in 1960 in 2000 U.S. dollars on a proportionate scale for 112 countries. The vertical axis shows the growth rate of real GDP per person for each country from 1960 to 2000. The red line is the straight line that provides a best fit to the relation between the growth rate of real GDP per person (the variable on the vertical axis) and the level of real GDP per person (on the horizontal axis). Although this line slopes upward, the slope is—in a statistical sense—negligibly different from zero. Hence, the growth rate is virtually unrelated to the level of real GDP per person. Thus, this broad group of countries does not display convergence.

initially poorer states to grow faster than the initially richer ones over the 120 years after 1880. This convergence tendency does not reflect only the recovery of the southern states, which were defeated during the U.S. Civil War (1861–1865). The convergence pattern applies if we examine economic performance within any of the four main regions—Northeast, South, Midwest, and West. Researchers have found results similar to those in Figure 4.1 for regions of some other advanced countries.

Figures 4.9 to 4.11 tell us that similar economies tend to converge, whereas dissimilar economies display no relationship between the level of real GDP per person and the growth rate. Thus, the convergence pattern is strongest for regions of an advanced country (Figure 4.11), next strongest among a group of rich countries (Figure 4.10), and weakest—in fact, absent—for the full worldwide sample of countries (Figure 4.9).

## Conditional Convergence in the Solow Model

The Solow model's prediction of convergence seems to explain growth patterns in similar economies, and it seems to fail when we examine a dissimilar array of economies. Do these findings mean that the model is flawed? Are there changes we can make to improve its predictions?

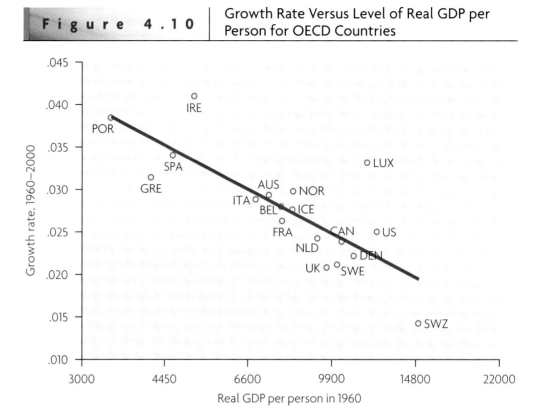

**Figure 4.10** | Growth Rate Versus Level of Real GDP per Person for OECD Countries

The horizontal axis shows real GDP per person in 1960 in 2000 U.S. dollars on a proportionate scale for 18 of the 20 founding members of the OECD (excluding Germany and Turkey). The abbreviation identifies each country. (AUS stands for Austria; Australia was not a founding member of the OECD.) The vertical axis shows the growth rate of real GDP per person for each country from 1960 to 2000. The red line is the straight line that provides a best fit to the relation between the growth rate of real GDP per person (the variable on the vertical axis) and the level of real GDP per person (on the horizontal axis). The line has a clear negative slope—therefore, a lower level of real GDP per person in 1960 matches up with a higher growth rate of real GDP per person from 1960 to 2000. Thus, the group of OECD countries exhibit convergence.

To find the flaw and try to correct it, let's reexamine the Solow model. One key assumption was that the determinants of the steady-state capital per worker, $k^*$, were the same for all economies. This assumption is reasonable for similar economies but is less plausible for a broad sample of countries with sharply different economic, political, and social characteristics. In particular, the assumption is unreasonable for the worldwide sample of countries considered in Figure 4.9. To explain the lack of convergence for this group, we have to allow for differences in the steady-state positions, $k^*$.

Suppose that countries differ with respect to some of the determinants of $k^*$ in equation (4.7) and Table 4.1. For example, $k^*$ could vary because of differences in saving rates, $s$, levels of technology, $A$, and population growth rates, $n$.[6] Figure 4.12 on page 86 modifies Figure 4.7 to show how differences in saving rates affect convergence. Economy 1 has the saving rate $s_1$, and economy 2 has the higher saving rate $s_2$. We assume, as in Figure 4.7, that economy 1 has lower initial capital per worker; that is, $k(0)_1$ is less than

---

[6] Levels of population and the labor force vary greatly across countries, but the level of labor input, represented by $L(0)$, does not affect $k^*$ in the model. The depreciation rate, $\delta$, probably does not vary systematically across countries.

| Figure 4.11 | Growth Rate Versus Level of Income per Person for U.S. States, 1880–2000 |

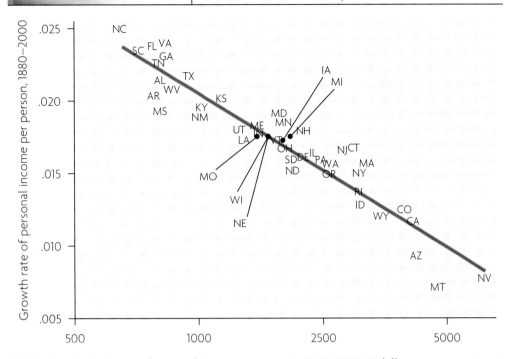

The horizontal axis shows real personal income per person in 1982–1984 U.S. dollars on a proportionate scale for 47 U.S. states. The two-letter abbreviation identifies the state. (Alaska, the District of Columbia, Hawaii, and Oklahoma are excluded.) The vertical axis shows the growth rate of real personal income per person for each state from 1880 to 2000. The solid line is the straight line that provides a best fit to the relation between the growth rate of income per person (the variable on the vertical axis) and the level of income per person (on the horizontal axis). The line has a clear negative slope—therefore, a lower level of income per person in 1880 matches up with a higher growth rate of income per person from 1880 to 2000. Thus, the U.S. states exhibit convergence.

$k(0)_2$. Remember that the growth rate of capital per worker, $\Delta k/k$, equals the vertical distance between the $s \cdot (y/k)$ curve and the $s\delta + n$ line. We see from Figure 4.12 that it is uncertain whether the distance between the $s \cdot (y/k)$ curve and the $s\delta + n$ line is greater initially for economy 1 or economy 2. The lower capital per worker, $k(0)$, tends to make the distance greater for economy 1, but the lower saving rate, $s$, tends to make the distance smaller for economy 1. In the graph, these two forces roughly balance, so that $\Delta k/k$ is about the same for the two economies. That is, the distance marked with the blue arrows is similar to the one marked with the red arrows. Therefore, the poorer economy, economy 1, does not necessarily converge toward the richer economy, economy 2.

To get the result in Figure 4.12, we had to assume that the economy with lower $k(0)$—economy 1—had a lower saving rate, $s$. This assumption is reasonable because an economy with a lower $s$ has a lower steady-state capital per worker, $k^*$. In the long run, an economy's capital per worker, $k$, would be close to its steady-state value, $k^*$. Therefore, it is likely when we examine countries at an arbitrary date, such as date 0, that $k(0)$ will be lower in the economy with the lower $s$—$k(0)$ tends to be lower in economy 1 than in economy 2. Thus, the pattern that we assumed—a low saving rate matched with a low $k(0)$—is likely to apply in practice.

| Figure 4.12 | Failure of Convergence in the Solow Model: Differences in Saving Rates |

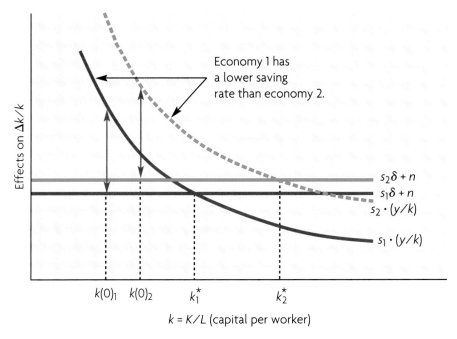

As in Figure 4.7, economy 1 starts with lower capital per worker than economy 2—$k(0)_1$ is less than $k(0)_2$. However, we now assume that economy 1 also has a lower saving rate; that is, $s_1$ is less than $s_2$. The two economies have the same technology levels, $A$, and population growth rates, $n$. Therefore, $k_1^*$ is less than $k_2^*$. In this case, it is uncertain which economy grows faster initially. The vertical distance marked with the blue arrows may be larger or smaller than the one marked with the red arrows.

We get a similar result if we consider other reasons for differences in the steady-state capital per worker, $k^*$. Suppose that the two economies have the same saving rates but that economy 1 has a lower technology level, $A$, than economy 2. In this case, the two curves for $s \cdot (y/k)$ again look as shown in Figure 4.12.[7] Therefore, it is again uncertain whether the vertical distance between the $s \cdot (y/k)$ curve and the $s\delta + n$ line is greater for economy 1 or economy 2. The lower capital per worker, $k(0)$, tends to make the distance greater for economy 1, but the lower $A$ tends to make the distance smaller for economy 1. As before, it is possible that the two forces roughly balance, so that $\Delta k/k$ is about the same for the two economies. Thus, the poorer economy, economy 1, need not converge toward the richer economy, economy 2.

To get this result, we had to assume that the economy with the lower starting capital per worker, $k(0)$—economy 1—had the lower technology level, $A$. This assumption is reasonable because an economy with a lower $A$ has a lower steady-state capital per worker, $k^*$. Therefore, it is again likely when we look at the two economies at date 0 that $k(0)$ will be lower in economy 1 than economy 2.

The same conclusions apply if we consider differences in population growth rates. In Figure 4.13, the two economies have the same saving rates and technology levels, but economy 1 has a higher population growth rate, $n$. Hence, the $s\delta + n$ line is higher for economy 1. It is again uncertain whether the vertical distance between the $s \cdot (y/k)$ curve

---

[7] In this case, unlike in Figure 4.12, the $\delta s + n$ lines are the same for the two countries.

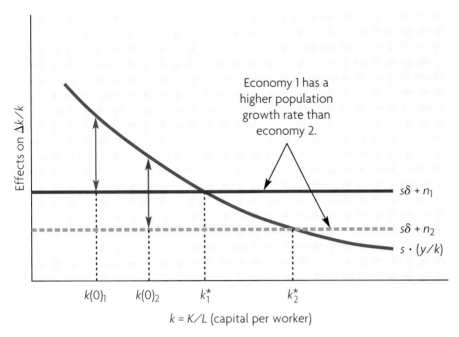

**Figure 4.13** | Failure of Convergence in the Solow Model: Differences in Population Growth Rates

As in Figure 4.12, economy 1 starts with lower capital per worker than economy 2—$k(0)_1$ is less than $k(0)_2$. The two economies now have the same saving rates, $s$, and technology levels, $A$, but economy 1 has a higher population growth rate, $n$; that is, $n_1$ is greater than $n_2$. Therefore, as in Figure 4.12, $k_1^*$ is less than $k_2^*$. It is again uncertain which economy grows faster initially. The vertical distance marked with the blue arrows may be larger or smaller than the one marked with the red arrows.

and the $\delta s + n$ line is greater for economy 1 or economy 2. The lower capital per worker, $k(0)$, for economy 1 tends to make the distance greater for economy 1, but the higher $n$ tends to make the distance smaller for economy 1. As in our other cases, it is possible that the two forces roughly balance, so that $\Delta k/k$ would be about the same in the two economies—the distance marked with the blue arrows is similar to the one marked with the red arrows. Thus, economy 1 again need not converge toward economy 2.

To get this result, we had to assume that the economy with the lower starting capital per worker, $k(0)$—economy 1—had the higher population growth rate, $n$. This assumption makes sense because an economy with a higher $n$ has a lower steady-state capital per worker, $k^*$. Therefore, it is again likely when we look at the two economies at date 0 that $k(0)$ will be lower in economy 1 than economy 2.

Now let's generalize the conclusions from our three cases. In each case, economy 1 had a characteristic—lower saving rate, $s$, lower technology level, $A$, higher population growth rate, $n$—that led to a lower steady-state capital per worker, $k^*$. For a given starting capital per worker, $k(0)$, each of the three characteristics tended to make country 1's initial growth rate less than economy 2's initial growth rate. We see these effects in Figures 4.12 and 4.13. At a given $k(0)$, the vertical distance between the $s\cdot(y/k)$ curve and the $s\delta + n$ line is smaller if $s$ or $A$ is lower or if $n$ is higher.

Since economy 1 has lower $k^*$, it is also likely to have lower initial capital per worker, $k(0)$. The lower $k(0)$ tends to make economy 1 grow faster than economy 2—the convergence

## Figure 4.14 | Failure of Convergence and Transition Paths for Two Economies

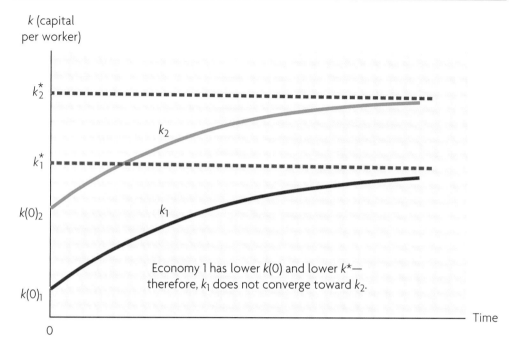

As in Figures 4.12 and 4.13, economy 1 has a lower starting capital per worker—$k(0)_1$ is less than $k(0)_2$—and also has a lower steady-state capital per worker—$k_1^*$ (the dashed brown line) is less than $k_2^*$ (the dashed blue line). Each capital per worker converges over time toward its own steady-state value: $k_1$ (the red curve) toward $k_1^*$, and $k_2$ (the green curve) toward $k_2^*$. However, since $k_1^*$ is less than $k_2^*$, $k_1$ does not converge toward $k_2$.

force shown in Figure 4.7. Whether economy 1 grows faster or slower overall than economy 2 depends on the offset of two forces. The lower $k(0)$ generates faster growth in economy 1, but the lower $k^*$ generates slower growth in economy 1. It is possible that the two forces roughly balance, so that the two economies grow at about the same rate. That is, we need not find convergence.

Figure 4.14 shows the transition paths of capital per worker, $k$, for the two economies. We assume that economy 1 starts with a lower capital per worker—$k(0)_1$ is less than $k(0)_2$—and also has a lower steady-state capital per worker—$k_1^*$ is less than $k_2^*$. The graph shows that capital per worker in each economy converges toward its own steady-state level—$k_1$ toward $k_1^*$, and $k_2$ toward $k_2^*$. However, since $k_1^*$ is less than $k_2^*$, $k_1$ does not converge toward $k_2$.

We can summarize our findings for the growth rate of capital per worker in an equation:

Key equation (conditional convergence in the Solow model):

(4.9) $$\Delta k/k = \varphi[k(0), k^*]$$

$$(-)\quad(+)$$

*growth rate of capital per worker = function of initial and steady-state capital per worker*

The function $\varphi$ indicates how $\Delta k/k$ depends on the initial capital per worker, $k(0)$, and the steady-state capital per worker, $k^*$. The minus sign under $k(0)$ signifies that, for given $k^*$, a decrease in $k(0)$ raises $\Delta k/k$. The plus sign under $k^*$ means that, for given $k(0)$, a rise in $k^*$ increases $\Delta k/k$.

We can interpret the effects in equation (4.9) from the perspective of our equation for the growth rate of capital per worker:

(4.3) $$\Delta k/k = sA \cdot f(k)/k - s\delta - n$$

The negative effect of $k(0)$ in equation (4.9) corresponds in equation (4.3) to a lower initial average product of capital, $A \cdot f(k)/k$. The positive effect of $k^*$ in equation (4.9) corresponds in equation (4.3) to a higher saving rate, $s$, a higher technology level, $A$, or a lower population growth rate, $n$.

One important result in equation (4.9) is that the negative effect of $k(0)$ on the growth rate, $\Delta k/k$, holds only in a conditional sense—that is, for a given $k^*$. This pattern is called **conditional convergence**: a lower $k(0)$ predicts a higher $\Delta k/k$, conditional on $k^*$. In contrast, the prediction that a lower $k(0)$ raises $\Delta k/k$ without any conditioning is called **absolute convergence**.

Recall from Figure 4.9 that we do not observe absolute convergence for a broad group of countries. We see from equation (4.9) that we can use the Solow model to explain the lack of convergence in this diverse group. Suppose that some countries have low saving rates, low technology levels, or high population growth rates and, therefore, have low steady-state capital per worker, $k^*$. In the long run, capital per worker, $k$, will be close to $k^*$. Therefore, when we look at date 0 (say, 1960), we tend to find that low values of $k(0)$ match up with low values of $k^*$. A low value of $k(0)$ makes the growth rate of capital per worker, $\Delta k/k$, high, but a low value of $k^*$ makes $\Delta k/k$ low. Thus, the data may show little relation between $k(0)$ and $\Delta k/k$. This pattern is consistent with the one found in Figure 4.9 for growth rates and levels of real GDP per person.

## Where Do We Stand with the Solow Model?

When we first considered convergence, we observed that the lack of absolute convergence for a broad group of countries, as in Figure 4.9, was a failing of the Solow model. Then we found that an extension of the model to consider conditional convergence explained this apparent failure. We show in the next chapter that conditional convergence allows us to understand many other features of economic growth in the world.

Although the Solow model has many strengths, we should be clear about what the model does not explain. Most important is the failure to explain how real GDP per person grows in the long run—for example, at a rate of about 2% per year for well over a century in the United States and other advanced countries. In the model, capital per worker—and, hence, real GDP per worker and per person—are constant in the long run. Thus, a key objective of the next chapter is to extend the model to explain long-run economic growth.

## Key Terms and Concepts

absolute convergence
conditional convergence

convergence
subsistence level

## Questions and Problems

**A.** Review questions

1. If the initial level of labor input, $L(0)$, doubles, why does the steady-state capital stock, $K^*$, double? That is, Figure 4.4 implies that steady-state capital per worker, $k^*$, does not change. How does this result depend on constant returns to scale in the production function?

2. Does population growth, $n > 0$, lead to growth of output in the long run? Does it lead to growth of output per worker in the long run?

3. What is the meaning of the term *convergence*? How does absolute convergence differ from conditional convergence?

4. For 112 countries, Figure 4.9 shows that the growth rate of real per capita GDP from 1960 to 2000 bears little relation to the level of real GDP in 1960. Does this finding conflict with the Solow model of economic growth? How does this question relate to the concept of conditional convergence?

**B.** Problems for discussion

5. Variations in the saving rate

Suppose that the saving rate, $s$, can vary as an economy develops.

a. The equation for the growth rate of capital per worker, $k$, is given by

$$\text{(4.1)} \qquad k/k = s \cdot (y/k) - s\delta - n$$

Is this equation still valid when $s$ is not constant?

b. Suppose that $s$ rises as an economy develops; that is, rich countries save at a higher rate than poor countries. How does this behavior affect the results about convergence?

c. Suppose, instead, that $s$ falls as an economy develops; that is, rich countries save at a lower rate than poor countries. How does this behavior affect the results about convergence?

d. Which case seems more plausible—b. or c. above? Explain.

6. Variations in the population growth rate

Suppose that the population growth rate, $n$, can vary as an economy develops.

a. The equation for the growth rate of capital per worker, $k$, is again given from

$$\text{(4.1)} \qquad \Delta k/k = s \cdot (y/k) - s\delta - n$$

Is this equation still valid when $n$ is not constant?

b. Suppose that $n$ falls as an economy develops; that is, rich countries have lower population growth rates than poor countries. How does this behavior affect the results about convergence?

c. Suppose, instead, that $n$ rises as an economy develops; that is, rich countries have higher population growth rates than poor countries. How does this behavior affect the results about convergence?

d. Which case seems more plausible—b. or c. above? Explain, giving particular attention to the views of Malthus about endogenous population growth.

# Appendix

## The Rate of Convergence

We assess here how fast convergence takes place in the Solow model. Figure 4.15 starts by reproducing the construction from Figure 3.10. The horizontal line is again at $s\delta + n$, and the capital per worker starts at $k(0)$. The saving curve is shown in blue as $s \cdot (y/k)^{\mathrm{I}}$. The growth rate of capital per worker, $\Delta k/k$, equals the vertical distance between the $s \cdot (y/k)^{\mathrm{I}}$ curve and the $s\delta + n$ line.

As stressed before, the source of convergence in the Solow model is the diminishing average product of capital, $y/k$. Recall that this average product is given by

$$y/k = A \cdot f(k)/k$$

The tendency for the average product to fall as $k$ increases is the reason that the $s \cdot (y/k)^{\mathrm{I}}$ curve slopes downward. The slope of the curve determines how fast convergence occurs, and this slope will depend on the form of the function $f(k)/k$.

To understand the role of the slope of the $s \cdot (y/k)$ curve, Figure 4.15 includes a second saving curve, $s \cdot (y/k)^{\mathrm{II}}$, shown in red. In comparison with the first curve, the second

**F i g u r e   4 . 1 5** | Determining the Speed of Convergence

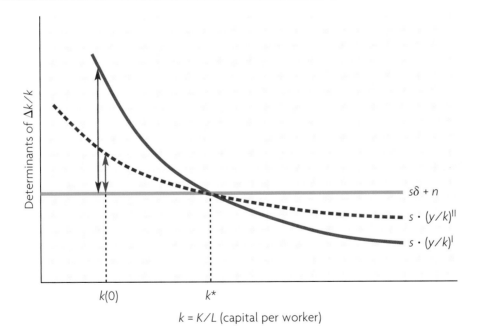

$k = K/L$ (capital per worker)

This graph modifies Figure 4.4. The first saving curve, $s \cdot (y/k)^{\mathrm{I}}$, is the same as before. The second saving curve, $s \cdot (y/k)^{\mathrm{II}}$, does not slope downward as much as the first one. The reason is that the average product of capital, $y/k$, diminishes less rapidly with $k$ in the second case. At $k(0)$, the distance between the $s \cdot (y/k)$ curve and the $s\delta + n$ line is greater in the first case (the brown arrows) than in the second (the green arrows). Therefore, the initial $\Delta k/k$ is higher in the first case, and the convergence to the steady state is faster. The conclusion is that convergence is faster when the average product of capital diminishes more rapidly with $k$.

one has the same saving rate, $s$, and technology level, $A$, but a different form of the function $f(k)/k$. This different form means that the relation between $k$ and $y/k$ is different for curve II than for curve I. Specifically, at any value of $k$, the second curve does not slope downward as much as the first one. That is, the average product of capital, $y/k$, diminishes less rapidly with $k$ in the second case than in the first one.

To ease the comparison, we set up the graph so that the two saving curves intersect the $s\delta + n$ line at the same point. Hence, the steady-state capital per worker, $k^*$, is the same in the two cases. However, at the initial capital per worker, $k(0)$, the vertical distance between the saving curve and the $s\delta + n$ line is larger in the first case than in the second. In the graph, the first distance is shown by the brown arrows, and the second distance by the green arrows. Therefore, at $k(0)$, $\Delta k/k$ is higher in the first case. The higher growth rate means that $k$ converges more rapidly toward its steady-state level, $k^*$. Hence, we have shown that the rate of convergence is higher when the average product of capital diminishes more rapidly with $k$.

For a given technology level, $A$, the relation between the average product of capital, $y/k$, and $k$ depends on the form of the function $f(k)/k$. To take a concrete example, consider the Cobb-Douglas production function, introduced in the Appendix, Part C to Chapter 3, where $f(k) = k^\alpha$. In this case, the average product of capital is

$$y/k = A \cdot f(k)/k$$

$$= Ak^\alpha/k$$

$$= Ak^\alpha \cdot k^{-1}$$

$$= Ak^{(\alpha-1)}$$

(4.10)
$$y/k = Ak^{-(1-\alpha)}$$

Since $0 < \alpha < 1$, the average product of capital, $y/k$, falls as $k$ rises. The value of $\alpha$ determines how fast $y/k$ falls as $k$ rises. If $\alpha$ is close to 1, equation (4.10) says that $y/k$ falls slowly as $k$ rises (curve II in Figure 4.15 is like this). If $\alpha$ is close to zero, $y/k$ falls quickly as $k$ rises (curve I is like this). Generally, the lower $\alpha$ is, the more quickly $y/k$ falls as $k$ rises.

To get a quantitative idea about the rate of convergence, consider an intermediate case in which $\alpha = 0.5$. In this case, the average product of capital is

$$y/k = Ak^{-(1/2)}$$

$$y/k = A/\sqrt{k}$$

That is, the average product of capital declines with the square root of $k$.

Recall that the growth rate of $k$ is given by

(4.1)
$$\Delta k/k = s \cdot (y/k) - s\delta - n$$

If we substitute $y/k = A/\sqrt{k}$, we get

(4.11)
$$\Delta k/k = sA/\sqrt{k} - s\delta - n$$

If we specify values for the saving rate, $s$, the technology level, $A$, the depreciation rate, $\delta$, the rate of population growth, $n$, and the initial capital per worker, $k(0)$, we can use

## Table 4.2 | The Transition Path in the Solow Model

| Year | $k/k^*$ | $y/y^*$ |
|------|---------|---------|
| 0 | 0.50 | 0.71 |
| 5 | 0.56 | 0.75 |
| 10 | 0.61 | 0.78 |
| 15 | 0.66 | 0.81 |
| 20 | 0.71 | 0.84 |
| 25 | 0.74 | 0.86 |
| 30 | 0.78 | 0.88 |
| 35 | 0.81 | 0.90 |
| 40 | 0.83 | 0.91 |
| 45 | 0.86 | 0.93 |
| 50 | 0.88 | 0.94 |

**Note:** The table shows the solution of the Solow model for capital per worker, $k$, and real GDP per worker, $y$. The results are expressed as ratios to the steady-state values, $k/k^*$ and $y/y^*$. The transitional behavior of $k$ and $y$ comes from equation (4.11), which assumes $y = A \cdot \sqrt{k}$. The calculations assume that $k/k^*$ starts at 0.5 and uses the values $n = 0.01$ per year and $\delta = 0.05$ per year. The values of $s$, $A$, and $L(0)$ turn out not to affect the results. The initial value for $k/k^*$ also does not matter for the speed of convergence.

equation (4.11) to calculate the time path of $k$. Since we know $k(0)$, equation (4.11) determines $k$ at the next point in time, $k(1)$. Then, given $k(1)$, we can use the equation to calculate $k(2)$. Proceeding in this way, we can calculate $k(t)$ at any time $t$.

Table 4.2 shows the solution for the path of $k(t)$. The calculations assume that the initial capital per worker, $k(0)$, is one-half of its steady-state value, $k^*$. The table reports the values of $k/k^*$ and $y/y^*$ that prevail after 5 years, 10 years, and so on. Note that it takes about 25 years—roughly a generation—to eliminate half of the initial gap between $k$ and $k^*$. By analogy to radioactive decay in physics, we can define the time for half of the convergence to the steady state to occur as the *half-life*. Since the ratio $k/k^*$ starts at 0.5 and the half-life of the convergence process is 25 years, the ratio reaches 0.75 in 25 years and 0.875 in 50 years. Hence, although capital per worker, $k$, converges toward $k^*$, the Solow model predicts that this process takes a long time. The same numerical results on half-lives turn out to apply to the adjustment of real GDP per worker, $y$, to its steady-state level, $y^*$.

If $\alpha$ is greater than 0.5, the average product of capital, $y/k$, declines more slowly as $k$ rises, and the convergence to the steady state is less rapid. Therefore, the half-life is more than 25 years. Conversely, if $\alpha$ is less than 0.5, $y/k$ declines more quickly as $k$ rises, and the convergence to the steady state is more rapid. In this case, the half-life is less than 25 years.

Many interesting applications have been made for speeds of convergence and half-lives calculated from the Solow model. One implication involves the aftermath of the U.S. Civil War, which ended in 1865. The model says that the southern states from the defeated Confederacy would converge only slowly in terms of real income per person to the richer northern states. (The war reduced the income per person in the south from roughly 80%

of the northern level to about 40%.) The quantitative prediction, which turns out to be accurate, is that the convergence process would take more than two generations to be nearly complete.

Similarly, with the unification of Germany in 1990, the model predicts that the poor eastern parts from the formerly Communist East Germany would converge, but only slowly, to the richer western regions. (In 1990, the GDP per person of the eastern regions was about 1/3 of the western level.) This prediction for gradual convergence of real GDP per person accords with the German data for the 1990s.

# C h a p t e r 5

## Conditional Convergence and Long-Run Economic Growth

In the previous two chapters, we developed and extended the Solow model of economic growth. The most important results for short-run analysis concerned convergence during the transition to the steady state. We show in the first part of this chapter how to use these results to understand patterns of economic growth in the world.

We observed at the end of Chapter 4 that the major deficiency of the Solow model was its failure to explain long-run economic growth. In the steady state, the growth rate of real GDP per worker was zero. In the second part of this chapter, we extend the model to analyze long-run growth.

## Conditional Convergence in Practice

We found that the Solow model predicted convergence across economies in capital per worker, $k$. We summarized this conclusion in an equation for the growth rate of capital per worker, $\Delta k/k$:

(4.9)
$$\Delta k/k = \varphi[k(0), k^*],$$
$$(-) \ (+)$$

where $k^*$ is the steady-state value of $k$. For a given $k^*$, a lower $k(0)$ matches up with a higher $\Delta k/k$. Thus, the model has a convergence property for $k$. The convergence is conditional in the sense of depending on variables that affect $k^*$. For given $k(0)$, an increase in $k^*$ raises $\Delta k/k$.

The production function relates real GDP per worker, $y$, to capital per worker, $k$:

(4.2)
$$y = A \cdot f(k)$$

We can use equation (4.2) in equation (4.9) to replace $\Delta k/k$ by $\Delta y/y$, $k(0)$ by $y(0)$, and $k^*$ by $y^*$ to get

---

Key equation (conditional convergence for real GDP per worker):

(5.1)
$$\Delta y/y = \varphi[y(0), y^*]$$
$$(-) \quad (+)$$

growth rate of real GDP per worker = function of initial and steady-state real GDP per worker

---

Equation (5.1) shows that the Solow model determines the growth rate of real GDP per worker, $\Delta y/y$, as a function of initial real GDP per worker, $y(0)$, and steady-state real GDP per worker, $y^*$. For given $y^*$, an increase in $y(0)$ lowers $\Delta y/y$. For given $y(0)$, an increase in $y^*$ raises $\Delta y/y$. This relation exhibits the convergence property because a poorer economy—with lower $y(0)$—has a higher growth rate, $\Delta y/y$. However, the convergence is conditional in the sense of depending on variables that influence the steady-state position, $y^*$.

In our discussion in Chapter 4, we focused on three variables that influenced the steady-state capital and real GDP per worker, $k^*$ and $y^*$: the saving rate, $s$, the technology level, $A$, and the population growth rate, $n$. Economists have extended the Solow model to allow for additional variables that affect $k^*$ and $y^*$. We can understand these effects, without working through the details, by taking a broader view of the technology level, $A$. The important feature of a higher $A$ is that it raises productivity; that is, it allows real GDP to rise for given inputs of capital and labor. Many variables that are not strictly technological also influence an economy's productivity. These other influences affect economic growth in ways analogous to changes in $A$.

As an example, productivity depends on the degree of market efficiency. Economies can enhance efficiency by removing restrictions due to government regulations, by lowering tax rates, and by promoting competition, possibly through anti-trust enforcement. Another way for markets to work better, discussed in Chapter 17, is for governments to allow free trade in goods and services across international borders. This kind of international openness allows countries to specialize in the production of the goods and services in which they have natural advantages. Hence, greater international openness tends to raise world productivity. A country's legal and political system also influences its productivity. Productivity tends to rise if governments do better at enforcing property rights, if the judicial system runs more smoothly, and if official corruption declines.

## Recent Research on the Determinants of Economic Growth

Recent research has used the equation for conditional convergence, given in equation (5.1), as a framework to analyze the determinants of economic growth across countries. The idea is to measure an array of variables that influence a country's steady-state real GDP per worker, $y^*$. Equation (5.1) then tells us two things. First, if we hold fixed $y^*$ (by holding fixed the variables that influence $y^*$), the growth rate of real GDP per worker, $\Delta y/y$, should exhibit convergence. That is, for given $y^*$, a lower $y(0)$ should match up with a higher $\Delta y/y$. Second, any variable that raises or lowers $y^*$ should correspondingly raise or lower $\Delta y/y$ for given $y(0)$. In practice, because of difficulties in measuring numbers of workers, most studies have measured $y$ by real GDP per person, rather than real GDP per worker.

| F i g u r e  5 . 1 | Growth Rate Versus Level of Real GDP per Person: Conditional Convergence for a Broad Group of Countries |

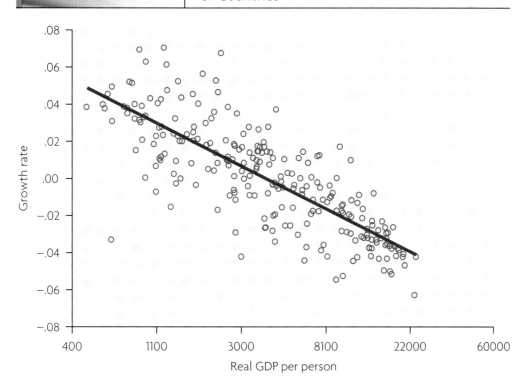

The horizontal axis shows real GDP per person in 2000 U.S. dollars on a proportionate scale. The data are for 71 countries in 1965, 85 countries in 1975, and 82 countries in 1985. (The sample was based on the availability of data—86 countries appear at least once.) The vertical axis shows the corresponding growth rates of real GDP per person—for 1965–75, 1975–85, and 1985–95. Each of the growth rates filters out (and, therefore, holds constant) the estimated effects of the variables discussed in the text. The red line is the straight line that provides a best fit to the relation between the growth rate of real GDP per person (the variable on the vertical axis) and the level of real GDP per person (on the horizontal axis). The line has a clear negative slope. Therefore, once we hold constant the other variables, a lower level of real GDP per person matches up with a higher growth rate of real GDP per person. This relation is called "conditional convergence."

Figure 5.1 shows empirical results for the relation between the growth rate and level of real GDP per person. The cross-country data are for a broad group of countries and are essentially the same as those plotted in Figure 4.9.[1] However, because we are holding fixed variables that determine the steady-state real GDP per worker, $y^*$, the graph looks very different from before. With the other variables held constant, the convergence pattern becomes clear—low levels of real GDP per person match up with high growth rates of real GDP per person, and high levels of real GDP per person match up with low growth rates. Thus, there is evidence for conditional convergence across a broad group of countries.

---

[1] One new feature is that the data are for the three 10-year periods from 1965 to 1995. A country's real GDP per person in 1965 is matched with its growth rate of real GDP per person from 1965 to 1975; the real GDP per person in 1975 is matched with the growth rate of real GDP per person from 1975 to 1985; and so on. If the data are available, each country appears three times in the graph. In contrast, in Figure 4.9, a country's real GDP per person in 1960 is matched with its growth rate of real GDP per person from 1960 to 2000. Therefore, each country appeared only once in this graph.

The relation shown in Figure 5.1 applies when we hold constant a list of variables that influence $y^*$. The particular list used to construct the graph is

- a measure of the saving rate
- the fertility rate for the typical woman (which influences population growth)
- subjective measures of maintenance of the rule of law and democracy
- the size of government, gauged by the share of government consumption purchases in GDP
- the extent of international openness, measured by the volume of exports and imports
- changes in the terms of trade (the ratio of prices of exported goods to prices of imported goods)
- measures of investment in education and health
- the average rate of inflation, which is an indicator of macroeconomic policy

One reason that we considered these variables is to isolate conditional convergence, as shown in Figure 5.1. Equally important, however, is that we learn how the variables in the list affect economic growth. The research shows that the growth rate of real GDP per person rises in response to a higher saving rate, lower fertility, better maintenance of the rule of law, smaller government consumption purchases, greater international openness, improvement in the terms of trade, greater quantity and quality of education, better health, and lower inflation. Democracy has a less clear effect—if a country starts from a totalitarian system, increases in democracy seem to favor economic growth. However, after a country reaches a midrange of democracy (characteristic in recent years of Indonesia, Turkey, and several countries in Latin America), further democratization seems to reduce growth.

Research on the determinants of economic growth has been lively since the early 1990s. This research has suggested numerous additional variables that influence growth. The variables considered include the scope of banking and financial markets, the degree of income inequality, the extent of official corruption, the role of colonial and legal origins, and the intensity of religious participation and beliefs. In the Back To Reality box, we consider two other variables: debt relief and foreign aid.

These kinds of empirical results have raised our understanding of the determinants of economic growth, but our knowledge remains incomplete. For one thing, economists have isolated only some of the variables that influence growth. The problems relate partly to data—for example, it is difficult to quantify government distortions from regulations and taxation or to measure various aspects of legal and political systems. Another problem is that many variables influence economic growth, and it is impossible to isolate all of these effects with the limited data available. Moreover, it is often difficult to be sure whether a variable—for example, maintenance of the rule of law or the levels of investment in education and health—affects economic growth or is affected by growth. In practice, both directions of causation are often important.

## Examples of Conditional Convergence

If we look at history, we find examples of conditional convergence. At the end of World War II, the economies of many nations were destroyed. Cities were leveled, factories bombed, and farmland used as battlefields. By 1946, Japan, Germany, France, and other countries in Europe suffered sharp reductions in physical capital. Human capital also fell sharply, but the reductions in physical capital were larger. In our model, these events generated low starting values of capital and real GDP per worker, $k(0)$ and $y(0)$. But these countries also had characteristics that were favorable to rapid economic recovery—including strong human capital in the forms of education and health, and good legal and

# Back To Reality

In the summer of 1999, I met Bono, the lead singer of the rock group U2. Bono wanted to discuss the Jubilee 2000 campaign, which was a global movement aimed at canceling the international debts of the world's poorest countries. I told him that I was an unlikely candidate to support Jubilee 2000. Bono said that was precisely why he wanted to talk with me. He wanted to see whether a hard-thinking economist could be persuaded of the soundness of the campaign.[2] In particular, he was not interested in a global welfare project but rather wanted to push debt relief as a way to promote sound economic policies and rapid economic growth. He even said that the relief would be conditioned on a country's commitment to use the freed-up money for productive investments.

I was shocked to hear these arguments from a rock star. Nevertheless, I recovered to say that this commitment was unenforceable and that debt relief would not be on the top 10 list of policies for growth promotion in poor countries. More important were well-functioning legal and political systems, openness to markets at home and abroad, investments in education and health, and sound macroeconomic policy. I mentioned the musical line "money for nothing" (from a song by Dire Straits) and said that it applied to a number of ways in which a country received unearned money. These included debt relief, debt default, foreign aid, and natural resources such as oil. Experience showed that all of these forms of free money tended to reduce economic growth. I also argued that growth would be encouraged if a country gained a reputation for honoring foreign debts and other contracts.

Bono agreed that it was important for a country to fulfill its debt obligations, especially those that originated from sensible commercial transactions. However, he argued that most of the international debts of African and other poor countries derived from poorly designed projects conceived by the World Bank, other international organizations, and donor countries such as the United States. Many of these loans were made to corrupt dictators, who diverted the funds for personal gain. He noted that these debts could never be repaid. Bono said that the idea of the term Jubilee 2000 was that it was a one-time happening and would, therefore, not encourage default on newly incurred debts. (I was a little worried here, because the Bible says that Jubilees are supposed to occur every 50 years.)

In the end, I was not convinced to put debt relief on the top 10 list of growth-promoting policies for poor countries. But, since the arguments I heard were better than I had anticipated, I was pleased at the time to offer two restrained cheers for Jubilee 2000.

In retrospect, my response was two cheers too many. William Easterly (2001) has argued convincingly that the problem of high foreign debt for poor countries is not new and that the remedy of debt relief is neither new nor effective. Easterly noted that we have already been trying debt forgiveness for two decades, with little of the salutary results promised by Jubilee 2000. He also documented that the main response to debt relief has been for countries to run up new debts, most used to finance nonproductive projects. There is no evidence that past debt relief operations helped the poor, who were Bono's intended target. So, why would one expect new debt relief to work any better?

Although I had doubts about the efficacy of Bono's proposals, he nevertheless achieved many successes since our meeting in summer 1999. His campaign brought him into contact

---

2 The "hard-thinking" phrase was Bono's.

with numerous world leaders, including then President Bill Clinton and Pope John Paul II (who is said to have tried on Bono's famous sunglasses). Bono swayed numerous politicians and economists to his cause, and his great exercise in persuasion culminated in the $435 million U.S. debt relief legislation of November 2000.

Because I hold Bono in high esteem, I wish I could believe that this and future programs of debt relief would help to spur economic growth. But economic analysis keeps me from believing these things. I wonder what would happen if Bono, instead, directed his persuasive talents to furthering ideas that seem to matter for economic growth. I have in mind property rights, the rule of law, free markets, and small government. And, I would be happy to include investments in education and health. But, of course, this is just a dream.

political traditions that encouraged markets and trade. We can represent these favorable characteristics as high values of steady-state capital and real GDP per worker, $k^*$ and $y^*$. Hence, conditional convergence—summarized in equation (5.1)—predicts that these countries would have high growth rates of real GDP per person in the aftermath of World War II. This prediction fits the facts.

As another example of conditional convergence, in the 1960s, many East Asian countries, such as South Korea and Taiwan, were poor and, therefore, had low values of capital and real GDP per worker, $k(0)$ and $y(0)$. However, these countries also had reasonably good legal systems, satisfactory programs in education and health, and relatively high openness to international trade. Therefore, the steady-state values, $k^*$ and $y^*$, were high. Hence, we predict the high growth rates of real GDP per person from 1960 to 2000.

The typical sub-Saharan African country was also poor in the 1960s; that is, capital and real GDP per worker, $k(0)$ and $y(0)$, were low. Hence, from the perspective of absolute convergence, we would predict high growth rates of real GDP per person in Africa—whereas, in fact, the growth rates were the lowest in the world from 1960 to 2000. Conditional convergence can explain this outcome, because the African countries had poorly functioning legal and political systems, weak education and health programs, high rates of population growth, and large corrupt governments. Thus, the steady-state values, $k^*$ and $y^*$, were low, and the sub-Saharan African countries failed to grow.

We see from these examples that the idea of conditional convergence allows us to understand many apparently dissimilar experiences about economic growth. This idea helps us to understand growth rates of real GDP per person in rich countries after World War II, as well as in East Asian and sub-Saharan African countries from 1960 to 2000. More generally, the idea of conditional convergence helps to explain the range of growth rates experienced by a broad group of countries since 1960.

## Long-Run Economic Growth

Thus far, the Solow model does not explain how capital and real GDP per worker, $k$ and $y$, grow in the long run. In the model, these variables are fixed in the long run at their steady-state values, $k^*$ and $y^*$. Thus, the model does not explain how real GDP per person grew at around 2% per year for well over a century in the United States and other currently rich countries.

We will now consider extensions of the Solow model that explain long-run growth of capital and real GDP per worker, $k$ and $y$. We begin with a model in which the average product of capital, $y/k$, does not diminish as $k$ rises. Then we allow for technological progress in the sense of continuing growth of the technology level, $A$. We will consider first a model in which this technological progress is just assumed—that is, $A$ grows in an exogenous manner. Then we will consider theories in which technological progress is explained within the model—that is, endogenous growth models. We will also consider models of technological diffusion, in which a country's technology level, $A$, rises through imitation of advanced technologies from other countries.

## Models with Constant Average Product of Capital

The diminishing average product of capital, $y/k$, plays a major role in the Solow model's transition to the steady state. As capital per worker, $k$, increases, the decline in $y/k$ reduces the growth rate of capital per worker, $\Delta k/k$. Eventually, the economy approaches a steady state, in which $k$ reaches a fixed value, $k^*$, and $\Delta k/k$ is zero. This sketch of the transition suggests that the conclusions would differ if $y/k$ did not decline as $k$ rose. Thus, we now consider a modified model in which $y/k$ does not change as $k$ rises. We are particularly interested in whether this modification can explain long-run growth of capital and real GDP per worker.

Recall that, in the Solow model, the growth rate of capital per worker, $k$, is given by

(4.1) $$\Delta k/k = s \cdot (y/k) - s\delta - n$$

Now we want to reconsider our assumption that the average product of capital, $y/k$, falls as $k$ rises. This diminishing average product makes sense if we interpret capital narrowly—for example, as machines and buildings. If a business keeps expanding its machines and buildings, without adding any workers, we would expect the marginal and average products of capital to fall. In fact, if labor input does not increase, we would expect the marginal product of capital eventually to get close to zero. If no one is available to operate an extra machine, the marginal product of that machine would be nil.

Another view is that we should interpret capital more broadly to include human capital in the forms of formal education, on-the-job training, and health. Human capital is productive, and the quantity of this capital can be increased by investment. Hence, human capital is analogous to machines and buildings. We might go further to include **infrastructure capital**, which is the capital often owned by government to provide services such as transportation, electric power, and water.

The tendency for capital's marginal and average products to fall as capital per worker, $k$, rises is less pronounced and may be absent if we view capital in this broad sense. That is, if we double not only machines and buildings but also human and infrastructure capital, real GDP may roughly double. All we are holding constant here, aside from the technology level, $A$, is the quantity of raw labor, $L$. If raw labor is not a critical input to production, capital's marginal and average products may not decline as capital accumulates.

To see the consequences of this modification, consider a case in which capital—broadly defined to include human and infrastructure capital—is the only factor input to production. Then, instead of the usual production function,

(4.2) $$y = A \cdot f(k)$$

we might have

(5.2)
$$y = Ak$$

Equation (5.2) is the special case of equation (4.2) in which $f(k) = k$. For obvious reasons, the new model is called the **Ak model**.

In the $Ak$ model, the average product of capital is constant. If we divide both sides of equation (5.2) by capital per worker, $k$, we get

(5.3)
$$y/k = A$$

Hence, the average product of capital equals the technology level, $A$. (The marginal product of capital also equals $A$.) If we substitute $y/k = A$ into equation (4.1), we get that the growth rate of $k$ is

(5.4)
$$\Delta k/k = sA - s\delta - n$$

We can use a graph analogous to Figure 3.9 to study the determination of the growth rate of capital per worker, $\Delta k/ks$, in the $Ak$ model. The new feature in Figure 5.2 is that the term $s \cdot (y/k) = sA$ is not downward sloping versus $k$—instead, it is a horizontal line at $sA$. The other horizontal line, at $s\delta + n$, is the same as before. Also as before, $\Delta k/k$

---

**Figure 5.2** | Economic Growth with Constant Average Product of Capital

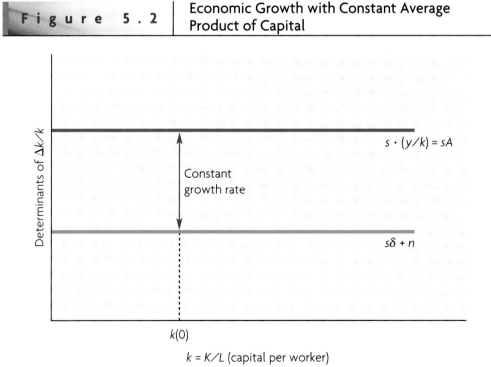

This graph modifies Figure 3.9 to allow for an unchanging average product of capital, $y/k$. In this $Ak$ model, $y/k$ equals the technology level, $A$. Therefore, the $s \cdot (y/k)$ curve becomes the horizontal line $sA$. If $sA$ is greater than $s\delta + n$, as shown, the growth rate of capital per worker, $\Delta k/k$, is a positive constant equal to the vertical distance between the two horizontal lines. This distance is shown by the red arrows.

equals the vertical distance between the two lines. However, now this distance is constant, rather than diminishing as $k$ rises.

Two important conclusions follow from Figure 5.2. First, instead of being zero, the long-run growth rate of capital per worker, $\Delta k/k$, is greater than zero and equal to $sA - s\delta - n$, as shown in the graph and in equation (5.4). This growth rate is greater than zero because we assumed that $sA$ was greater than $s\delta + n$. This condition is more likely to hold the higher the saving rate, $s$,[3] and the technology level, $A$, and the lower the population growth rate, $n$, and the depreciation rate, $\delta$.

If $sA$ is greater than $s\delta + n$, as assumed in Figure 5.2, growth of capital per worker, $k$, continues forever at the rate $sA - s\delta - n$. Moreover, since $y = Ak$, real GDP per worker, $y$, grows forever at the same rate. In this case, a higher saving rate, $s$, or a higher technology level, $A$, raises the long-run growth rates of capital and real GDP per worker, $\Delta k/k$ and $\Delta y/y$. Conversely, a higher population growth rate, $n$, or a higher depreciation rate, $\delta$, lowers the long-run values of $\Delta k/k$ and $\Delta y/y$. In contrast, in the standard Solow model, $\Delta k/k$ and $\Delta y/y$ were zero in the steady state and, therefore, did not depend on $s$, $A$, $\delta$, and $n$. The reason for the different result is that the standard model assumed diminishing average product of capital, $y/k$.

The second important result from Figure 5.2 and equation (5.4) is the absence of convergence. The growth rates of capital and real GDP per worker, $\Delta k/k$ and $\Delta y/y$, do not change as capital and real GDP per worker, $k$ and $y$, rise. Consequently, poor economies—with low $k$ and $y$—do not tend to grow faster than rich economies.

Economists have developed more sophisticated models in which the average product of capital does not change as capital accumulates. Some models distinguish human from nonhuman capital and allow for an education sector that produces human capital. However, two basic shortcomings apply to most of these models. First, the loss of the convergence prediction is a problem, because we do observe conditional convergence in cross-country data. Therefore, we cannot be satisfied with a growth model that fails to predict conditional convergence. Second, a common view among economists is that diminishing marginal and average products of capital apply eventually to the accumulation of capital even when interpreted in a broad sense to include human and infrastructure capital. If we reintroduced diminishing average product of capital, growth of capital and real GDP per worker could not continue in the long run just by accumulating capital. Therefore, we now turn to another explanation for long-run economic growth: technological progress.

## Exogenous Technological Progress

In Chapter 4, we studied the effects of a one-time increase in the technology level, $A$. This change raised the growth rates of capital and real GDP per worker, $\Delta k/k$ and $\Delta y/y$, during the transition to the steady state. However, the economy still approached a steady state in which $\Delta k/k$ and $\Delta y/y$ were zero. Thus, we cannot explain long-run growth in $k$ and $y$ from a single increase in $A$. Rather, we have to allow for continuing increases in $A$. This regular process of improvement in technology is called **technological progress**.

Solow did extend his growth model to allow for technological progress, but he did not try to explain the sources of this progress. He just assumed that technological progress occurred and then examined the consequences for economic growth. In other words, he assumed **exogenous technological progress**—the improvements in technology were not explained within the model. This approach would be reasonable if most improvements in

---

[3] We are assuming $A > \delta$; otherwise, real net domestic product is less than zero.

technology came by luck—in particular, if they did not depend much on purposeful effort by businesses (including nonprofit enterprises, such as universities), workers, and the government. In this section, we follow Solow's practice by assuming that the technology level, $A$, grows exogenously at a constant rate $g$:

$$\Delta A / A = g$$

In a later section, we discuss **endogenous growth theory**, which tries to explain the rate of technological progress within the model.

**The steady-state growth rate**   The growth-accounting equation worked out in Chapter 3 is again

(3.3)   $$\Delta Y / Y = \Delta A / A + \alpha \cdot (\Delta K / K) + (1 - \alpha) \cdot (\Delta L / L)$$

where $Y$ is real GDP, $K$ is the capital stock, and $L$ is labor input. If we substitute $\Delta A / A = g$ and $\Delta L / L = n$, the population growth rate, we get

(5.5)   $$\Delta Y / Y = g + \alpha \cdot (\Delta K / K) + (1 - \alpha) \cdot n$$

Recall that the growth rate of real GDP per worker, $\Delta y / y$, is given by

(3.6)   $$\Delta y / y = \Delta Y / Y - \Delta L / L$$

so that, with $\Delta L / L = n$,

(5.6)   $$\Delta y / y = \Delta Y / Y - n$$

If we substitute for $\Delta Y / Y$ from equation (5.5), we get

$$\Delta y / y = g + \alpha \cdot (\Delta K / K) + (1 - \alpha) \cdot n - n$$
$$= g + \alpha \cdot (\Delta K / K) + n - \alpha n - n$$
$$= g + \alpha \cdot (\Delta K / K - n)$$

The growth rate of capital per worker, $\Delta k / k$, is given by

(3.7)   $$\Delta k / k = \Delta K / K - \Delta L / L$$

so that, with $\Delta L / L = n$,

(5.7)   $$\Delta k / k = \Delta K / K - n$$

If we substitute $\Delta k / k$ for $\Delta K / K - n$ in the formula for $\Delta y / y$, we get

(5.8)   $$\Delta y / y = g + \alpha \cdot (\Delta k / k)$$

Therefore, real GDP per worker grows because of technological progress, $g$, and growth of capital per worker, $\Delta k / k$.

The growth rate of capital per worker, $\Delta k/k$, is still determined in the Solow model by

(4.3) $$\Delta k/k = sA \cdot f(k)/k - s\delta - n$$

If we substitute this expression for $\Delta k/k$ into equation (5.8), we get

---

Key equation (growth rate of real GDP per worker with technical progress):

(5.9) $$\Delta y/y = g + \alpha \cdot [sA \cdot f(k)/k - s\delta - n]$$

---

In our previous analysis, where $A$ was fixed, increases in $k$ led to reductions in the average product of capital, $y/k = A \cdot f(k)/k$. Consequently, in the long run, the economy approached a steady state in which the average product of capital was low enough so that $\Delta k/k$ equaled zero in equation (4.3). Then, with $g = 0$, $\Delta y/y$ also equals zero in equations (5.8) and (5.9).

The difference now is that each increase in $A$ raises the average product of capital, $y/k = A \cdot f(k)/k$, for given $k$. Hence, the negative effect of rising $k$ on $y/k$ is offset by a positive effect from rising $A$. The economy will tend toward a situation in which these two forces balance. That is, $k$ will increase in the long run at a constant rate, and $y/k$ will be unchanging. We call this situation **steady-state growth**.

Since the average product of capital, $y/k$, does not change during steady-state growth, the numerator of the ratio, $y$, must grow at the same rate as the denominator, $k$. Therefore, we have

(5.10) $$(\Delta y/y)^* = (\Delta k/k)^*$$

where the asterisks designate values in steady-state growth.

We know from equation (5.10) that capital and real GDP per worker, $k$ and $y$, grow at the same rate in steady-state growth. Now we want to determine the steady-state growth rate. Equation (5.8) implies that, in steady-state growth:

(5.11) $$(\Delta y/y)^* = g + \alpha \cdot (\Delta k/k)^*$$

Using equation (5.10), we can replace $(\Delta k/k)^*$ on the right-hand side by $(\Delta y/y)^*$ to get

$$(\Delta y/y)^* = g + \alpha \cdot (\Delta y/y)^*$$

If we move the term $\alpha \cdot (\Delta y/y)^*$ from the right side to the left side, we get

$$(\Delta y/y)^* - \alpha \cdot (\Delta y/y)^* = g$$

which implies, after we combine the terms on the left,

$$(1 - \alpha) \cdot (\Delta y/y)^* = g$$

If we divide both sides by $1 - \alpha$, we get the steady-state growth rate of real GDP per worker:

---

Key equation (steady-state growth rate with technological progress):

(5.12) $$(\Delta y/y)^* = g/(1 - \alpha)$$

---

Since $0 < \alpha < 1$, equation (5.12) tells us that *the steady-state growth rate of real GDP per worker, $(\Delta y/y)^*$, is greater than the rate of technological progress, g.* As an example, if $\alpha = 1/2$, we have

$$(\Delta y/y)^* = 2g$$

Thus, when $\alpha = 1/2$, $(\Delta y/y)^*$ is twice the rate of technological progress, $g$.

The reason that the growth rate of real GDP per worker, $(\Delta y/y)^*$, is greater than $g$ is that the steady-state growth rate of capital per worker, $(\Delta k/k)^*$, is greater than zero, and this growth rate adds to $g$ to determine $(\Delta y/y)^*$—see equation (5.11). In fact, we know from equation (5.10) that the growth rates of $k$ and $y$ are the same in steady-state growth:

$$(\Delta k/k)^* = (\Delta y/y)^*$$

Therefore, equation (5.12) implies

**(5.13)**
$$(\Delta k/k)^* = g/(1-\alpha)$$

The important finding from equations (5.12) and (5.13) is that exogenous technological progress at the rate $\Delta A/A = g$ leads to long-term growth in real GDP and capital per worker, $k$ and $y$, at the rate $g/(1-\alpha)$. The technological progress offsets the tendency for the average product of capital, $y/k$, to fall when $k$ rises and, thereby, allows for long-term growth of $k$ and $y$.

Recall from our discussion in Chapter 3 that the growth rate of real GDP per person in the United States averaged 2% per year from 1869 to 2005. Similar long-term growth rates of real GDP per person applied to other advanced economies. To explain this long-term growth within the Solow model, we have to look at the model's predictions for steady-state growth.

Since the labor-force participation rate is constant in the model, the growth rate of real GDP per person equals the growth rate of real GDP per worker. Therefore, to get long-term growth of real GDP per person at around 2% per year, we need the steady-state growth rate of real GDP per worker, which equals $g/(1-\alpha)$ from equation (5.12), to be around 2% per year. If we think of $\alpha$ as the share of capital income and use values for $\alpha$ between 1/3 and 1/2, the required value for $g$ is a little over 1% per year. In other words, if the technology improves exogenously at a rate around 1% per year, the Solow model's prediction for the long-term growth rate of real GDP per person matches the long-term growth rates observed in the United States and other advanced countries.

**Steady-state saving**    Now we consider how technological progress affects steady-state saving. The growth rate of capital per worker, $\Delta k/k$, is again

**(4.1)**
$$\Delta k/k = s \cdot (y/k) - s\delta - n$$

In steady-state growth, we can replace $\Delta k/k$ from equation (5.13) with $g/(1-\alpha)$ to get

$$g/(1-\alpha) = s \cdot (y/k) - s\delta - n$$

We can then rearrange the terms to get

$$s \cdot [(y/k) - \delta] = n + g/(1-\alpha)$$

If we multiply through by $k$, we determine saving per worker, $s \cdot (y - \delta k)$, in steady-state growth:

*In steady-state growth*:

(5.14)
$$s \cdot (y - \delta k) = nk + [g/(1 - \alpha)] \cdot k$$

When $g = 0$, steady-state saving per worker equals $nk$, the amount required to provide the growing labor force with capital to work with. When $g$ is greater than zero, steady-state saving also includes the term $[g/(1 - \alpha)] \cdot k$. Since $g/(1 - \alpha)$ equals the steady-state growth rate of capital per worker, $\Delta k/k$ (equation [5.13]), this term is

$$[g/(1 - \alpha)] \cdot k = (\Delta k / k) \cdot k$$
$$= \Delta k$$

Therefore, this term is the saving per worker needed in the steady state to provide for increasing capital per worker.

**The transition path and convergence**   In Figure 3.11, we analyzed the transition path for capital per worker, $k$, in the Solow model without technological progress. We found that $k$ gradually approached its steady-state value, $k^*$. Thus, $k^*$ was the target that $k$ was approaching. The model with exogenous technological progress still has a transition path for $k$. However, we have to think of $k^*$ as a moving target, rather than a fixed point. That is, $k^*$ moves over time along a steady-state path.

In steady-state growth, equation (5.13) says that capital per worker rises at the rate $(\Delta k/k)^* = g/(1 - \alpha)$. Hence, capital per worker, $k$, varies over time in the steady state—it grows at the rate $g/(1 - \alpha)$. We now define $k^*$ to be the value that $k$ takes at each point in time along the steady-state path. We just have to remember that $k^*$ rises over time when $g$ is greater than zero.

Capital per worker, $k$, again starts at some initial value, $k(0)$. The model still has a transition in which $k$ moves from $k(0)$ to its steady-state path. However, we have to represent the steady-state path not by a fixed point, but rather by the blue line labeled $k^*$ in Figure 5.3. This line has a positive slope because capital per worker grows in the steady state. The graph shows that $k$ begins at $k(0)$, rises over time along the red curve, and gradually approaches its moving target, $k^*$.

Along the steady-state path, $k = k^*$ grows at the rate $g/(1 - \alpha)$ (equation [5.13]). Therefore, in order for $k$ to approach $k^*$, as shown in Figure 5.3 on the next page, the growth rate of $k$, $\Delta k/k$, must be greater than $g/(1 - \alpha)$, the growth rate of $k^*$. Otherwise, $k$ could not catch up during the transition to its moving target, $k^*$.

The results for the transitional behavior of $k$ again tell us about convergence across economies. As before, convergence depends on whether different economies have the same or different steady states. Figure 5.4 on page 109 shows a case in which two economies have the same steady-state paths, $k^*$. Economy 1 begins at the capital per worker $k(0)_1$, and economy 2 at the higher capital per worker $k(0)_2$. The graph shows that $k_1$ and $k_2$ converge toward the steady-state path, $k^*$, and that $k_1$ also converges toward $k_2$. Therefore, economy 1 has a higher growth rate of capital per worker, $\Delta k/k$, than economy 2 during the transition to the steady-state path. In other words, if the two economies have the same steady-state paths, absolute convergence holds, and the poorer economy (with lower $k[0]$) has a higher $\Delta k/k$. These results are similar to those found in Figure 4.8 for the model without technological progress, where $g = 0$.

Figure 5.5 on page 110 considers a case in which the two economies have different steady-state paths, $k^*$. We assume that economy 1—with lower $k(0)$—also has a lower $k^*$.

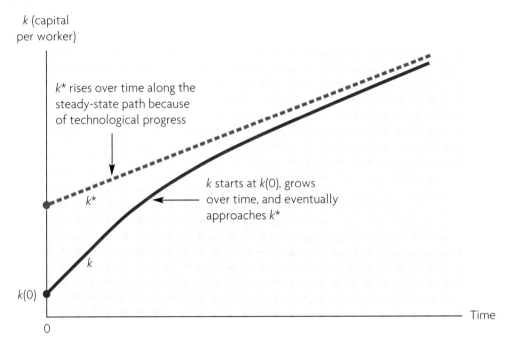

| Figure 5.3 | The Transition Path for Capital per Worker in the Solow Model with Technological Progress |

*k* (capital per worker)

*k\** rises over time along the steady-state path because of technological progress

*k\**

*k* starts at *k*(0), grows over time, and eventually approaches *k\**

*k*

*k*(0)

0 — Time

In the Solow model with technological progress at the rate $g$, the steady-state level of capital per worker, *k\**, is not fixed; *k\** rises over time along the steady-state path shown by the blue line. (Since we use a proportionate scale on the vertical axis, the straight line means that *k\** grows along the steady-state path at a constant rate, given by $g/[1-\alpha]$.) In the transition, capital per worker, *k*, starts at *k*(0), rises over time along the red curve, and gradually approaches the *k\** line. (We assume that *k*(0) lies below the *k\** line.)

We discussed in Chapter 4 why an economy with low $k^*$ tends also to have low $k$ when observed at an arbitrary time, such as date 0. The graph shows that each economy converges over time toward its own steady-state path—$k_1$ toward $k_1^*$, and $k_2$ toward $k_2^*$. Since $k_1(0)$ is less than $k_2(0)$, and $k_2^*$ is less than $k_2^*$, we cannot be sure which economy has the higher growth rate of capital per worker, $\Delta k/k$, during the transition. The lower $k(0)$ tends to make $\Delta k/k$ higher in economy 1, but the lower $k^*$ tends to make $\Delta k/k$ lower in economy 1. Thus, convergence need not hold in an absolute sense. However, conditional convergence still applies—if we hold fixed the steady-state path, $k^*$, a lower $k(0)$ leads to higher growth rates of capital per worker, $\Delta k/k$, during the transition.

We expressed all the results about convergence in terms of capital per worker, $k$. However, the results also hold for real GDP per worker, $y$, once we make use of the production function, $y = A \cdot f(k)$. Therefore, we can also use Figures 5.4 and 5.5 to assess convergence of real GDP per worker across economies.

## Endogenous Growth Theory

The inclusion of exogenous technological progress allows the Solow model to match the long-term growth rates of real GDP per person observed in the United States and other advanced countries. However, many economists have criticized this fix of the model because the technological progress comes from nowhere—it is not explained by the model. For that reason, economists led by Paul Romer in the late 1980s and early 1990s tried to

| | Convergence and Transition Paths for |
|---|---|
| **F i g u r e   5 . 4** | Two Economies in the Solow Model with Technological Progress |

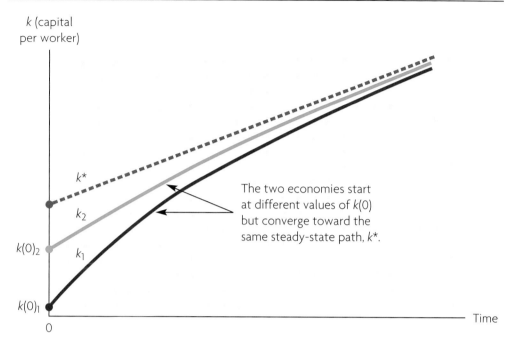

As in Figure 5.3, the steady-state capital per worker, $k^*$, rises over time along the steady-state path shown by the dashed blue line. The first economy starts at $k(0)_1$, and the second economy starts at the higher value $k(0)_2$. During the transitions, capital per worker in each economy, $k_1$ or $k_2$, gradually approaches the common steady-state path, $k^*$. The first economy (the red curve) has a higher growth rate of capital per worker, $\Delta k/k$, than the second economy (the green curve), so that $k_1$ converges toward $k_2$. Therefore, absolute convergence applies.

extend the model to explain why technological progress occurs. The models that Romer and others developed are called endogenous growth theory because, first, the models explain the rate of technological progress, and, second, as in the Solow model, the technological progress leads to long-run growth of real GDP and capital per worker.

Most endogenous growth models focus on investments in **research and development**, or **R&D**. Successful R&D projects lead to the discovery of new products, better products, or superior methods of production. In the Solow growth model, we can think of these research successes as increases in the technology level, $A$. However, in contrast to the Solow model with exogenous technological progress, the growth rate of $A$ is explained within the model. Therefore, we can use endogenous growth models to understand how government policies and other variables influence R&D investment and, thereby, the rate of technological progress and the long-run growth rate of real GDP per person.

Theories of technological progress specify a connection between R&D investment and the amount of technological advance, represented by increases in $A$. Because research entails discovery, the outcomes are uncertain. For example, when working on new medicines, computer designs, or other original products or processes, a researcher does not know the degree of success in advance. This uncertainty is greater for basic research than for refinements of existing products or methods of production. However, we can say generally that a greater amount of R&D investment leads to a larger expected increase in

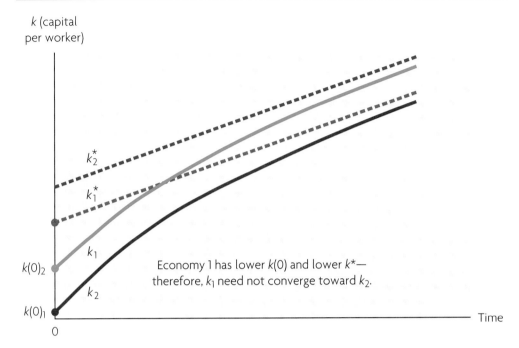

Figure 5.5 Failure of Convergence and Transition Paths for Two Economies in the Solow Model with Technological Progress

As in Figure 5.4, the first economy starts at $k(0)_1$, and the second economy starts at the higher value $k(0)_2$. However, economy 1 now has a lower steady-state path of capital per worker; that is, the dashed brown line for $k_1^*$ lies below the dashed blue line for $k_2^*$. During the transitions, $k_1$ and $k_2$ gradually approach their respective steady-state paths, $k_1^*$ and $k_2^*$. However, the growth rate of capital per worker, $\Delta k/k$, need not be higher in economy 1 than economy 2. Therefore, $k_1$ (the red curve) does not necessarily converge toward $k_2$ (the green curve). Hence, absolute convergence need not hold.

the technology level, $A$. Therefore, to have more technological progress on average, innovators must be motivated to raise R&D outlays. For private businesses, the motivation comes from greater prospective profit. The government may affect the profit motive by subsidizing research, some of which is carried out by nonprofit organizations, such as universities. The government may also contract directly for research projects, such as in defense industries and the space program.

In many respects, R&D investment resembles the familiar investment in physical capital. The R&D outlays correspond to investment expenditure, and the technology level, $A$, corresponds to the stock of capital, $K$. However, there are two important differences between technological progress and increases in the stock of capital. One has to do with diminishing returns and the other with ownership rights.

A key question is whether diminishing returns apply to R&D investment. Specifically, as the technology level, $A$, grows, does it become increasingly expensive in terms of R&D outlays to generate expected further increases in $A$? If so, the R&D process exhibits diminishing returns, and it may be impossible for R&D investments to sustain technological progress and long-run growth of real GDP per worker. If not, it may be possible for R&D investments to maintain technological progress and long-run growth of real GDP per worker.

To understand how ownership rights differ between technology and the stock of capital, think of the technology level, $A$, as representing an idea about how to use factor inputs, $K$ and $L$, to produce output, $Y$. In contrast, think of the stock of capital, $K$, as a machine or a building. If $A$ represents an idea, all producers can use the idea simultaneously. If producer 1 uses the idea to create goods and services, producer 2 can use the same idea at the same time to create other goods and services. In a physical sense, an idea is a **non-rival good**—any number of producers can use the idea simultaneously without reducing the amount of the idea available to others. Examples of non-rival ideas are mathematical formulas in calculus, chemical formulas for drugs, codes for computer software, and the notes in a song. An important point about a non-rival idea is that, once discovered, efficiency dictates sharing with all potential users.

The stock of capital differs from the stock of ideas. If one business uses a machine to produce goods, it is physically impossible for other businesses to use the same machine at the same time. This property holds also for labor input and most other goods and services. Economists say that each of these is a **rival good**.

Suppose, however, that all ideas were freely available once discovered. In this case, profit-seeking businesses would devote few resources to making inventions. The learning of an idea typically requires R&D investment, but there is no individual payoff—no profit motive—for making the discovery. As an example, the invention of a chemical formula for a new drug typically entails substantial R&D outlays. If the formulas for successful drugs were distributed widely and all firms were allowed to use these formulas without charge, there would be no way for the innovating company to recoup its research expenses. Then—if we are relying on profit-seeking private enterprises, rather than governments— little R&D would take place, and little technological progress would occur.

Profit-seeking companies invest in R&D only if they can maintain some rights in the (good) ideas that they discover. These rights are called **intellectual property rights**. In some areas, the enforcement of intellectual property rights involves a **patent** (typically for 17 or 20 years) or a **copyright** (usually for the lifetime of the author plus 50 years). These legal protections are especially important for pharmaceuticals, software, books, music, and movies.

Many basic discoveries have no patent protection, partly because of legal limitations and partly because of practical considerations in defining the scope of an idea. For example, Isaac Newton did not have patent protection for his mathematical innovations in calculus, Solow did not have property rights in his growth model, and Henry Ford did not have exclusive use over the assembly line. For a more recent example, Toyota Motors did not have property rights over the idea of just-in-time inventory management, the practice of having suppliers deliver product components just before they're needed in a production process instead of storing raw materials in physical inventory. Other automobile manufacturers, Dell Computer, and many other companies copied this idea to reduce their inventory costs.

In many cases, businesses that make patentable inventions do not seek patents, sometimes because the approval process is costly and, more often, because businesses do not want to reveal the information needed to gain approval. Such information tends to aid competitors even when patents are granted. In the absence of formal patent protection, the main methods of maintaining intellectual property rights are secrecy and the advantages gained from moving first into a new area.

Paul Romer (1990) constructed the first model that linked R&D investment and intellectual property rights to a theory of technological progress and economic growth. In his model, an inventor retained perpetual monopoly rights over his or her invention. However, this extreme form of intellectual property rights is not necessary for Romer's main results. The basic idea is that some form of intellectual property rights ensured that successful innovators were rewarded for their discoveries.

# Back To Reality

The story of Napster and Viagra

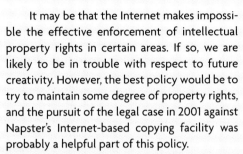

What do Napster (the once popular Internet site for copying music) and proposals to limit prescription drug prices have in common? Both seek to reduce prices of goods that cost little to produce now but were expensive to create initially. Cutting prices today looks great for users and, arguably, for society as a whole. If it costs virtually nothing to copy a CD over the Internet, why should people not be able to copy and listen to the music, rather than having to pay $10 at the local store? If it costs only a few dollars to produce and distribute a standard quantity of Viagra, why should people not be able to use the drug if they are willing to pay $10, rather than $100?

The problem is that the "high" prices are the rewards for the costly efforts that came before. Music companies and artists expend time and money to create hits, and the bulk of the expenses are for failed projects. To compensate for these efforts and to provide incentives for future hits, the industry has to reap large profits on its few successes.

Piracy is a problem for producers of music and similar products, such as books, movies, and computer software. The incentive to abridge intellectual property rights reflects the big gap between the prices charged by the copyright owners and the actual costs of copying and distribution. Innovations in the Internet and computer technology have dramatically lowered these costs. On the one hand, these advances are desirable, because they allow products to reach a vastly expanded audience. On the other hand, the down side is the threat to intellectual property rights. These rights are partly a matter of fairness, in the philosophical sense that inventors ought to be able to control the use of their discoveries. But, more concretely, if intellectual property rights disappear and no other effective means of compensating creativity is implemented, society will see much less future greatness in music, books, movies, and software.

It may be that the Internet makes impossible the effective enforcement of intellectual property rights in certain areas. If so, we are likely to be in trouble with respect to future creativity. However, the best policy would be to try to maintain some degree of property rights, and the pursuit of the legal case in 2001 against Napster's Internet-based copying facility was probably a helpful part of this policy.

Prescription drugs are similar in many respects. One way to see that retail prices of patented drugs exceed current costs of production is to compare U.S. prices with the lower ones prevailing in some other countries. For example, many drugs sell in Canada at about one-half the U.S. price. Some people conclude that the United States ought to adopt Canada's policies for pricing of prescription drugs or, alternatively, allow reimportation of the cheaper drugs into the United States. A more reasonable view is that the incentives for drug research and innovation created by high U.S. prices give Canada, Mexico, and other small markets what economists call a *free ride*. The idea of a free ride is that it allows some people—in this case, Canadians and Mexicans—to enjoy the fruits of someone else's labor without having to share fully in the costs. Specifically, these small countries can benefit from low prices of prescription drugs without having to worry about the effects on the overall market and, hence, on the incentives for companies to develop new drugs.

The United States does not have the option to free ride because it is such a large part of the market for prescription drugs. If the United States were to follow Canada's lead, fewer new drugs would be available for the whole world. Thus, for the United States, the choice is whether to have many effective new drugs at high prices or to have few new drugs at low prices. This choice is the relevant one for society as a whole, but many people fantasize that they can have low prices *and* many new drugs. Unfortunately, it just ain't so.

The Romer model distinguishes the return to society from an invention from the private return, which is the reward to the inventor. The private return is greater than zero because of the intellectual property rights, but the social return tends to exceed the private one. For example, the social benefits from the invention of the transistor or the microchip were much greater than the payoffs to the individuals and businesses that made the discoveries.[4] For this reason, the resources devoted to R&D and the resulting rate of technological progress tend to be too low from a social perspective. This reasoning is often used to justify government subsidy of innovative activity, especially basic research. However, government subsidies also create problems, including the politics of choosing what to subsidize and the necessity to raise revenues to pay for the subsidies.

Romer equated technology with ideas, and he assumed that the returns from generating new ideas did not diminish as the technology level advanced. His reasoning was that the number of potentially good ideas was unlimited, so the stock of remaining ideas would not be depleted as more things were discovered. Thus, at least as a working hypothesis, we might assume that the returns to the creation of ideas are constant. This assumption turns out to be consistent with a constant, steady-state growth rate of real GDP per worker, driven by technological progress at a constant rate. That is, the results look like those in the Solow model when the technology level, $A$, grows exogenously at the constant rate $g$.

In the Romer model, where R&D investment is carried out by profit-seeking businesses, the rate of technological progress depends on the private rewards from making discoveries. These rewards depend on a number of factors:

- The private return to R&D investment is higher if the costs of R&D are lower. Some of these costs depend on government policies. Costs are lower if the government subsidizes R&D. Costs are higher if there are large expenses for gaining government approval (of new drugs, for example) or satisfying government regulations.
- The reward from successful innovations depends on how much they raise sales revenue or reduce production costs. One consideration is the size of the market over which the benefits from a discovery can be spread. A bigger market, which includes domestic and foreign sales, encourages more R&D.
- The private return is higher if intellectual property rights over the use of an invention are more secure and long lasting. In many cases, these rights will be better protected domestically than internationally. Another consideration is the ease with which competitors, domestic or foreign, can imitate successful innovations. The easier the imitation, the lower the intellectual property rights over an innovation and, hence, the smaller the incentive for R&D investment.

Changes in any of these factors influence the rate of technological progress and, therefore, the economy's steady-state growth rate of real GDP per worker. These effects are analogous to those from changes in the rate of exogenous technological progress, $g$, in the Solow model.

Advanced countries spend the most on R&D. They have the most scientists and engineers, and are granted most of the patents. (India is an exception to the usual pattern, as a poor country with many innovations in computer software.) One reason for the concentration of R&D in rich countries is the complementary resources that support research, including a large supply of skilled workers and strong educational institutions. The large domestic market available to wealthy countries is also significant. However, a small country can successfully innovate if it is well connected to other markets through international trade, and if intellectual property rights are respected in foreign countries. As examples, Sweden and Finland have been leaders in pharmaceuticals and telecommunications.

---

[4] Theoretically, the private returns could exceed the social ones. This situation can apply if resources are wasted when competing researchers strive to be the first to make a discovery, or if the main consequence from an improved product is the transfer of monopoly profits from the old industry leader to the new one. However, it is hard to present convincing empirical examples of this theoretical possibility.

At the start of this chapter, we discussed cross-country empirical research on convergence and other aspects of economic growth. These empirical findings match up well with the version of the Solow growth model that includes exogenous technological progress. Thus far, less cross-country empirical work has been done on the endogenous growth models. One finding, however, is that countries that spend more on R&D investment tend to have higher growth rates of real GDP per person.[5]

## The Diffusion of Technology

For the world as a whole, the only way to raise the technology level, $A$, is for someone to discover something new. However, for an individual country or producer, it is possible to raise $A$—the technology level available to that country or producer—by imitating or adapting someone else's innovation. For example, color television sets were invented in the United States by RCA (Radio Corporation of America), but the technology for producing televisions was copied and improved in Japan. Similarly, the technology for operating steel mini-mills in the United States was based on innovations in Germany and elsewhere.

The term **diffusion of technology** describes the imitation and adaptation of one country's technology by another country. For low-income countries, imitation and adaptation tend to be less expensive than invention as ways to improve methods of production and introduce new and better products. Therefore, low-income countries tend to focus on diffusion of technology as the way to raise technology levels.

Businesses have used many methods to imitate leading technologies. A multinational firm from an advanced country can use an advanced technology in a foreign subsidiary. Domestic entrepreneurs then learn from the foreign-owned operations about products and production processes. These channels of technological diffusion were important in the textile industries in Hong Kong and Mauritius (an economically successful island off the east coast of Africa).

Sometimes the transfer of technology occurs through observation and analysis of products exchanged in international trade. For example, an importer of a good may be able to deduce how the good was produced by taking it apart (through a process of "reverse engineering"). In other cases, a foreign company licenses or sells its processes to domestically owned businesses. For example, Nucor—the first steel mini-mill producer in the United States—purchased technological designs from a German company. In still other cases, domestic residents work or study at a business or university in an advanced country and bring back the technology to their home countries.

The diffusion of technology is another mechanism for poor countries to converge toward rich ones. Low-income countries are poor partly because they lack access to leading technologies. Therefore, these countries can grow rapidly by imitating better technologies from advanced countries. However, as imitation proceeds, the supply of useful uncopied technologies decreases, and the cost of further imitation tends to rise. This rising cost of imitation is similar to the decreasing average product of capital, $y/k$, in the Solow model. Therefore, growth rates of follower countries tend to decline, and their levels of real GDP per worker tend to converge toward those in the advanced countries.

Studies show that the rate of technological diffusion to a developing country is high when the country trades a lot with rich countries, has high education levels, and has well-functioning legal and political systems, as in some East Asian countries.[6] Therefore, these characteristics help to explain the high rates of economic growth in East Asia since the 1960s.

---

[5] See David Coe and Elhanan Helpman (1995). For evidence on the relation between R&D and productivity at the level of industries and firms, see Zvi Griliches (1998).

[6] See, for example, Florence Jaumotte (2000) and Francesco Caselli and Wilbur Coleman (2001).

# Back To Reality

## Hybrid corn: A case of technological diffusion

In 1957, Zvi Griliches published one of the first studies of the diffusion of technology. He investigated the spread of hybrid corn. The basic idea—crossing specially selected strains of corn to develop types suitable to local conditions—was familiar to agricultural scientists since the early 20th century. However, the first successful commercial application did not occur until the 1930s in Iowa. Researchers then needed time to develop hybrids that grew well in other states. The delay in application to a new state depended on the costs of the necessary refinements and on the potential gains in crop yields and market sizes. The speed of acceptance within a state also depended on the economic benefits from the hybrids. Figure 5.6 shows the time of introduction of hybrid corn in various states and the speed with which each state adopted the new strain. One reason for the delay in the southern states was that these hybrids had to be substantially modified from those used in Iowa. Applications of the Griliches model to technological diffusion in other industries include Michael Gort and Steven Klepper (1982) and Boyan Jovanovic and Saul Lach (1997).

| Figure 5.6 | Technological Diffusion for Hybrid Corn |

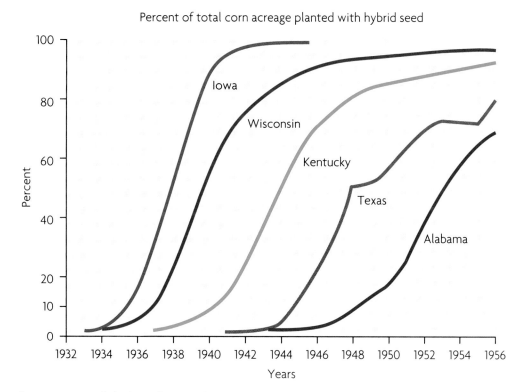

The innovations in hybrid corn began in the United States in Iowa in the early 1930s. This innovation spread later to other agricultural states, as shown in the graphs. Each curve shows the fraction of corn acreage planted in various years with hybrid seed.

# What Do We Know About Economic Growth?

We began our study of economic growth in Chapter 3 with the Solow growth model. In the first phase of this model, capital and real GDP per worker rise from their initial levels to their steady-state levels. The second phase is the steady state. In Chapters 3 and 4, capital and real GDP per worker did not grow in the steady state. However, in the present chapter, the inclusion of technological progress led to growth of capital and real GDP per worker in the steady state.

In Chapter 4, we used the Solow model to predict short- and long-run effects from changes in the saving rate, the technology level, the size of the labor force, and the population growth rate. The transition phase of the model predicted convergence—poor economies tend to grow faster than rich ones and, therefore, tend to catch up over time to rich ones. Although this prediction conflicted with observations for a broad group of countries, a modified concept—conditional convergence—fit well with the data. Conditional convergence allows for differences in steady-state positions, due to variations in saving rates, technology levels, and population growth rates. In extended models, the differences can reflect other variables, including legal and political systems, openness to international trade, and the efficiency of education and health programs.

In the present chapter, we showed that the concept of conditional convergence explains many historical patterns of economic growth. We can understand why some war-ravaged OECD countries grew rapidly after World War II. We can also explain why, from 1960 to 2000, most East Asian countries grew fast but most sub-Saharan African countries grew slowly or not at all.

The basic Solow model does not explain long-run growth of real GDP per person, a pattern that applies for well over a century to the United States and other advanced countries. The model does explain long-term per capita growth at around 2% per year if we assume exogenous technological progress at about 1% per year. Endogenous growth models rely on R&D investment as the source of improvements in technology. These models predict how intellectual property rights, research subsidies, and other variables affect the rate of technological progress and, hence, the long-run growth rate of real GDP per person.

Technological diffusion is the main method by which low-income countries raise their technology levels. This diffusion helps to explain convergence of poor countries toward rich countries but does not explain technological progress for the whole world.

Although we understand a lot about economic growth, there is much that remains unexplained. For example, economists have isolated only some of the variables that underlie differences across countries in steady-state positions. In the long-run context, we are still uncertain about the sources of technological progress. In particular, we cannot say with confidence how government policies that affect incentives for R&D investment influence long-run economic growth in a single country or in the world. Thus, although we have learned a lot, there is still much to do.

## Key Terms and Concepts

*Ak* model
copyright
diffusion of technology
endogenous growth theory
exogenous technological progress
infrastructure capital
intellectual property rights

non-rival good
patent
research and development (R&D)
rival good
steady-state growth
technological progress

## Questions and Problems

**A.** Review questions

1. Suppose that the technology level, $A$, grows exogenously at a positive rate, $g > 0$. Does the level of output, $Y$, grow in the long run? Does output per worker, $Y/L$, grow in the long run?

2. Most countries in sub-Saharan Africa grew at a low rate from 1960 to 2000, while many countries in East Asia grew at a high rate. How can the concept of conditional convergence help to explain these observations?

**B.** Problems for discussion

3. Convergence and the dispersion of income (difficult)

Consider a group of economies that satisfies absolute convergence; that is, poor economies tend to grow faster than rich ones.

a. Does this convergence property imply that a measure of the dispersion of income per person—or income inequality—across the economies will narrow over time? (This question relates to Galton's fallacy, an idea applied by Galton to the distribution of heights and other characteristics in a population. If a parent is taller than average, the child tends to be taller than average but shorter than the parent. That is, there is reversion to the mean, an effect that parallels the idea of absolute convergence. Does the presence of reversion to the mean imply that the distribution of heights across the population will narrow over time? The answer is no, but you are supposed to explain why.)

b. We found in Figure 4.11 that absolute convergence held for the U.S. states from 1880 to 2000. A measure of the dispersion of per capita income across the states declined for most of the period from 1880 to 1970 (except for the 1920s and 1930s). Dispersion did not change a great deal from 1970 to 2000. Can you relate these observations to your answer from question a.?

c. We found in Figure 4.9 that absolute convergence did not hold for a broad group of countries from 1960 to 2000. We did find in Figure 5.1 that conditional convergence held for these countries. A measure of the dispersion of per capita real GDP across these countries shows a mild, but persistent, increase from 1960 to 2000. How would you account for this pattern?

# Appendix

## The Steady-State Path in the Solow Model with Exogenous Technological Progress

We now derive the steady-state path, $k^*$, in the model with exogenous technological progress. The path is shown graphically in Figure 5.3. This appendix provides an algebraic derivation.

The growth rate of capital per worker is given by

(4.1) $$\Delta k / k = s \cdot (y/k) - s\delta - n$$

Hence, along a steady-state path, the growth rate is

(5.15) $$(\Delta k / k)^* = s \cdot (y/k)^* - s\delta - n$$

where $(y/k)^*$ is the unchanging average product of capital in a position of steady-state growth. We also know that, in a situation of steady-state growth, $k$ grows at the rate

(5.13) $$(\Delta k/k)^* = g/(1-\alpha)$$

Therefore, if we substitute $g/(1-\alpha)$ for $(\Delta k/k)^*$ on the left-hand side of equation (5.15), we get

$$g/(1-\alpha) = s \cdot (y/k)^* - s\delta - n$$

We can rearrange the terms to get

$$s \cdot (y/k)^* = s\delta + n + g/(1-\alpha)$$

Then, if we divide by $s$, we get a formula for the steady-state average product of capital:

(5.16) $$(y/k)^* = \delta + (1/s) \cdot [n + g/(1-\alpha)]$$

Note that the right-hand side of the equation is constant. Therefore, this result verifies that the average product of capital, $(y/k)^*$, does not change in steady-state growth.

Since the production function is

$$y = A \cdot f(k)$$

we can write the average product of capital, $y/k$, as

$$y/k = A \cdot f(k)/k$$

Therefore, if we define $k^*$ to be the time-varying value for $k$ during steady-state growth, the steady-state average product of capital is

(5.17) $$(y/k)^* = A \cdot f(k^*)/k^*$$

Equations (5.16) and (5.17) give us two expressions for $(y/k)^*$. Therefore, the two right-hand sides must be equal:

(5.18) $$A \cdot f(k^*)/k^* = \delta + (1/s) \cdot [n + g/(1-\alpha)]$$

The right-hand side is constant, and the technology level, $A$, on the left-hand side grows over time at the rate $g$. Therefore, if we specify the form of the production function, $f$, we can use equation (5.18) to determine the steady-state path, $k^*$.

Suppose that the production function, $f(k)$, takes the Cobb-Douglas form,

(3.24) $$y = Ak^\alpha$$

which we discussed in Appendix, Part C to Chapter 3. In this case,

$$
\begin{aligned}
A \cdot f(k)/k &= Ak^\alpha/k \\
&= Ak^\alpha k^{-1} \\
&= Ak^{\alpha-1} \\
A \cdot f(k)/k &= Ak^{-(1-\alpha)}
\end{aligned}
$$

Therefore, we can substitute $A \cdot f(k^*)^{-(1-\alpha)}$ in equation (5.18) to get

$$A \cdot (k^*)^{-(1-\alpha)} = \delta + (1/s) \cdot [n + g/(1 - \alpha)]$$

If we multiply through by $(k^*)^{1-\alpha}$ and $s$, divide through by $[s\delta + n + g/(1 - \alpha)]$, and rearrange terms, we get

(5.19)
$$(k^*)^{1-\alpha} = \frac{sA}{[s\delta + n + g/(1 - \alpha)]}$$

On the right-hand side, everything except $A$ does not vary over time. If $A$ were constant, $k^*$ would be constant, as in the Solow model without technological progress ($g = 0$). If $A$ grows at the rate $g$, equation (5.19) implies that $k^*$ grows at the rate $g/(1 - \alpha)$, consistent with the result in equation (5.13).

# Economic Fluctuations

Part

3

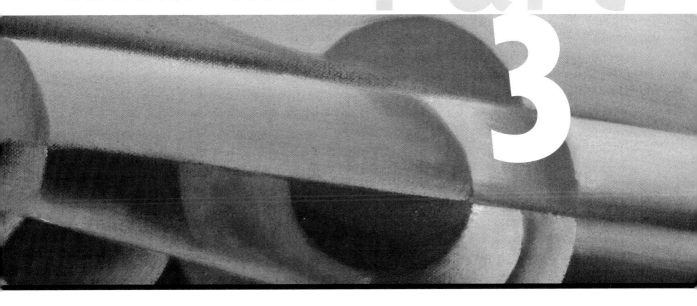

# Chapter 6
## Markets, Prices, Supply, and Demand

People care a lot about whether the economy is expanding or contracting. During a boom, when real GDP rises, consumption and investment tend to be strong, employment tends to rise, and unemployment tends to fall. Conversely, during a recession, when real GDP falls, consumption, investment, and employment tend to be weak, and unemployment tends to increase. During recessions, people find it hard to locate good jobs, and more workers lose jobs than find them. The inability to keep or find a good job causes hardship for job seekers and their families.

In this part of the book, our main goal is to understand these economic fluctuations—that is, the increases of real GDP during booms and the decreases during recessions. These fluctuations typically apply to relatively short periods, such as one or two years. In contrast, our study of economic growth in Chapters 3 through 5 focused on the long term: 5–10 years or even 20–30 years or longer.

To build a model of economic fluctuations, we start by working out the model's microeconomic foundations. These foundations describe how individual consumers and producers make choices. In the present chapter, we will focus on the markets for labor and capital services. In Chapter 7, we extend the analysis to consumption and saving.

An example of a microeconomic choice is a worker's decision about how much to work. Another example is a producer's decision about how many workers to hire. In these decisions, an individual worker or producer takes as given the prices that it faces. One of these prices is the *real wage rate*, which specifies the quantity of goods that a worker can buy with an hour of labor.

A key assumption in our model is that individual workers, consumers, and producers are too small to have a significant impact on the prices that influence their decisions. To take a concrete example—which we detail later—consider a simple analysis of the labor market. Suppose that, in choosing how much labor to supply, each worker takes as given the real wage rate. Similarly, in deciding how much labor to demand, each producer takes as given the real wage rate. Thus, the individual choices of quantities supplied and

| Figure 6.1 | An Example of Market Clearing: The Labor Market |

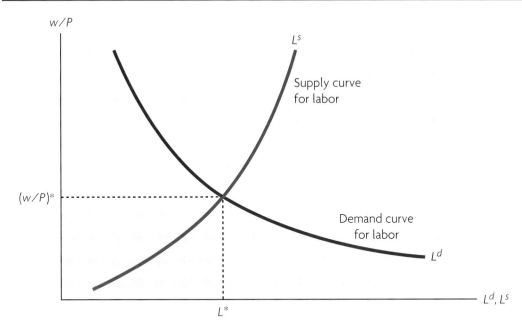

This figure gives a simple example of how a market—in this case, the labor market—clears. The labor-demand curve, $L^d$, slopes downward versus the real wage rate, $w/P$. The labor-supply curve, $L^s$, slopes upward versus $w/P$. Market clearing corresponds to the intersection of the two curves. The market-clearing real wage rate is $(w/P)^*$, and the market-clearing quantity of labor is $L^*$.

demanded are made at given market prices. Economists say that this assumption applies under perfect competition. With perfect competition, each market participant assumes that he or she can sell or buy any quantity desired at the going price. In particular, each participant is small enough that changes in his or her quantity supplied and demanded have a negligible impact on the market price.

When we add up the individual choices, we determine aggregate or market supply and demand functions. For example, we determine the market supply of and demand for labor as a function of the real wage rate, $w/P$; Figure 6.1 shows this case. The aggregate quantity of labor supplied, $L^s$, is assumed to rise as $w/P$ increases (along the blue curve). Therefore, the $L^s$ curve slopes upward. The aggregate quantity of labor demanded, $L^d$, is assumed to decline as $w/P$ rises (along the red curve). Therefore, the $L^d$ curve slopes downward.

Once we know the market supply and demand functions, we have to consider how these functions determine the quantities and prices in the economy. Our main approach relies on **market-clearing conditions**. As an example, in Figure 6.1, the market supply of and demand for labor each depends on the real wage rate, $w/P$. Our assumption is that $w/P$ adjusts to clear the labor market—that is, to equate the quantity of labor supplied to the quantity demanded. Thus, the market-clearing real wage rate is the value $(w/P)^*$ on the vertical axis, and the market-clearing quantity of labor is the value $L^*$ on the horizontal axis.

With this background about markets in mind, we will now start the construction of the microeconomic foundations for our macroeconomic model. We begin by specifying the structure of the markets in the model.

# Markets in the Macroeconomy

Our macroeconomic model contains several markets on which exchanges occur. In this section, we describe the participants in each market and identify the goods and services exchanged on each market.

We simplify by assuming that households perform all of the functions in the economy. Each household runs a family business and uses labor, $L$, and capital, $K$, to produce goods, $Y$, through the production function, which we introduced in Chapter 3:

$$(3.1) \qquad\qquad Y = A \cdot F(K, L)$$

More realistically, the production of goods might take place in a large corporation or a small business. However, if we included these private businesses in our model, we would have to take into account that they must ultimately be owned by households, possibly through shares traded on a **stock market**. When we think of businesses as parts of households, we avoid the complexities of ownership structure. Since we end up with the same macroeconomic results, this simplification is worth making.

## The Goods Market

In the real world, the typical household uses little of the goods that it helps to produce in the marketplace. Usually, a person works on one or a few products and receives income from the sale of these products, or from the sale of labor services, which help to produce the products. The person then spends this income on an array of goods. The model would become too complex if we tried to capture this variety of goods.

We simplify by imagining that households sell all the goods they produce on a **goods market**. Then households buy back from this market the goods that they want. One reason that a household buys goods is for *consumption*. Another reason is to increase the stock of goods in the form of capital—machines and buildings—used for production. This use of goods is called *investment*.

## The Labor Market

Households supply labor on a **labor market**. To simplify at the outset, we assume that the quantity supplied, $L^s$, is a constant, $L$. This assumption is not harmless, and we eventually change it in Chapter 8. As in previous chapters, we measure labor as the flow quantity of person-hours per year. For example, if a person works 40 hours per week, 52 weeks per year, the flow of person-hours per year is 2080.

Households, as managers of family businesses, demand labor in the quantity $L^d$ from the labor market. The labor demanded is used as an input to the production of goods. Notice that each household wears two hats in our simplified economy. When wearing the first hat, the household supplies labor and, thereby, looks like an employee, hired by the person who buys the labor. When wearing the second hat, the household demands labor and, thereby, looks like an employer, who hires the person who sells the labor.

## The Rental Market

Next we consider the capital input to production. Households own the capital stock, $K$. An individual household can add to its stock by buying goods from the goods market and can lower its stock by selling goods on the goods market. We can think of these trades as resales of used capital goods. For example, a household might sell a used automobile or house, which are forms of capital goods. In our model, where households run businesses, we also imagine that households might sell a used machine or a whole used factory.

The stock of capital, $K$, is measured in units of goods—for example, numbers of automobiles or numbers of machines. Conceptually, we should distinguish this stock of goods from the flow of capital services. For example, suppose that a household owns a single machine. If the machine operates 8 hours per day, 5 days per week, 52 weeks per year, the machine is used for 2080 hours per year. We think of these 2080 machine-hours per year—a flow variable—as the quantity of capital services. This flow is analogous to the flow of labor services, measured in person-hours per year.

We simplify at the outset by assuming that each unit of capital—say, each machine—is used for a fixed number of hours per year, perhaps 2080. In this case, the flow of capital services is a constant multiple of the capital stock—each machine represents 2080 machine-hours per year. Therefore, in this case, we will not get into any trouble if we enter the capital stock, $K$, as an input to the production function, as we did in equation (3.1). This stock really represents the flow of capital services, but this flow is a fixed multiple of the stock. Since the multiple is a constant—say, 2080—we do not have to show it explicitly in the production function, $F(K, L)$.

Although a household owns a particular unit of capital—say, a machine—it does not necessarily use that capital for its own production of goods. Rather, the household can rent the capital to another household, which then uses it as an input to production. For example, a household might rent its house or automobile to another household. In our model, we extend this idea of rentals to all types of capital, including machines and factories.

We shall find it convenient to assume that each household rents out all of the capital that it owns on a **rental market**. Thus, if a household owns a machine, it offers for rent all of the capital services—say, 2080 machine-hours per year—that this machine provides. In the real world, we can think of Hertz Rent A Car as owning automobiles and renting them to users. Other real-world examples are rentals of furniture from a company such as Cort Furniture, rentals of tools from a store such as Home Depot, and rentals of taxis and truck cabs from their owners. The important assumption in our model is that households do not allow any of their capital to sit idle and, rather, provide all of it for use on the rental market.

The amount of capital offered on the rental market is analogous to the amount of labor offered or supplied to the labor market, $L^s$. Therefore, we think of the capital offered on the rental market as the supply of capital services, $K^s$. Since we have assumed that each household rents out all of its capital, we have $K^s = K$. (More precisely, we should multiply by 2080 to convert from capital stock—numbers of machines—to capital services—machine-hours per year. But since 2080 is a constant, we can ignore it.) Our assumption that the supply of capital services is constant is analogous to our assumption that the supply of labor is constant. Again, the assumption is not harmless, and we change our assumption about capital services in Chapter 9.

So far, we have assumed that each household rents out all the capital that it owns. However, households, as managers of family businesses, also use capital services to produce goods. To get this capital input, households rent it from the rental market. The amount of capital rented on the rental market is analogous to the amount of labor purchased or demanded from the labor market, $L^d$. Therefore, we think of the capital rented on the rental market as the demand for capital services, $K^d$.

Notice that we are assuming that each household rents out all of its capital, $K^s = K$, and then rents back the quantity $K^d$. If $K^s$ is greater than $K^d$, we could think instead of the household as retaining the quantity $K^d$ of its own capital for use in production of goods and then renting out only the remainder, $K^s - K^d$. Analogously, if $K^s$ is less than $K^d$, we can think of the household as using the entire quantity $K^s$ of its own capital for use in production of goods, and then renting the additional amount, $K^d - K^s$. The results would be the same under these alternative assumptions. Therefore, we shall find it convenient to stick with the assumption that the household rents out all of its capital, $K^s = K$, and then rents back the quantity, $K^d$, that it uses as an input to production.

## The Bond Market

The last market that we introduce is one in which households borrow or lend. A borrowing household receives a loan from another household, whereas a lending household provides a loan to another household. In the real world, this lending and borrowing would typically occur through financial institutions, such as banks. However, as in our neglect of private businesses, we simplify by assuming that households carry out all lending and borrowing directly.

We assume that a household that makes a loan receives a piece of paper—a form of contract—that specifies the terms of the loan. We call this piece of paper a *bond*, and we call the market on which households borrow or lend the **bond market**. The holder of a bond—the lender—has a claim to the amount owed by the borrower.

# Money as a Medium of Exchange

Households buy and sell goods on the goods market, labor on the labor market, capital services on the rental market, and bonds on the bond market. We assume that the exchanges on each of these markets use a single form of **medium of exchange**. In general, a medium of exchange is an object held, not for its own sake, but rather to trade fairly soon for something else, such as goods and services. We call the medium of exchange in our model **money**. Historically, money has taken many forms, including precious commodities such as gold and silver, or sometimes beads and shells. However, in our model, we assume that money is just a piece of paper, analogous to a paper **currency** issued by a government.

Money is denominated in an arbitrary unit, such as a "dollar." For example, a household may have $100 of U.S. currency. Dollar amounts are in **nominal** terms. Thus, $100 is the value of the household's currency in dollar or nominal units. One important property

# Back To Reality

Historically, most governments have issued their own currency. However, there is now a trend toward the formation of groups of countries that share a **common currency**, which is a single form of money used by several countries. This kind of group is called a **currency union**. The most important example of a currency union since 1999–2001 is the twelve Western European countries that use the same money, the *euro*, issued by the European Central Bank. These countries are Austria, Belgium, Finland, France, Germany, Greece, Ireland, Italy, Luxembourg, Netherlands, Portugal, and Spain. Some other European countries are considering the adoption of the euro, although the United Kingdom, Denmark, and Sweden have rejected the idea.

A number of small countries have been joined together in currency unions for some time. Examples are the 15 African countries that use the CFA franc (linked most of the time to the French franc and now the euro) and the 7 Caribbean countries in the Eastern Caribbean Currency Area (ECCA) that use the Caribbean dollar (linked to the U.S. dollar). Proposals exist for the creation of new currency unions in northeast Asia (China, Japan, and South Korea), southern and western Africa, the Persian Gulf, Central America, and between Australia and New Zealand. In addition, a number of small countries use the currency of a large country—examples are Panama, Ecuador, Bermuda, Liechtenstein, Luxembourg, and San Marino.

of paper money is that it bears no interest. That is, if a household has $100 of money and just leaves it under the mattress, the amount of money held is still $100 the following week and the following year (assuming that it is not lost). In contrast, bonds will earn interest.

We use the symbol $M$ for the dollar quantity of money that a household holds. The sum of the individual holdings of money equals the aggregate quantity of money in the economy. We assume, for now, that this aggregate quantity of money is a given constant. Therefore, the total money held by all households must end up equaling this constant.

## Markets and Prices

The key macroeconomic variables in our model will be determined by the interactions of households who trade on the various markets. We will now describe the details of each market.

### The Goods Market

We assume that there is a single type of good, which can be used for consumption or investment. The goods market is the place in which households exchange goods for money. The price in this market, denoted by $P$, expresses the number of dollars that exchange for one unit of goods. We call $P$ the **price level**. The consumer price index, or CPI, which we discussed in Chapter 2, is a real-world counterpart of the price level. The CPI measures the dollar cost of a representative market basket of goods and services.[1] Alternatively, we can

---

[1] More precisely, the CPI measures the dollar cost of a market basket of goods in a particular year—say, 2007—expressed relative to the dollar cost of the market basket of goods in a base year—say, 1996.

think of the deflator for the gross domestic product (the GDP deflator), which is a price index related to the economy's overall production of goods and services (the real GDP). In the model, which has just one type of good, the price level, $P$, corresponds to the CPI or the GDP deflator. We assume, for now, that there is no inflation, which is the change over time in the price level. That is, we assume that $P$ does not change over time.

Recall that households produce goods in the flow quantity $Y$ per year, where $Y$ is given from the production function as

(3.1)
$$Y = A \cdot F(K, L)$$

Since all of these goods are sold on the goods market, the variable $Y$ will also represent the quantity of goods per year sold and bought on the goods market. The quantity $PY$ is the dollar value per year of the goods bought and sold on the goods market.

For a seller of goods, the price level, $P$, is the number of dollars obtained for each unit of goods sold. In contrast, for a buyer, $P$ is the number of dollars paid per unit of goods. Since $P$ dollars buy 1 unit of goods, \$1 buys $1/P$ units of goods. The expression $1/P$ is, therefore, the value of \$1 in terms of the goods that it buys. Similarly, $M$ dollars exchange for

$$(M) \cdot (1/P) = M/P$$

units of goods. The quantity $M$ is the value of money in dollars, and the quantity $M/P$ is the value of this money in terms of the goods that it buys. An expression like $M/P$ is in **real terms**—in units of goods—whereas a quantity like $M$ is in dollar or nominal terms.

As an example, if a household has \$100 of money and the price level is 5, the real value of the household's money is

$$100/5 = 20$$

That is, the household could buy 20 units of goods with its \$100 of money. Hence, 100 is the dollar or nominal value of the household's money, and 20 is the real value of this money, measured in terms of the quantity of goods that it buys. To put it another way, each \$1 of money can buy 1/5th of a unit of goods. Hence, 1/5th is the real value of each dollar.

## The Labor Market

Households buy and sell labor in the labor market at the dollar or **nominal wage rate**, $w$. Since we measure labor, $L$, in units of hours worked per year, the wage rate, $w$, has the units of dollars per hour worked. A household that buys the amount of labor $L^d$ pays the nominal amount $wL^d$ per year, and then gets to use the labor as an input to production. A household that sells the quantity of labor $L^s$ receives the nominal wage income of $wL^s$ per year.

The **real wage rate** is $w/P$. This real wage rate is the value in goods per hour received by a supplier of labor and paid by a demander of labor. For example, if the dollar wage rate is $w = \$10$ per hour and the price level is $P = 5$, the real wage rate is

$$w/P = 10/5 = 2$$

This real wage rate—2 goods per hour worked—determines the quantity of goods that can be bought with the nominal wage ($10) paid for an hour of work. Since people care about the goods that they get, we shall find that household decisions depend on the real wage rate, $w/P$, rather than the nominal wage rate, $w$.

## The Rental Market

In the rental market, households rent out capital, $K$, for dollars at the dollar or **nominal rental price**, $R$. The price $R$ is expressed in dollars per unit of capital per year. For example, if $R = \$100$ per year, a household receives $100 per year for each unit of capital (say, a machine or an automobile) that the household rents out on the rental market.

A household that rents the amount of capital $K^d$ pays the nominal amount $RK^d$ per year and then gets to use the capital as an input to production. A household that rents out the quantity of capital $K^s$ receives the nominal rental income of $RK^s$ per year.

The **real rental price** is $R/P$. This real rental price is the value in goods per unit of capital per year received by the supplier and paid by the demander. For example, if the dollar rental price is $R = \$100$ and the price level is $P = 5$, the real rental price is

$$R/P = 100/5 = 20$$

This real rental price—20 goods per unit of capital per year—gives the quantity of goods that can be bought with the rental payments ($100) for each unit of capital over a year. Again, since people care about the goods that they get, we shall find that household decisions depend on the real rental price, $R/P$, rather than the nominal rental price, $R$.

## The Bond Market

Our model has a simple form of bond market in which households borrow and lend from each other. For example, a household might make a loan to another household that wants to buy a car, a house, a machine, or a factory. A **bond** is the piece of paper that lays out the terms of the loan contract.

A bond could be an I.O.U. that says that household $a$ owes a certain number of dollars to the holder of the bond. Initially, the borrower owes the money to household $b$, which is the household that advanced the money. However, we assume that bonds can be sold on the bond market to another household, perhaps household $c$, which becomes the holder of the bond. Household $a$ then owes the money to household $c$.

We define units so that each unit of bonds commits the borrower to repay $1 to the holder of the bond. This $1 is the **principal** of each bond. The principal is the initial amount advanced on a loan.

We simplify by thinking of all bonds as having very short **maturity**, by which we mean the time at which the principal must be paid back. At any point in time, the issuer of a bond—the borrower—is entitled to buy back the bond for the fixed $1 of principal. That is, the borrower can retire the loan by giving back the $1 to the holder of the bond. Similarly, the holder of the bond is entitled to return the bond to the borrower at any time in exchange for $1. That is, the holder can cancel the loan by demanding the $1 of principal.

These assumptions are not so realistic. For example, with a student loan, the lender (which might be a bank) cannot demand repayment until many years in the future; that is, the maturity is long. Similarly, home mortgages often have long maturities, although borrowers can usually pay back the principal at any time. Despite these real-world complications, our assumption that maturities are very short will capture the most important aspects of interest rates in a tractable way.

We assume that, as long as a bond is neither retired nor cancelled, each unit of bonds commits the borrower to pay the holder a flow of interest payments of $i per year. The variable $i$ is the interest rate, which is the ratio of the interest payment, $i, to the principal, $1. The interest rate, $i$, can vary over time.

As an example, suppose that a household borrows $1000, so that the principal amount outstanding is $1000. Assume that the interest rate, $i$, is 5% per year. In this case, the annual interest payment is

$$\text{interest payment} = \text{interest rate} \cdot \text{principal}$$
$$\$50 = 5\% \cdot \$1000$$

For the holder of a bond, the interest rate, $i$, determines the return per year to lending. For the issuer of a bond, $i$ determines the cost per year of borrowing.

One complication is that a borrower receives dollars today—say, $1000—and pays interest over time—say, $50 per year—with dollars in the future. If the price level, $P$, were changing—that is, if the inflation rate were not zero—today's dollars and future dollars would differ in their real values. Thus, when we allow for inflation in Chapter 11, we have to distinguish two concepts of interest rates—the *nominal interest rate* and the *real interest rate*. However, for now, we do not have to worry about this complication because the inflation rate is zero.

We simplify by assuming that all bonds are alike, regardless of the household that issued the bond. Most importantly, we neglect differences among issuers in the risk that payments of interest and principal will not be made. One type of risk is that a borrower will default on a loan by refusing to pay or by disappearing. Since we ignore these risks, the interest rate, $i$, will have to be the same on all bonds. Otherwise, borrowers would want to do all their borrowing at the lowest interest rate, whereas lenders would want to do all their lending at the highest interest rate. Since all bonds are identical, borrowers and lenders can be matched only if the interest rates on all bonds are the same.

Let $B$ represent the number of bonds in dollar or nominal units that a household holds. This amount may be greater than zero or less than zero for an individual household. Notice, however, that for any dollar borrowed by one household, there must be a corresponding dollar lent by another household. Hence, the total of positive bond holdings for lenders must exactly match the total of negative bond holdings for borrowers. Therefore, when we sum up over all households, the total of the $B$s must always be zero.

Finally, we consider the price of bonds. One unit of bonds was defined to have a principal of $1—that is, each unit can always be exchanged for $1 by canceling the loan. Therefore, the nominal price of these bonds must always be $1 per unit.[2] However, the important variable for our analysis is the interest rate, $i$. We can think of $i$ as the cost or price of credit. A higher $i$ means that obtaining credit—borrowing—is more expensive in terms of the interest that has to be paid. At the same time, a higher $i$ means that extending credit—lending—is more rewarding in that it yields a higher flow of interest income.

---

[2] The price is fixed at $1 per unit because we are considering bonds with very short maturity. Longer-term bonds commit the borrower to pay the bondholder a stream of nominal payments (in interim payments called *coupons* and in a final payment called the *principal*) over a period, up to the maturity date. We can define the units so that each unit of bonds commits the borrower to pay the holder $1 at the maturity date. The nominal price of these bonds will vary when the interest rate, $i$, changes.

# Constructing the Budget Constraint

The quantities and prices determined on the four markets will determine household income. Households will receive income from managing the family business, wages, rentals of capital services, and interest received. These flows of income are **sources of funds** for households. Households use their sources of funds to buy goods or increase their assets—that is, to *save*. The purchases of goods and assets are **uses of funds** for households. The important point is that the total sources of funds must equal the total uses of funds. This equality is called the household **budget constraint**, which we derive in this chapter. In Chapter 7, we use the budget constraint to understand how households choose consumption and saving.

## Income

Begin by considering household income. Households receive income in four forms: profit from the family business, wage income, rental income, and interest income. We consider each of these in turn.

**Profit**    Households may earn **profit**—an excess of revenue over costs—from their business activities. If a household uses the quantity of labor $L^d$ and the quantity of capital $K^d$ as inputs to production, the amount of goods produced, $Y$, is given by the production function:

(6.1) $$Y = A \cdot F(K^d, L^d)$$

Since all goods sell at the price level, $P$, the nominal income from sales is $PY$ per year.

Households pay the nominal amounts $wL^d$ per year for labor input and $RK^d$ per year for capital input. The difference between the income from sales and the payments to labor and capital is the nominal profit per year from running the family business. This nominal profit, which we represent by $\Pi$, is given by

$$profit = income\ from\ sales - wage\ and\ rental\ payments$$
$$\Pi = PY - (wL^d + RK^d)$$

If we substitute $A \cdot F(K^d, L^d)$ for $Y$, we get

(6.2) $$\Pi = PA \cdot F(K^d, L^d) - (wL^d + RK^d)$$

This expression is useful because it shows how profit, $\Pi$, depends on households' business decisions, which are the quantities demanded of capital and labor input, $K^d$ and $L^d$.

**Wage income**    If households supply the quantity of labor $L^s$ to the labor market, they receive the nominal wage income of $wL^s$ per year. As already mentioned, we assume for now that the quantity of labor supplied is the fixed amount $L$. Therefore, the nominal wage income is $wL$.

**Rental income**    If households supply the quantity of capital $K^s$ to the rental market, they receive the nominal rental income of $RK^s$ per year. Since households supply all of their available capital, $K$, to the rental market, so that $K^s = K$, the nominal rental income is $RK$.

We assume, as in Chapter 3, that capital depreciates at the rate $\delta$. Therefore, the quantity $\delta K$ of capital disappears each year. The dollar value of this lost capital is $P \cdot \delta K$ per year. Hence, the net nominal rental income from ownership of capital is

$$net\ nominal\ rental\ income = nominal\ rental\ income - value\ of\ depreciation$$
$$= RK - \delta PK$$

We want to calculate the rate of return that households get by owning capital. To compute this rate of return, we have to manipulate the expression for net nominal rental income. Start by dividing and multiplying the first term by $P$ to get

$$net\ nominal\ rental\ income = (R/P) \cdot PK - \delta PK$$

Next, combine the terms on the right-hand side to get

(6.3)    $$net\ nominal\ rental\ income = (R/P - \delta) \cdot PK$$

The right-hand side expresses the net nominal rental income as the product of two terms: $R/P - \delta$ and $PK$. The second term, $PK$, is the dollar value of the capital owned by households. The first term, $R/P - \delta$, is the rate of return on each dollar held in the form of capital. The important result is the formula for the rate of return on capital:

(6.4)    $$rate\ of\ return\ on\ owning\ capital = R/P - \delta$$

The rate of return on owning capital is the real rental price, $R/P$, less the rate of depreciation, $\delta$.

**Interest income**    If a household's nominal bond holdings are $B$, the flow of nominal interest income received is $iB$ per year. Notice that interest income is greater than zero for a holder of bonds (when $B$ is greater than zero) and less than zero for an issuer of bonds (when $B$ is less than zero). That is, an issuer of bonds—someone who owes money to another person—has to pay out interest rather than receive it. Since $B$ equals zero for the whole economy, we have that the total of interest income equals zero. The amount paid to holders of bonds (lenders) exactly balances the amount paid by issuers of bonds (borrowers).

**Total income**    We can put the four types of income together to calculate households' total nominal income per year. The result is

$$household\ nominal\ income = nominal\ profit + nominal\ wage\ income$$
$$+ nominal\ net\ rental\ income + nominal\ interest\ income$$

If we substitute $\Pi$ for nominal profit (from equation [6.2]), $wL$ for nominal wage income, $(R/P - \delta) \cdot PK$ for nominal net rental income (from equation [6.3]), and $iB$ for nominal interest income, we get

(6.5)    $$household\ nominal\ income = \Pi + wL + (R/P - \delta) \cdot PK + iB$$

## Consumption

So far, we have discussed household income. Now we will consider household expenditures on goods. Households consume goods in the quantity $C$ per year. Since the price level is $P$, the nominal amount spent on consumption per year is

$$household\ nominal\ consumption = P\,C$$

### Assets

Now we will work out how households' incomes and expenditures relate to households' assets. Households hold assets in three forms: money, $M$; bonds, $B$; and ownership of capital, $K$. Money pays no interest. Bonds pay interest at the rate $i$ per year. Ownership of capital yields the rate of return $R/P - \delta$ per year (from equation [6.4]). We assume that households can divide their assets any way they wish among the three forms. That is, at any point in time, households can exchange dollars of money for dollars of bonds and can exchange dollars of money for units of capital at the price level, $P$. So, when would households choose to hold all three forms of assets?

Bonds seem to be more attractive than money if the interest rate, $i$, is greater than zero. Households would, however, hold some money for convenience, because they use money as a medium of exchange—for example, to buy or sell goods and labor. In contrast, our assumption is that bonds are not readily accepted in exchange for goods or labor—usually, the holder of a bond has to sell the bond for money before buying goods or labor. The special role of money in making exchanges motivates households to have a positive *demand for money*. We will postpone our study of this demand for money until Chapter 10. For now, we assume that households hold a fixed amount of money in dollar terms; that is, we assume that the change over time of a household's nominal money holdings is zero. If we use the symbol $\Delta$ to represent a change over time, we have

$$\Delta M = 0$$

As an example, a family might want to hold $200 on average to cover expenses for groceries, gasoline, and other goods. The amount of money held by an individual household would vary over time, sometimes rising above $200 and sometimes falling below $200. However, if the average money held by each household is always $200, then the total money held at every point in time by all households would tend not to vary much. Our assumption is that the change in the total amount of money held by all households, $\Delta M$, is zero.

In considering whether to hold assets as bonds or capital, households would compare the rate of return on bonds—the interest rate, $i$—with the rate of return on ownership of capital—$R/P - \delta$. Would households be willing to hold both forms of assets if the rates of return differed? They might be willing to hold both types if the assets differed by characteristics other than the rate of return. In the real world, the most important difference is the *riskiness* of the returns. Some types of bonds, such as U.S. Treasury Bills with three-month maturity, are nearly risk-free.[3] Forms of owning capital, such as stock in Ford

---

[3] The holder of a three-month U.S. Treasury Bill has virtual certainty of receiving the promised dollar amount three months in the future. However, the real value of this payment is uncertain because the future price level is unknown; that is, the inflation rate is uncertain. Thus, U.S. Treasury Bills have risk in their real returns. Since 1997, the U.S. Treasury has issued inflation-protected securities (indexed bonds). These assets, if held to maturity, provide a guaranteed real return.

Motor Company, provide uncertain returns. In these situations, the risky asset (stock in Ford) typically has to pay an expected rate of return greater than the interest rate on U.S. Treasury Bills to induce people to hold the risky asset.

To keep things manageable in our model, we do not consider risk in the returns paid on bonds or capital. That is, we assume that, aside from rates of return, bonds and capital look the same to households as ways to hold assets. In this case, if bonds offered a higher rate of return, households would hold no capital. In contrast, if capital offered a higher rate of return, households would want to borrow a lot to hold a lot of capital (actually, an infinite amount). Since the economy's stock of capital is greater than zero but less than infinity, the two rates of return must be equal. This condition is

---

Key equation:

$$\text{rate of return on bonds} = \text{rate of return on ownership of capital}$$

(6.6) $$i = R/P - \delta$$

---

If we use this result to substitute $i$ for $R/P - \delta$ in the expression for household nominal income in equation (6.5), we get

(6.7) $$\text{household nominal income} = \pi + wL + i \cdot (B + PK)$$

The last term shows that assets held as bonds or ownership of capital yield the same rate of return per year, given by the interest rate, $i$.

## Household Budget Constraint

Now we will use the results on household income to construct the household budget constraint. This constraint relates changes in households' assets to the flows of income.

At a point in time, a household has assets in the form of money, bonds, and ownership of capital:

$$\text{nominal value of assets} = M + B + PK$$

We define **nominal saving** to be the change over time in the nominal value of assets. Therefore, if we again use the symbol $\Delta$ to represent a change over time, we have

$$\text{nominal saving} = \Delta(\text{nominal assets})$$
$$= \Delta M + \Delta B + P \cdot \Delta K$$

If we use our assumption that $\Delta M = 0$, we get

(6.8) $$\text{nominal saving} = \Delta B + P \cdot \Delta K$$

That is, a household's saving corresponds to changes in its holdings of bonds and capital.

A household's nominal saving depends on its income and consumption. If income is greater than consumption, the difference will be saved and, therefore, added to assets. If income is less than consumption, nominal saving is less than zero, and the difference will subtract from nominal assets. Therefore, we have

$$\text{nominal saving} = \text{nominal income} - \text{nominal consumption}$$

9038.0
18.860
7.7577
61.851

# Extending The Model

## Allowing for a risk premium on ownership of capital

We can make our model more realistic by allowing for a difference between the rate of return on ownership of capital, $R/P - \delta$, and the interest rate on bonds, $i$. We can write the relationship between the two rates of return as

$$R/P - \delta = i + risk\ premium$$

$$rate\ of\ return = interest\ rate + risk\ premium$$
$$on\ capital$$

Thus, the **risk premium** is the excess of the anticipated rate of return on capital—for example, the expected rate of return on holding corporate stock—over the expected rate of return on a nearly risk-free asset, such as U.S. Treasury Bills. The risk premium normally has to be greater than zero to induce households to hold the riskier asset. If the risk premium is constant, our analysis would not change by allowing for this premium. More interesting (and more difficult) would be to allow the risk premia to vary over time. Some reasons that risk premia change are: first, the perceived riskiness of capital changes; second, households become more or less willing to absorb risk; and, third, innovations in the financial markets or the legal system make it easier for households to reduce the overall risk in their assets and incomes.

If we substitute for nominal income from equation (6.7) and replace nominal consumption by $PC$, we get

(6.9) $$nominal\ saving = \Pi + wL + i \cdot (B + PK) - PC$$

Equations (6.8) and (6.9) are two ways of representing nominal saving. Therefore, the right-hand sides of the equations must be equal:

(6.10) $$\Delta B + P \cdot \Delta K = \Pi + wL + i \cdot (B + PK) - PC$$

This equation says that nominal saving, $\Delta B + P \cdot \Delta K$ on the left-hand side, equals the difference between nominal income, $\Pi + wL + i \cdot (B + PK)$, and nominal consumption, $PC$, on the right-hand side.

If we rearrange equation (6.10) to put nominal consumption, $PC$, on the left-hand side, we get

---

Key equation (household budget constraint in nominal terms):

(6.11) $$PC + \Delta B + P \cdot \Delta K = \Pi + wL + i \cdot (B + PK)$$

nominal consumption + nominal saving = nominal income

---

The right-hand side has total nominal income, $\Pi + wL + i \cdot (B + PK)$. Equation (6.11) says that households are constrained to divide this total nominal income between the two terms on the left-hand side: nominal consumption, $PC$, and nominal saving, $\Delta B + P \cdot \Delta K$. Thus, equation (6.11) is the **household budget constraint in nominal terms**.

We shall find it useful to express the household budget constraint in real terms by dividing all the terms in equation (6.11) by the price level, $P$. After we do this division, we get

---

Key equation (household budget constraint in real terms):

**(6.12)**   $$C + (1/P) \cdot \Delta B + \Delta K = \Pi/P + (w/P) \cdot L + i \cdot (B/P + K)$$

consumption + real saving = real income

---

This equation is the **household budget constraint in real terms**. The right-hand side has total real income, $\Pi/P + (w/P) \cdot L + i \cdot (B/P + K)$. The left-hand side has consumption, $C$, and the change in the real value of assets, $(1/P) \cdot \Delta B + \Delta K$. We refer to the change in the real value of assets as **real saving**. Notice that nominal saving, $\Delta B + P \cdot \Delta K$, which appears on the left-hand side of equation (6.11), gives the change in the nominal value of assets. In contrast, real saving, $(1/P) \cdot \Delta B + \Delta K$, which appears on the left-hand side of equation (6.12), gives the change in the real value of assets.

Figure 6.2 shows graphically the household budget constraint from equation (6.12). Suppose that a household has a given total real income, $\Pi/P + (w/P) \cdot L + i \cdot (B/P + K)$,

### F i g u r e   6 . 2 | The Household Budget Constraint

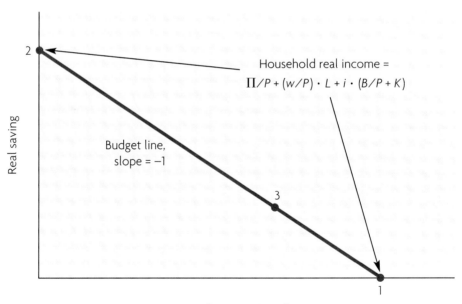

Households have a given total of real income, $\Pi/P + (w/P) \cdot L + i \cdot (B/P + K)$. This total must be divided between consumption, $C$, and real saving, $(1/P) \cdot \Delta B + \Delta K$. Thus, if real saving is zero, $C$ equals the total of real income along the horizontal axis at point 1. If $C$ is zero, real saving equals the total of real income along the vertical axis at point 2. The budget constraint in equation (6.12) allows the household to select any combination of consumption and real saving along the budget line, shown in red, such as point 3. The budget line has a slope of $-1$. Therefore, along this line, one unit less of consumption corresponds to one unit more of real saving.

on the right-hand side of the equation. The budget constraint says that this real income must be divided between consumption, $C$, and real saving, $(1/P) \cdot \Delta B + \Delta K$. One possibility is that the household sets real saving to zero, so that $C$ equals the total real income. This choice corresponds to point 1, shown on the horizontal axis where $C$ equals total real income. Another possibility is that the household sets $C$ to zero, so that real saving equals total real income. This choice corresponds to point 2, shown on the vertical axis where real saving equals total real income. More commonly, the household would choose an intermediate point, such as point 3, where $C$ and real saving are both greater than zero. The full range of possibilities is shown by the downward-sloping red line in the figure. This line is called a **budget line**. The budget constraint in equation (6.12) tells us that, along a budget line, each increase in $C$ by one unit corresponds to a decrease in real saving by one unit. Hence, the slope of a budget line is $-1$.

# Clearing of the Markets for Labor and Capital Services

Now that we have worked out the household budget constraint, we can consider the choices that households make. We begin by considering decisions about the family business. These decisions determine the demands for labor and capital services. Once we know these demands, we can study the clearing of the markets for labor and capital services.

### Profit Maximization

The two business decisions that households make are the quantities of labor and capital services to demand, $L^d$ and $K^d$. These decisions determine the amount of goods produced and sold on the goods market, $A \cdot F(K^d, L^d)$, and, therefore, the amount of nominal profit from

(6.2)
$$\Pi = P A \cdot F(K^d, L^d) - wL^d - RK^d$$

To calculate real profit, we can divide through equation (6.2) by the price level, $P$, to get

(6.13)
$$\Pi / P = A \cdot F(K^d, L^d) - (w/P) \cdot L^d - (R/P) \cdot K^d$$

*real profit = output − real wage payments − real rental payments*

We can see from the right-hand side of the household budget constraint in equation (6.12) that an increase in profit, $\Pi/P$, raises household real income. Figure 6.3 on the next page shows how an increase in real income affects households. An increase in real income moves the budget line outward from the red line to the blue one. In comparison with the red budget line, the blue line allows households to choose higher consumption, $C$, for any given value of real saving, $(1/P) \cdot \Delta B + \Delta K$. Therefore, as long as households like more consumption, they prefer more real income to less. This result tells us that households, as managers of family businesses, will seek to make real profit, $\Pi/P$, as high as possible. That is, households will choose their demands for labor and capital services, $L^d$ and $K^d$, to maximize $\Pi/P$, as given in equation (6.13).

We assume that an individual household takes as given the real wage rate for labor, $w/P$, and the real rental price for capital, $R/P$. As mentioned before, these assumptions are standard for competitive markets—an individual household is too small to have a

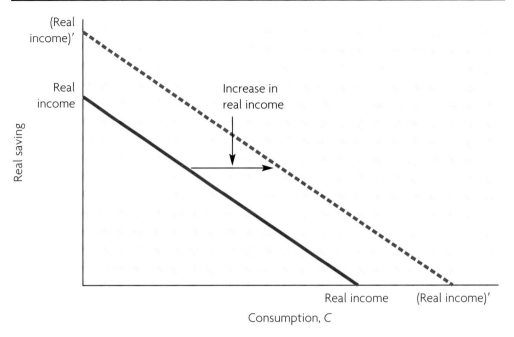

| | Effect of an Increase in Real Income on the |
|---|---|
| **F i g u r e   6 . 3** | Household Budget Constraint |

If household real income, $\Pi/P + (w/P) \cdot L + i \cdot (B/P + K)$, rises, the budget line moves outward from the red line to the blue line. That is, in the graph, (real income)$'$ is larger than (real income). In comparison with the red line, the blue line allows the household to have more consumption, $C$, for any given value of real saving, $(1/P) \cdot \Delta B + \Delta K$. Since households like more consumption, they prefer more real income to less.

noticeable effect on the market prices. In this situation, each household can buy or sell whatever quantity of labor it wants at the going real wage rate, $w/P$, and can rent or rent out whatever amount of capital it wants at the going real rental price, $R/P$. Therefore, the household will demand quantities of labor and capital services, $L^d$ and $K^d$, that maximize real profit, $\Pi/P$, for given values of $w/P$ and $R/P$.

## The Labor Market

We will now consider the demand for labor and the supply of labor. Then we will determine the real wage rate, $w/P$, from the market-clearing condition for the labor market: the quantity of labor demanded equals the quantity supplied.

**Demand for labor**   The demand for labor, $L^d$, comes from the objective of profit maximization. Consider the effect of an increase in labor input, $L^d$, by one unit on real profit, $\Pi/P$, as given in equation (6.13). The increase in $L^d$ raises output, $A \cdot F(K^d, L^d)$, on the right-hand side by increasing production and, hence, sales of goods on the goods market. We know from Chapter 3 that an increase in $L^d$ by one unit raises production by the marginal product of labor (MPL). An increase in $L^d$ also raises the second term on the right-hand side, the real wage payments, $(w/P) \cdot L^d$. For a given real wage rate, $w/P$, an

**F i g u r e   6 . 4** | Labor Demand

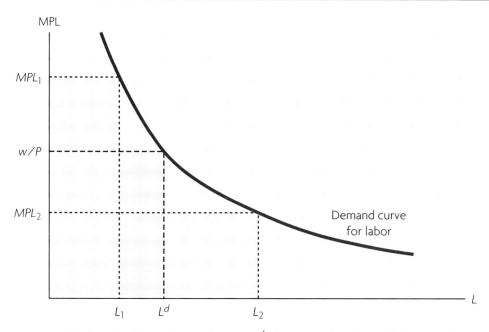

For a given technology level, $A$, and capital input, $K^d$, the marginal product of labor, MPL, decreases as labor input, $L$, increases. Therefore, the MPL, given by the red curve, declines on the vertical axis as $L$ rises on the horizontal axis. The household chooses labor input, $L^d$, where the MPL equals the real wage rate, $w/P$. At a lower labor input, such as $L_1$, $MPL_1$ is greater than $w/P$, and at a higher labor input, such as $L_2$, $MPL_2$ is less than $w/P$. If $w/P$ decreases, $L^d$ increases.

increase in $L^d$ by one unit raises these payments by the amount $w/P$. Therefore, the overall effect from an increase in $L^d$ by one unit is to change real profit by

$$\Delta(\Pi/P) = \Delta[A \cdot F(K^d, L^d)] - w/P$$
$$= MPL - w/P$$

*change in real profit = marginal product of labor − real wage rate*

We know from Chapter 3 that the MPL depends on the quantity of labor input, $L^d$. As $L^d$ rises, the MPL falls. This relation is shown by the downward-sloping red curve in Figure 6.4. This curve applies for a given technology level, $A$, and capital input, $K^d$.

Suppose that the household selects a low labor input, such as $L_1$ in Figure 6.4, where the marginal product of labor, $MPL_1$, is greater than $w/P$. In this case, an increase in $L^d$ by an additional unit would raise real profit, $\Pi/P$. The reason is that the addition to output—by $MPL_1$ units—is larger than the addition to wage payments—by $w/P$ units. However, as $L^d$ rises, the MPL falls and eventually gets as low as $w/P$. If the household continues to raise $L^d$, the MPL falls below $w/P$, such as at $L_2$ in the figure. In that situation, further increases in $L^d$ lower $\Pi/P$. Thus, to maximize real profit, the household should stop at the point where the MPL equals $w/P$. The graph shows that this equality occurs where the value along the curve for the MPL equals $w/P$.

For a given real wage rate, $w/P$, on the vertical axis, the graph in Figure 6.4 shows on the horizontal axis the quantity of labor demanded, $L^d$. We can see that a decrease in $w/P$ raises $L^d$. Hence, if we graph $L^d$ versus $w/P$, we map out a downward-sloping demand curve. That is, the labor-demand curve looks as shown in Figure 6.1.

Each household determines its labor demand, $L^d$, as shown in Figure 6.4. Therefore, when we add up across all the households, we end up with an aggregate or market demand for labor that also looks like the curve shown in the figure. In particular, a decrease in the real wage rate, $w/P$, raises the market quantity of labor demanded, $L^d$.

**Supply of labor**   We are assuming that each household supplies a fixed quantity of labor to the labor market. Therefore, the aggregate or market supply of labor, $L^s$, is the given amount $L$. More realistically, the quantity of labor supplied would depend on the real wage rate, $w/P$. For example, we might have the upward-sloping labor-supply curve shown in Figure 6.1. However, we neglect until Chapter 8 this dependence of $L^s$ on $w/P$.

**Clearing of the labor market**   The market labor demand, $L^d$, is determined from Figure 6.4 as a downward-sloping function of the real wage rate, $w/P$. We reproduce this curve in Figure 6.5. The market labor supply, $L^s$, is assumed to be the constant $L$. We show this fixed labor supply as the vertical line at $L$. Now we can determine the equilibrium value of $w/P$ from the market-clearing condition for the labor market. Specifically, we

| **F i g u r e   6 . 5** | Clearing of the Labor Market |

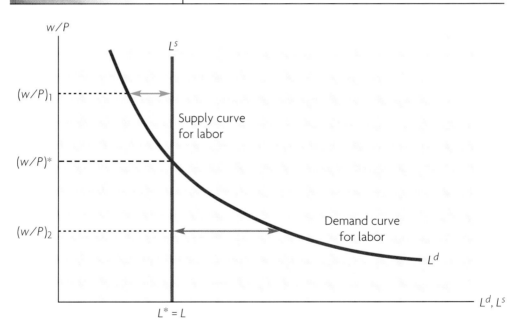

The downward-sloping labor-demand curve, $L^d$, comes from Figure 6.4. We assume that labor supply, $L^s$, is fixed at $L$. The market-clearing real wage rate is $(w/P)^*$. The market-clearing quantity of labor input is $L^* = L$. At a higher real wage rate, such as $(w/P)_1$, the quantity of labor supplied, $L^s$, exceeds the quantity demanded, $L^d$, in the amount shown by the green arrows. At a lower real wage rate, such as $(w/P)_2$, the quantity of labor supplied, $L^s$, falls short of the quantity demanded, $L^d$, in the amount shown by the brown arrows.

assume that $w/P$ is determined to equate the aggregate quantity of labor demanded, $L^d$, to the aggregate quantity supplied, $L$. This market-clearing value of $w/P$ corresponds in Figure 6.5 to the intersection of the $L^d$ curve with the vertical line at $L$. The market-clearing value for $w/P$ is denoted by $(w/P)^*$ on the vertical axis. The corresponding market-clearing quantity of labor input, $L^*$, equals $L$ on the horizontal axis.

The equality between $L$ and $L^d$ means that the market-clearing real wage rate, $(w/P)^*$, equals the marginal product of labor, MPL:

**(6.14)** $$(w/P)^* = MPL\,(evaluated\ at\ L)$$

By *MPL* (evaluated at $L$), we are referring in Figure 6.4 to the value for the marginal product of labor that corresponds to the quantity of labor $L$.[4]

Why do we assume that the labor market clears? The idea is that only at this market-clearing position would the real wage rate, $w/P$, tend neither to rise nor fall. If $w/P$ were below $(w/P)^*$, for example, at $(w/P)_1$ in Figure 6.5, the aggregate quantity of labor demanded would exceed the quantity supplied in the amount shown by the green arrows. In this case, demanders of labor would compete to hire scarce workers by raising $w/P$.[5] Conversely, if $w/P$ were above $(w/P)^*$, for example, at $(w/P)_2$ in Figure 6.5, the aggregate quantity of labor demanded would fall short of the quantity supplied in the amount shown by the brown arrows. In this case, the eager suppliers of labor would bid down $w/P$. In equilibrium, $w/P$ will be determined to clear the labor market—that is, so that the aggregate quantity of labor supplied, $L$, equals the quantity demanded, $L^d$.

## The Market for Capital Services

We will now consider the demand for capital services and the supply of capital services. Then we will determine the real rental price, $R/P$, from the market-clearing condition for the market for capital services: the quantity of capital services demanded equals the quantity supplied.

**Demand for capital services**  As with the demand for labor, the demand for capital services, $K^d$, comes from the objective of profit maximization. Consider the effect of an increase in $K^d$ by one unit on a household's real profit, as given again by

**(6.13)** $$\Pi/P = A \cdot F(K^d, L^d) - (w/P) \cdot L^d - (R/P) \cdot K^d$$
$$real\ profit = output - real\ wage\ payments - real\ rental\ payments$$

We know from Chapter 3 that an increase in capital input, $K^d$, by one unit raises output, $A \cdot F(K^d, L^d)$, the first term on the right-hand side, by the marginal product of capital (MPK). An increase in $K^d$ also raises the real rental payments, $(R/P) \cdot K^d$, the last term on the right-hand side. For a given real rental price, $R/P$, an increase in $K^d$ by one unit raises real rental payments by the amount $R/P$. Therefore, the overall effect from an increase in $K^d$ by one unit is to change real profit by

$$\Delta(\Pi/P) = \Delta[A \cdot F(K^d, L^d)] - R/P$$
$$= MPK - R/P$$
$$change\ in\ real\ profit = marginal\ product\ of\ capital - real\ rental\ price$$

---

[4] Note that the curve for MPL in Figure 6.4 applies for a given capital stock, $K$. A change in $K$ would shift the MPL associated with a given value of $L$ and would therefore change $(w/P)^*$ in Figure 6.5.

[5] This description views the participants in the labor market as directly setting the real wage rate, $(w/P)$. However, our story would be the same if, instead, the price level, $P$, were given, and the participants in the labor market adjusted the nominal wage rate, $w$.

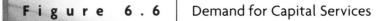

**Figure 6.6** | Demand for Capital Services

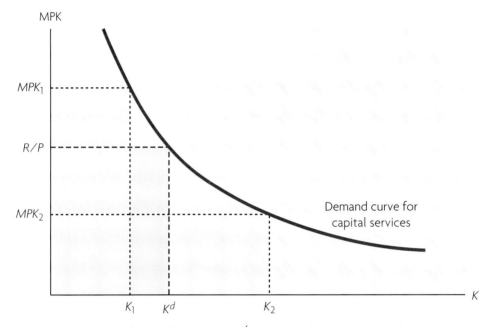

For a given technology level, $A$, and labor input, $L^d$, the marginal product of capital, MPK, decreases as capital input, $K$, increases. Therefore, the MPK, given by the red curve, declines on the vertical axis as $K$ rises on the horizontal axis. The household chooses capital input, $K^d$, where the MPK equals the real rental price, $R/P$. In contrast, at a lower capital input, such as $K_1$, $MPK_1$ is greater than $R/P$, and at a higher capital input, such as $K_2$, $MPK_2$ is less than $R/P$. If $R/P$ decreases, $K^d$ increases.

We know from Chapter 3 that the MPK depends on the amount of capital input, $K^d$. As $K^d$ rises, MPK falls. This relation is shown by the downward-sloping red curve in Figure 6.6. This curve applies for a given technology level, $A$, and labor input, $L^d$.

Suppose that the household selects a low value of capital input, $K^d$, such as $K_1$ in Figure 6.6, at which the marginal product of capital, $MPK_1$, is greater than $R/P$. In this case, an increase in $K^d$ by an additional unit would raise real profit, $\Pi/P$. The reason is that the addition to output (by $MPK_1$ units) is greater than the increase in real rental payments (by $R/P$ units). However, as $K^d$ rises, the MPK falls and eventually gets as low as $R/P$. If the household continues to raise $K^d$, the MPK falls below $R/P$, such as at $K_2$ in the figure. In that case, further increases in $K^d$ lower $\Pi/P$. Thus, to maximize real profit, the household should stop at the point where the MPK equals $R/P$. The graph shows that this equality occurs where the value along the curve for the MPK equals $R/P$.

For a given real rental price, $R/P$, on the vertical axis, the graph in Figure 6.6 shows on the horizontal axis the quantity of capital services demanded, $K^d$. We can see that a decrease in $R/P$ increases $K^d$. Hence, if we graph $K^d$ versus $R/P$, we determine a downward-sloping demand curve.

Each household sets its demand for capital services, $K^d$, as shown in Figure 6.6. Therefore, when we add up across all the households, we end up with an aggregate or market demand for capital services that also looks like the curve shown in the figure. In particular, a decrease in the real rental price, $R/P$, raises the market quantity of capital services demanded, $K^d$.

| Figure 6.7 | Clearing of the Market for Capital Services |

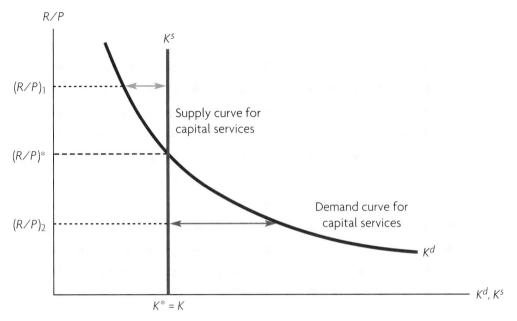

The downward-sloping demand curve for capital services, $K^d$, comes from Figure 6.6. The supply of capital services, $K^s$, is fixed at $K$. The market-clearing real rental price is $(R/P)^*$. The market-clearing quantity of capital services is $K^* = K$. At a higher real rental price, such as $(R/P)_1$, the quantity of capital services supplied, $K^s = K$, exceeds the quantity demanded, $K^d$, in the amount shown by the green arrows. At a lower real rental price, such as $(R/P)_2$, the quantity of capital services supplied, $K^s = K$, falls short of the quantity demanded, $K^d$, in the amount shown by the brown arrows.

**Supply of capital services** For the economy as a whole, the aggregate quantity of capital, $K$, is given from past flows of investment. That is, in the short run, the economy has a given stock of houses, cars, machines, and factories. This capital stock is owned by households, and all of the services from this stock are supplied to the rental market. Therefore, in the short run, the aggregate or market quantity of capital services supplied, $K^s$, equals $K$.

**Clearing of the market for capital services** The market demand for capital services, $K^d$, is determined from Figure 6.6 as a downward-sloping function of the real rental price, $R/P$. We reproduce this curve in Figure 6.7. The market supply of capital services, $K^s$, is the constant $K$. We show this fixed supply of capital services as the vertical line at $K$. As with the labor market, we assume that the equilibrium value of $R/P$ is determined to clear the market—that is, so that the aggregate quantity of capital services supplied, $K$, equals the aggregate quantity demanded, $K^d$. This market-clearing value of $R/P$ corresponds in Figure 6.7 to the intersection of the $K^d$ curve with the vertical line at $K$. The market-clearing value for $R/P$ is denoted by $(R/P)^*$ on the vertical axis. The corresponding market-clearing quantity of capital services, $K^*$, equals $K$ on the horizontal axis.

The equality between $K$ and $K^d$ means that the market-clearing real rental price, $(R/P)^*$, equals the marginal product of capital, MPK:

(6.15) $$(R/P)^* = MPK\,(evaluated\ at\ K)$$

By $MPK$ (evaluated at $K$), we are referring in Figure 6.6 to the value for the marginal product of capital that corresponds to the capital input $K$.[6]

We can ask again why we assume that the market clears. The idea is that only at this market-clearing position would the real rental price, $R/P$, tend neither to rise nor fall. If $R/P$ were below $(R/P)^*$, for example, at $(R/P)_1$ on the vertical axis in Figure 6.7, the aggregate quantity of capital services demanded would exceed the quantity supplied in the amount shown by the green arrows. In this case, demanders of capital services would compete to hire scarce capital by bidding up $R/P$. Conversely, if $R/P$ were above $(R/P)^*$, for example, at $(R/P)_2$ on the vertical axis in Figure 6.7, the aggregate quantity of capital services demanded would fall short of the quantity supplied in the amount shown by the brown arrows. In this case, the suppliers of capital services would compete by lowering $R/P$. In equilibrium, $R/P$ will be determined to clear the market—that is, so that the aggregate quantity of capital services supplied, $K$, equals the aggregate quantity demanded, $K^d$.

**The interest rate**   The market-clearing solution for the real rental price will allow us to determine the interest rate, $i$. We found before that $i$ equals the rate of return to owning capital:

(6.6) 
$$i = R/P - \delta$$

*rate of return on bonds = rate of return on ownership of capital*

Therefore, if we substitute for $R/P$ from the formula for $(R/P)^*$ in equation (6.15), we get

> Key equation (equilibrium interest rate):
>
> (6.16) 
> $$i = MPK\,(evaluated\ at\ K) - \delta$$

Thus, once we determine $R/P$, we also determine the interest rate, $i$.

This last result is important. It says that the interest rate, $i$, cannot change unless something changes the MPK. For a given technology level, $A$, the MPK depends on the inputs of capital services, $K$, and labor, $L$. In our present setting, $K$ and $L$ are given. Therefore, $i$ will also be given. In the real world, the interest rate, $i$, tends to fluctuate a good deal. Thus, to capture this aspect of reality, we have to extend our model to allow for variations in the MPK. We introduce in Chapters 8 and 9 some sources of changes in the MPK and, therefore, in the interest rate, $i$.

## Profit in Equilibrium

We determined households' demands for labor and capital services, $L^d$ and $K^d$, from the objective of profit maximization. Households as business managers chose $L^d$ and $K^d$ to make real profit, $\Pi/P$, as high as possible. Now we will consider the level of $\Pi/P$ that households receive when the labor and rental markets clear.

When the labor and rental markets clear, so that $L^d = L$ and $K^d = K$, real profit is given from equation (6.13) by

(6.17) 
$$\Pi/P = A \cdot F(K, L) - (w/P) \cdot L - (R/P) \cdot K$$

Since the labor and rental markets clear, we also have, from equations (6.14) and (6.15),

$$w/P = MPL$$
$$R/P = MPK$$

---

[6] Note that the curve for MPK in Figure 6.6 applies for a given labor input, $L$. A change in $L$ would shift the MPK associated with a given value of $K$ and would therefore change $(R/P)^*$ in Figure 6.7.

# Back To Reality

**Economic profit versus accounting profit**

Our definition of profit differs from the standard accounting definition. The reason for the difference is the treatment of rental payments on capital. Suppose, for example, that a household (or, more realistically, a business) owns capital and uses the capital to produce goods. In that case, the household pays no explicit rental payments on the capital that it uses in production. The rental payments are only implicit—the household should think of paying rentals to itself on the capital that it owns and uses. These implicit rental payments represent the income that the household could have received by renting the capital to another producer. Thus, the foregone rental payments should be treated as a cost (called an *opportunity cost*) of using one's own capital to produce goods.

However, standard accounting practices, including the national-income accounts, do not include most forms of implicit rental payments as costs.[7] For this reason, the usual accounting measure of rental payments understates the rental payments that are appropriate from an economic perspective. Since rental payments are a negative item for real profit, $\Pi/P$, in equation (6.17), we also get that the accounting measure overstates real profit from an economic standpoint. Since the economic profit is zero in equilibrium, the accounting measure of profit must be greater than zero in equilibrium. The accounting measure of profit really measures the uncounted part of the rental income on capital.

where MPL and MPK are evaluated at the given values of $L$ and $K$. If we substitute these formulas for $w/P$ and $R/P$ into equation (6.17), we get

**(6.18)** $$\Pi/P = A \cdot F(K, L) - MPL \cdot L - MPK \cdot K$$

We show in the Appendix that the expression on the right-hand side of equation (6.18) equals zero. That is, when the values for $w/P$ and $R/P$ satisfy the market-clearing conditions for labor and capital services, the real profit, $\Pi/P$, ends up being zero. Another way to say this is that real GDP, which equals $A \cdot F(K, L)$, just covers the payments to the two factor inputs, $(w/P) \cdot L$ for labor and $(R/P) \cdot K$ for capital services. Output equals the total of these real factor incomes, and all of this income goes to either labor or capital. Nothing is left over for profit.

We therefore have something of a paradox. Households as business managers select their demands for labor and capital services, $L^d$ and $K^d$, to maximize profit. However, when $w/P$ and $R/P$ satisfy market-clearing conditions, the resulting real profit, $\Pi/P$, is zero. That is, the highest real profit that households can attain is zero. The Back to Reality box on the top of this page notes that accounting measures of profit include part of rental payments to capital and tend, therefore, to be greater than zero.

From an economic perspective, the reason that profit ends up being zero in our model is that profit represents the return to a household from managing a business. We have assumed that all households are equally good at business management and that the process of managing takes no effort. Therefore, in equilibrium, business management receives zero compensation (profit is nil).

---

[7] If a business borrows money to finance purchases of capital goods, the usual accounting practice treats the interest payments on the business's debt as costs. Therefore, interest expenses—which represent the rental payments on debt-financed capital—enter as a negative item into the accounting definition of profit. Thus, standard accounting procedures include rental payments on capital as costs when the capital is debt financed but not when the capital is owned outright by a business. In the case of corporations, this ownership corresponds to finance of capital by issue of equity shares (corporate stock) or *retained earnings* (after-tax profit not paid out as dividends to shareholders).

Another point is that households as business owners are the *residual claimants* on business earnings. That is, profit income is the residual after subtracting from sales the costs of factor inputs, labor and capital. In our model, profit is not risky—it equals zero in equilibrium with complete certainty. More realistically, profit involves uncertainties about sales and costs. In most circumstances, the average profit has to be greater than zero to compensate business owners for assuming the risks of being a residual claimant.

## Summing Up

We set up the market structure and microeconomic foundations for our macroeconomic model. We began by describing the economy's four markets—for goods, labor, rental of capital, and bonds. The dollar prices on the first three markets are the price level, $P$, the wage rate, $w$, and the rental price, $R$. The price of short-term bonds is fixed at \$1, but the interest rate, $i$, can vary. We can think of $i$ as the price of credit. We showed how the sales and purchases on the various markets determined household income from wages, returns on assets, and profit.

We examined in detail the markets for labor and capital services. As managers of family businesses, households determine their demands for labor, $L^d$, and capital services, $K^d$. We derived these demands from the objective of profit maximization, assuming that each household took as given the real wage rate, $w/P$, and the real rental price, $R/P$. We assumed that the supply of labor, $L^s$, was fixed at $L$ and that the supply of capital services, $K^s$, was fixed at $K$.

We found from the labor market that the market-clearing real wage rate, $(w/P)^*$, equaled the marginal product of labor, MPL. We found from the market for capital services that the market-clearing real rental price, $(R/P)^*$, equaled the marginal product of capital, MPK. The two marginal products, MPL and MPK, were evaluated at the given values of $L$ and $K$. We also showed that the market-clearing real rental price, $(R/P)^*$, determined the interest rate, $i$.

The results from this chapter provide essential building blocks for our model of economic fluctuations. In the next chapter, we extend the analysis to consumption, saving, and investment. Then, in Chapters 8 and 9, we show how to use the model to explain real-world features of economic fluctuations.

## Key Terms and Concepts

bond
bond market
budget constraint
budget line
common currency
currency
currency union
goods market
household budget constraint in nominal terms
household budget constraint in real terms
labor market
market-clearing conditions
maturity
medium of exchange
money
nominal

nominal rental price
nominal saving
nominal wage rate
price level
principal (of bond)
profit
real rental price
real saving
real terms
real wage rate
rental market
risk premium
sources of funds
stock market
uses of funds

# Questions and Problems

A. Review questions

1. Why would households be interested only in the real values of consumption, income, and assets such as bonds? Think about how households would feel if the nominal values of consumption, income, and assets all doubled, and the price level, $P$, also doubled.

2. Distinguish clearly between a household's initial asset position and the change in that position. If a household has negative saving, is that household necessarily a borrower in the sense of having a negative position in bonds?

3. Derive the budget line shown in Figure 6.2. What does this line show?

4. How does an increase in the real wage rate, $w/P$, affect the quantity of labor demanded, $L^d$? Where does the assumption of diminishing marginal product of labor (MPL) come in?

5. How does an increase in the real rental price, $R/P$, affect the quantity of capital services demanded, $K^d$? Where does the assumption of diminishing marginal product of capital (MPK) come in?

B. Problems for discussion

6. Discount bonds

The bonds in our model have a maturity close to zero; they just pay interest in accordance with the current interest rate, $i$, as a flow over time. We could consider, instead, a discount bond, such as a U.S. Treasury Bill. This type of asset has no explicit interest payments (called *coupons*) but pays a principal of, say, $1000 at a fixed date in the future. A Bill with one-year maturity pays off one year from the issue date, and similarly for three-month or six-month Bills. Let $P^B$ be the price of a discount bond with one-year maturity and principal of $1000.

  a. Is $P^B$ greater than or less than $1000?
  b. What is the one-year interest rate on these discount bonds?
  c. If $P^B$ rises, what happens to the interest rate on these bonds?
  d. Suppose that, instead of paying $1000 in one year, the bond pays $1000 in two years. What is the interest rate per year on this two-year discount bond?

7. Term structure of interest rates

Suppose that the economy has discount bonds (discussed in question 6) with one- and two-year maturities. Let $i_t^1$ be the interest rate on a one-year bond issued at the start of year $t$, and $i_{t+1}^1$ the interest rate on a one-year bond issued at the start of year $t+1$. Let $i_t^2$ be the interest rate (per year) on a two-year bond issued at the start of year $t$. We can think of $i_t^1$ as the current short-term interest rate and $i_t^2$ as the current long-term interest rate.

  a. Assume that, at the start of year $t$, everyone knows not only $i_t^1$ and $i_t^2$, but also the next year's one-year rate, $i_{t+1}^1$. What must be the relation of $i_t^2$ to $i_t^1$ and $i_{t+1}^1$? Explain the answer by considering the incentives of lenders and borrowers.
  b. If $i_{t+1}^1 > i_t^1$, what is the relation between $i_t^2$, the long-term interest rate, and $i_t^1$, the short-term interest rate? The answer is an important result about the term structure of interest rates.

c. How would the results change if we assumed, more realistically, that there was uncertainty in year $t$ about the future one-year interest rate, $i_{t+1}^1$?

8. Financial intermediaries

Consider a financial intermediary, such as a bank, that participates in the credit market. This intermediary borrows from some households and lends to others. (The loan from a customer to a bank often takes the form of a deposit account.)

a. Does the existence of intermediaries affect the result that the aggregate amount of loans is zero?
b. What interest rates would the intermediary charge to its borrowers and pay to its lenders? Why must there be some spread between these two rates?
c. Can you provide some reasons to explain why intermediaries might be useful?

# Appendix

## Output Equals Real Factor Incomes and Profit Equals Zero

We show here that, when capital and labor are each paid their marginal products, the total of real income payments to capital and labor equals the output or real GDP. Hence, profit is zero. These results are shown most easily using calculus.

Start with the production function for real GDP, $Y$:

$$(3.1) \qquad Y = A \cdot F(K, L)$$

In Chapter 3, we assumed that the production function satisfied constant returns to scale in capital and labor, $K$ and $L$. Therefore, if we multiply $K$ and $L$ each by $1/L$, we also multiply $Y$ by $1/L$:

$$Y/L = A \cdot F(K/L, 1)$$

Thus, output per unit of labor, $Y/L$, depends only on capital per unit of labor, $K/L$. If we multiply through each side of the equation by $L$, we get another way to write the production function:

$$(6.19) \qquad Y = AL \cdot F(K/L, 1)$$

We can use calculus to calculate the MPK from equation (6.19). The MPK is the derivative of $Y$ with respect to $K$, while holding fixed $A$ and $L$:

$$MPK = AL \cdot F_1 \cdot (1/L)$$

where $F_1$ is the derivative of the function $F$ with respect to its first argument, $K/L$. We get the last term, $1/L$, from the chain rule for differentiation. That is, $1/L$ is the derivative of $K/L$ with respect to $K$, while holding fixed $L$. If we cancel out $L$ and $(1/L)$, we get

$$(6.20) \qquad MPK = AF_1$$

The MPL is the derivative of $Y$ with respect to $L$, while holding fixed $A$ and $K$. Since $L$ appears in two places on the right-hand side of equation (6.19), we have to calculate the derivative with respect to $L$ of the product of two terms, $AL$ and $F(K/L, 1)$. The first part of the answer is the derivative of the first term, $A$, multiplied by the second term, $F(K/L, 1)$. The second part is the first term, $AL$, multiplied by the derivative of the second term. This derivative is $F_1 \cdot (-K/L^2)$, where $F_1$ is again the derivative of the function $F$ with respect to its first argument, $K/L$. The term $-K/L^2$ comes from the chain rule for differentiation. That is, $-K/L^2$ is the derivative of $K/L$ with respect to $L$, while holding fixed $K$. Putting the results together, we get

$$MPL = A \cdot F(K/L, 1) + A\cancel{L} \cdot F_1 \cdot (-K/L^2)$$

(6.21)
$$MPL = A \cdot F(K/L, 1) - A \cdot (K/L) \cdot F_1$$

If the factor inputs are each paid their marginal products, so that $w/P = MPL$ and $R/P = MPK$, we can use equations (6.20) and (6.21) to calculate the total payments to labor and capital:

$$
\begin{aligned}
(w/P) \cdot L + (R/P) \cdot K &= MPL \cdot L + MPK \cdot K \\
&= [A \cdot F(K/L, 1) - A \cdot (K/L) \cdot F_1] \cdot L + (AF_1) \cdot K \\
&= AL \cdot F(K/L, 1) - \cancel{AK \cdot F_1} + \cancel{AK \cdot F_1} \\
&= AL \cdot F(K/L, 1)
\end{aligned}
$$

Equation (6.19) tells us that the last term equals real GDP $Y$, which equals $A \cdot F(K, L)$. Therefore, we have shown:

(6.22)
$$(w/P) \cdot L + (R/P) \cdot K = A \cdot F(K, L)$$

Thus, the total real payments to labor and capital, $(w/P) \cdot L + (R/P) \cdot K$, equal real GDP, $A \cdot F(K, L)$.[8]

Recall that real profit is given by

(6.17)
$$\Pi/P = A \cdot F(K, L) - (w/P) \cdot L - (R/P) \cdot K$$

Therefore, the result in equation (6.22) proves that $\Pi/P$ is zero in equilibrium, as claimed in the text.

---

[8] This result is called Euler's Theorem.

# C h a p t e r 7

## Consumption, Saving, and Investment

The previous chapter introduced the four markets in our model of the macro economy—goods, labor, capital services, and bonds. We related household income to the prices and quantities in the four markets. We began the construction of the model's microeconomic foundations by considering how households, as managers of family businesses, determined their demands for labor and capital services. Then we investigated the clearing of the markets for labor and capital services. For given values of labor, $L$, and capital, $K$, these market-clearing conditions determined the real wage rate, $w/P$, the real rental price of capital, $R/P$, and the interest rate, $i$.

In this chapter, we extend our microeconomic analysis of households to the choices of consumption and saving. Then we will use these results to determine economy-wide levels of consumption, saving, and investment. These results will form the basis for an equilibrium business-cycle model, which we will use in Chapters 8 and 9 to analyze macroeconomic fluctuations.

## Consumption and Saving

In this section, we study an individual household's choice of consumption, $C$. In making this decision, the household also determines how much to save.

Start with the household budget constraint from equation (6.12) of Chapter 6:

(6.12) $$C + (1/P) \cdot \Delta B + \Delta K = \Pi/P + (w/P) \cdot L + i \cdot (B/P + K)$$

We showed in Chapter 6 that real profit, $\Pi/P$, equaled zero when the markets for labor and capital services cleared. Therefore, we can set $\Pi/P = 0$ to get a simplified form of the household budget constraint:

(7.1) $$C + (1/P) \cdot \Delta B + \Delta K = (w/P) \cdot L + i \cdot (B/P + K)$$

$$consumption + real\ saving = real\ income$$

Recall that the expression $(1/P) \cdot \Delta B + \Delta K$ represents real saving—the change in the real value of assets held as bonds, $B$, and ownership of capital, $K$. Real income consists of real wage income, $(w/P) \cdot L$, plus real asset income, $i \cdot (B/P + K)$.

We want to explore how the household chooses consumption and real saving. In making these choices, we assume, as in Chapter 6, that an individual household takes as given the real wage rate, $w/P$. This assumption is standard for a competitive market—the individual household is too small to have a noticeable effect on $w/P$. Now we go further by assuming that an individual household takes the interest rate, $i$, as given. This assumption is also standard for a competitive market—the individual household is too small to have a noticeable effect on $i$. Notice that, in this setup, each household can lend or borrow as much as it wants at the going interest rate. A household would borrow by issuing a bond that pays the interest rate, $i$. A household would lend by buying a bond that pays the interest rate, $i$.

Suppose that a household has given labor, $L$, and real assets, $(B/P + K)$. Then, since the real wage rate, $w/P$, and the interest rate, $i$, are given by the market to an individual household, the total of household real income, $(w/P) \cdot L + i \cdot (B/P + K)$, is determined on the right-hand side of equation (7.1).

With a given real income, the household's only choice is how to divide this income between consumption, $C$, and real saving, $(1/P) \cdot \Delta B + \Delta K$. That is, the household budget constraint in equation (7.1) constrains the total of consumption and real saving on the left-hand side. A household would like to have more of both, but this desire cannot be met for a given real income.

Figure 7.1 (similar to Figure 6.2 in Chapter 6) shows how the budget constraint from equation (7.1) allows the household to choose between consumption, C, and real saving,

---

**Figure    7 . 1** | The Household Budget Constraint

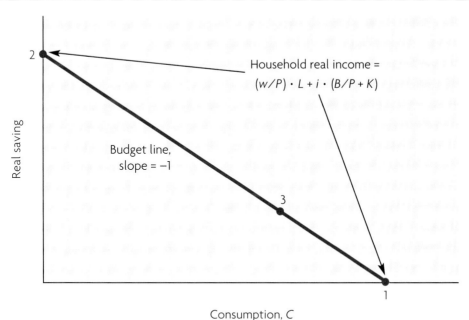

Households have a given total of real income, $(w/P) \cdot L + i \cdot (B/P + K)$. This total must be divided between consumption, $C$, and real saving, $(1/P) \cdot \Delta B + \Delta K$. Thus, if real saving is zero, $C$ equals the total of real income along the horizontal axis at point 1. If $C$ is zero, real saving equals the total of real income along the vertical axis at point 2. The budget constraint in equation (7.1) allows the household to select any combination of consumption and real saving along the budget line, shown in red, such as point 3. The budget line has a slope of $-1$. Along this line, one unit less of consumption corresponds to one unit more of real saving.

$(1/P) \cdot \Delta B + \Delta K$. One option is to set real saving to zero, so that $C$ equals the total real income. This choice corresponds to point 1, shown on the horizontal axis where $C$ equals total real income. Another option is to set $C$ to zero, so that real saving equals total real income. This choice corresponds to point 2, shown on the vertical axis where real saving equals total real income. More typically, the household would opt for an intermediate position, where $C$ and real saving are both greater than zero. For example, the household could pick point 3 in the graph.

The full range of possibilities is shown by the downward-sloping red budget line in Figure 7.1. The budget constraint in equation (7.1) tells us that, along a budget line, each increase in $C$ by one unit of goods corresponds to a decrease in real saving by one unit. Hence, the slope of a budget line is $-1$. The important point is that if the household wants one unit more of consumption, it must give up one unit of real saving.

So far, we have considered only the choice between consumption and saving at a point in time. But the reason for saving is to raise future assets, which will allow for higher consumption in the future. Thus, the essence of the household's choice between today's consumption and today's saving is the choice between today's consumption and tomorrow's consumption. By today and tomorrow, we mean that today's consumption has to be considered as part of a long-term plan—perhaps a lifetime plan, or even a longer one that considers the well-being of one's children. The key idea is that, to understand the choice between consumption and saving, we have to study the household's choices of consumption at different points in time.

The household budget constraint, equation (7.1), applies at every point in time. The link between today's budget constraint and tomorrow's budget constraint comes from the effect of today's real saving, $(1/P) \cdot \Delta B + \Delta K$, on tomorrow's real assets, $B/P + K$. We can go a long way in exploring this linkage by considering just two periods. To be concrete, think of the first period as the current year and the second period as the following year. Once we understand this two-period framework, we can readily extend the model to determine consumption and saving over many periods.

## Consumption Over Two Years

For the current year, year 1, we can write the budget constraint from equation (7.1) as

(7.2) $$C_1 + (B_1/P + K_1) - (B_0/P + K_0) = (w/P)_1 \cdot L + i_0 \cdot (B_0/P + K_0)$$

*consumption in year 1 + real saving in year 1 = real income in year 1*

On the left-hand side, $C_1$ is year 1's consumption. The real assets $B_1/P$ and $K_1$ are the amounts held at the end of year 1. The real assets $B_0/P$ and $K_0$ are the amounts held at the end of the previous year, year 0, and therefore also the amounts held at the *beginning* of year 1. Thus, $(B_1/P + K_1) - (B_0/P + K_0)$ is the change in real assets—or real saving—in year 1.

On the right-hand side of equation (7.2), the real wage rate for year 1 is $(w/P)_1$, and the real wage income for the year is $(w/P)_1 \cdot L$. Since we assume that labor, $L$, is fixed over time, we do not include a year subscript. The interest rate for assets held at the end of year 0 is $i_0$. Thus, the real asset income for year 1 is $i_0 \cdot (B_0/P + K_0)$. When we add real wage income to real asset income, we get total real income for year 1 on the right-hand side.

The budget constraint in equation (7.2) is for year 1. The same form of budget constraint applies to year 2:

(7.3) $$C_2 + (B_2/P + K_2) - (B_1/P + K_1) = (w/P)_2 \cdot L + i_1 \cdot (B_1/P + K_1)$$

*consumption in year 2 + real saving in year 2 = real income in year 2*

Our next task is to combine the budget constraints in equations (7.2) and (7.3) to describe a household's choice between consuming this year, $C_1$, and next year, $C_2$. Notice that both budget constraints include the assets held at the end of year 1, $B_1/P + K_1$. We can use equation (7.2) to solve out for this term by moving $C_1$ and $B_0/P + K_0$ from the left-hand side to the right-hand side and rearranging terms to get

(7.4) $\qquad B_1/P + K_1 = B_0/P + K_0 + i_0 \cdot (B_0/P + K_0) + (w/P)_1 \cdot L - C_1$

$$\underset{\substack{year\,1}}{real\,assets\,end} = \underset{\substack{end\,year\,0}}{real\,assets} + \underset{\substack{year\,1}}{real\,income} - \underset{\substack{year\,1}}{consumption}$$

Figure 7.2 shows this relation visually. The red bin has the real assets at the end of year 0, $B_0/P + K_0$, which is the first term on the right-hand side of equation (7.4). Add to this amount the blue bin, which contains the real income in year 1,

**F i g u r e   7 . 2** | Change in Real Assets in Year 1

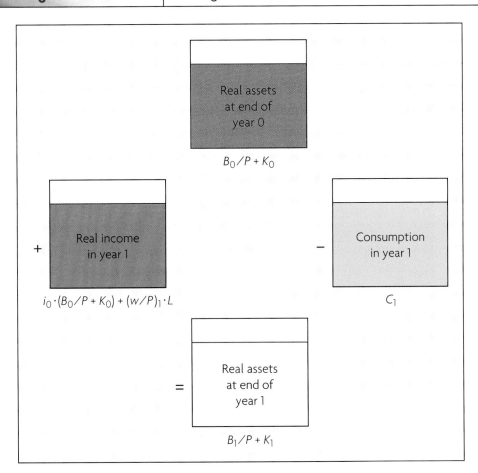

The red bin has the real assets at the end of year 0, $B_0/P + K_0$, the first term on the right-hand side of equation (7.4). The real income for year 1, $i_0 \cdot (B_0/P + K_0) + (w/P)_1 \cdot L$ in the blue bin, corresponds to the second term on the right-hand side of equation (7.4) and adds to the red bin. The consumption for year 1, $C_1$ in the green bin, corresponds to the third term on the right-hand side of equation (7.4) and subtracts from the red bin. The final result is the real assets at the end of year 1, $B_1/P + K_1$ in the yellow bin. This amount is the left-hand side of equation (7.4).

$i_0 \cdot (B_0/P + K_0) + (w/P)_1 \cdot L$. This income is the second term on the right-hand side of equation (7.4). Then subtract the green bin, which contains consumption in year 1, $C_1$, the final term on the right-hand side. We end up with the yellow bin, which contains the real assets at the end of year 1, $B_1/P + K_1$, the term on the left-hand side of equation (7.4).

The same analysis applies to year 2. The analog to equation (7.4) is

(7.5)
$$B_2/P + K_2 = B_1/P + K_1 + i_1 \cdot (B_1/P + K_1) + (w/P)_2 \cdot L - C_2$$

$$\underset{year\ 2}{real\ assets\ end} = \underset{end\ year\ 1}{real\ assets} + \underset{year\ 2}{real\ income} - \underset{year\ 2}{consumption}$$

Figure 7.3, similar to Figure 7.2, shows this relationship visually.

---

**F i g u r e   7 . 3** | Change in Real Assets in Year 2

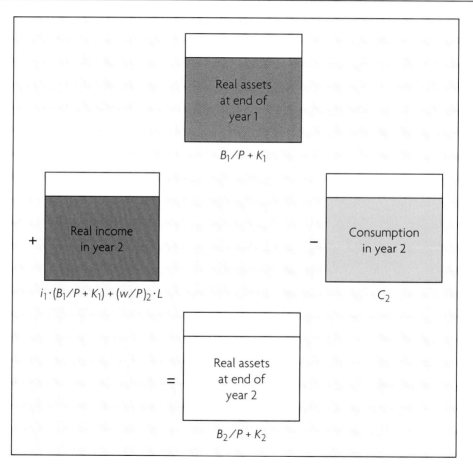

The red bin has the real assets at the end of year 1, $B_1/P + K_1$, the first term on the right-hand side of equation (7.5). The real income for year 2, $i_1 \cdot (B_1/P + K_1) + (w/P)_2 \cdot L$ in the blue bin, corresponds to the second term on the right-hand side of equation (7.5) and adds to the red bin. The consumption for year 2, $C_2$ in the green bin, corresponds to the third term on the right-hand side of equation (7.5) and subtracts from the red bin. The final result is the real assets at the end of year 2, $B_2/P + K_2$ in the yellow bin. This amount is the left-hand side of equation (7.5).

Going back to equation (7.4), we can combine the two terms involving $B_0/P + K_0$ on the right-hand side to get

(7.6) $$B_1/P + K_1 = (1 + i_0) \cdot (B_0/P + K_0) + (w/P)_1 \cdot L - C_1$$

Notice, on the right-hand side, that we multiply $B_0/P + K_0$ by the term $1 + i_0$. The "1" represents the principal of year 0's assets, and the "$i_0$" represents the interest paid on these assets.

We see on the right-hand side of equation (7.6) that, if the household lowers year 1's consumption, $C_1$, by one unit, the real assets held at the end of year 1, $B_1/P + K_1$, rise by one unit on the left-hand side. Visually, in Figure 7.2, suppose that we take one unit of goods out of the green $C_1$ bin and do not change the red and blue bins. Since the green bin enters with a minus sign, taking one unit out of it means that there will be one unit more left in the yellow bin, which has $B_1/P + K_1$.

If we combine the two terms involving $B_1/P + K_1$ on the right-hand side of the second year's budget constraint in equation (7.5), we get

(7.7) $$B_2/P + K_2 = (1 + i_1) \cdot (B_1/P + K_1) + (w/P)_2 \cdot L - C_2$$

This expression takes the same form as equation (7.6), except that everything is updated by one year. Notice, on the right-hand side, that a higher value of $B_1/P + K_1$, the assets held at the end of year 1, allows the household to raise year 2's consumption, $C_2$, also on the right-hand side. Visually, in Figure 7.3, an increase in $B_1/P + K_1$ by one unit means that we add one unit to the red bin (which has the assets at the end of year 1) and $i_1$ units to the blue bin (which includes the interest income on the assets from the end of year 1). Suppose that we do not change the yellow bin, which has the assets held at the end of year 2, $B_2/P + K_2$. In this case, we must have $1 + i_1$ units more in the green bin, which contains $C_2$. Note that $C_2$ can be increased by $1 + i_1$ units without having to change the assets held at the end of year 2, $B_2/P + K_2$.

We now have the building blocks to establish the link between consuming this year, $C_1$, and next year, $C_2$. Recall from equation (7.6) and Figure 7.2 that a reduction in $C_1$ by one unit allows the household to increase assets at the end of year 1, $B_1/P + K_1$, by one unit. We also have from equation (7.7) and Figure 7.3 that an increase in $B_1/P + K_1$ by one unit can be used to raise $C_2$ by $1 + i_1$ units. Thus, if $C_1$ decreases by one unit, the household can increase $C_2$ by $1 + i_1$ units. Moreover, the household can make this switch between $C_1$ and $C_2$ without changing $B_2/P + K_2$, the real assets carried over to year 3 (and shown as the yellow bin in Figure 7.3). Thus, the household can change the timing of consumption between this year and next year, $C_1$ and $C_2$, without shortchanging or enriching the future—that is, without altering the assets available for year 3 and beyond.

To construct the full two-year budget constraint algebraically, first replace $B_1/P + K_1$ on the right-hand side of equation (7.7) by the right-hand side of equation (7.6) to get

$$B_2/P + K_2 = (1 + i_1) \cdot [(1 + i_0) \cdot (B_0/P + K_0) + (w/P)_1 \cdot L - C_1] + (w/P)_2 \cdot L - C_2$$

If we multiply the terms inside the large brackets by $1 + i_1$, we get

(7.8) $$B_2/P + K_2 = (1 + i_1) \cdot (1 + i_0) \cdot (B_0/P + K_0) + (1 + i_1) \cdot (w/P)_1 \cdot L \\ - (1 + i_1) \cdot C_1 + (w/P)_2 \cdot L - C_2$$

Notice the effects of the interest-rate terms on the right-hand side of equation (7.8). The first term includes the assets from the end of year 0, $B_0/P + K_0$, which pay the return $i_0 \cdot (B_0/P + K_0)$ in year 1. If the household holds these assets, it ends up with $(1 + i_0) \cdot (B_0/P + K_0)$ in assets at the end of year 1. Hence, each unit of assets from the end of year 0 is multiplied by $1 + i_0$ to get assets at the end of year 1.

Equivalently, in Figure 7.2, if $B_0/P + K_0$ rises by one unit, the red bin rises by one unit and the blue bin rises by $i_0$ units. Therefore, if the green bin, which contains $C_1$, does not change, the yellow bin increases by $1 + i_0$ units.

The same calculation applies for year 2. Each unit of assets held at the end of year 1 is multiplied by $1 + i_1$ to get assets at the end of year 2. In Figure 7.3, if $B_1/P + K_1$ rises by one unit, the red bin rises by one unit and the blue bin rises by $i_1$ units. Therefore, if the green bin, which contains $C_2$, does not change, the yellow bin increases by $1 + i_1$ units. If we put this result together with the result for year 1, we find that each unit of assets held for two periods—from the end of year 0 to the end of year 2—ends up as $(1 + i_1) \cdot (1 + i_0)$ units of assets. This interest-rate term is the one that multiplies $B_0/P + K_0$ on the right-hand side of equation (7.8).

Similarly, the household could save its wage income in year 1, $(w/P)_1 \cdot L$, and thereby have more assets at the end of year 1. (In Figure 7.2, the blue and yellow bins each rise by one unit.) Each unit of these assets becomes $1 + i_1$ units at the end of year 2. (In Figure 7.3, the red bin rises by one unit, the blue bin rises by $i_1$ units, and the yellow bin increases by $1 + i_1$ units.) Therefore, $(w/P)_1 \cdot L$ is multiplied by $1 + i_1$ in equation (7.8). In contrast, the wage income $(w/P)_2 \cdot L$ appears by itself because the household receives this income too late to get any asset returns in year 2.

To think about the consumption terms, notice in equation (7.6) that year 1's consumption, $C_1$, enters in the same way as year 1's real wage income, $(w/P)_1 \cdot L$, but with a minus sign.[1] The reason is that real saving is the difference between real income and consumption. We therefore find in equation (7.8) that $C_1$, like $(w/P)_1 \cdot L$, is multiplied by $1 + i_1$. Similarly, year 2's consumption, $C_2$, enters into equation (7.7) in the same way as year 2's real wage income, $(w/P)_2 \cdot L$, except for the sign.[2] Therefore, $C_2$, like $(w/P)_2 \cdot L$, appears in equation (7.8) without any interest-rate terms.

If we divide through everything in equation (7.8) by $1 + i_1$ and rearrange the terms to put the ones involving consumption on the left-hand side, we get

---

Key equation (two-year household budget constraint):

(7.9)
$$C_1 + C_2/(1 + i_1) = (1 + i_0) \cdot (B_0/P + K_0) + (w/P)_1 \cdot L$$
$$+ (w/P)_2 \cdot L/(1 + i_1) - (B_2/P + K_2)/(1 + i_1)$$

---

We get this result by using the budget constraints for years 1 and 2, as given in equations (7.2) and (7.3). Therefore, we call equation (7.9) the **two-year budget constraint**.

Observe how the wage incomes, $(w/P)_1 \cdot L$ and $(w/P)_2 \cdot L$, enter on the right-hand side of equation (7.9). We do not add the two together but rather divide $(w/P)_2 \cdot L$ by $1 + i_1$ before combining it with $(w/P)_1 \cdot L$. Similarly, on the left-hand side, we make the same adjustment to $C_2$ before combining it with $C_1$. To understand these adjustments, we have to explore the concept of **present value**.

---

[1] Equivalently, in Figure 7.2, an increase by one unit in the blue bin, which contains $(w/P)_1 \cdot L$, has the same effect as a decrease by one unit in the green bin, which contains $C_1$.

[2] Equivalently, in Figure 7.3, an increase by one unit in the blue bin, which contains $(w/P)_2 \cdot L$, has the same effect as a decrease by one unit in the green bin, which contains $C_2$.

**Present value**    If the interest rate, $i_1$, is greater than zero, one dollar held as assets in year 1 becomes more than one dollar in year 2. Therefore, $1 received or spent in year 1 is equivalent to more than $1 in year 2. Or, viewed in reverse, dollars received or spent in year 2 must be **discounted** to make them comparable to dollars in year 1. The general idea of discounting is that dollars received later are not worth as much as dollars received earlier. Here we apply the general notion of discounting to a comparison of year 1 with year 2.

To be concrete, suppose that the interest rate is $i_1 = 5\%$ per year. Assume that a household has $100 of income in year 1 but plans to spend this income a year later, in year 2. Then the household can buy $100 of bonds at the start of year 1 and have $105 at the start of year 2. Hence, $100 received in year 1 is worth as much as $105 received in year 2. Equivalently, the $105 from year 2 has to be discounted to get the income needed in year 1 to generate $105 in year 2. We find this amount by solving the equation:

$$\textit{income needed in year}\ 1 \times (1 + 5\%) = \$105$$

The required amount of income in year 1 is $105/1.05 = $100.

More generally, if we substitute $i_1$ for 5%, the income for year 2 has to be divided by $1 + i_1$ to find the equivalent amount for year 1. Hence, if the wage income received in year 2 is $(w/P)_2 \cdot L$, the present value (or year 1 value) of this income is $(w/P)_2 \cdot L/(1 + i_1)$. The term $1 + i_1$ is an example of what economists call a **discount factor**. When we discount by this factor—that is, divide by $1 + i_1$—we determine the present value of year 2's income. If we went beyond year 2, we would have a different discount factor for each year.

The two-year budget constraint in equation (7.9) shows that we express year 2's wage income as a present value, $(w/P)_2 \cdot L/(1 + i_1)$, before combining it with year 1's income, $(w/P)_1 \cdot L$. The sum, $(w/P)_1 \cdot L + (w/P)_2 \cdot L/(1 + i_1)$, is the total present value of wage income for years 1 and 2. Similarly, we express year 2's consumption as the present value $C_2/(1 + i_1)$ before combining it with year 1's consumption, $C_1$. The sum, $C_1 + C_2/(1 + i_1)$, is the total present value of consumption for years 1 and 2.

Our next task is to analyze a household's choices of how much to consume in year 1 and year 2. We know that these choices have to respect the two-year budget constraint, given in equation (7.9). But the household still has a lot of leeway in deciding among the feasible combinations of $C_1$ and $C_2$. We have to figure out which combination the household will prefer among those that satisfy the two-year budget constraint.

**Choosing consumption: income effects**    To understand choices of consumption, we have to bring in *household preferences* about consuming at different points in time. By preferences, we mean a ranking of time paths of consumption in terms of the satisfaction that the household gets. Economists use the term **utility** as a synonym for satisfaction or happiness.[3] Our assumption is that the household chooses the time path of consumption—in this case, $C_1$ and $C_2$—to maximize utility, subject to the budget constraint in equation (7.9).

We assume that, other things the same, utility increases if $C_1$ or $C_2$ (or consumption in any other year) rises. We assume further that a household likes to consume at similar levels at different points in time, rather than consuming at high levels some of the time and at low levels other times. For example, a household prefers having $C_1$ and $C_2$ both equal to 100, rather than having $C_1$ equal to 0 and $C_2$ equal to 200. These preferences motivate a household to *smooth consumption* even when income is irregular. By "smooth," we mean that the planned levels of consumption chosen for different years, such as $C_1$ and $C_2$, tend to be close to each other, rather than varying greatly from one year to the next.

---

[3] The term **utility function** is used to express the relation between the utility obtained and the time path of consumption—in this case, the values of $C_1$ and $C_2$.

Consider some intuitive examples of consumption smoothing. Suppose that a person gets an unexpected windfall of income, perhaps from winning the lottery or receiving a surprise check in the mail. The usual response is to spread the extra money over consumption at various dates, rather than spending it all at once. Similarly, because people anticipate that their incomes will go down when they retire, they tend to save in advance to avoid sharply lower consumption during retirement.

To see how the household chooses $C_1$ and $C_2$, return to the two-year budget constraint:

(7.9)
$$C_1 + C_2/(1 + i_1) = (1 + i_0) \cdot (B_0/P + K_0) + (w/P)_1 \cdot L$$
$$+ (w/P)_2 \cdot L/(1 + i_1) - (B_2/P + K_2)/(1 + i_1)$$

$p.v.$ of consumption = value of initial assets
$\qquad\qquad$ + $p.v.$ of wage incomes − $p.v.$ of assets end year 2

where we use $p.v.$ as an abbreviation for present value. The first term on the right-hand side, $(1 + i_0) \cdot (B_0/P + K_0)$, is the value in year 1 of initial assets. This term adds to the present value of wage incomes received in years 1 and 2, $(w/P)_1 \cdot L + (w/P)_2 \cdot L/(1 + i_1)$. We shall find it convenient to combine these two terms into a single measure, $V$, of the present value of the household's sources of funds received through year 2. Thus, we define $V$ by

(7.10)
$$V = (1 + i_0) \cdot (B_0/P + K_0) + (w/P)_1 \cdot L + (w/P)_2 \cdot L/(1 + i_1)$$

$p.v.$ of sources of funds = value of initial assets + $p.v.$ of wage incomes

If we substitute this definition of $V$ into equation (7.9), we get

(7.11)
$$C_1 + C_2/(1 + i_1) = V - (B_2/P + K_2)/(1 + i_1)$$

$p.v.$ of consumption = $p.v.$ of sources of funds − $p.v.$ of assets end year 2

The last term on the right-hand side of equation (7.11), $(B_2/P + K_2)/(1 + i_1)$, is the present value of the real assets held at the end of year 2. These assets will help to pay for consumption in years 3 and later. We assume, for now, that this term is fixed. That is, we analyze the choices of $C_1$ and $C_2$ while holding constant the assets that a household provides for year 3 and beyond. This simplifying device allows us to carry out a two-period analysis, where we study just the choices of $C_1$ and $C_2$.

Suppose that $V$, the present value of the sources of funds, increases due to a rise in initial assets, $(B_0/P + K_0)$, or wage incomes, $(w/P)_1 \cdot L$ and $(w/P)_2 \cdot L$. Since we are holding fixed the term $(B_2/P + K_2)/(1 + i_1)$, equation (7.11) tells us that the total present value of consumption, $C_1 + C_2/(1 + i_1)$, must rise by the same amount as $V$. Since households like to consume at similar levels in the two years, we predict that $C_1$ and $C_2$ will rise by similar amounts. These responses of consumption to increases in initial assets or wage incomes are called **income effects**. An increase in $V$, the present value of the sources of funds, leads to higher consumption in each year, $C_1$ and $C_2$.

### Choosing consumption: the intertemporal-substitution effect
The income effects that we just studied tell us about the overall level of consumption—for example, the responses of $C_1$ and $C_2$ to a change in initial assets and wage incomes. The other major decision is how much to consume in one year compared to the other year. We have already assumed that households like to have similar levels of $C_1$ and $C_2$. However, this

preference is not absolute. Households would be willing to deviate from equal consumption levels if there were an economic incentive to deviate. The interest rate, $i_1$, provides this incentive.

Consider again the two-year budget constraint:

(7.11)     $C_1 + C_2/(1 + i_1) = V - (B_2/P + K_2)/(1 + i_1)$

*p.v. of consumption = p.v. of sources of funds − p.v. of assets end year 2*

The left-hand side has the present value of consumption, $C_1 + C_2/(1 + i_1)$. This expression shows that $C_2$ is discounted by $1 + i_1$ before adding it to $C_1$. This discounting means that a unit of $C_2$ is effectively cheaper than a unit of $C_1$. The reason is that, if a household defers consumption from year 1 to year 2, it can hold more assets (or borrow less) at the end of year 1. Since each unit of assets becomes $1 + i_1$ units in year 2 (see equation [7.7]), one unit less of $C_1$ can be replaced by $1 + i_1$ units more of $C_2$.

As an example, suppose that you are considering taking a vacation this summer. If the interest rate is $i_1 = 5\%$, you might prefer to postpone the vacation until next summer. The reward is that you could spend 5% more and have a better vacation.

We can also use this example to see how the household responds to an increase in the interest rate. If the interest rate rises to $i_1 = 10\%$, the reward for waiting increases— now you could spend 10% more on the delayed vacation. Thus, our prediction is that the vacation is more likely to be postponed when the interest rate, $i_1$, rises. Hence, $C_1$, consumption of vacations in year 1, falls, and $C_2$, consumption of vacations in year 2, rises.

The general point is that an increase in the interest rate, $i_1$, lowers the cost of $C_2$ compared to $C_1$. That is, a higher $i_1$ provides a greater reward for deferring consumption. Therefore, the household responds to an increase in $i_1$ by lowering $C_1$ and raising $C_2$. Economists call this response an **intertemporal-substitution effect**. By "intertemporal," we mean that the effect refers to substitution *over time*. The household shifts consumption away from one point in time, such as year 1, and toward another point, such as year 2.[4] The By The Numbers box on the following page describes empirical estimates of the strength of the intertemporal-substitution effect in U.S. data.

Although we analyzed the intertemporal-substitution effect in terms of consumption in different years, we can view the results through a different lens to determine the responses of saving. That is, we can figure out the effects of the interest rate on the household's saving.

Return to the household budget constraint for year 1:

(7.2)     $C_1 + (B_1/P + K_1) - (B_0/P + K_0) = (w/P)_1 \cdot L + i_0 \cdot (B_0/P + K_0)$

*consumption in year 1 + real saving in year 1 = real income in year 1*

We know from the intertemporal-substitution effect that an increase in the interest rate, $i_1$, motivates the household to postpone consumption, so that this year's consumption, $C_1$, falls on the left-hand side. Since year 1's real income, $(w/P)_1 \cdot L + i_0 \cdot (B_0/P + K_0)$ on the right-hand side of equation (7.2), is given, the decline in $C_1$ must be matched by a rise in

---

[4] Economists usually assume that households prefer to consume earlier rather than later. In this case, the interest rate, $i_1$, has to be greater than zero—perhaps 2% per year—to motivate households to choose equal values of $C_1$ and $C_2$. If $i_1$ is greater than 2%, the household sets $C_1$ below $C_2$, whereas if $i_1$ is less than 2%, the household sets $C_1$ above $C_2$. The main point is still that an increase in $i_1$ reduces $C_1$ and raises $C_2$.

$$9038.0$$
$$18.860$$
$$7.7577$$
$$61.851$$

# By The Numbers

## Empirical evidence on intertemporal substitution of consumption

The intertemporal-substitution effect predicts that a higher interest rate motivates households to reduce current consumption compared to future consumption. A study by David Runkle (1991) isolated the effect of interest rates on consumption by examining food outlays for 1100 U.S. households from 1973 to 1982. (The data are from the *Panel Study of Income Dynamics*, or PSID, conducted at the University of Michigan.) Runkle found that an increase in the annual interest rate by one percentage point raises the typical family's growth rate of consumption by about one-half percentage point per year.

The isolation of intertemporal-substitution effects in aggregate consumption data has proven to be more difficult, as discussed by Robert Hall (1989). However, a study of U.S. non-durable consumption by Joon-Ho Hahm (1998) estimated that a rise in the annual interest rate by one percentage point increases the growth rate of aggregate consumption by around one-third percentage point per year. Thus, the intertemporal-substitution effect does apply to aggregate consumption data.

year 1's seal saving, $(B_1/P + K_1) - (B_0/P + K_0)$. That is, the intertemporal-substitution effect motivates the household to save more when the interest rate rises.

Our analysis of interest rates is incomplete because we have considered only the intertemporal-substitution effect. We have not yet considered whether a change in the interest rate also has an income effect.

**The income effect from a change in the interest rate**    We can understand the income effect from a change in the interest rate, $i_1$, by examining the household budget constraint for year 2:

(7.3)    $$C_2 + (B_2/P + K_2) - (B_1/P + K_1) = (w/P)_2 \cdot L + i_1 \cdot (B_1/P + K_1)$$

*consumption in year 2 + real saving in year 2 = real income in year 2*

We can see the income effect from $i_1$ in the yellow shaded term, $i_1 \cdot (B_1/P + K_1)$, which gives the income on assets in year 2. We can break this term down into its two parts, $i_1 \cdot (B_1/P)$ and $i_1 K_1$.

Consider first the part $i_1 \cdot (B_1/P)$, which is the interest income on bonds. This interest income is greater than zero for a holder of bonds (the lender), for whom $B_1/P$ is greater than zero. However, this term is less than zero for an issuer of bonds (the borrower), for whom $B_1/P$ is less than zero. For a holder of bonds, the income effect from an increase in $i_1$ is positive, because the interest income received on a given amount of bonds, $B_1/P$, is larger. For an issuer of bonds, the income effect from an increase in $i_1$ is negative, because the interest paid on a given amount of bonds, $B_1/P$, is larger. For the economy as a whole, lending and borrowing must balance—any outstanding bond has both a holder and an issuer. Therefore, for the average household, $B_1/P$ has to be zero. Hence, for the average household, the income effect from the term $i_1 \cdot (B_1/P)$ is zero.

Households also hold assets in the form of ownership of capital, and the $i_1 K_1$ part of the yellow shaded term in equation (7.3) represents the income received on these assets in year 2. For the economy as a whole, the capital stock, $K_1$, is, of course, greater than zero. Thus, in contrast to bonds, the average household's holding of claims on capital, $K_1$, is greater than zero. Therefore, when we consider the term $i_1 K_1$, the income effect from an increase in $i_1$ is positive.

To put the results together, in the aggregate, the income effect from an increase in $i_1$ consists of a zero effect from the term $i_1 \cdot (B_1/P)$ and a positive effect from the term $i_1 K_1$. Therefore, the full income effect from an increase in $i_1$ is positive.

**Combining income and substitution effects**   In many circumstances, an economic change will involve both income and substitution effects. Consider, for example, the effect of an increase in the interest rate, $i_1$, on year 1's consumption, $C_1$. The intertemporal-substitution effect motivates the household to reduce $C_1$. However, an increase in $i_1$ also has a positive income effect, which motivates the household to raise $C_1$. Therefore, the overall effect from an increase in $i_1$ on $C_1$ is ambiguous. Year 1's consumption, $C_1$, falls if the intertemporal-substitution effect dominates but rises if the income effect dominates. In the next section, we will use the *multiyear budget constraint* to assess the strength of the income effect. In some cases, this analysis allows us to determine whether the income effect is likely to be stronger or weaker than the substitution effect.

Figure 7.4 on the next page provides a visual summary of the intertemporal-substitution and income effects from a change in the interest rate, $i_1$. The upper part shows that the intertemporal-substitution effect predicts that an increase in $i_1$ will lower year 1's consumption, $C_1$, and, therefore, raise year 1's real saving, $(B_1/P + K_1) - (B_0/P + K_0)$. If $i_1$ falls, these intertemporal-substitution effects are in the opposite direction. The lower part shows that the income effects always offset the intertemporal-substitution effects. For example, if $i_1$ rises, the income effects predict that $C_1$ will rise and, hence, real saving, $(B_1/P + K_1) - (B_0/P + K_0)$, will fall.

### Consumption Over Many Years

We now extend the household budget constraint to include consumption over many years. We start with the two-year budget constraint:

(7.9)
$$C_1 + C_2/(1 + i_1) = (1 + i_0) \cdot (B_0/P + K_0) + (w/P)_1 \cdot L$$
$$+ (w/P)_2 \cdot L/(1 + i_1) - (B_2/P + K_2)/(1 + i_1)$$

*p.v. of consumption = value of initial assets + p.v. of wage incomes*
*− p.v. of assets end year 2*

We now relax our simplifying assumption that the household could not change the present value of assets held at the end of year 2—that is, the yellow shaded term, $(B_2/P + K_2)/(1 + i_1)$, in equation (7.9). These assets are, in fact, not fixed. A change in $(B_2/P + K_2)$ means that the household provides more or less assets for consumption in years 3 and beyond. To understand the choice of $(B_2/P + K_2)$, we have to consider consumption and income in future years. The Appendix describes in detail how to make this extension. Here we provide an intuitive analysis.

The left-hand side of equation (7.9) is the present value of consumption for years 1 and 2. When we consider many years, the left-hand side becomes the present value of consumption over these many years. The first term added is the present value of year 3's

rise by nearly one unit on the left-hand side. That is, the **propensity to save** in year 1 out of an extra unit of year 1's income is nearly one when the extra income is temporary. Saving goes up so much because additional assets are needed to provide for the planned increases in consumption in future years.

Consider, as a contrast, a permanent increase in wage income, where $(w/P)_1 \cdot L$, $(w/P)_2 \cdot L$, $(w/P)_3 \cdot L$, and so on each rise by one unit. An example would be a wage increase that an employee expects to be permanent. The multiyear budget constraint in equation (7.12) shows that it would be possible for the household to respond by increasing consumption by one unit in each year—in that case, for any $t = 1, 2, 3$, and so on, each rise in $C_t$ would match each rise in $(w/P)_t \cdot L$. Moreover, we predict that the household would respond roughly this way because this behavior is consistent with the desire to have similar levels of consumption each year. Thus, the prediction is that the propensity to consume out of an extra unit of year 1's income would be high—close to one—when the extra income is permanent.

For the response of saving, we can again look at year 1's budget constraint in equation (7.2). If $(w/P)_1 \cdot L$ rises by one unit on the right-hand side, and $C_1$ rises by roughly one unit on the left-hand side, year 1's real saving, $(B_1/P + K_1) - (B_0/P + K_0)$, must change by little or not at all. In other words, the propensity to save in year 1 out of an extra unit of year 1's income is small when the extra income is permanent. Saving does not change much because, in this case, the household does not need additional assets to provide for the planned increases in future consumption. These increases can be paid for by the higher future wage incomes: $(w/P)_2 \cdot L$, $(w/P)_3 \cdot L$, and so on.

Our findings about temporary and permanent changes of income correspond to Milton Friedman's famous concept of **permanent income**.[6] His idea was that consumption depends on a long-term average of incomes—which he called permanent income—rather than current income. If a change in income is temporary, permanent income and, hence, consumption change relatively little. Therefore, as in our analysis, the propensity to consume out of temporary income is small. The By The Numbers box on the following page discusses empirical evidence on the propensity to consume.

We can also assess the effects from changes in anticipated future incomes. The multiyear budget constraint is again

(7.12)     $C_1 + C_2/(1 + i_1) + C_3/[(1 + i_1) \cdot (1 + i_2)] + \cdots = (1 + i_0) \cdot (B_0/P + K_0)$

            $+ (w/P)_1 \cdot L + (w/P)_2 \cdot L/(1 + i_1) + (w/P)_3 \cdot L/[(1 + i_1) \cdot (1 + i_2)] + \cdots$

*overall present value of consumption = value of initial assets*

*+ overall present value of wage incomes*

Suppose, to begin, that real wage incomes, $(w/P)_t \cdot L$, for $t = 1, 2$, and so on, are all the same. Then, assume in year 1 that the household learns that it will be getting a permanent raise the following year. Hence, expected future wage incomes, $(w/P)_2 \cdot L$, $(w/P)_3 \cdot L$, and so on, all rise. Alternatively, the household might learn in year 1 that it would be receiving in the future an inheritance payment or an insurance settlement.

The household would react to higher expected future incomes by raising consumption by similar amounts in each year: $C_1$, $C_2$, and so on. In particular, year 1's consumption, $C_1$, increases even though no higher income has yet shown up.

---

[6] See Friedman (1957). Chapters 2 and 3.

9038.0
18.860
7.7577
61.851 | # By The Numbers

## Empirical evidence on the propensity to consume

Economists have found strong evidence that the propensity to consume out of permanent changes in income is much larger than that for temporary changes. Some of the clearest evidence comes from special circumstances in which people received windfalls of income, which were clearly temporary and at least partly unanticipated.

One example is the receipt by Israeli citizens of lump-sum, nonrecurring restitution payments from Germany in 1957–58 (see Mordechai Kreinin [1961] and Michael Landsberger [1970]). The payments were large and roughly equal to an average family's annual income. The typical family increased its consumption expenditure during the year of the windfall by about 20% of the amount received. However, consumption expenditure includes consumer durables, which last for many years and should be regarded partly as saving rather than consumption. Therefore, the true propensity to consume was less than 20%.

Another example is the payment in 1950 to U.S. World War II veterans of an unanticipated, one-time life insurance dividend of about $175, roughly 4% of an average family's annual income at the time. In this case, consumption expenditure rose by about 35% of the windfall (see Roger Bird and Ronald Bodkin [1965]). However, since consumption expenditure includes consumer durables, the true propensity to consume was less than 35%.

Broader studies of consumer behavior show that the propensity to consume out of permanent changes in income is large and not much different from unity. In contrast, the propensity to consume out of temporary income is about 20 to 30% (see Robert Hall [1989]). Although this response to temporary changes is greater than that predicted by our theory, the important point is that the response of consumption to permanent changes in income is much larger than that to temporary changes.

Consider a case where wage incomes starting in year 2—$(w/P)_2 \cdot L$, $(w/P)_3 \cdot L$, and so on—increase by one unit. Because these increases in wage incomes were anticipated in year 1, we predicted that $C_1$, $C_2$, $C_3$, and so on would rise by similar amounts. Therefore, although year 2 has higher wage income than year 1—$(w/P)_2 \cdot L$ is greater than $(w/P)_1 \cdot L$—we do not predict that the rise in wage income in year 2 will be matched by a rise in consumption. That is, we predict that $C_1$ and $C_2$ will be similar. We get this result because the anticipated increase in income from year 1 to year 2 was already reflected in a higher $C_1$. The important prediction is that the household's consumption will not respond to an increase in income when that increase was already expected. The By The Numbers box discusses empirical evidence on this proposition.

# Consumption, Saving, and Investment in Equilibrium

We will now use our analysis of a single household's choices of consumption and saving to determine the aggregate quantities of consumption and saving. This analysis will allow us to determine the aggregate quantity of investment. Once we finish this section, we will

9038.0
18.860
7.7577
61.851

# By The Numbers

## The response of consumption to anticipated income changes

In our model, the household's consumption would not respond to changes in income that were anticipated beforehand. To assess this prediction empirically, we have to isolate variations in income that households would have predicted in advance. The most convincing tests of this hypothesis involve responses of individual consumption in special circumstances where income variations are clearly predictable.

A study by Chang-Tai Hsieh (2003) examines the response of consumption by Alaskans to predictable payments from the Alaska Permanent Fund, which was created in 1976 as a device to distribute part of the state's oil royalties to Alaskan residents. These payments have been substantial; $1,964 per person ($7,856 for a family of four) in 2000. Since 1994, the payments have been made each October through a system of direct deposits to individuals' bank accounts. Hsieh's main finding is that individual consumption expenditure on a quarterly basis did not respond to the sizable income variations created by the large royalty payments in the fourth quarter of each year. Thus, as predicted, households smoothed their consumption over the year—effectively using their high fourth quarter income to pay for roughly the same amount of consumption in each quarter.

Empirical results are different for seemingly predictable variations in income that are smaller and, perhaps, less easy to forecast accurately. For example, Jonathan Parker (1999) found that household consumption reacted to increases in after-tax income associated with reaching the ceiling on income subject to the Social Security payroll tax. We discuss this tax in Chapter 13; for present purposes, the important point is that the tax for the main Social Security program applies only to wage earnings up to a maximum amount each year—in 2006, the ceiling was $94,200. Parker's estimate was that nondurable consumption expenditure rose by about 20 cents for each dollar of predictable increase in after-tax income. This result departs from our model if most individuals knew in advance that their wage incomes would rise enough later in the year so that they would not have to pay the Social Security payroll tax for the rest of the year.

Similarly, Nicholas Souleles (1999) found that household consumption responded to the receipt of refunds from the federal individual income tax. This result conflicts with our model if a substantial part of these tax refunds were anticipated. However, Souleles's estimated propensities to consume for nondurable consumption were not large—less than 10%.

Overall, the empirical evidence supports the model's prediction that households would react in advance to forecastable variations in income. The data are inconsistent with the proposition that consumption is invariant to all predictable income changes. However, the departures are not that large and seem to arise mainly in cases where the income involved is relatively minor.

have all the building blocks in place to study economic fluctuations. Our analysis of that topic begins in Chapter 8.

We have discussed how a household divides its real income between consumption and real saving. Now we will determine the aggregates of consumption and real saving. These quantities are the amounts that arise when the various markets clear. That is, as in Chapter 6, we go from microeconomic foundations—the behavior of individual households—to aggregate variables by using market-clearing conditions.

Consider again the household budget constraint at a point in time:

$$\text{(7.1)} \qquad C + (1/P) \cdot \Delta B + \Delta K = (w/P) \cdot L + i \cdot (B/P + K)$$

$$\textit{consumption} + \textit{real saving} = \textit{real income}$$

If we separate real income on assets, $i \cdot (B/P + K)$, into its two parts, $i \cdot (B/P)$ and $iK$, we get the revised budget constraint:

$$C + (1/P) \cdot \Delta B + \Delta K = (w/P) \cdot L + i \cdot (B/P) + iK$$

We know from Chapter 6 that the interest rate, $i$, is determined from

$$\text{(6.6)} \qquad i = (R/P - \delta)$$

$$\textit{rate of return on bonds} = \textit{rate of return on ownership of capital}$$

If we substitute $(R/P - \delta)$ for $i$ in the $iK$ term of the budget constraint, we get

$$C + (1/P) \cdot \Delta B + \Delta K = (w/P) \cdot L + i \cdot (B/P) + (R/P) \cdot K - \delta K$$

Since this equation applies for each household, it also applies when we add up across all the households. That is, the equation can be applied to the aggregate variables. However, we know for the aggregate of households that the total quantity of bonds, $B$, must be zero. That is, when the bond market clears, households in the aggregate hold a zero net quantity of bonds. The condition that $B = 0$ at every point in time also implies that the change in aggregate bond holdings, $\Delta B$, must always be zero. If we substitute $B = 0$ and $\Delta B = 0$ into the equation, we find that, in the aggregate, the household budget constraint becomes

$$C + \Delta K = (w/P) \cdot L + (R/P) \cdot K - \delta K$$

We know from Chapter 6 that, when the labor and rental markets clear, the total payments to factors—$(w/P) \cdot L$ for labor plus $(R/P) \cdot K$ for capital—equal real gross domestic product (real GDP), $Y$. (See the Appendix to Chapter 6.) If we substitute $Y$ for $(w/P) \cdot L + (R/P) \cdot K$ in the equation, we find that the aggregate household budget constraint becomes

---

Key equation (aggregate form of household budget constraint):

$$\text{(7.13)} \qquad C + \Delta K = Y - \delta K$$

$$\textit{consumption} + \textit{net investment} = \textit{real GDP} - \textit{depreciation}$$

$$= \textit{real net domestic product}$$

---

Recall that the real gross domestic product is determined from the production function by $Y = A \cdot F(K, L)$. Therefore, on the right-hand side of equation (7.13), the real net domestic product, $Y - \delta K$, is determined, for a given technology level, $A$, by the given values of

$K$ and $L$. Therefore, the left-hand side of the equation implies that the economy's net investment, $\Delta K$, is determined by households' choices of consumption, $C$. Given the real net domestic product, one unit more of consumption, $C$, means one unit less of net investment, $\Delta K$. In Chapter 8, we investigate how much households choose to consume, $C$, given that the interest rate, $i$, is determined from equation (6.6) to equal the rate of return on capital, $R/P - \delta$. This choice of $C$ determines $\Delta K$ from equation (7.13).

Notice that, when the bond market clears, net investment, $\Delta K$, equals economy-wide real saving. For an individual household, real saving equals $(1/P) \cdot \Delta B + \Delta K$—the change in the real value of assets held as bonds or capital. However, for the economy as a whole, $\Delta B$ equals zero, and real saving equals $\Delta K$.

## Summing Up

We extended the microeconomic foundations of our model from Chapter 6 to consider a household's choices of consumption and saving. The whole point of saving is to increase assets, which will allow for more consumption in the future. Therefore, the essence of the household's choice between today's consumption and today's saving is the choice between today's consumption and tomorrow's consumption.

Using this perspective, we analyzed consumption choices in terms of income effects and intertemporal-substitution effects. Higher initial assets, or higher current or future real wage incomes, raise consumption in all years through income effects. A higher interest rate today motivates the household to lower today's consumption compared to future consumption. Through this channel, a higher interest rate raises current saving. However, a higher interest rate also has a positive income effect, which leads to more consumption and less saving today. Therefore, the overall effect of the interest rate on today's saving is ambiguous.

We distinguished a permanent change in wage income from a temporary change. For a permanent change, the propensity to consume is high, and the propensity to save is low. In contrast, for a temporary change, the propensity to consume is low, and the propensity to save is high.

By aggregating the household budget constraint and using market-clearing conditions, we were able to determine economy-wide levels of consumption, saving, and investment. As we show in the next chapter, aggregate consumption can be derived by considering income and intertemporal-substitution effects. Net investment is then the difference between real net domestic product and consumption. If the quantities of capital, $K$, and labor, $L$, are given, the real net domestic product is determined. Hence, the model will determine the aggregates of consumption and net investment.

## Key Terms and Concepts

discount factor
discounted
finite horizon
income effects
infinite horizon
infinite-horizon budget constraint
intertemporal-substitution effect
life-cycle models
multiyear budget constraint

permanent income
planning horizon
present value
propensity to consume
propensity to save
two-year budget constraint
utility
utility function

# Questions and Problems

**A.** Review questions

1. Derive the two-year household budget constraint shown in equation (7.9). According to this constraint, if a household reduces this year's consumption, $C_1$, by one unit, how much would next year's consumption, $C_2$, rise (if nothing else changes in the equation)?

2. Show how taking a present value gives different weights to income and consumption in different years. Why is a unit of real income in the present more valuable than a unit of real income next year? Why is a unit of consumption next year cheaper than a unit this year?

3. What factors determine whether the propensity to consume out of an additional unit of income is less than or equal to one? Can the propensity be greater than one?

4. Discuss the effects on this year's consumption, $C_1$, from the following changes:

a. An increase in the interest rate, $i_1$
b. A permanent increase in real wage income, $(w/P) \cdot L$
c. An increase in current real wage income, $(w/P)_1 \cdot L$, but no change in future real wage incomes
d. An increase in future real wage income, $(w/P)_t \cdot L$, for $t = 2, 3$, and so on
e. A one-time windfall, which raises initial real assets, $(B_0/P + K_0)$

**B.** Problems for discussion

5. Permanent income

The idea of permanent income is that consumption depends on a long-run average of income, rather than current income. Operationally, we can define permanent income as the hypothetical, constant income that has the same present value as a household's sources of funds on the right-hand side of the multiyear budget constraint:

(7.12)  $C_1 + C_2/(1 + i_1) + C_3/[(1 + i_1) \cdot (1 + i_2)] + \cdots = (1 + i_0) \cdot (B_0/P + K_0)$

$\quad + (w/P)_1 \cdot L + (w/P)_2 \cdot L/(1 + i_1) + (w/P)_3 \cdot L/[(1 + i_1) \cdot (1 + i_2)] + \cdots$

a. Use equation (7.12) to get a formula for permanent income, when evaluated in year 1.
b. What is the propensity to consume out of permanent income?
c. If consumption, $C_t$, for $t = 1, 2$, and so on is constant over time, what is the value of permanent income?

6. Income effects

Consider again the household's multiyear budget constraint in equation (7.12). What are the income effects from the following:

a. An increase in the price level, $P$, for a household that has a positive value of initial nominal bonds, $B_0$. What if $B_0$ is zero or negative?
b. An increase by 1% per year in every year's interest rate, $i_t$. Assume here that $B_0 = 0$.

# Appendix

## The Multiyear Budget Constraint and the Planning Horizon

We show here how to calculate the household budget constraint over many years. When we considered two years, we got the budget constraint

$$(7.9) \qquad C_1 + C_2/(1+i_1) = (1+i_0) \cdot (B_0/P + K_0) + (w/P)_1 \cdot L + (w/P)_2 \cdot L/(1+i_1)$$
$$- (B_2/P + K_2)/(1+i_1)$$

To extend to many years, we will begin with year 3.

The real assets held at the end of year 2 are given by

$$(7.5) \qquad (B_2/P + K_2) = (1+i_1) \cdot (B_1/P + K_1) + (w/P)_2 \cdot L - C_2$$

The real assets held at the end of year 3 are given by an analogous formula, with everything updated by one year:

$$(7.14) \qquad (B_3/P + K_3) = (1+i_2) \cdot (B_2/P + K_2) + (w/P)_3 \cdot L - C_3$$

We found before that we could express the real assets held at the end of year 2 by

$$(7.8) \qquad (B_2/P + K_2) = (1+i_1) \cdot (1+i_0) \cdot (B_0/P + K_0) + (1+i_1) \cdot (w/P)_1 \cdot L$$
$$- (1+i_1) \cdot C_1 + (w/P)_2 \cdot L - C_2$$

If we replace $(B_2/P + K_2)$ on the right-hand side of equation (7.14) by the right-hand side of equation (7.8), we get

$$(B_3/P + K_3) = (1+i_2) \cdot [(1+i_1) \cdot (1+i_0) \cdot (B_0/P + K_0) + (1+i_1) \cdot (w/P)_1 \cdot L$$
$$- (1+i_1) \cdot C_1 + (w/P)_2 \cdot L - C_2] + (w/P) \cdot L - C_3$$

If we multiply the terms inside the brackets by the term $1 + i_2$, we get

$$(7.15) \qquad (B_3/P + K_3) = (1+i_2) \cdot (1+i_1) \cdot (1+i_0) \cdot (B_0/P + K_0)$$
$$+ (1+i_2) \cdot (1+i_1) \cdot (w/P)_1 \cdot L - (1+i_2) \cdot (1+i_1) \cdot C_1$$
$$+ (1+i_2) \cdot (w/P)_2 \cdot L - (1+i_2) \cdot C_2 + (w/P)_3 \cdot L - C_3$$

The important result involves interest rates. The initial real assets, $(B_0/P + K_0)$, now accumulate interest over three years, up to the end of year 3. Thus, these assets are multiplied on the right-hand side of equation (7.15) by $(1+i_2) \cdot (1+i_1) \cdot (1+i_0)$. Year 1's real wage income, $(w/P)_1 \cdot L$, accumulates interest over two years and is therefore multiplied by $(1+i_2) \cdot (1+i_1)$. The other real income and consumption terms enter in an analogous way.

If we divide through everything in equation (7.15) by $(1+i_2) \cdot (1+i_1)$ and rearrange the terms to put only those involving consumption on the left-hand side, we get the three-year budget constraint.

**(7.16)** $C_1 + C_2/(1 + i_1) + C_3/[(1 + i_1) \cdot (1 + i_2)] = (1 + i_0) \cdot (B_0/P + K_0) + (w/P)_1 \cdot L$

$+ (w/P)_2 \cdot L/(1 + i_1) + (w/P)_3 \cdot L/[(1 + i_1) \cdot (1 + i_2)] - (B_3/P + K_3)/[(1 + i_1) \cdot (1 + i_2)]$

This result extends the two-year budget constraint from equation (7.9) to three years. Everything in equation (7.16) appears as a present value (or year 1 value). But now the budget constraint includes the real wage income and consumption from year 3, $(w/P)_3 \cdot L$ and $C_3$, and these amounts are discounted for the accumulation of interest over two years—that is, by $(1 + i_1) \cdot (1 + i_2)$. The real assets held at the end of year 3, $(B_3/P + K_3)$, now appear on the right-hand side and are also discounted by $(1 + i_1) \cdot (1 + i_2)$.

By now, we see how to extend the budget constraint to any number of years. Each time we push forward one more year, we bring in the real income and consumption from that year. We also bring in the real assets held at the end of the new year and drop the real assets held at the end of the previous year. All of the new terms are discounted to reflect the accumulation of interest from year 1 up to the future year. For example, if we consider $j$ years, where $j$ is greater than 3, we get the j-year budget constraint.

**(7.17)** $C_1 + C_2/(1 + i_1) + C_3/[(1 + i_1) \cdot (1 + i_2)] + \cdots$

$+ Cj/[(1 + i_1) \cdot (1 + i_2) \cdot \cdots \cdot (1 + i_{j-1})] = (1 + i_0) \cdot (B_0/P + K_0)$

$+ (w/P)_1 \cdot L + (w/P)_2 \cdot L/(1 + i_1) + (w/P)_3 \cdot L/[(1 + i_1) \cdot (1 + i_2)]$

$+ \cdots + (w/P)_j \cdot L/[(1 + i_1) \cdot (1 + i_2) \cdot \cdots \cdot (1 + i_{j-1})]$

$- (B_j/P + K_j)/[(1 + i_1) \cdot (1 + i_2) \cdot \cdots \cdot (1 + i_{j-1})]$

We want to use equation (7.17) to understand how the household chooses year 1's consumption, $C_1$. That is, the household now makes this choice as part of a long-term plan that considers future consumptions and real incomes out to year $j$. These future values relate to the current choice through the $j$-year budget constraint. We can think of the number $j$ as the **planning horizon**—that is, the number of years over which the household plans its choices of consumption and saving.

How long is the horizon that the typical household considers when making decisions? Because we are dealing with households that have access to borrowing and lending, a long horizon is appropriate. By borrowing or lending, households can effectively use future income to pay for current consumption, or current income to pay for future consumption. When expressed as a present value, future incomes are as pertinent for current decisions as today's income.

Economists often assume that the typical household's planning horizon is long but finite. For example, in theories called **life-cycle models**, the horizon, $j$, represents an individual's expected remaining lifetime.[7] If people do not care about things that occur after their death, they have no reason to carry assets beyond year $j$. Accordingly, they plan so as to set to zero the final stock of assets, $(B_j/P + K_j)$, in equation (7.17).[8] That is, each person plans to end up with no assets when he or she dies.

It is straightforward to define the anticipated lifetime and, thereby, the planning horizon for an isolated individual. The appropriate horizon is, however, not so obvious for a family in which individuals have spouses and children. Since a person cares about his or her spouse and children, the applicable horizon extends beyond a person's expected lifetime, and households give weight to the expected future real incomes and consumptions

---

[7] Life-cycle models are associated particularly with the economist Franco Modigliani. See Franco Modigliani and Richard Brumberg (1954), and Albert Ando and Franco Modigliani (1963).

[8] We have to rule out the possibility of dying with negative assets. Otherwise, each person would like to set $(B_j/P + K_j)$ to be a large negative number.

of children. Further, since children care about their prospective children, should they have any, there is no clear point at which to draw the line.

Instead of imposing a **finite horizon** (where $j$ is a finite number), we can think of each household's plan as having an **infinite horizon**. That is, the planning period, $j$, extends arbitrarily far out into the future and can be thought of as being infinite. There are two good reasons to make this assumption:

- First, if we think of the typical person as part of a family that cares about members of future generations—children, grandchildren, and so on—into the indefinite future, this setup is appropriate.
- Second, although it is not obvious at this point, an infinite horizon is the simplest assumption.

If we use an infinite horizon, we allow the number $j$ to become arbitrarily large in equation (7.17). In that case, there is no final year, $j$, and we do not have to worry about the last term on the right-hand side, which involves $(B_j/P + K_j)$.[9] Thus, the **infinite-horizon budget constraint**—the constraint that applies to an infinite planning period—is the one we used before:

(7.12)    $C_1 + C_2/(1 + i_1) + C_3/[(1 + i_1) \cdot (1 + i_2)] + \cdots = (1 + i_0)] \cdot (B_0/P + K_0)$

$+ (w/P)_1 \cdot L + (w/P)_2 \cdot L/(1 + i_1) + (w/P)_3 \cdot L/[(1 + i_1) \cdot (1 + i_2)] + \cdots$

The ellipses signify that we are including terms involving $C_t$ and $(w/P)_t \cdot L$ for $t = 1, 2$, and so on—that is, extending out to arbitrarily large values of $t$.

---

[9] Because of the discounting by $(1 + i_1) \cdot (1 + i_2) \cdot \cdots \cdot (1 + i_{j-1})$, the present value of the assets left over, $(B_j/P + K_j)$, tends to become negligible as $j$ gets very large.

# Chapter 8

## An Equilibrium Business-Cycle Model

This chapter uses the framework developed in Chapters 6 and 7 to study the short-term economic fluctuations called business cycles. A business cycle involves phases in which real gross domestic product (real GDP) is expanding or contracting. A period of expanding real GDP—a boom—is typically accompanied by increases in other macroeconomic variables, such as consumption, investment, and employment, and with decreases in the unemployment rate. Conversely, a period of contraction— a recession—tends to feature decreases in consumption, investment, and employment, along with rises in the unemployment rate.

The economy's total output, real GDP, is the key indicator of whether the economy is in a phase of expansion or contraction. Thus, to understand the nature of economic fluctuations, we will look first at the behavior of U.S. real GDP during the post-World War II period.

## Cyclical Behavior of Real GDP—Recessions and Booms

The blue graph in Figure 8.1 shows U.S. real GDP on a quarterly basis from 1947.1 (the first quarter of 1947) to 2006.1 (the first quarter of 2006). This graph is analogous to the one showing annual data since 1869 in Figure 1.1 of Chapter 1.

If we look at the graph of real GDP in Figure 8.1 on the next page, we can think of the movements as reflecting two forces. First, there is the overall upward movement or *trend* in real GDP from 1947 to 2006. We think of this trend as reflecting long-term economic growth, the subject of Chapters 3–5. Second, there are shorter-term fluctuations of real GDP around its trend. We think of these economic fluctuations as stemming from the business cycle—that is, from booms and recessions. In this and the next chapter, we seek to understand these economic fluctuations.

We imagine that real GDP has two parts:

(8.1)  *real GDP = trend real GDP + cyclical part of real GDP*

To break down real GDP into trend and cycle, we start by estimating the trend. A good measure of the trend is a reasonably smooth curve fit to the data on real GDP. In Figure 8.2 on

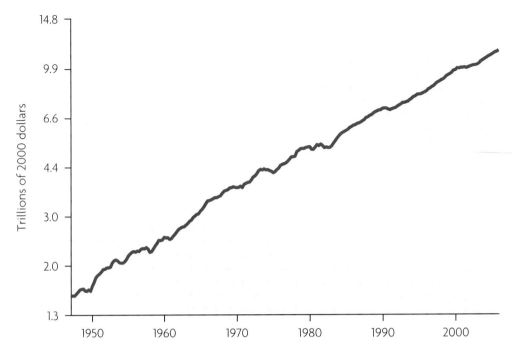

| Figure 8.1 | U.S. Real GDP, 1947–2006 |

The graph shows U.S. real GDP from 1947.1 to 2006.1. The data are quarterly, seasonally adjusted, and mea-sured in dollars from the base year, 2000. We use a proportionate (or logarithmic) scale. Therefore, each change along the vertical axis represents the same proportionate or percentage change in real GDP.

page 175, the blue graph shows real GDP. **Trend real GDP** is the red curve.[1] This graph is a smooth curve drawn through the blue graph.

Once we know trend real GDP, displayed in red in Figure 8.2, we can calculate the deviation from the trend. If we rearrange the terms in equation (8.1), we get

(8.2)        *cyclical part of real GDP = real GDP − trend real GDP*

We call the difference between real GDP and its trend the **cyclical part of real GDP**, because we view this part as coming from the business cycle—that is, from short-term economic fluctuations.

Figure 8.2 demonstrates that the most important property of U.S. real GDP from 1947 to 2006 is the overall upward trend, shown in red. In fact, it is not so easy in this graph to discern the cyclical part, which is the difference between real GDP and its trend. In subse-quent graphs, we magnify the cyclical part to get a clearer picture. However, we should remember that the trend in real GDP is the main determinant of how the typical person's standard of living in the United States in 2006 compares with that 10, 20, or 50 years earlier. Therefore, in the long run, economic growth is more important than economic fluctuations.

---

[1] The trend is called a Hodrick-Prescott filter (H-P filter), named after the economists Robert Hodrick and Edward Prescott. The general idea is to determine the position of the trend to fit the movements in real GDP without fluctuating too much. The procedure allows the slope of the trend to change slowly over time in response to observed changes in the growth rate of real GDP.

| F i g u r e   8 . 2 | Calculating the Trend of U.S. Real GDP, 1947–2006 |

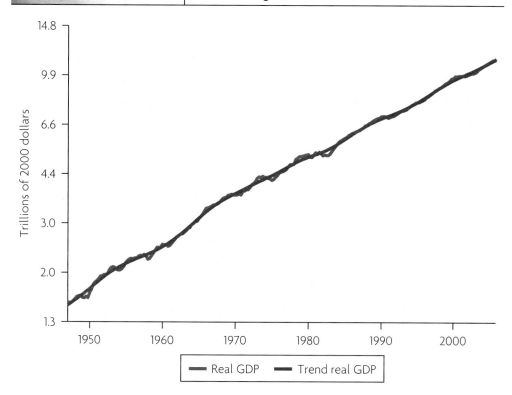

The blue graph shows U.S. real GDP from Figure 8.1. The red curve is a smooth trend drawn through the GDP data. We think of this trend curve as reflecting long-run economic growth.

Although economic fluctuations are typically small compared to long-term trends, the fluctuations do influence the typical person's well-being. For example, people are harmed during recessions because they have lower real incomes and less consumption, and often lose their jobs. Most discussions in the news media focus on fluctuations rather than trends. This focus probably exists because trends represent long-term forces that are usually not news, whereas fluctuations reflect recent events that do constitute news. In addition, it is easier (even if usually wrong) to blame economic fluctuations, especially an ongoing recession, on the current political administration. It is more difficult to assign responsibility for long-term economic growth.

Figure 8.3 on the next page shows a magnified version of the cyclical part of real GDP. This cyclical part is the difference between real GDP and its trend from Figure 8.2. By changing the scale on the vertical axis, we get a clear picture in Figure 8.3 of when real GDP was above or below its trend.

The variability of the cyclical part of real GDP is a good way to gauge the extent of economic fluctuations. To get a quantitative measure, we use a statistic called the **standard deviation**.[2] In Figure 8.3, the standard deviation of the cyclical part of real GDP

---

[2] The standard deviation is the square root of the variance. The variance is the average of the squared deviation of a variable from its mean. In the present case, the mean of the cyclical part of real GDP is close to zero (because of the way we constructed the trend in Figure 8.2). Therefore, the variance is just the average squared value of the cyclical part of real GDP.

## Figure 8.3 | Cyclical Part of U.S. Real GDP, 1947–2006

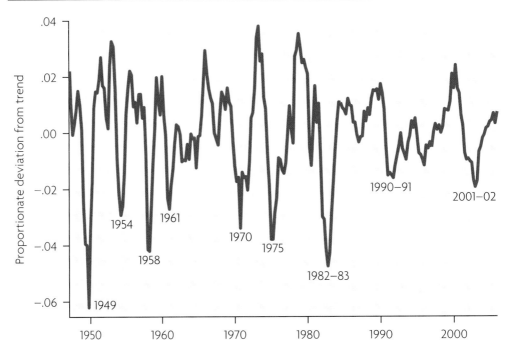

The graph plots the difference between real GDP (the blue graph in Figure 8.2) and its trend (the red graph in Figure 8.2). The resulting series—the cyclical part of real GDP—shows the deviations of real GDP from its trend. This cyclical part is measured in a proportionate sense; for example, 0.02 means that real GDP is 2% above trend, and −0.02 means that real GDP is 2% below trend. The recession years marked are those in which the cyclical part of real GDP was negative and reached at least 1.5% in magnitude.

is 1.7%. This value means that the typical range of fluctuation of U.S. real GDP from 1947 to 2006 was between 1.7% below and 1.7% above trend.[3]

The low points, or troughs, in Figure 8.3 pick out the nine U.S. recessions from 1947 to 2006. The general notion of a recession is a period of low economic activity, gauged by real GDP and other macroeconomic variables. In our case, we make this definition operational by looking at periods in which the cyclical part of real GDP was negative and reached at least 1.5% in magnitude. By this definition, recessions occurred in 1949, 1954, 1958, 1961, 1970, 1975, 1982–83, 1990–91, and 2001–02. The departures of real GDP from trend ranged from the mild recessions of 1990–91 (where the largest shortfall from trend was 1.6%), 2001–02 (1.9%), and 1961 (2.7%), to the more severe recessions of 1949 (6.2%), 1982–83 (4.7%), 1958 (4.2%), and 1975 (3.8%).

The semi-official arbiter of when U.S. recessions begin and end is the National Bureau of Economic Research (NBER), which is a think tank located near Harvard University in Cambridge, Massachusetts. The NBER does not have a strict definition of what constitutes a recession but does take into account a number of macroeconomic variables observed at monthly frequencies, including employment, retail sales, personal income, and

---

[3] If a variable is normally distributed (a reasonable approximation for the cyclical part of real GDP), about two-thirds of the time the variable is between one standard deviation below and one standard deviation above its mean. About 95% of the time, the variable is between two standard deviations below and two standard deviations above its mean.

9038.0
18.860
7.7577
61.851

# By The Numbers

## Recessions in long-term U.S. history

The recessions of the post-World War II period, shown in Figure 8.3, were mild compared to some earlier ones, especially the Great Depression of the early 1930s. We can measure U.S. recessions back to 1869 using the annual data on real GDP from Figure 1.1 of Chapter 1.

Figure 8.4 on the next page shows the cyclical part of real GDP from 1869 to 2005. The method for calculating the cyclical part is the same as that used for post-World War II data in Figures 8.2 and 8.3, except that the long-term data are annual. To focus on major contractions, we label as recessions in Figure 8.4 only cases in which the cyclical part of real GDP was negative and at least 3% in magnitude. With this more stringent cutoff (compared to 1.5% in Figure 8.3), some of the post-World War II

recessions—including those for 1990–91 and 2001–02—are too mild to be marked.

The Great Depression dwarfs any of the recessions experienced since World War II. In the worst year, 1933, real GDP fell short of trend by 19%. Two other large recessions during the inter-war period occurred in 1920–22 and 1938–40—real GDP was 9% below trend in both cases.

The pre-World War I period does not contain any recessions as large as those of the inter-war years. In fact, the period from 1869 to 1914 does not differ greatly from the period since 1947, in terms of the extent of economic fluctuations. It is hard to be precise, however, because the pre-1929 national-accounts data are less reliable.[4]

industrial production. Despite the differences between our definition of a recession and the NBER concept, the dates shown in Figure 8.3 correspond well to those announced by the NBER.

We can also use Figure 8.3 to isolate economic booms, represented by the high points, or peaks, in the cyclical part of real GDP. The most recent peak was at 2.4% above trend in the second quarter of 2000. This peak coincided with large investments in the Internet and other forms of advanced technology.

# An Equilibrium Business-Cycle Model

## Conceptual Issues

To model economic fluctuations, we start by assuming that these fluctuations reflect **shocks** to the economy. An example of a shock is a change in the technology level, $A$, which enters into the production function introduced in equation (3.1) of Chapter 3 and repeated here:

(8.3) $$Y = A \cdot F(K, L)$$

[4] Christina Romer's (1986, 1988) analysis shows that the pre-World War I period was only slightly more variable than the post-World War II period in terms of the extent of economic fluctuations.

The real challenge for the model is to predict how other macroeconomic variables move along with real GDP during economic fluctuations. As an example, we want to see what the model predicts for the changes in consumption and investment during booms and recessions. Similarly, we can assess the behavior of the real wage rate, the real rental price of capital, and the interest rate. Later, when we drop the assumption that $L$ is fixed, we can look at the behavior of employment and unemployment. The general idea is that we will test our equilibrium business-cycle model by making predictions about the relationship between real GDP and other macroeconomic variables, and then looking at the data to see if these predictions are accurate. We will now start our analysis of macro-economic variables.

**The marginal product of labor and the real wage rate**   We know from the production function in equation (8.3) that an increase in the technology level, $A$, raises the marginal product of labor, MPL, for given inputs of capital, $K$, and labor, $L$. We show the effects from a higher schedule for the MPL in Figure 8.5. We consider two technology levels, $A$ and $A'$, where $A'$ is greater than $A$. We assume that the capital stock is fixed at $K$. The downward-sloping blue curve shows how the MPL varies with $L$ when the technology level is $A$. If the real wage rate is $w/P$, on the vertical axis, the quantity of labor demanded is the amount $L^d$ on the horizontal axis. The downward-sloping red curve shows the MPL when the technology level is $A'$. The MPL is higher for any $L$ on this second curve than on the first one. Therefore, at the given real wage rate, $w/P$, the quantity of labor demanded, $(L^d)'$ on the horizontal axis, is greater than $L^d$.

| **F i g u r e   8 . 5** | Effect of an Increase in the Technology Level on the Demand for Labor |
|---|---|

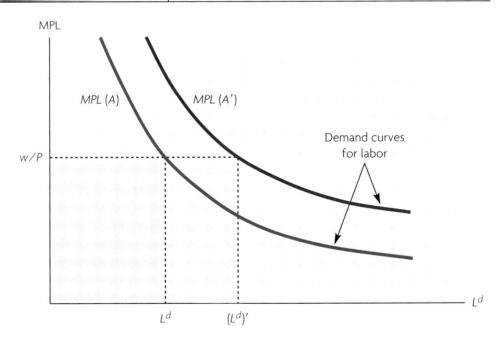

When the technology level is $A$, the MPL is given by the blue curve, labeled $MPL\,(A)$. At the real wage rate $w/P$, shown on the vertical axis, the quantity of labor demanded is $L^d$ on the horizontal axis. The technology level $A'$ is greater than $A$. Therefore, the MPL, given by the red curve labeled $MPL\,(A')$, is higher at any labor input than the value along the blue curve. When the technology level is $A'$ and the real wage rate is $w/P$, the quantity of labor demanded is $(L^d)'$, which is greater than $L^d$.

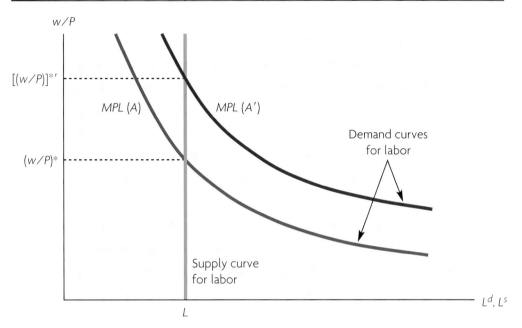

| Figure 8.6 | Effect of an Increase in the Technology Level on the Real Wage Rate |

Labor supply is the given value $L$, shown on the horizontal axis. If the technology level is $A$, the schedule for the MPL determines the blue labor-demand curve, labeled $MPL$ $(A)$. Therefore, the market-clearing real wage rate is $(w/P)^*$, shown on the vertical axis. The technology level $A'$ is greater than $A$, as in Figure 8.5. Therefore, the schedule for the MPL is given by the red labor-demand curve, labeled $MPL$ $(A')$. In this case, the market-clearing real wage rate is $[(w/P)^*]'$, which is greater than $(w/P)^*$.

The two labor-demand curves in Figure 8.6 come from Figure 8.5. For labor supply, we assume for now that the quantity of labor supplied is fixed at the value $L$ on the horizontal axis. That is, the labor-supply curve is a vertical line at $L$.

If the technology level is $A$, the labor-demand curve is given in Figure 8.6 by the downward-sloping blue curve. Therefore, the labor market clears—the quantity of labor demanded equals the quantity supplied—when the real wage rate, $w/P$, equals the market-clearing value $(w/P)^*$, shown on the vertical axis. The real wage rate $(w/P)^*$ equals the marginal product of labor, MPL, evaluated at $L$ (when the technology level is $A$ and the capital stock is fixed at $K$).

If the technology level rises to $A'$, the labor-demand curve is given in Figure 8.6 by the downward-sloping red curve. In this case, the market-clearing real wage rate equals $[(w/P)^*]'$ on the vertical axis. Since the MPL is higher, at the given $L$, on the red curve than on the blue one, the market-clearing real wage rate is higher. That is, $[(w/P)^*]'$ is greater than $(w/P)^*$.

One way to think about the result is that, at the initial real wage rate, $(w/P)^*$, the rise in the MPL means that the quantity of labor demanded, $(L^d)'$, exceeds the quantity supplied, which is fixed at $L$. Therefore, employers (households in their role as business managers) compete for the scarce labor and drive up the real wage rate to $[(w/P)^*]'$.

We found that an increase in the technology level, $A$, raises the real wage rate, $w/P$. Hence, the model predicts that an economic boom—where real GDP is high because $A$ is high—will have a relatively high $w/P$. In contrast, a recession will have a relatively low $w/P$.

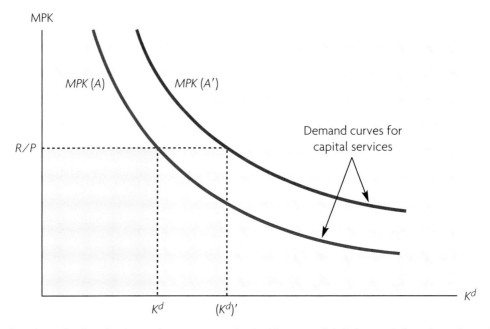

| Figure 8.7 | Effect of an Increase in the Technology Level on the Demand for Capital Services |

When the technology level is *A*, the MPK is given by the blue curve, labeled *MPK* (*A*). At the real rental price *R/P*, shown on the vertical axis, the quantity of capital demanded is $K^d$ on the horizontal axis. The technology level *A′* is greater than *A*. Therefore, the MPK, given by the red curve labeled *MPK* (*A′*), is higher at any capital input than the value along the blue curve. When the technology level is *A′* and the real rental price is *R/P*, the quantity of capital demanded is $(K^d)′$, which is greater than $K^d$.

**Marginal product of capital, real rental price, and the interest rate**    We know from the production function in equation (8.3) that an increase in the technology level, *A*, raises the marginal product of capital, MPK, for given inputs of capital, *K*, and labor, *L*. We show the effects of a higher MPK in Figure 8.7. This figure again considers two technology levels, *A* and *A′*, where *A′* is greater than *A*. We still assume that labor input is fixed at *L*. The downward-sloping blue curve shows how the MPK varies with *K* when the technology level is *A*. If the real rental price is *R/P* on the vertical axis, the quantity of capital demanded is the amount $K^d$ on the horizontal axis. The downward-sloping red curve shows the MPK when the technology level is *A′*. The MPK is higher at any given *K* on this second curve than on the first one. Therefore, at the given real rental price, *R/P*, the quantity of capital demanded, $(K^d)′$ on the horizontal axis, is greater than $K^d$.

The two demand curves for capital services in Figure 8.8 come from Figure 8.7. We assume that the quantity of capital services supplied is fixed at *K* on the horizontal axis. That is, the supply curve is a vertical line at *K*.

If the technology level is *A*, the demand curve for capital services is given in Figure 8.8 by the downward-sloping blue curve. Therefore, the market for capital services clears—the quantity of capital services demanded equals the quantity supplied—when the real rental price, *R/P*, equals the market-clearing value $(R/P)^*$ on the vertical axis. The real rental price $(R/P)^*$ equals the marginal product of capital, MPK, evaluated at *K* (when the technology level is *A* and labor input is fixed at *L*).

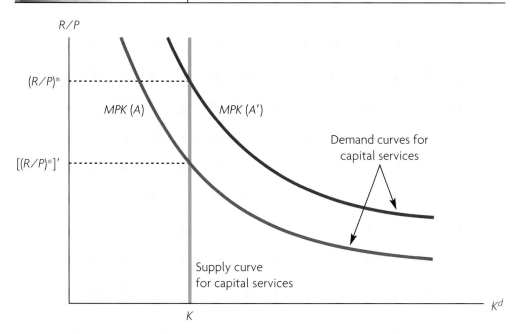

**Figure 8.8** | Effect of an Increase in the Technology Level on the Real Rental Price of Capital

The supply of capital services is the given value $K$, shown on the horizontal axis. If the technology level is $A$, the schedule for the MPK is given by the blue curve, labeled *MPK* $(A)$. This curve gives the demand for capital services when the technology level is $A$. The market-clearing real rental price is $(R/P)^*$, shown on the vertical axis. The technology level $A'$ is greater than $A$, as in Figure 8.7. Therefore, the schedule for the MPK is given by the red curve, labeled *MPK* $(A')$. This curve gives the demand for capital services when the technology level is $A'$. In this case, the market-clearing real rental price is $[(R/P)^*]'$, which is greater than $(R/P)^*$.

If the technology level rises to $A'$, the demand curve for capital services is given in Figure 8.8 by the downward-sloping red curve. In this case, the market-clearing real rental price equals $[(R/P)^*]'$ on the vertical axis. Since the MPK is higher, at the given $K$, on the red curve than on the blue one, the market-clearing real rental price is higher. That is, $[(R/P)^*]'$ is greater than $(R/P)^*$.

We conclude that an increase in the technology level, $A$, raises the real rental price of capital, $R/P$. Hence, the model predicts that an economic boom—where real GDP is high because $A$ is high—will have a relatively high $R/P$. In contrast, a recession will have a relatively low $R/P$.

Recall from our analysis in Chapter 6 that the interest rate is given by

(6.6) $$i = R/P - \delta$$
*rate of return on bonds = rate of return on ownership of capital*

We know from Figure 8.8 that, when the market for capital services clears, the real rental price, $R/P$, equals the marginal product of capital, MPK, evaluated at the given values of capital, $K$, and labor, $L$. Therefore, the interest rate is given by

(8.4) $$i = MPK \ (\textit{evaluated at given K and L}) - \delta$$

An increase in the technology level raises the marginal product of capital, MPK, at given inputs of capital, $K$, and labor, $L$. Therefore, equation (8.4) implies that the interest rate, $i$, rises. Hence, the model predicts that an economic boom will have a relatively high interest rate, whereas a recession will have a relatively low interest rate.

**Consumption, saving, and investment**   Now we will use our microeconomic analysis from Chapter 7 to determine how much households consume and save. A rise in the technology level, $A$, raises the interest rate, $i$, and a higher $i$ motivates households to defer consumption from the present to the future (the intertemporal-substitution effect). On this ground, we predict that current consumption would fall. However, our analysis is incomplete, because we have to allow for income effects.

Consider the household budget constraint at each point in time from Chapter 7:

(7.1)
$$C + (1/P) \cdot \Delta B + \Delta K = (w/P) \cdot L + i \cdot (B/P + K)$$

$$consumption + real\ saving = real\ income$$

Income effects enter through real wage income, $(w/P) \cdot L$, and real asset income, $i \cdot (B/P + K)$. An increase in $A$ raises real wage income, because $w/P$ rises and $L$ does not change. An increase in $A$ also raises real asset income, because $i$ rises, $B/P$ is unchanged (at zero in the aggregate), and $K$ does not change in the short run. Therefore, an increase in $A$ raises overall household real income.

Another way to see the effect on overall income is to use the aggregate household budget constraint from Chapter 7 that applies when the markets for bonds, labor, and capital services clear:

(7.13)
$$C + \Delta K = Y - \delta K$$

$$consumption + net\ investment = real\ GDP - depreciation$$

$$= real\ net\ domestic\ product$$

If we substitute $Y = A \cdot F(K, L)$ from the production function (equation [8.3]), we get

(8.5)
$$C + \Delta K = A \cdot F(K, L) - \delta K$$

Since depreciation, $\delta K$, is fixed in the short run, the income effect from a change in $A$ boils down to its effect on real GDP, $Y = A \cdot F(K, L)$. Since an increase in $A$ raises real GDP for given $K$ and $L$, we again see that a rise in $A$ raises overall real income.

The increase in real income motivates households to raise current consumption (as well as future consumption). This response is the familiar income effect. This effect works against the intertemporal-substitution effect, which tends to reduce current consumption. Therefore, we are unsure whether an increase in the technology level, $A$, leads to more or less current consumption, $C$. The net change depends on whether the income effect is stronger or weaker than the intertemporal-substitution effect.

We can sharpen our prediction because the size of the income effect depends on how long the change in the technology level, $A$, lasts. For the rest of this section, we assume that the change in $A$ is permanent. This situation would apply to a literal technological advance, because producers tend not to forget these advances. In this case, the increases in real income tend also to be permanent. Therefore, we should consider the case from Chapter 7 in which real income rises by similar amounts each year. The prediction for this case was that the propensity to consume out of higher income would be close to one. Hence, if an increase in $A$ raises real GDP, $Y = A \cdot F(K, L)$, by one unit, then—from the standpoint of the income effect—current consumption, $C$, would rise by roughly one unit.

To compute the overall effect on current consumption, we have to balance the income effect—whereby consumption rises by roughly as much as real GDP—against the intertemporal-substitution effect, which lowers current consumption. Quantitative estimates of the intertemporal-substitution effect show that it has less of an impact than this large income effect. Hence, when the increase in $A$ is permanent, current consumption will rise. However, as long as the intertemporal-substitution operates at all, the increase in current consumption will be less than the increase in real GDP.

In equation (7.1), the change on the left-hand side in $C$ is less than the change on the right-hand side in real income, which corresponds to the change in real GDP, $Y$. Therefore, household real saving must rise on the left-hand side. That is, part of the extra household real income goes to consumption and another part goes to real saving.

In the aggregate household budget constraint in equation (7.13), we found that current consumption, $C$, rises, but by less than the increase in real GDP, $Y$. Therefore, net investment, $\Delta K$, must increase—the increase in real GDP shows up partly as more $C$ and partly as more $\Delta K$. Since net investment, $\Delta K$, equals real saving, this result is consistent with our finding that real saving increased.

# Matching the Theory with the Facts

Our equilibrium business-cycle model makes a number of predictions about how fluctuations in macroeconomic variables match up with variations in real GDP. Now we will examine the predictions for consumption, investment, the real wage rate, the real rental price of capital, and the interest rate. We will focus on U.S. data since 1954; the difference from Figures 8.1 to 8.3 is that we are leaving out the years 1947 to 1953. That period is unusual because of the heavy influences from the aftermath of World War II and the Korean War. We will consider the economic effects of wartime in Chapter 12.

## Consumption and Investment

We can measure consumption, $C$, from the national-income accounts by real consumer expenditure. This expenditure accounted, on average, for 64% of U.S. GDP from 1954 to 2006. We calculate the cyclical part of real consumer expenditure by using the method applied to real GDP in Figure 8.2. The result is the blue graph in Figure 8.9 on the next page. This graph shows the proportionate deviation of real consumer expenditure from its trend. We also show, as the red graph, the cyclical part of real GDP (copied from Figure 8.3).

Two important findings emerge from Figure 8.9. First, real consumer expenditure typically fluctuates in the same direction as real GDP.[6] When a variable fluctuates, like real consumer expenditure, in the same direction as real GDP, we say that the variable is **procyclical**. A procyclical variable moves in the same direction as the business cycle—it tends to be high relative to its trend in a boom and low relative to its trend in a recession. (A variable that fluctuates in the opposite direction from real GDP is **countercyclical**. One that has little tendency to move in a particular direction during a business cycle is **acyclical**.) Second, real consumer expenditure fluctuates in a proportional sense by less than real GDP. From 1954.1 to 2006.1, the standard deviation of the cyclical part of real consumer expenditure was 1.2%, compared with 1.6% for the cyclical part of real GDP. Thus, in a proportionate sense, real consumer expenditure varies by less than real GDP in booms and recessions.

We can measure gross investment, $I$, from the national-income accounts by real gross domestic private investment. This expenditure accounted, on average, for 16% of GDP from 1954 to 2006. We again use the method from Figure 8.2 to calculate the cyclical part

---

[6] From 1954.1 to 2006.1, the correlation of the cyclical part of real consumer expenditure with the cyclical part of real GDP was 0.88.

Figure 8.9 | Cyclical Behavior of U.S. Real GDP and Consumer Expenditure

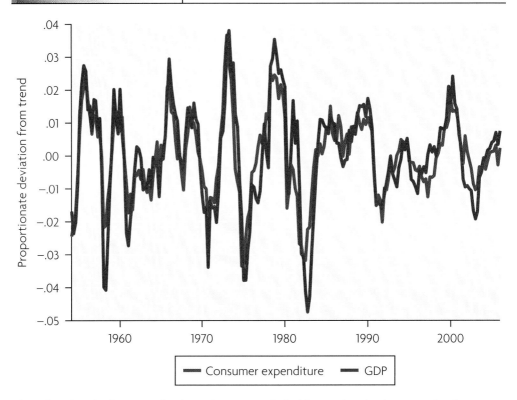

The red graph is the deviation of real GDP from its trend. The blue graph is the deviation of real consumer expenditure from its trend. These deviations are measured in a proportionate sense. The data on GDP and consumer expenditure are quarterly and seasonally adjusted. Real consumer expenditure is procyclical—it fluctuates closely with real GDP but is less variable than real GDP.

of real gross investment. The result is the blue graph in Figure 8.10. This graph shows the proportionate deviation of real investment from its trend. The cyclical part of real GDP is again the red graph.

One finding from Figure 8.10 is that, like real consumer expenditure, real gross investment is procyclical; that is, it typically fluctuates in the same direction as real GDP.[7] Hence, investment is high relative to its trend in a boom and low relative to its trend in a recession. Another finding is that real gross investment fluctuates, in a proportional sense, much more than real GDP. In terms of the standard deviations of the cyclical parts, the one for gross investment was 7.2%, compared to 1.6% for real GDP.[8] Thus, in a proportionate sense, real investment fluctuates much more than real GDP in booms and recessions. The volatility of investment means that it represents far more of the fluctuations in real GDP than we would expect from the average ratio of gross investment to GDP (16%).

---

[7] From 1954.1 to 2006.1, the correlation of the cyclical part of real gross domestic private investment with the cyclical part of real GDP was 0.92.

[8] Consumer expenditure includes purchases of consumer durables, such as automobiles, furniture, and appliances, as well as spending on nondurables and services. We should think of consumer durables as forms of capital owned by households. Therefore, we should view the purchases of these durables as forms of gross investment. Hence, we could combine the purchases of consumer durables with gross investment to get a broader measure of investment. We would then represent consumption by a narrower measure—real consumer expenditure on nondurables and services. If we make these changes, we find that the narrower measure of real consumer expenditure fluctuates, in a proportional sense, less than the one shown in Figure 8.9—that is, we get a stronger pattern of consumption being less variable than real GDP.

| **Figure 8.10** | Cyclical Behavior of U.S. Real GDP and Investment |
|---|---|

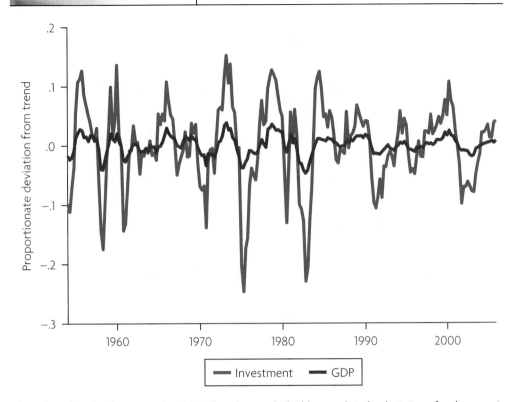

The red graph is the deviation of real GDP from its trend. The blue graph is the deviation of real gross private domestic investment from its trend. These deviations are measured in a proportionate sense. The data on GDP and investment are quarterly and seasonally adjusted. Real gross investment is procyclical—it fluctuates closely with real GDP but is far more variable than real GDP.

Going back to the model, permanent shifts in the technology level, $A$, match up with some of the empirical patterns found in Figures 8.9 and 8.10. Specifically, increases in $A$ generate economic booms, where real GDP increases, and these increases show up partly as more consumption and partly as more investment. In reverse, decreases in $A$ create recessions, where real GDP, consumption, and investment all decline.

Does the model explain why investment fluctuates proportionately far more than consumption? Recall that, because the changes in the technology level, $A$, are permanent, the income effects are strong. On this ground, consumption would change by roughly the same amount as real GDP. However, we also found that an increase in $A$ led to a rise in the interest rate, which reduced current consumption and raised current real saving. This effect means that, during a boom, consumption rises proportionately by less than real GDP. Analogously, during a recession, consumption falls proportionately by less than real GDP. Thus, to match the observation that consumption is less variable than real GDP, the model relies on the intertemporal-substitution effect from the interest rate. One problem, however, is that empirical studies have found evidence only for small intertemporal-substitution effects on consumption and saving. Therefore, it may be important to find additional reasons to explain why consumption is proportionately less variable than real GDP. We explore an important reason in a later section, which allows for the change in the technology level, $A$, to be partly temporary.

## The Real Wage Rate

The model predicts that the real wage rate, $w/P$, will be relatively high in booms and relatively low in recessions. A good measure of the nominal wage rate, $w$, is the average hourly nominal earnings of production workers in the total private economy (these data start in 1964). We can measure the real wage rate, $w/P$, by dividing nominal earnings by a broad measure of the price level, the deflator for the gross domestic product. The results are similar if we use the consumer price index (CPI).

We calculate the cyclical part of the real wage rate, $w/P$, by the procedure used for real GDP in Figure 8.2. The result is the blue graph in Figure 8.11. This graph shows the proportionate deviation of $w/P$ from its trend. We again show as the red graph the cyclical part of real GDP (from Figure 8.3). We see that the real wage rate is procyclical—it tends to be above its trend during booms and below its trend during recessions.[9] This finding accords with the model's predictions.

| **F i g u r e   8 . 1 1** | Cyclical Behavior of U.S. Real GDP and the Real Wage Rate |

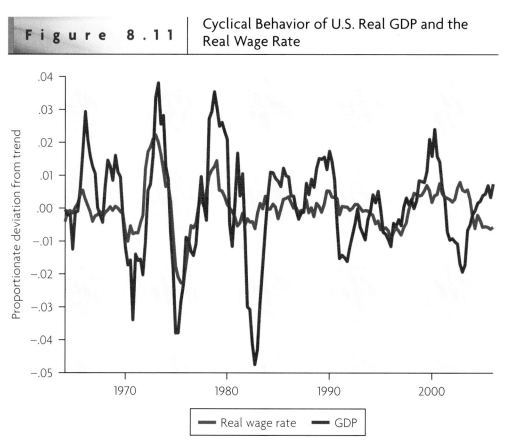

The red graph is the deviation of real GDP from its trend. The blue graph is the deviation of the real wage rate from its trend. These deviations are measured in a proportionate sense. The real wage rate is average hourly nominal earnings of production workers in the total private, nonagricultural economy divided by the price deflator for the GDP. The data on GDP and wage rates are quarterly and seasonally adjusted. (The underlying data on wage rates are monthly.) The real wage rate is procyclical—it fluctuates with real GDP but is not as variable as real GDP.

---

[9] From 1964.1 to 2006.1, the correlation of the cyclical part of the real wage rate with the cyclical part of real GDP was 0.58.

## The Real Rental Price

The model predicts that the real rental price of capital, $R/P$, will be relatively high in booms and relatively low in recessions. The main problem in testing this proposition is that the rental price is difficult to measure for the whole economy. The reason is that most forms of capital—such as structures and equipment owned by corporations—are not explicitly rented out. These types of capital are typically used by their owners. In effect, businesses rent capital to themselves, but we cannot observe the implicit rental price for this capital. (The national-income accounts estimate an implicit rental price for owner-occupied housing by calculating what the rental price would have been if the homeowner had rented out the house.)

Casey Mulligan (2001) estimated the implicit real rental price, $R/P$, for capital owned by the U.S. corporate sector. He made this calculation by dividing total payments to corporate capital by the total quantity of this capital. The blue graph in Figure 8.12 is the cyclical part of Mulligan's $R/P$ series. This graph shows the proportionate deviation of $R/P$ from its trend. We again show as the red graph the cyclical part of real GDP. We see that $R/P$ is procyclical—it tends to be above its trend in booms and below its trend during recessions.[10] This finding fits the model's predictions.

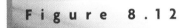

| **F i g u r e    8 . 1 2** | Cyclical Behavior of U.S. Real GDP and the Real Rental Price of Capital |

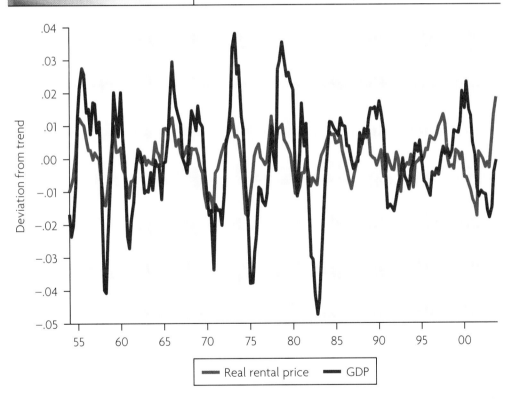

The red graph is the deviation of real GDP from its trend (in a proportionate sense). The blue graph is the deviation of the real rental price of corporate capital from its trend. The real rental price was calculated by Casey Mulligan (2001), based on after-tax payments to capital per unit of capital in the U.S. corporate sector. The real rental price is procyclical—it fluctuates with real GDP.

---

[10] From 1954.1 to 2003.4 (over which the data on the real rental price are available), the correlation of the cyclical part of the real rental price with the cyclical part of real GDP was 0.52.

## The Interest Rate

The model predicts that booms will have a high interest rate, $i$, whereas recessions will have a low interest rate. This pattern looks right; that is, interest rates tend to be above trend during booms and below trend during recessions.[11] However, to get a full picture, we have to consider the effect of inflation on nominal and real interest rates. We will consider inflation in Chapter 11.

# Temporary Changes in the Technology Level

In our model, all changes in the technology level, $A$, were permanent. This assumption is reasonable for technological advances but less compelling for other interpretations of $A$. For example, if a decrease in $A$ represents a harvest failure or a general strike, the change would be temporary. To allow for these cases, we now assume that the change in $A$ is temporary. Think of the change as lasting for one year.

The change in the assumption about the technology level, $A$, does not affect most of our analysis. If $A$ increases temporarily, real GDP, $A \cdot F(K, L)$, still rises for fixed values of $K$ and $L$. The marginal product of capital, MPK, and the interest rate, $i$, also rise as before. The intertemporal-substitution effect from the higher $i$ still motivates households to reduce current consumption, $C$, and raise current real saving.

There are some new results about income effects. The overall change in current consumption, $C$, again depends on the size of the income effect. In our previous case—where the increase in the technology level, $A$, was permanent—the income effect raised consumption by about as much as the increase in real GDP. This change worked against the intertemporal-substitution effect, which reduced current consumption. For a permanent rise in $A$, the income effect more than offset the intertemporal-substitution effect, and current consumption increased.

When the increase in the technology level, $A$, is temporary, the income effect is weak. Therefore, the income effect now raises current consumption, $C$, by only a small amount. Since the income effect is weak, we can no longer be confident that it more than offsets the intertemporal-substitution effect. Hence, current consumption may rise or fall. In any event, current consumption does not rise by nearly as much as real GDP.

Consider again the aggregate budget constraint that applies when the markets for bonds, labor, and capital services clear:

(7.13)
$$C + \Delta K = Y - \delta K$$

*consumption* $+$ *net investment* $=$ *real GDP* $-$ *depreciation*

$=$ *real net domestic product*

Real GDP, $Y = A \cdot F(K, L)$, rises, and consumption, $C$, either falls or rises by a small amount. Hence, net investment, $\Delta K$, rises by nearly as much as—or possibly by even more than—real GDP. The model therefore predicts that an economic boom would feature high real GDP and investment. However, consumption would rise by, at most, a small amount. Conversely, a recession would have low real GDP and investment, but consumption would decline by, at most, a modest amount.

---

[11] From 1954.1 to 2006.1, the correlation of the cyclical part of the interest rate on three-month U.S. Treasury Bills with the cyclical part of real GDP was 0.39.

These patterns conflict with the data, because consumption is clearly procyclical—it rises well above trend during booms and falls well below trend in recessions. Thus, if the underlying shocks were purely temporary changes in the technology level, $A$, the model would not explain the behavior of consumption. Our conclusion is that we cannot rely solely on temporary changes in $A$ as the main source of economic fluctuations. However, the model does work better if we allow for changes in $A$ to be less than fully permanent, even if not purely temporary.

Consider again the empirical observation that consumption fluctuates proportionately by less than real GDP. When we assumed that the changes in the technology level, $A$, were permanent, the model could explain the smaller variability of consumption only if the intertemporal-substitution effect on consumption was substantial. However, if the changes in $A$ are less than fully permanent, we have another reason why consumption is less variable than real GDP. If a change in $A$ lasts for a long time, but not forever, the income effect will be strong. However, the income effect will not be strong enough to raise consumption by as much as the change in real GDP. Thus, consumption can fluctuate proportionately less than real GDP even if the intertemporal-substitution effect on consumption is weak. This reasoning suggests that the model works best to fit the data when the underlying shocks to $A$ are long lasting but less than fully permanent. This form of shock to technology has typically been assumed in real business-cycle models.

## Variations in Labor Input

An important shortcoming of the model worked out thus far is its failure to fit the observed behavior of labor input during economic fluctuations. Labor input, $L$—measured by employment or total hours worked—varies with the business cycle. As we detail later, $L$ is high in booms and low in recessions; that is, it is clearly procyclical. We cannot give our model a high grade unless we can use it to explain this important phenomenon.

To fit the facts on labor input, we will now extend the model to allow for a variable supply of labor, $L^s$. This extension will be important for two reasons. First, we will be able to explain short-term variations in labor input, $L$. Second, changes in real GDP will reflect the variations in $L$, as well as the direct effect from changes in the technology level, $A$. We first extend the microeconomic foundations of the model to allow for variable $L^s$. Then we will use our equilibrium business-cycle model to assess how labor input, $L$, moves during economic fluctuations.

### Labor Supply

Start with a modified form of the household budget constraint worked out in equation (7.1) of Chapter 7:

(8.6)
$$C + (1/P) \cdot \Delta B + \Delta K = (w/P) \cdot L^s + i \cdot (B/P + K)$$

*consumption + real saving = real income*

The left-hand side is the total of consumption, $C$, and real saving, $(1/P) \cdot \Delta B + \Delta K$. The right-hand side is household real income, which is the sum of real wage income, $(w/P) \cdot L^s$, and real asset income, $i \cdot (B/P + K)$. The difference from before is that we replaced $L$ by the quantity of labor supplied, $L^s$, to allow for a variable labor supply.

Since each household has a fixed amount of time each year, a higher quantity of labor supplied, $L^s$, means a smaller amount of leisure time. From the perspective of a household, a higher $L^s$ can mean either that working family members work more hours per year or that more members work. In the latter case, the rise in labor supply shows up as an increase in labor-force participation. Either way, more labor supplied means less leisure time for the family.

We have already assumed that households like consumption, C. Now we assume that households also like more leisure time. To put it differently, households dislike work effort, represented by the quantity of labor supplied, $L^s$.

As with consumption and saving, the choice of $L^s$ involves substitution and income effects. We start with the *substitution effect for leisure and consumption*.

**The substitution effect for leisure and consumption**    Consider the household budget constraint in equation (8.6). The right-hand side includes the real wage rate, $w/P$, and the interest rate, $i$, each of which an individual household takes as given. Suppose that we also hold fixed the real assets, $B/P + K$, on the right-hand side, and the real saving, $(1/P) \cdot \Delta B + \Delta K$, on the left-hand side. In this case, a household can raise or lower the quantity of labor supplied, $L^s$, and thereby raise or lower real wage income, $(w/P) \cdot L^s$. Since we are holding everything else fixed in equation (8.6), the higher or lower real wage income will increase or decrease consumption, C. In other words, if the household chooses to work one more hour and thereby have one less hour of leisure, the extra $w/P$ of real wage income pays for $w/P$ more units of consumption. Therefore, the household can substitute one less hour of leisure for $w/P$ more units of consumption.

If the real wage rate, $w/P$, rises, the household gets a better deal by working more because it gets more consumption for each extra hour worked. Since the deal is better, we predict that the household responds to a higher $w/P$ by working more. Another way to view the result is that a higher $w/P$ makes leisure time more expensive compared to consumption: $w/P$ tells the household how much consumption it gives up by taking an extra hour of leisure. An increase in $w/P$ motivates the household to substitute away from the object that got more expensive—leisure time—and toward the one that got cheaper—consumption. Therefore, a higher real wage rate, $w/P$, raises the quantity of labor supplied, $L^s$.

**Income effects on labor supply**    As usual, we also have to consider income effects. Consider again the budget constraint

$$(8.6) \qquad C + (1/P) \cdot \Delta B + \Delta K = (w/P) \cdot L^s + i \cdot (B/P + K)$$

*consumption + real saving = real income*

We see from the yellow shaded term that a change in the real wage rate, $w/P$, has an income effect. For a given quantity of labor supplied, $L^s$, a higher $w/P$ means higher real wage income, $(w/P) \cdot L^s$. Our prediction is that the household spends the extra income on consumption and leisure time. Thus, on this ground, a higher $w/P$ leads to a smaller quantity of labor supplied, $L^s$. Since the substitution effect from a higher $w/P$ favors higher $L^s$, the overall effect is ambiguous. An increase in the real wage rate, $w/P$, raises $L^s$ if the substitution effect is stronger than the income effect.

We may be able to resolve the ambiguity by considering whether the income effect is strong or weak. We found in Chapter 7 that the strength of the income effect depended on whether the change in income was permanent or temporary. To see how this works, consider a modified form of the multiyear budget constraint worked out in Chapter 7 in equation (7.12):

$$(8.7) \quad C_1 + C_2/(1 + i_1) + C_3/[(1 + i_1) \cdot (1 + i_2)] + \cdots = (1 + i_0) \cdot (B_0/P + K_0)$$
$$+ (w/P)_1 \cdot L_1^s + (w/P)_2 \cdot L_2^s/(1 + i_1) + (w/P)_3 \cdot L_3^s/[(1 + i_1) \cdot (1 + i_2)] + \cdots$$

*present value of consumption = value of initial assets + present value of wage incomes*

The difference from before is that we replaced the fixed quantity of labor, $L$, by the quantity of labor supplied in each year, $L_t^s$, where $t = 1, 2$, and so on.

When we examined income effects on consumption in Chapter 7, we found that households responded to higher real wage rates by consuming more each year. That is, the income effect was positive for each year's consumption. However, the income effect was much stronger if the change in the real wage rate was permanent and applied to $(w/P)_2$, $(w/P)_3$, and so on, rather than just to $(w/P)_1$.

The same reasoning applies to labor supply. A permanent increase in real wage rates results in a large income effect. In this case, we are unsure whether an increase in $(w/P)_1$ (accompanied by increases in future real wage rates, $[w/P]_2$, $[w/P]_3$, and so on) raises or lowers year 1's quantity of labor supplied, $L_1^s$. The income effect, which lowers labor supply, may be stronger or weaker than the substitution effect, which raises labor supply.

In contrast, if the change in year 1's real wage rate, $(w/P)_1$, is temporary, the income effect is small. In this case, we can be confident that the income effect will be weaker than the substitution effect. Therefore, a temporary increase in year 1's real wage rate, $(w/P)_1$ (when $[w/P]_2$, $[w/P]_3$, and so on do not change), would raise year 1's quantity of labor supplied, $L_1^s$.

### Intertemporal-substitution effects on labor supply

We found in Chapter 7 that a change in the interest rate, $i$, had an intertemporal-substitution effect on consumption. Now we will study intertemporal-substitution effects on labor supply. We will first consider effects from interest rates and then study new effects from variations over time in real wage rates.

The multiyear budget constraint is again

$$(8.7) \quad C_1 + C_2/(1 + i_1) + C_3/[(1 + i_1) \cdot (1 + i_2)] + \cdots = (1 + i_0) \cdot (B_0/P + K_0)$$
$$\blacksquare\blacksquare\blacksquare\blacksquare\blacksquare\blacksquare\blacksquare\blacksquare\blacksquare\blacksquare\blacksquare\blacksquare + (w/P)_3 \cdot L_3^s/[(1 + i_1) \cdot (1 + i_2)] + \cdots$$

The yellow shaded terms show that an increase in year 1's interest rate, $i_1$, makes year 2's consumption, $C_2$, cheaper compared with year 1's, $C_1$. Therefore, an increase in $i_1$ lowered $C_1$ and raised $C_2$. In other words, households substituted away from the object that got more expensive—current consumption—and toward the one that got cheaper—future consumption.

The pink shaded terms in equation (8.7) show that year 2's real wage income, $(w/P)_2 \cdot L_2^s$, is discounted by $1 + i_1$ to get a present value before combining it with year 1's real wage income, $(w/P)_1 \cdot L_1^s$. If the interest rate, $i_1$, rises, a unit of year 2's real wage income, $(w/P)_2 \cdot L_2^s$, becomes less valuable as a present value compared to a unit of year 1's real wage income, $(w/P)_1 \cdot L_1^s$. We therefore predict that the household would increase $L_1^s$ and decrease $L_2^s$. This change is an intertemporal-substitution effect on labor supply— a higher interest rate favors more labor supply today and less in the future.

Another way to view this result is through leisure time. A higher interest rate, $i_1$, means that future consumption and leisure time are cheaper in present-value terms compared to current consumption and leisure time. Therefore, the household substitutes toward the cheaper objects—future consumption and leisure time—and away from the more expensive ones—current consumption and leisure time.

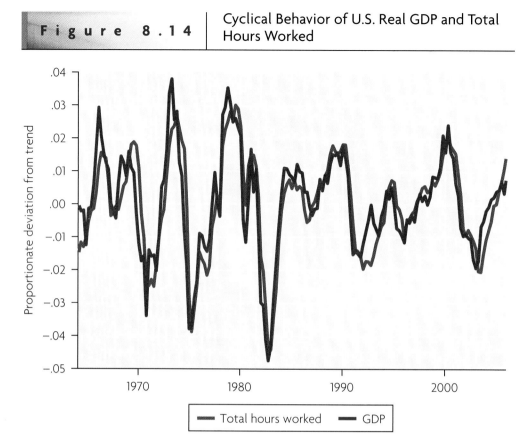

| Figure 8.14 | Cyclical Behavior of U.S. Real GDP and Total Hours Worked |

The red graph is the deviation of real GDP from its trend. The blue graph is the deviation of total hours worked from its trend. These deviations are measured in a proportionate sense. Total hours worked is employment (from Figure 8.13) multiplied by average weekly hours of persons working. The data for weekly hours, available since 1964, come from the BLS payroll survey and refer to the private, nonagricultural economy. The data on real GDP and total hours are quarterly and seasonally adjusted. (The underlying data on total hours worked are monthly.) Total hours worked is procyclical—it fluctuates closely with real GDP and is about as variable as real GDP.

graphs show the proportionate deviation of employment or total hours worked from trend. As before, the red graphs show the cyclical parts of real GDP.

We see from the graphs that both measures of labor input are procyclical: they move in the same direction as real GDP during booms and recessions.[13] That is, employment and total hours worked are both high relative to trend during booms and low relative to trend during recessions. The variability of labor input is nearly as great as that of real GDP—the standard deviations of the cyclical parts were 1.3% for employment and 1.5% for total hours worked, compared with 1.6% for real GDP. Thus, in a proportionate sense, employment and total hours worked vary by nearly as much as real GDP during booms and recessions.

---

[13] From 1954.1 to 2006.1, the correlation of the cyclical part of employment with the cyclical part of real GDP was 0.81. From 1964.1 to 2006.1, the correlation of the cyclical part of total hours worked with the cyclical part of real GDP was 0.88.

**Figure  8.15** | Clearing of the Labor Market

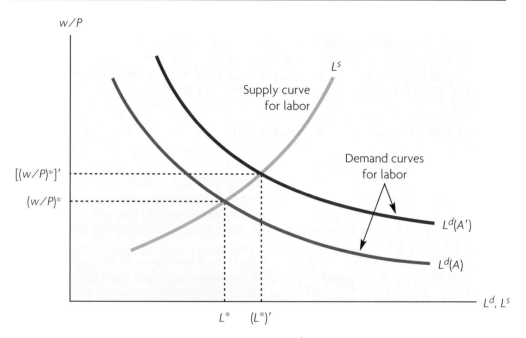

At the technology level $A$, the demand for labor, labeled $L^d(A)$ along the blue curve, slopes downward versus the real wage rate, $w/P$. At the higher technology level, $A'$, the demand for labor, labeled $L^d(A')$ along the red curve, is larger at any given $w/P$. These two curves are from Figure 8.5. The supply of labor, $L^s$, shown in green, slopes upward versus $w/P$ because we assume that the substitution effect from a change in $w/P$ dominates the income effect. The increase in the technology level from $A$ to $A'$ raises the real wage rate from $(w/P)^*$ to $[(w/P)^*]$ on the vertical axis, and increases labor input from $L^*$ to $(L^*)'$ on the horizontal axis.

**The cyclical behavior of labor input: theory**   We will now work out the equilibrium business-cycle model with variable labor supply. We assume again that economic fluctuations reflect shocks to the technology level, $A$. These shocks are long lasting but not permanent.

Figure 8.15 shows how an increase in the technology level, $A$, affects the labor market. The downward-sloping labor-demand curves come from Figure 8.5. The blue curve shows market labor demand, $L^d$, at an initial technology level, $A$. This curve slopes downward, as usual, because a decrease in the real wage rate, $w/P$, raises the quantity of labor demanded. The downward-sloping red curve is for a higher technology level, $A'$.

Figure 8.15 shows an upward-sloping curve for labor supply, $L^s$. This curve slopes upward because we assume that the substitution effect from a higher current real wage rate, $w/P$, dominates the income effect. We already noted that this upward slope is likely to apply if the changes in $w/P$ are not fully permanent. The same curve for $L^s$ applies for the two technology levels. That is, for a given $w/P$, we assume that the labor-supply curve does not shift when the technology level rises from $A$ to $A'$. This assumption is not fully accurate because it neglects effects on $L^s$ from an increase in the interest rate (which occur when the technology level rises). However, the inclusion of an interest-rate effect would not change our main results.

We reach two important conclusions from Figure 8.15. First, as before, the real wage rate rises, from $(w/P)^*$ to $[(w/P)^*]'$ on the vertical axis. Second, aggregate labor input

## Figure 9.2 | Effect of an Increase in the Technology Level on the Demand for Capital Services

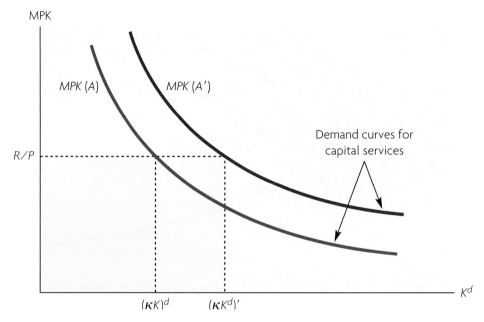

When the technology level is $A$, the MPK is given by the blue curve, labeled $MPK$ $(A)$. At the real rental price $R/P$, shown on the vertical axis, the quantity of capital services demanded is $(\kappa K)^d$ on the horizontal axis. The technology level $A'$ is greater than $A$. Therefore, the MPK, given by the red curve labeled $MPK$ $(A')$, is higher at any capital input than the value along the blue curve. When the technology level is $A'$ and the real rental price is $R/P$, the quantity of capital services demanded is $(\kappa K^d)'$, which is greater than $(\kappa K)^d$.

Owners of capital choose the utilization rate, $\kappa$, to maximize their net real income from supplying capital services:

$$net\ real\ income\ from\ supplying\ capital\ services = real\ rental\ payments - depreciation$$
$$= (R/P) \cdot \kappa K - \delta(\kappa) \cdot K$$

If we take the variable $K$ outside, we can write the result as

(9.3)    $net\ real\ income\ from\ supplying\ capital\ services = K \cdot [(R/P) \cdot \kappa - \delta(\kappa)]$

Thus, the net real income equals the capital owned, $K$, multiplied by the term $(R/P) \cdot \kappa - \delta(\kappa)$. To understand this term, note that the first part, $(R/P) \cdot \kappa$, is the product of the real rental per machine-hour, $R/P$, and the machine-hours per year, $\kappa$, from each machine. Thus, $(R/P) \cdot \kappa$ is the real rental income per year on each unit of capital. When we subtract the depreciation rate, $\delta(\kappa)$, we get the net real rental income per unit of capital, $(R/P) \cdot \kappa - \delta(\kappa)$. This term gives the rate of return from owning capital:

Key equation (rate of return on capital):

(9.4)        $rate\ of\ return\ from\ owning\ capital = (R/P) \cdot \kappa - \delta(\kappa)$

<table>
<tr><td>F i g u r e   9 . 3</td><td>Choosing the Capital Utilization Rate</td></tr>
</table>

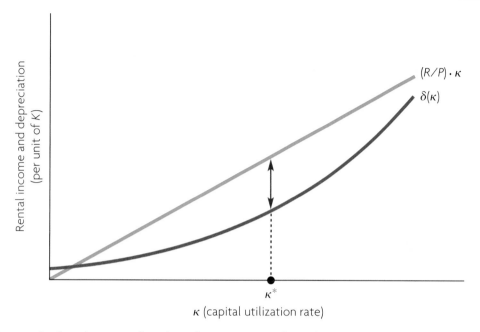

The green line from the origin is the real rental income per unit of capital, $(R/P) \cdot \kappa$. The blue curve shows the depreciation rate, $\delta(\kappa)$, as an upward-sloping function of the capital utilization rate, $\kappa$. The gap between the green line and the blue curve equals the rate of return from owning capital, $(R/P) \cdot \kappa - \delta(\kappa)$, given in equation (9.3). Owners of capital choose $\kappa$ to maximize this vertical distance—this maximization occurs when $\kappa = \kappa^*$ on the horizontal axis.

For a given capital stock, $K$, the maximization of the net real income from supplying capital services boils down to maximizing the net real return from owning capital, $(R/P) \cdot \kappa - \delta(\kappa)$, in equation (9.4). Figure 9.3 graphs the two parts of this return against the capital utilization rate, $\kappa$. The straight green line shows the first part, $(R/P) \cdot \kappa$. This line starts from the origin, and its slope equals the real rental price, $R/P$. As in our previous analysis, an individual household takes $R/P$ as given.

The second part of the rate of return from owning capital in equation (9.4) is the negative of the depreciation rate, $\delta(\kappa)$. We graph $\delta(\kappa)$ versus $\kappa$ in Figure 9.3 as the blue curve. We assume that $\delta(\kappa)$ is greater than zero when $\kappa$ equals zero; that is, capital depreciates even when it sits idle (perhaps because it gets rusty). Second, $\delta(\kappa)$ rises as $\kappa$ increases above zero, so that a higher $\kappa$ leads to a higher depreciation rate, $\delta(\kappa)$.[2]

The rate of return from owning capital, given by equation (9.4), equals the vertical distance between the green line and the blue curve in Figure 9.3. Owners of capital (households) select the utilization rate, $\kappa$, that maximizes this distance. In the graph, this maximization occurs when $\kappa = \kappa^*$ on the horizontal axis. At $\kappa^*$, the vertical distance between the line and the curve is shown by the red arrows. Typically, $\kappa^*$ will be set below its maximum feasible value of 8,736 hours per year. Owners avoid this extremely high rate of capital utilization because it leads to rapid depreciation of the

---

[2] We also assume that $\delta(\kappa)$ gets more sensitive to $\kappa$ as $\kappa$ increases. Graphically, the curve $\delta(\kappa)$ has a convex shape—it bows out toward the horizontal axis.

## Figure 9.10 | Distribution of Real Wage Offers

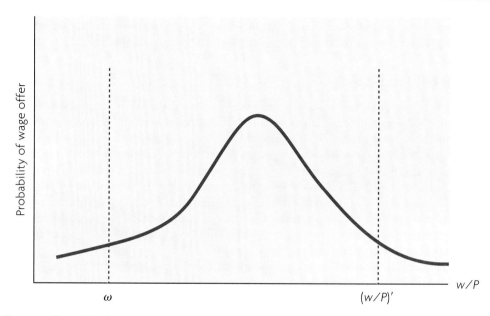

The curve shows the chances of receiving offers of real wages, $w/P$, of different sizes. The higher the curve, the more likely that real wage offers of that size will be received. On the horizontal axis, $\omega$ is the effective real income received while unemployed, and $(w/P)'$ is the reservation real wage. Job offers are accepted if they pay at least as much as $(w/P)'$, and are otherwise rejected.

spent unemployed will usually be brief. However, a low $(w/P)'$ also means that Hillary will likely end up on a job with a low $w/P$.

The optimal reservation real wage, $(w/P)'$, depends on the shape of the wage-offer distribution in Figure 9.10, as well as the effective real income while unemployed, $\omega$, and the expected duration of a job.[6] For our purposes, we do not have to go through the details of the determination of the optimal $(w/P)'$. We can get the main results by describing the important properties that come out of this analysis.

Since some job offers are unacceptable—that is, $w/P < (w/P)'$ for some offers— it typically takes time for Hillary to find an acceptable position. In the interim, she is "unemployed," although engaged in job search. Thus, incomplete information about where to find the best job can explain why unemployment is greater than zero.

An increase in the effective real income while unemployed, $\omega$, motivates Hillary to raise her standards for job acceptance; that is, $(w/P)'$ increases. This effect is particularly strong if Hillary's likely offers of real wages, $w/P$, are not much above $\omega$. For example, an increase in $\omega$ caused by a rise in unemployment insurance benefits will have a strong impact on $(w/P)'$ if the benefits are high compared to usual wage offers. In the United States, where unemployment insurance benefits are not so high, a small increase in benefits would not have a major effect on $(w/P)'$ for the typical job seeker. In contrast, in countries such as France and Germany, which have very generous unemployment insurance programs, a rise in benefits would have a much greater impact on the typical $(w/P)'$.

---

[6] For a discussion of job search models that involve a reservation wage, see Belton Fleisher and Thomas Kniesner (1984, pp. 477–507).

For a given distribution of wage offers in Figure 9.10, an increase in $\omega$ makes it more likely that $w/P < (w/P)'$ will apply, because $(w/P)'$ increases. Hence, job offers will be rejected more often. It follows that job searchers, such as Hillary, tend to take longer to find a position when $\omega$ increases. For a group of persons, we therefore predict that a rise in $\omega$ reduces the **job-finding rate**, which is the rate at which job seekers find positions. Correspondingly, a rise in $\omega$ raises the expected **duration of unemployment**, which is the amount of time that the typical unemployed person stays unemployed.

Suppose that the entire distribution of wage offers improves. For example, a favorable shock to the technology level, $A$, could raise the MPL of all workers—say, by 10%. Since each real wage offer, $w/P$, equals the value of a worker's potential marginal product, the distribution of real wage offers in Figure 9.10 shifts to the right—the typical real wage offer, $w/P$, rises by 10%. Therefore, if the reservation real wage, $(w/P)'$, does not change, job offers fall more often in the acceptable range, where $w/P > (w/P)'$. Hence, the job-finding rate rises, and the expected duration of unemployment falls.

We have to consider, however, that a better distribution of wage offers tends to raise the reservation real wage, $(w/P)'$. Job seekers, such as Hillary, become more selective—raise $(w/P)'$—if they anticipate that the better distribution of real wage offers will persist into the future. For example, a permanent improvement in technology would tend to have a long-run impact on real wage offers. In this case, $(w/P)'$ would rise. The increase in $(w/P)'$ works against our predicted rise in the job-finding rate. In the example where all real wage offers, $w/P$, increase by 10%, the job-finding rate will rise only if the increase in $(w/P)'$ is by less than 10%.

There are two reasons why the increase in the reservation real wage, $(w/P)'$, tends to be smaller in proportion than the rise in the typical real wage offer, $w/P$. First, if the rise in workers' MPL is not permanent, future real wage offers will tend to rise by less than current offers. In this case, $(w/P)'$ will also rise proportionately less than the typical real wage, $w/P$, offered currently to job searchers.

Second, even if the improvement in real wage offers is permanent, $(w/P)'$ will rise proportionately by less than the typical real wage offer, $w/P$, if the effective real income received while unemployed, $\omega$, does not change. To see why, we can compare three scenarios, as follows.

- Scenario 1 is the initial situation, where offers of real wage rates, $w/P$, are given by the distribution in Figure 9.10, and the effective real income received while unemployed is $\omega$.
- Scenario 2 is the new situation, where the typical real wage offer, $w/P$, is permanently higher by 10%, and $\omega$ is unchanged.
- Scenario 3 is a hypothetical situation, where the typical real wage offer, $w/P$, is permanently higher by 10%, and $\omega$ is also permanently higher by 10%.

Compare Scenario 1 with Scenario 3: the only difference is that everything is scaled upward by 10% in Scenario 3. Therefore, in weighing the trade-off between accepting or rejecting a job offer, it seems reasonable (and is, in fact, optimal) that a person would set the reservation real wage, $(w/P)'$, higher by 10% in Scenario 3. Therefore, the probability of receiving an acceptable job offer is the same in Scenario 3 as in Scenario 1. Hence, the job-finding rate is the same in these two cases.

Now compare Scenario 3 with Scenario 2. The only difference is that the real income received while unemployed, $\omega$, is higher by 10% in Scenario 3. Therefore, a job seeker would set the reservation real wage, $(w/P)'$, higher in Scenario 3 than in Scenario 2, and the job-finding rate is lower in Scenario 3 than in Scenario 2.

Now put the results together. Scenario 3 has the same job-finding rate as Scenario 1. Scenario 2 has a higher job-finding rate than Scenario 3. We have therefore shown that the

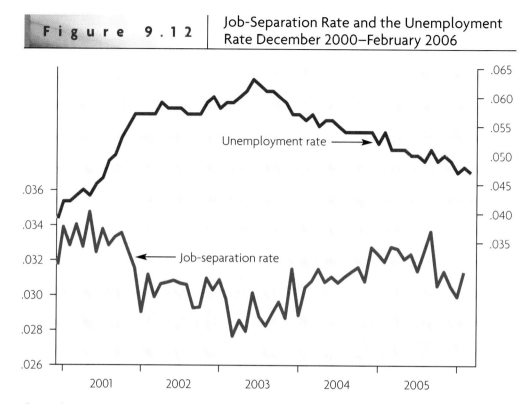

**Figure 9.12** | Job-Separation Rate and the Unemployment Rate December 2000–February 2006

The graph covers the period of data availability for the Job Openings and Labor Turnover Survey (JOLTS) from the BLS (http://www.bls.gov). The blue graph and the left scale are for the job-separation rate, calculated as the ratio of monthly total job separations to the number of persons employed. The red graph and the right scale are for the unemployment rate.

per month. Since the labor force is constant, all those who lose jobs move from category $L$ to category $U$. We are ignoring the fact that many job losers find new jobs immediately, without ever becoming unemployed.

Since December 2000, the BLS has carried out the Job Openings and Labor Turnover Survey (JOLTS), which estimates the job-separation rate for the total nonfarm economy. This rate is the ratio of total job separations over a month to civilian employment. From December 2000 to February 2006, the separation rate averaged 3.1% per month, and the average number of monthly separations was 4.32 million. This number is staggering—the U.S. job market has an enormous flow of persons out of jobs (and, as we shall see, also into jobs).

Figure 9.12 shows how the job-separation rate varied from December 2000 to February 2006. Note that late 2000 was the end of a boom period (see Figure 8.3). The red graph in Figure 9.12 shows that the unemployment rate rose from 3.9% in December 2000 to a peak of 6.3% in June 2003. Then the economy recovered, and the unemployment rate fell to 4.7% in March 2006.

The blue graph in Figure 9.12 shows that the job-separation rate did not vary much from December 2000 to February 2006—only between 2.8% and 3.5% per month. In particular, the job-separation rate changed little during the recession of 2001–02 and the strong economy of 2003–06. Thus, these data—though available only for a few years—suggest that the job-separation rate may not have a strong association with recessions and booms.[7]

---

[7] For a discussion of this behavior of the job-separation rate, see Robert Hall (2005).

The other part of the story is the rate at which people find jobs. In Figure 9.11, the arrow pointing from $U$ to $L$ represents the number of unemployed persons who find jobs during a month. We are again not being completely realistic, because we are ignoring movements out of and into the labor force. Some of the unemployed, $U$, may become discouraged about job prospects during a recession and therefore drop out of the labor force. This phenomenon is called **discouraged workers**. However, we are also neglecting opposing forces that motivate people to intensify job search during a recession. For example, if a person loses his or her job, the person's spouse might enter the labor force. As already mentioned, we know that variations in the labor force are a small part of short-run fluctuations in labor input. Therefore, the assumption of a constant labor force may be a satisfactory approximation.

We can use the BLS survey, JOLTS, to gauge the job-finding rate. From December 2000 to February 2006, the ratio of job hirings over a month to civilian employment averaged 3.2%, and the average monthly number of hirings was 4.45 million. In other words, while 4.32 million persons separated from their jobs each month, 4.45 million (not necessarily the same persons) were hired each month. Thus, there are tremendous gross flows of persons out of and into employment.

To measure the job-finding rate, we have to express the number of jobs found in relation to the number of persons seeking jobs—that is, the number of persons unemployed, $U$, rather than the number employed, $L$. Thus, we have

$$job - finding\ rate = (number\ of\ hires\ per\ month)/U$$

When defined this way, the job-finding rate measured by the BLS survey, JOLTS, averaged 0.58 per month from December 2000 to February 2006—roughly half of the unemployed found a job within one month. This number overstates the job-finding rate for the unemployed, because many job hires come from people who moved from one job to another (without becoming unemployed) and some came from people outside of the labor force (who were never recorded as unemployed). If we could adjust the number of hires per month to include only hirings that come from the unemployed, we would calculate a smaller job-finding rate. However, we lack the data to make this adjustment.

Although the job-finding rate estimated from the available data likely overstates the level of the rate, the movements in the estimated rate over time probably give a good indication of changes in the job-finding rate. The blue graph in Figure 9.13 on the next page shows the pattern of the calculated job-finding rate from December 2000 to February 2006. By comparing with the red graph, we see that the job-finding rate mirrored the unemployment rate. The job-finding rate fell from a peak of 0.90 in December 2000 to a low point of 0.44 in spring 2003, then recovered along with the economy to 0.70 in early 2006. Thus, the data show clearly that the job-finding rate falls during a recession and rises in a boom.

The job-separation and job-finding rates determine the dynamics of persons employed and unemployed. To get a realistic example, we will use numbers for the job-separation and job-finding rates that mirror the U.S. data. Specifically, assume that the job-separation rate is 0.03 per month and the job-finding rate is 0.5 per month, as shown in Figure 9.11. We assume, for now, that these rates are constant. This assumption may be satisfactory for the job-separation rate but not for the job-finding rate, which tends to fall below average during a recession and rise above average during a boom.

Table 9.1 on page 223 assumes that the labor force is fixed at 150 million people (roughly the U.S. number in 2006). Suppose that the economy starts in month 1 with an unemployment rate, $u$, of 10%, indicating a serious recession. Employment, $L$, starts at 135 million, and unemployment, $U$, starts at 15 million.

# Back To Reality

**Seasonal fluctuations**

Our analysis views economic fluctuations as resulting from shocks to the technology level, *A*. Shocks other than technological changes, such as harvest failures and strikes, have effects that resemble those from changes in *A*. Seasonal changes also resemble shifts to the technology.

As noted in Chapter 2, economists usually use seasonally adjusted data to study economic fluctuations. The seasonal adjustment eliminates the normal change in a variable, such as real GDP, from winter (the first quarter) to spring (the second quarter), and so on. In the unadjusted data, real GDP tends to rise each year toward a peak in the fourth quarter. This systematic quarter-to-quarter pattern does not appear in the seasonally adjusted numbers.

Robert Barsky and Jeffrey Miron (1989) studied the seasonally unadjusted numbers. They found that the seasonal fluctuations in quantities—real GDP, consumption, investment, employment, and unemployment—are larger than the variations associated with typical recessions and booms. From 1948 to 1985, over 80% of the quarterly fluctuations in real GDP and over 60% of those in the unemployment rate reflected seasonal factors (Barsky and Miron, 1989, Table 1). Further, the seasonal

patterns of co-movement among real GDP and its major components and between real GDP and employment look similar to those found in economic fluctuations (*ibid.*, Table 2). For example, in the seasonal pattern, investment and consumption move along with real GDP, and investment fluctuates much more than consumption. J. Joseph Beaulieu and Jeffrey Miron (1992) show that the U.S. findings apply also to 25 industrialized or semi-industrialized countries.

Seasonal fluctuations reflect influences of weather and holidays. We can think of some of these effects as variations in technology, such as the adverse impact of winter on the construction industry. Other effects correspond to variations in household preferences, such as the positive impact of Christmas on consumer demand and the negative impact of summer vacations on labor supply. The magnitude of the seasonal fluctuations shows that these kinds of disturbances can be quantitatively important in the short run. That is, the seasonal evidence weakens the argument made by some economists that shocks to technology and preferences are not large enough to account for the observed magnitude of recessions and booms.

The horizontal axis in Figure 9.15 shows the cyclical part of the unemployment rate, *u*. The vertical axis shows the cyclical part of the help-wanted advertising index. Note the clear downward slope—the correlation between the two series is −0.93. Thus, the data strongly confirm that a low unemployment rate matches up with high vacancies, whereas a high unemployment rate matches up with low vacancies.

## Summing Up

We began by extending the equilibrium business-cycle model to allow for variable capital utilization and, therefore, for a variable supply of capital services in the short run. This extension predicts that the capital-utilization rate will be procyclical—high in booms and low in recessions. The data on capacity utilization accord with this prediction.

In the U.S. data, labor input—measured, for example, by total worker-hours—is strongly procyclical. Worker-hours can be broken down into three components: the labor force, the employment rate (the fraction of the labor force with jobs), and the average hours worked per worker. The most important part of the fluctuations in worker-hours is the employment rate. Changes in average hours worked rank second in importance, and movements in the labor force rank third. Our analysis in Chapter 8 applies to the last two of these components but does not explain the most important part: the fluctuations in the employment rate.

This chapter extends the equilibrium business-cycle model to allow workers to search for good jobs and employers to search for productive workers. This extension explains why the unemployment rate would be greater than zero—that is, why the employment rate would be less than 100%. The analysis shows why the unemployment rate would be countercyclical, so that the employment rate would be procyclical. In addition, the model predicts that the job vacancy rate would move opposite to the unemployment rate—that is, job vacancies are procyclical. Overall, this extended version of the equilibrium business-cycle model gives us a better understanding of why labor input is high in booms and low in recessions.

## Key Terms and Concepts

capital utilization rate  
discouraged workers  
duration of unemployment  
employment rate  
help-wanted advertising  
job-finding rate  
job-separation rate  

natural unemployment rate  
reservation real wage  
unemployment insurance  
user costs  
vacancies  
vacancy rate  

## Questions and Problems

A. Review questions
1. Explain how the quantity of capital services depends on the stock of capital, $K$, and the capital utilization rate, $\kappa$. Why is the rate of return on capital given by equation (9.4)?
2. Use Figure 9.4 to study the capital utilization rate, $\kappa$. How does $\kappa$ change when

 a. the real rental price, $R/P$, rises?
 b. the depreciation rate, $\delta(\kappa)$, rises for each value of $\kappa$?

3. What is the definition of the unemployment rate? Since it does not include persons who are "out of the labor force," does it underestimate the true unemployment rate? Can you think of reasons why the reported numbers may overestimate the true unemployment rate?

4. Suppose that a job seeker receives a real wage offer, $w/P$, that exceeds his or her effective real income while unemployed, $\omega$. Why might the person reject the offer?

5. Once a job seeker and a firm find a job match, why might they choose subsequently to end the match? List some influences on the job-separation rate.

6. What is the natural rate of unemployment, $u^n$? Why might the unemployment rate, $u$, differ from $u^n$? Can $u^n$ change over time?

**B.** Problems for discussion

   7. The job-finding rate

   Discuss the effects on the job-finding rate and the expected duration of unemployment from the following:

   a. an increase in unemployment insurance benefits
   b. an increase in the allowable duration of unemployment insurance benefits
   c. a technological change, such as the Internet, that improves the matching of workers and jobs

   8. The job-finding rate, the job-separation rate, and the dynamics of the unemployment rate

   Suppose that the labor force is fixed at 100 million people, of whom 92 million initially have jobs and 8 million are unemployed. Assume that the job-separation rate is 2% per month and the job-finding rate is 40% per month. Trace out the time paths of employment and unemployment. What is the natural unemployment rate?

   9. Cyclical behavior of the labor force

   Figure 9.7 shows that the labor force is weakly procyclical. What pattern would you predict on theoretical grounds? (Hint: think first about people's incentives to leave the labor force—that is, to stop looking for work—during a recession. Are there also incentives for people to enter the labor force during a recession?)

   10. Job vacancies

   Suppose that economic fluctuations are caused by shocks to the technology level, $A$. What do you predict for the cyclical behavior of job vacancies? How then would fluctuations in vacancies relate to fluctuations in the unemployment rate? How does your answer relate to the Beveridge curve shown in Figure 9.15?

# Money and Prices

**Part 4**

# Chapter 10

## The Demand for Money and the Price Level

Our model has three forms of assets: money, bonds, and ownership of capital. So far, we have not analyzed how much money households hold or how these holdings change over time. We therefore carried out our analysis in Chapters 6–9 under the assumption that each household held a constant stock of money, $M$. Now we extend the microeconomic foundations of the model to explain why a household holds part of its assets as money; that is, we explain the **demand for money**. By demand for money, we refer to the quantity of money that a household decides to hold as a function of the price level, $P$, the interest rate, $i$, and other variables.

As mentioned in Chapter 6, we assume in the model that money is the sole medium of exchange in the economy. Households exchange money for goods on the goods market, money for labor on the labor market, money for capital services on the rental market, and money for bonds on the bond market. However, households do not directly exchange goods for goods (a process called **barter**), bonds for goods, and so on.

## Concepts of Money

The money in our model matches up with paper currency issued by a government. For example, the money could be U.S. dollar notes issued by the Federal Reserve, euro notes issued by the European Central Bank, and almost 200 other forms of paper currency issued by the world's governments. These currencies are sometimes called **fiat money** because they have value due to government fiat, rather than through intrinsic value. In earlier times, societies tended to rely more on **commodity money**, such as gold and silver coins, which do have intrinsic value. These coins are valued, in part, for their content of gold or silver. In the box below, we discuss how another commodity, the cigarette, served as money in a prisoner-of-war camp. In our model, money has no intrinsic value; it is just a piece of paper issued by the government. Therefore, we do not have to consider any resources used up when intrinsically valuable goods serve as money.

# Back To Reality

## Money in a prisoner-of-war camp

R.A. Radford (1945) described his experience with the economy of a German prisoner-of-war (P.O.W.) camp during World War II. He observed that cigarettes became the primary medium of exchange, with many goods being exchanged for cigarettes, which were then used to buy other goods. In addition, most prices were expressed in units of cigarettes, for example, as four cigarettes per ration of treacle (a form of syrup).

Radford noted that cigarettes had several attractive characteristics as money (p. 194): "homogeneous, reasonably durable, and of convenient size for the smallest or, in packets, for the largest transactions." One drawback, applicable also to other commodity moneys, was the resource cost of using cigarettes as a medium of exchange. That is, the cigarettes used as money could not simultaneously be smoked and, worse yet, might deteriorate physically over time.

Radford discussed an attempt to introduce paper money as an alternative medium of exchange. This money was issued by the camp restaurant and was supposed to be redeemable for a fixed quantity of food. However, problems arose with respect to the credibility of the promised food value of the paper money, and cigarettes remained the primary medium of exchange. For our purposes, an interesting lesson from Radford's story is that a medium of exchange is important in any economy, even a P.O.W. camp.

If we think of money as paper currency issued by the government, there are several reasons why this money might occupy the dominant position as an economy's medium of exchange. First, the government may impose legal restrictions that prevent private parties, such as Microsoft Corporation, from issuing small-size, interest-bearing bonds that could serve conveniently as hand-to-hand currency. Further, the government may enact statutes that reinforce the use of its money. As an example, there is the proclamation that the U.S. dollar is "**legal tender** for all debts public and private." The term "legal tender" means that U.S. dollar currency has to be accepted in some forms of trade, such as payments of taxes to the government. However, since the legal-tender requirement does not specify the price, $P$, at which exchanges have to occur, the content of the legal-tender provision is unclear—what would legal tender mean if $P$ were infinity? Perhaps more significant is that U.S. courts are more inclined to enforce contracts that are denominated in U.S. dollars rather than other units.

Another consideration is the cost of establishing one's money as reliable and convenient. These costs include prevention of counterfeiting, replacement of worn-out notes, willingness to convert notes into different denominations, and so on. Because of these costs, money would always tend to bear interest at a rate lower than bonds. In fact, because of the inconvenience of paying interest on hand-to-hand currency, the interest rate on currency is typically zero. That is, if one holds $1 of currency and does not lose it, one will still have $1 of currency in the future.

We can relate our abstract concept of money to conventional measures of the money stock. The theoretical construct corresponds most closely to currency held by the public. In the real world, currency held by the public differs from *total currency in circulation*, which includes currency held in the vaults of banks and other depository institutions. (Currency in circulation does not include amounts held by the U.S. Treasury or by Federal

# Back To Reality

**Where is all the currency?**

As mentioned, in March 2006, the amount of U.S. currency held by the public was about $2,500 per person in the United States. To understand this surprisingly large number, start with the observation that, at the end of 2005, 72% of currency in circulation by value, including coins, was in $100 bills. (The data on currency by denomination are in the *Treasury Bulletin*.) Thus, much of the currency is likely not used for ordinary transactions. Because currency is anonymous, it is attractive for illegal activities, such as the drug trade. Currency transactions also facilitate tax evasion. However, the amount of U.S. currency held for these purposes is unknown.

More is known about the amounts of U.S. currency held abroad, mostly in the form of $100 bills. Foreigners like U.S. money as a store of value and a medium of exchange because the money has a reasonably stable value and can readily be exchanged for goods or other assets. In addition, transactions carried out in currency can usually be hidden from local governments, and this secrecy is particularly attractive when the government is oppressive. The foreign demand for U.S. currency is especially high in countries experiencing economic and political turmoil. A recent joint study by the Federal Reserve and the U.S. Treasury estimated that 55–60% of the total U.S. currency in circulation in 2002 was held abroad. The geographical division was estimated to be 25% in Latin America (with Argentina the highest demander), 20% in the Middle East and Africa, 15% in Asia, and 40% in Europe (with Russia and other former Soviet republics as particularly high users). For additional discussion, see Richard Porter and Ruth Judson (2001) and Board of Governors of the Federal Reserve System (2003).

Reserve Banks.) A further distinction is between total currency in circulation and **high-powered money**, which adds the deposits held by banks and other depository institutions at the Federal Reserve. Another name for high-powered money is the **monetary base**.

In March 2006, the amount of (seasonally adjusted) currency held by the public in the United States was $735 billion, which amounted to 5.6% of nominal gross domestic product (GDP). This amount of currency is surprisingly large—about $2,500 per U.S. resident. In the box below, we note that much of the currency is in $100 bills, many of which are held abroad, rather than by U.S. residents.

The term "money" often refers to a **monetary aggregate** that is broader than currency. A monetary aggregate is the total dollar stock of a group of financial assets defined to be money. The most common definition, called **M1**, attempts to classify as money the assets that serve regularly as media of exchange. This concept adds to currency held by the public the **checkable deposits** issued by banks and other financial institutions. Checkable deposits are deposits held at financial institutions that can be withdrawn by writing a check. The amount of these checkable deposits (including travelers' checks) in the United States in March 2006 was $649 billion, or 5.0% of nominal GDP.[1] Therefore, M1—the sum of

---

[1] The standard definition of checkable deposits includes travelers' checks issued by banks and other depository institutions. Other travelers' checks, amounting to $6.9 billion in March 2006, are included separately in M1, not as part of checkable deposits. Our measure of checkable deposits departs from the standard definition by including all travelers' checks.

currency and checkable deposits—was $1,384 billion, or 10.6% of nominal GDP. The total M1 was 53% in currency and 47% in checkable deposits (including travelers' checks). In earlier times, a much smaller proportion of M1 was in currency, and a much larger proportion was in checkable deposits. For example, in 1960, only 19% of M1 was in currency, whereas 81% was in checkable deposits. This change illustrates the declining importance of checkable deposits held at banks and other financial institutions. These checking accounts have been replaced to a considerable extent by other forms of financial assets, such as money-market accounts, which have become much easier to access.

Table 10.1 shows ratios of currency to nominal GDP for OECD countries (the rich countries in the Organization for Economic Cooperation and Development), plus China, in 1960, 1980, and 2000. Notice that the ratio of currency to GDP declined over time in most countries—a typical case, for France, showed a decrease from 0.133 in 1960 to

T a b l e   1 0 . 1  |  Ratios of Currency to Nominal GDP

| Country | 1960 | 1980 | 2000 |
|---|---|---|---|
| Australia | 0.054 | 0.036 | 0.041 |
| Austria | 0.119 | 0.078 | 0.071 |
| Belgium | 0.220 | 0.110 | 0.054 |
| Canada | 0.046 | 0.034 | 0.034 |
| China | — | — | 0.072 |
| Denmark | 0.068 | 0.032 | 0.029 |
| Finland | 0.036 | 0.025 | 0.025 |
| France | 0.133 | 0.052 | 0.035 |
| Germany | 0.072 | 0.062 | 0.070 |
| Greece | 0.103 | 0.130 | — |
| Ireland | 0.117 | 0.077 | 0.052 |
| Italy | — | 0.070 | 0.066 |
| Japan | 0.069 | 0.072 | 0.121 |
| Netherlands | 0.125 | 0.064 | 0.047 |
| New Zealand | 0.061 | 0.025 | 0.019 |
| Norway | 0.112 | 0.060 | 0.030 |
| Portugal | 0.177 | 0.131 | 0.057 |
| South Korea | 0.059 | 0.049 | 0.034 |
| Spain | 0.120 | 0.083 | 0.099 |
| Sweden | 0.090 | 0.064 | 0.043 |
| Switzerland | 0.197 | 0.141 | 0.093 |
| United Kingdom | 0.081 | 0.044 | 0.025 |
| United States | 0.056 | 0.042 | 0.059 |

**Note:** The table shows the ratio of currency held by the public to nominal GDP. The data are from International Monetary Fund, *International Financial Statistics*.

0.052 in 1980 and 0.035 in 2000. However, in some countries, the ratio leveled off or even rose from 1980 to 2000—this pattern applied to Canada, Finland, Germany, Japan, Spain, and the United States. In 2000, the highest currency ratio was 0.121 in Japan, and the lowest was 0.019 in New Zealand. The United States, at 0.059, was close to the median. Table 10.2 shows comparable figures with money defined to be M1.

Still broader definitions of money add in other kinds of deposits held at financial institutions. For example, **M2** ($6,777 billion in the United States in March 2006) includes household holdings of savings deposits, small-time deposits, and retail money-market mutual funds. However, the M2 definition goes beyond the concept of money as a medium of exchange. In our model, it is best to use a narrower definition of money, for example, as currency held by the public.

### T a b l e  1 0 . 2 | Ratios of M1 to Nominal GDP

| Country | 1960 | 1980 | 2000 |
|---|---|---|---|
| Australia | 0.228 | 0.126 | 0.211 |
| Austria | 0.197 | 0.151 | 0.280 |
| Belgium | 0.322 | 0.192 | 0.271 |
| Canada | 0.152 | 0.112 | 0.213 |
| China | — | — | 0.146 |
| Denmark | 0.246 | 0.201 | — |
| Finland | — | 0.080 | 0.307 |
| France | 0.468 | 0.280 | 0.224 |
| Germany | 0.160 | 0.170 | 0.288 |
| Greece | 0.151 | 0.196 | 0.288 |
| Ireland | — | — | 0.197 |
| Italy | — | 0.442 | 0.416 |
| Japan | 0.265 | 0.286 | 0.484 |
| Netherlands | 0.274 | 0.187 | 0.367 |
| New Zealand | 0.279 | 0.110 | 0.141 |
| Norway | 0.235 | 0.145 | 0.403 |
| Portugal | — | 0.390 | 0.427 |
| South Korea | 0.104 | 0.101 | 0.090 |
| Spain | 0.327 | — | 0.338 |
| Sweden | — | — | — |
| Switzerland | 0.489 | 0.362 | 0.396 |
| United Kingdom | — | — | — |
| United States | 0.294 | 0.169 | 0.146 |

**Note:** The table shows the ratio of M1 (currency held by the public plus checkable deposits) to nominal GDP. The data are from the International Monetary Fund, *International Financial Statistics*. Data on M1 were unavailable for Sweden and the United Kingdom.

# The Demand for Money

We will now extend the microeconomic foundations of our model to consider the demand for money. Since we identify money with hand-to-hand currency, we assume that the interest rate paid on money is zero. In contrast, the rate of return on bonds and ownership of capital equals the interest rate, $i$, which we assume is greater than zero. Henceforth, we refer to bonds and ownership of capital as **interest-bearing assets**, because these assets pay a positive return to the holder. The important point is that these assets yield a higher rate of return than money and are therefore better than money as long-term **stores of value**. Nevertheless, since households use money to make exchanges, households will hold some money for convenience, rather than always cashing in earning assets immediately prior to each exchange. That is, the demand for money will be greater than zero.

In Chapter 6, we wrote the household budget constraint in nominal terms in equation (6.11), which we repeat here:

$$(10.1) \qquad PC + \Delta B + P \cdot \Delta K = \Pi + wL + i \cdot (B + PK)$$

$$\text{nominal consumption} + \text{nominal saving} = \text{nominal income}$$

On the right-hand side, the household receives nominal profit, $\Pi$ (which is zero in equilibrium), nominal wage income, $wL$, and nominal asset income, $i \cdot (B + PK)$, all in the form of money. On the left-hand side, the household uses money to buy consumption goods, in the nominal amount $PC$, and to add to interest-bearing assets (that is, to save), in the nominal amount $\Delta B + P \cdot \Delta K$.

Although all of the income and spending terms in equation (10.1) use money, it would be possible for the household to hold little or no money at every point in time. If each inflow of income were perfectly synchronized with an equal outflow of expenditure on goods or purchases of interest-bearing assets, each household's money balance could always be close to zero. However, this synchronization would require a great deal of effort and planning. We assume, as a general matter, that the household can reduce its average money balance by incurring more **transaction costs**. By transaction costs, we mean any expenses of time or goods related to the timing and form of various exchanges. In the real world, examples of transaction costs are the time spent going to the bank or an automatic teller machine (ATM), and brokerage fees.

One way to maintain a low average money balance is to rush off to the store as soon as money wages are paid to spend one's entire weekly or monthly paycheck on goods. Another method would be to go immediately to a financial institution to convert all of one's wage income into interest-bearing assets. More realistically, a household might immediately deposit its paycheck into a bank account (or might arrange for the paycheck to be deposited directly into an account). In addition, if workers were paid wages more frequently—say, weekly rather than monthly—it would be easier for workers to maintain a lower average money balance.

The general idea is that, by putting more effort into money management and, thereby, incurring more transaction costs, the household can reduce its average holding of money, $M$. For a given total of nominal assets, $M + B + PK$, a reduction in the average level of $M$ raises the average holding of interest-bearing assets, $B + PK$. Since asset income is $i \cdot (B + PK)$, the rise in $B + PK$ raises asset income. Thus, a household's average holding of money, $M$, emerges from a trade-off. With a frequent transaction strategy, $M$ will be low and asset income will be high, but transaction costs will be high. With an infrequent transactions strategy, $M$ will be high and asset income will be low, but transaction costs will be low. The household's choice of average money holdings entails finding the right balance between additional asset income and added transaction costs.

price, $R$, would halve, so that the real wage rate, $w/P$, and the real rental price, $R/P$, would stay the same. As before, the decrease in $M^s$ has no effect on real GDP, $Y$. Hence, nominal GDP, $PY$, falls to half its initial value.

## The Neutrality of Money

The results in the previous section exhibit a property called the **neutrality of money**. One-time changes in the nominal quantity of money supplied, $M^s$, affect nominal variables but leave real variables unchanged. Money is neutral in the sense of not affecting real variables. The real variables include real GDP, $Y$; the real wage rate, $w/P$; the real rental price, $R/P$; and the quantity of real money balances, $M/P$. The interest rate, $i$, also does not change. We should think of $i$ as a real variable because it governs intertemporal-substitution effects for consumption and work. In Chapter 11, which introduces inflation, we distinguish the nominal interest rate from the real interest rate.

Almost all economists accept the neutrality of money as a valid long-run proposition. That is, in the long run, an increase or decrease in the nominal quantity of money supplied, $M^s$, influences nominal variables but not real ones. However, many economists believe that money is not neutral in the short run. In the short run, increases in $M^s$ are usually thought to increase real GDP, $Y$, whereas decreases in $M^s$ are thought to decrease $Y$. The main source of the difference in conclusions involves the flexibility of nominal prices—notably, the price level, $P$, and the nominal wage rate, $w$. These nominal prices are thought to be flexible up or down in the long run in response to increases or decreases in $M^s$. However, $P$ and $w$ are often viewed as less flexible in the short run, especially when decreases in $M^s$ mean that $P$ and $w$ have to decrease. In some models, the assumption of price flexibility is replaced by an assumption that $P$ or $w$ is *sticky* in the short run. We discuss sticky-price and sticky-wage models in Chapter 16.

## A Change in the Demand for Money

We mentioned that financial innovations could affect the real demand for money. To explore these effects, suppose that the nominal demand for money is again given initially by

(10.2) $$M^d = P \cdot L(Y, i)$$

where $L(Y, i)$ is the real demand for money. As before, the nominal money demand, $M^d$, is graphed versus the price level, $P$, as the upward-sloping red line in Figure 10.3.

Suppose now that an improvement in the technology for making financial transactions—perhaps increased use of credit cards or ATM machines—decreases the real demand for money to $[L(Y, i)]'$, so that the nominal demand becomes

$$(M^d)' = P \cdot [L(Y, i)]'$$

We graph the new nominal money demand, $(M^d)'$, as the upward-sloping green line in Figure 10.3. At any price level, $P$, the nominal quantity of money demanded is smaller along the green line than along the red line.

We assume that the nominal quantity of money supplied, $M^s$, is fixed at $M$, shown by the vertical blue line in Figure 10.3. Therefore, the initial equilibrium price level is $P^*$ on the vertical axis. At this point, $M^s$ equals the nominal quantity of money demanded, $M^d$. After the fall in the real demand for money, the equilibrium price level is $(P^*)'$ on the vertical axis. At this point, $M^s$ equals the new nominal quantity of money demanded, $(M^d)'$.

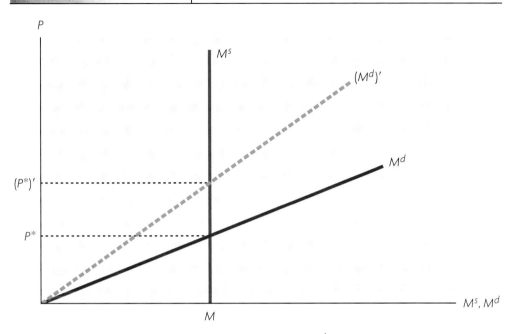

Figure 10.3 | A Decrease in the Real Demand for Money

The nominal demand for money is initially given by the red line, $M^d = P \cdot £(Y, i)$. We consider a decrease in the real demand for money, $£(Y, i)$. This real demand is lower along the dashed green line, $(M^d)'$, than along the red line. The nominal quantity of money supplied, $M^s$, is the constant $M$, shown by the vertical blue line. The decrease in the real demand for money raises the equilibrium price level from $P^*$ to $(P^*)'$ on the vertical axis.

Note that the decrease in the real demand for money leads to a higher price level; that is, $(P^*)'$ is above $P^*$. (As before, we assume that the price level adjusts rapidly to its equilibrium level.)

A decrease in the real demand for money is similar to an increase in the nominal quantity of money supplied, $M^s$, in that the price level, $P$, rises in each case. However, one difference is that a change in $M^s$ is fully neutral, whereas a change in the real demand for money is not fully neutral. To see why, note that the decrease in the real demand for money led to a rise in $P$, while $M^s$ was fixed at $M$. Therefore, the real quantity of money, $M/P$, decreased. In addition, the change in transactions technology that led to the decline in the real demand for money—such as expanded use of credit cards or ATM machines—would itself have real effects. For example, the resources used up in transaction costs would change. However, in most cases, the effects on macroeconomic variables, such as real GDP, will be small enough to neglect.

## The Cyclical Behavior of the Price Level

In Chapters 8 and 9, we used our equilibrium business-cycle model to study how shifts to the technology level, $A$, create economic fluctuations. Now we can use our analysis of the demand for money to determine how the price level, $P$, moves during economic fluctuations.

Recall that the nominal demand for money is given by

(10.2) $$M^d = P \cdot L(Y, i)$$

# Back To Reality

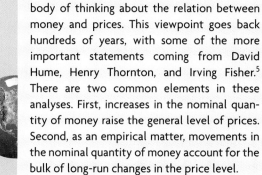

### The quantity theory of money

The **quantity theory of money** refers to a body of thinking about the relation between money and prices. This viewpoint goes back hundreds of years, with some of the more important statements coming from David Hume, Henry Thornton, and Irving Fisher.[5] There are two common elements in these analyses. First, increases in the nominal quantity of money raise the general level of prices. Second, as an empirical matter, movements in the nominal quantity of money account for the bulk of long-run changes in the price level.

Some economists refined the quantity theory to apply to changes in the nominal quantity of money measured relative to changes in the quantity of goods and services—real GDP—on which people spent their money. However, real GDP is only one variable that affects the real demand for money. Therefore, quantity theorists went further to argue that prices rose only when the nominal quantity of money expanded in relation to the real money balances that people wanted to hold. Hence, most variations in the price level would reflect movements in the nominal quantity of money if the fluctuations in this quantity were much greater than the fluctuations in the real quantity of money demanded. Milton Friedman (1956) stressed the stability of the real demand for money as the hallmark of a modern quantity theorist.

Sometimes economists identify the quantity theory of money with the proposition that changes in the nominal quantity of money are neutral. This idea corresponds to our previous result that changes in nominal money have no effects on real variables. Many quantity theorists regard this result as valid in the long run but not for short-run variations in the nominal quantity of money. Thus, in some versions of the quantity theory, changes in the nominal quantity of money have temporary effects on real variables, such as real GDP.

Think about a recession, in which real GDP, $Y$, falls. The decline in $Y$ reduces the real quantity of money demanded, given by $L(Y, i)$ on the right-hand side of equation (10.2). However, we also found that the interest rate, $i$, tends to fall in a recession. The decrease in $i$ raises the real quantity of money demanded, $L(Y, i)$. The overall change depends on the magnitudes of the decreases in $Y$ and $i$, and on the sensitivity of $L(Y, i)$ to $Y$ and $i$. Typical estimates indicate that the real quantity of money demanded, $L(Y, i)$, declines overall in this situation; the fall in $i$ tends to be small, and $L(Y, i)$ is not very responsive to changes in $i$. Therefore, we assume that, in a recession, the real quantity of money demanded, given by $L(Y, i)$, decreases overall.

We can use Figure 10.3 to determine the effect of an economic contraction on the price level, $P$. Recall that this figure applied to a decrease in the real demand for money, $L(Y, i)$, caused by a change in the transactions technology. However, the same construction applies if $L(Y, i)$ decreases for other reasons. In the present case, the real quantity of money demanded, $L(Y, i)$, falls overall because of the decreases in real GDP, $Y$, and the interest rate, $i$. Thus, we can use Figure 10.3 to study how the price level, $P$, changes during a recession.

We see from Figure 10.3 that, for a given nominal quantity of money supplied, $M^s$, the decrease in the real quantity of money demanded, $L(Y, i)$, raises the price level, $P$.

---

[5] See Hume's essay, "Of Money," in Eugene Rotwein (1970), Thornton (1802), and Fisher (1926).

| **F i g u r e   1 0 . 4** | Cyclical Behavior of U.S. Real GDP and the Price Level |

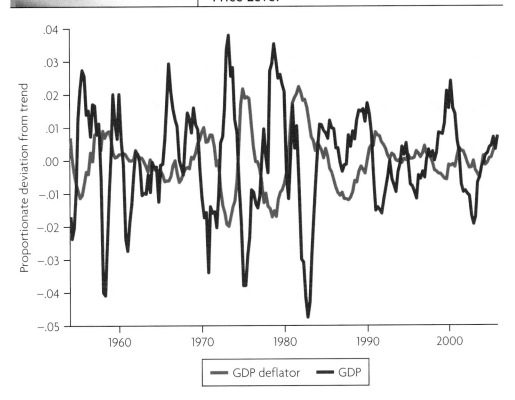

The red graph is the deviation of real GDP from its trend. The blue graph is the deviation of the GDP deflator from its trend. These deviations are measured in a proportionate sense. The GDP deflator is countercyclical—it fluctuates in the direction opposite to real GDP—and is less variable than real GDP.

Hence, in a recession, a relatively high $P$ tends to accompany the decrease in real GDP, $Y$. If we had done the analysis in reverse—to consider a boom in which the real quantity of money demanded, $L(Y, i)$, increased—we would get the opposite conclusion. That is, the price level, $P$, would fall. Thus, our model has a new prediction: if the nominal quantity of money supplied, $M^s$, does not vary, the price level, $P$, will be relatively high in recessions and relatively low in booms. That is, we predict that $P$ will be countercyclical.[6]

The result that the price level, $P$, is countercyclical may be counterintuitive. One might guess that, since real GDP is low in a recession, the low real income would lead to low consumer demand and tend, thereby, to reduce $P$. However, in our equilibrium business-cycle model, the underlying shocks come from the supply side, not the demand side. For example, a low technology level, $A$—the source of a recession in the model—means that goods and services are in low supply. When looked at this way, it makes sense that $P$ would tend to be high in a recession.

Now we will consider how the model's predictions about the price level, $P$, match up with the U.S. data. We measure $P$ by the deflator for the gross domestic product. We calculate the cyclical part of $P$ by using the method applied to real GDP in Figure 8.2. The result is the blue graph in Figure 10.4. This graph shows the proportionate deviation of $P$ from

---

[6] This result was first emphasized by Finn Kydland and Edward Prescott (1990).

its trend. We also show as the red graph the cyclical part of real GDP (from Figure 8.3). We can see from Figure 10.4 that $P$ typically fluctuates in the direction opposite to real GDP.[7] That is, as predicted, the price level is high—relative to trend—in recessions, and low—relative to trend—in booms. The results are similar if we use the consumer price index (CPI), rather than the GDP deflator, to measure the price level.

We see from the blue graph in Figure 10.4 that two of the largest positive deviations of the GDP deflator from its trend were in 1974–75 and 1981–82. These increases in the price level reflected, in part, the sharp rises in oil prices generated by the oil cartel run by the Organization of Petroleum Exporting Countries (OPEC). These periods also featured recessions in the United States, so that real GDP was well below its trend, as seen on the red graph. Thus, the price level and real GDP moved in opposite directions at the times of these oil shocks. However, the inverse relation between the price level and real GDP is not just the result of oil shocks—the pattern applies more generally to the period 1954–2006, shown in Figure 10.4.[8]

## Price-Level Targeting and Endogenous Money

A key assumption in our model is that the nominal quantity of money supplied, $M^s$, is independent of the nominal demand for money, $M^d = P \cdot L(Y, i)$. In other words, the monetary authority decides how much nominal money, $M$, to provide, and sticks with this quantity no matter what happens to nominal money demand, $M^d$. A formal way to say this is that the money-supply function, given in our case by $M^s = M$, is independent of the money-demand function.

This formulation is useful for studying exogenous changes in the nominal quantity of money supplied, $M^s$. By exogenous, we mean that the change comes from out of the blue, or at least from outside of the model. The trouble is that most changes in money supply are not like this in the real world. The head of the central bank does not just wake up in the morning and happen to think that it would be nice if the nominal quantity of money were higher or lower by 10%. Usually, the changes in $M^s$ are responses to economic events; the changes happen because the monetary authority is trying to accomplish some important economic objective. One common objective is to achieve a desired or *target* value of the price level, $P$. Related objectives, considered in later chapters, are to target the inflation rate and the nominal interest rate.

When the monetary authority seeks to attain a specified price level, $P$, it typically has to adjust the nominal quantity of money, $M$, in response to changes in the nominal quantity demanded, $M^d$. Another way to say this is that $M$ will be endogenous, or determined within the model. We therefore have a setting of **endogenous money**. To see how this works, we now assume that the monetary authority wants the price level, $P$, to equal a target level, which we call $\bar{P}$. This objective is called **price-level targeting**.

For present purposes, we assume that the monetary authority can determine the path of the nominal quantity of money, $M$, possibly subject to minor random errors. This assumption is reasonable in our model because we are taking a narrow view of money as currency. However, the assumption would be less satisfactory if we took a broader view of $M$, for example, to add the deposit accounts included in broader monetary aggregates, such as M1 and M2. Another reasonable assumption is that the monetary authority can

---

[7] From 1954.1 to 2006.1, the correlation of the cyclical part of the GDP deflator with the cyclical part of real GDP was −0.61. The GDP deflator is less variable than real GDP: the standard deviation of the cyclical part of the GDP deflator was 0.8%, compared with 1.6% for real GDP.

[8] The pattern is different before World War II. From 1880 to 1940 (using the available annual data), the correlation of the cyclical part of the GNP deflator with the cyclical part of real GNP was positive: 0.39. The main difference in the earlier period is the high frequency of banking panics, which tended to reduce broad monetary aggregates, such as M1, and the price level, along with output. This effect was especially important from 1931 to 1934, during the Great Depression.

control a monetary aggregate that is slightly broader than currency: the monetary base. This aggregate adds to total currency outstanding the reserves of financial institutions held at the central bank.

Since we assume that the monetary authority has no technical problems in controlling the quantity of nominal money, the changes in $M$ will reflect only intentional policy, not technical errors. In particular, changes in $M$ will occur because the underlying objective of price-level targeting, $P = \bar{P}$, dictates changes in $M$.

We still have equality at every point in time between the nominal quantity of money, $M$, and the nominal quantity demanded, $M^d$:

(10.6) $$M = P \cdot L(Y, i)$$

Before, we thought of $M$ as equal to an arbitrary quantity supplied, $M^s$. Now we will let $M$ be endogenous—determined by equation (10.6)—and assume that the monetary authority allows $M$ to adjust to achieve its price-level target:

(10.7) $$P = \bar{P}$$

If we substitute $P = \bar{P}$ from equation (10.7) into equation (10.6), we get a condition for determining the nominal quantity of money:

> Key equation (endogenous determination of money):
>
> (10.8) $$M = \bar{P} \cdot L(Y, i)$$
>
> *nominal quantity of money = price-level target · real quantity of money demanded*

The idea in equation (10.8) is that the price level, $P$, can be constant at its target value $\bar{P}$ only if the nominal quantity of money, $M$, varies on the left-hand side to compensate for changes in the real quantity of money demanded, $L(Y, i)$, on the right-hand side. For example, if $L(Y, i)$ doubles but $M$ stays the same, $P$ would have to fall to satisfy equation (10.6). Alternatively, if $L(Y, i)$ stays the same but $M$ doubles, $P$ would have to rise. To keep $P$ fixed at $\bar{P}$, proportionate changes in the real quantity of money demanded, $L(Y, i)$, have to be matched by equal proportionate changes in $M$. This condition tells us how price-level targeting determines the behavior of $M$ in equation (10.8). The general point is that the nominal quantity of money, $M$, will be endogenous and will react to changes in variables that affect the real quantity of money demanded, $L(Y, i)$. We now apply this analysis to determine $M$ in three settings: long-term growth, cyclical fluctuations, and seasonal movements.

**Trend growth of money**   To determine the trend in the nominal quantity of money, $M$, we have to allow for a long-run trend in the real quantity of money demanded, $L(Y, i)$, on the right-hand side of equation (10.8). The most important source of this trend is long-run economic growth—that is, an upward trend in real GDP, $Y$. We can use the Solow growth model from Chapter 5 to understand this trend. In the long-run or steady-state situation, real GDP, $Y$, grows at a constant rate due to technological progress and population growth.[9] This growth of $Y$ produces a continuing rise in the real quantity of money

---

[9] The interest rate, $i$, will be constant in this situation, because the marginal product of capital, MPK, will not be changing. Therefore, at least if we neglect financial innovations, the real quantity of money demanded, $L(Y, i)$, will be changing only because of the growth of real GDP, $Y$.

demanded, $L(Y, i)$. If we think of money as currency, the empirical estimates of money demand suggest that the growth rate of $L(Y, i)$ will be about the same as the growth rate of $Y$.[10]

Consider our condition for determining the nominal quantity of money, $M$:

$$(10.8) \qquad\qquad M = \bar{P} \cdot L(Y, i)$$

Since the price-level target, $\bar{P}$, is constant, continuing growth of the real quantity of money demanded, $L(Y, i)$, on the right-hand side requires $M$ to grow at the same rate on the left-hand side. Since $L(Y, i)$ grows at the same rate as real GDP, $Y$, we conclude that $M$ must grow at the same rate as $Y$. Thereby, the growth rate of the nominal quantity of money, $M$, matches the growth rate of the real quantity demanded, $L(Y, i)$, and allows the price level, $P$, to remain constant at its target level, $\bar{P}$.

The important conclusion is that a growing economy will have growth in its nominal quantity of money, $M$, assuming that the monetary authority seeks to stabilize the price level, $P$. This result accords with data considered in Chapter 11. We shall see there that growing $M$ applies to almost all countries in the world. However, we also allow in Chapter 11 for inflation—that is, for a continual upward movement in $P$.

**Cyclical behavior of money**  To study the cyclical behavior of money, we again use the condition for determining the nominal quantity of money, $M$:

$$(10.8) \qquad\qquad M = \bar{P} \cdot L(Y, i)$$

We know that the real quantity of money demanded, $L(Y, i)$, is high in a boom and low in a recession; this is because a change in real GDP, $Y$, moves $L(Y, i)$ in the same direction. (We assume that this effect dominates the impact from a change in the interest rate, $i$.) We also know that, if $M$ did not fluctuate, the price level, $P$, would fall in a boom and rise in a recession. That is, $P$ would be countercyclical—low relative to trend in booms and high relative to trend in recessions.

If the monetary authority wants to keep the price level, $P$, fixed at its target, $\bar{P}$, during economic fluctuations, it has to introduce a cyclical pattern into the nominal quantity of money, $M$. In particular, in equation (10.8), the cyclical fluctuations in $M$ on the left-hand side have to match the cyclical fluctuations in the real quantity of money demanded, $L(Y, i)$, on the right-hand side. Thus, $M$ will have to rise in a boom (along with the rise in $L[Y, i]$) and fall in a recession (along with the fall in $L[Y, i]$). In other words, $M$ should be procyclical.

Recall that we found that the price level, $P$, is countercyclical in the U.S. data. This pattern fit with our equilibrium business-cycle model when we assumed that the nominal quantity of money, $M$, did not vary over the business cycle. In other words, the monetary authority (the Federal Reserve) has not pursued a monetary policy that completely eliminated the countercyclical behavior of $P$: $M$ has not been sufficiently procyclical to avoid a countercyclical price level. Nevertheless, we would like to know whether the monetary authority has followed a policy that is somewhat procyclical; that is, whether nominal money, $M$, is high relative to trend during booms and low relative to trend during recessions. If so, this policy would have moderated the countercyclical pattern for $P$.

---

[10] With economies of scale in money demand, the real quantity of money demanded would grow at a slower rate than real GDP. As discussed before, the empirical evidence suggests that these economies of scale are important for checkable deposits but not for currency. We are also neglecting the possibility that continuing financial innovations affect the real demand for money.

Empirically, the nominal quantity of money, $M$, is weakly procyclical. For example, from 1954 to 2006, the correlation of the cyclical part of currency held by the public with the cyclical part of real GDP was only 0.08. Broader monetary aggregates are somewhat more procyclical: from 1959 to 2006, the correlations with the cyclical part of real GDP were 0.14 for M1 and 0.31 for M2. The weak procyclical pattern in monetary aggregates is consistent with our finding that the price level, $P$, is countercyclical. The monetary aggregates would have had to be more procyclical to eliminate the countercyclical pattern in $P$.

**Seasonal variations in money**    We have argued that, to achieve price-level stability, the monetary authority has to vary the nominal quantity of money, $M$, to match the changes in the real quantity demanded, $L(Y, i)$, that occur because of economic growth or fluctuations. An analogous argument applies to the variations in $L(Y, i)$ associated with the seasons.

Until the mid-1980s, the quantity of real currency held in December was about 2% higher than the average for the year, whereas the amount held in February was about 1% lower than average. If the monetary authority had kept the nominal quantity of currency, $M$, constant over the year, the price level, $P$, would have had the reverse seasonal pattern— low in December and high in February. To see how the monetary authority avoided this outcome, we can again use our condition for determining the nominal quantity of money, $M$:

(10.8)
$$M = \bar{P} \cdot L(Y, i)$$

To avoid a seasonal pattern in the price level, $P$, the Federal Reserve engineered a relatively high nominal quantity of currency, $M$, when the real quantity of money demanded, $L(Y, i)$, was high—for example, December—and a relatively low nominal quantity when $L(Y, i)$ was low—for example, February. Thus, the nominal quantity of currency, $M$, has a pronounced seasonal pattern, whereas the price level, $P$, does not have a substantial seasonal pattern. (That is, before seasonal adjustments, $P$ has little seasonal variation.)

The seasonal variations in the real demand for U.S. currency have declined substantially since the mid-1980s. For example, the December excess of real currency over the average for the year varied between 1.6% and 2.2% from 1950 to 1983, but then fell to an average of 0.9% in the 1990s and 0.7% from 2000 to 2005. A study by the Federal Reserve and the U.S. Treasury (Board of Governors of the Federal Reserve System, 2003) suggests that this change relates to the increased use of U.S. currency in foreign countries. The foreign demand for U.S. currency has less of a seasonal pattern than that found in domestic demand. Therefore, the full seasonal variation weakened when more of the currency was held by foreigners.

The pattern is different if we look at checkable deposits, the other main part of M1. The seasonal variations in the U.S. real demand for checkable deposits have not changed so much over time. For example, the December excess of real checkable deposits over the average for the year ranged between 2.4% and 3.3% from 1959 to 1997, then rose to an average of 3.6% from 1998 to 2005. The difference from currency probably arises because the foreign demand for U.S. checkable deposits is not nearly as important as the foreign demand for U.S. currency.

## Summing Up

We extended our macroeconomic model to add another equilibrium condition: the nominal quantity of money supplied, $M^s$, equals the nominal quantity demanded, $M^d$. We then have a general-equilibrium model that determines the price level, $P$, the nominal wage rate, $w$, and the nominal rental price, $R$. The three nominal prices are flexible and adjust rapidly to ensure that three equilibrium conditions hold: $M^s = M^d$, $L^s = L^d$ (clearing of the labor market), and $(\kappa K)^s = (\kappa K)^d$ (clearing of the market for capital services).

We extended the microeconomic foundations of the model to consider the determinants of the nominal demand for money, $M^d = P \cdot L(Y, i)$, where the function $L(Y, i)$ gives the quantity of money demanded in real terms, $M^d/P$. The real quantity demanded, $L(Y, i)$, rises with real GDP, $Y$, and falls with the interest rate, $i$. Shifts in financial technology also affect $L(Y, i)$.

An increase in the nominal quantity of money supplied, $M^s$, raises nominal variables—such as the price level, $P$; the nominal wage rate, $w$; and the nominal rental price, $R$—in the same proportion. Real variables—such as $w/P$, $R/P$, and real GDP, $Y$—do not change. This property is called neutrality of money. An increase in the real quantity of money demanded, $L(Y, i)$, lowers $P$ if $M^s$ is fixed. Therefore, the model predicts that $P$ would be countercyclical, as found in the U.S. data.

If the monetary authority seeks to keep the price level, $P$, equal to a fixed target, $\bar{P}$, the nominal quantity of money, $M$, becomes endogenous. In particular, shifts in the real quantity of money demanded, $L(Y, i)$, affect $M$ in the same direction. We applied this result in three contexts: long-term growth, economic fluctuations, and seasonal movements. With long-term growth in real GDP, $M$ is predicted to trend upward. In a cyclical context, $M$ has to be procyclical to avoid countercyclical fluctuations in the price level, $P$. However, empirically, $M$ has not been sufficiently procyclical to eliminate the countercyclical behavior of $P$. In a seasonal setting, $M$ would have to vary seasonally to avoid a seasonal pattern in $P$. We found evidence for this seasonal behavior of $M$.

## Key Terms and Concepts

| | |
|---|---|
| barter | M1 |
| checkable deposits | M2 |
| commodity money | monetary aggregate |
| demand for money | monetary base |
| economies of scale in cash management | neutrality of money |
| endogenous money | price-level targeting |
| fiat money | quantity theory of money |
| general equilibrium | real demand for money |
| high-powered money | stores of value |
| interest-bearing assets | transaction costs |
| legal tender | |

## Questions and Problems

**A.** Review questions

1. What are the costs of transacting between money and alternative financial assets? You might make a list and include such items as the time spent going to the bank or waiting in line. How were these costs affected by the development of automatic teller machines (ATMs)?

2. Consider the following changes and state whether the effect on the real quantity of money demanded is an increase, decrease, or no change:

a. an increase in the nominal interest rate, $i$
b. an increase in real transaction costs

c. an increase in real GDP, $Y$, caused by a rise in per capita real GDP with population held constant

d. an increase in real GDP, $Y$, caused by a rise in population with per capita real GDP held constant

e. an increase in the price level, $P$

3. Suppose that the nominal quantity of money, $M$, doubles once and for all.

a. The rise in the price level, $P$, suggests that workers will be worse off. Is this correct?

b. The rise in the nominal wage rate, $w$, suggests that workers will be better off. Is this right?

c. How do your results relate to the concept of the neutrality of money?

4. Economists who subscribe to the quantity theory of money believe that changes in the price level, $P$, are primarily the result of changes in the nominal quantity of money, $M$. Can this conclusion be based solely on theoretical reasoning?

5. Explain why a favorable shock to the production function tends to reduce the price level, $P$. How could the monetary authority prevent this fall in $P$?

6. Explain why it is important to distinguish between shifts in the nominal quantity of money, $M$, and shifts in the nominal demand for money, $M^d$. What association would we expect between the price level, $P$, and real GDP, $Y$, for periods in which both types of monetary shifts occurred?

7. What is the meaning of the term "endogenous money?" Under what circumstances would endogenous money generate a positive association between nominal money, $M$, and real GDP, $Y$?

B. Problems for discussion

8. Effects of other variables on the demand for money
Assume given values of real GDP, $Y$; population; the nominal interest rate, $i$; and real transaction costs. If these variables are given, would you say that the following statements about the real demand for money are true, false, or uncertain?

a. Agricultural societies have lower real money demand than industrial societies.

b. Dictatorships have higher real money demand than democracies.

c. Countries with a larger fraction of persons who are elderly have higher real money demand.

d. Countries with a higher literacy rate have lower real money demand.
For empirical evidence on these effects, see the study by Lawrence Kenny (1991).

9. Transaction frequency and the demand for money
Suppose that a household's consumption expenditure is $60,000 per year and is financed by monthly withdrawals from a savings account.

a. Show on a graph the pattern of the household's money holding over a year. What is the average money balance? Should we identify this average balance with the quantity of money demanded in our model?

b. Suppose now that the frequency of withdrawals from the savings account rises to two per month. What happens to the average money balance?

c. Return to question a., but assume now that consumption expenditure is $120,000 per year. If withdrawals from the savings account are still made monthly, what is the average money balance? How does this average compare to the one in question a.? Is it optimal for the frequency of withdrawals to remain the same when consumption expenditure increases? Explain.

10. Velocity of money

The velocity of money is the ratio of the dollar volume of transactions—say, nominal GDP—divided by the nominal quantity of money. How is the velocity of money affected by

a. an increase in the nominal interest rate, $i$?
b. an increase in real GDP, $Y$ caused by a rise in per capita real GDP with population held constant?
c. an increase in real GDP, $Y$ caused by a rise in population with per capita real GDP held constant?
d. an increase in the price level, $P$?
e. Why might nominal GDP not be the correct measure of transactions?
f. What do you predict happens to the velocity of money as an economy develops?

11. The payments period and the demand for money

Suppose that a worker has an annual income of $60,000. Assume that the worker receives wage payments twice per month. The worker keeps all of these payments in money, does not use any alternative financial assets, and pays for consumption expenditure of $60,000 per year from money holdings.

a. What is the worker's average money balance?
b. What would the average money balance be if the worker were paid monthly, rather than twice per month?
c. What is the general relation between the payments period and the demand for money?
d. How do the results change if the worker puts part of his or her monthly wage payments into a savings account and then makes withdrawals as needed from this account?

12. Shopping trips and the demand for money

Assume again the conditions in the first part of question 11, with a worker paid once per month. However, instead of making consumption expenditure as a uniform flow, the worker (or the worker's spouse) makes periodic shopping trips. During each trip, enough goods (groceries, for example) are bought to last until the next trip.

a. If the worker shops four times per month, what is the average money balance? Why is the answer different from that for part a. of question 11?
b. What happens if the worker shops only twice per month?
c. What is the general relation between the frequency of shopping trips and the demand for money?
d. Suppose that the cost of a shopping trip rises, perhaps because of an increase in the price of gasoline. What would happen to the frequency of shopping trips? What would happen to the demand for money?

13. Transaction costs and households' budget constraints

In our model, we neglected the resources that households use up in transaction costs. Suppose that these costs take the form of purchases of goods and services (such as fees paid to banks or brokers). Assume that real transaction costs decline because of the expansion of ATM machines.

a. How does this change show up in households' budget constraints?
b. What is the income effect on consumption and leisure?
c. Suppose that transaction costs represent the time required to go to a bank, rather than a purchase of goods and services. Is there a change in the results for questions a. and b.?

14. A currency reform

Suppose that the government replaces the existing monetary unit with a new one. For example, the United States might shift from the old dollar to the Reagan dollar, defined to equal 10 old dollars. People would be able to exchange their old currency for the new currency at the ratio of 10 to 1. Also, any contracts that were written in terms of old dollars are reinterpreted in Reagan dollars at the ratio 10 to 1.

a. What happens to the price level, $P$, and the interest rate, $i$?
b. What happens to real GDP, $Y$; consumption, $C$; and labor, $L$?
c. Do the results exhibit the neutrality of money?

15. Denominations of currency

Consider how people divide their holdings of currency between large bills (say, $100 bills) versus small ones. How would the dollar fraction of currency held in large bills depend on the following:

a. the price level, $P$?
b. real per capita GDP?
c. population?
d. incentives to avoid records of payments—for example, for tax evasion or to disguise illegal activities, such as the drug trade?
e. increased holdings of U.S. currency in foreign countries?

Given these results, the U.S. data on currency denominations are not so easy to explain. The fraction of the dollar value of currency (including coins) held in denominations of $100 and higher stayed nearly constant—between 20% and 22%—from 1944 to 1970. Then the fraction rose steadily to reach 72% at the end of 2005. What do you think explains these patterns?

We can think of $i_t$ as the nominal interest rate on a three-month T-bill issued on January 1 of year $t$. The rate $i_t$ is expressed at an annual rate, such as 0.02, or 2%, per year. The variable $\pi_t$ is the inflation rate, also expressed at an annual rate, from January to April. The problem is that this inflation rate is unknown in January, when the household buys the T-bill. The real interest rate, $r_t$, becomes known only later, when $\pi_t$ is observed.

Suppose that, in January, households expect the inflation rate from January to April to be $\pi_t^e$. This expected inflation rate determines the **expected real interest rate**, $r_t^e$, on the T-bill from equation (11.7):

(11.8) $$r_t^e = i_t - \pi_t^e$$

*expected real interest rate = nominal interest rate − expected inflation rate*

For example, if $i_t = 0.03$ per year and $\pi_t^e = 0.01$ per year, $r_t^e = 0.02$ per year. Formally, the expected real interest rate is the expectation, formed at the beginning of year $t$, of the real interest rate, $r_t$, over a period such as the next three months.

When households choose today's consumption and labor supply, they know the expected real interest rate, $r_t^e$, not the actual rate, $r_t$. Thus, intertemporal-substitution effects depend on $r_t^e$, which we would like to measure. To do so, we have to calculate the expected inflation rate, $\pi_t^e$.

**Measuring expected inflation**    Economists have used three methods to measure the expected inflation rate:

1. Ask a sample of people about their expectations.
2. Use the hypothesis of rational expectations, which says that expectations correspond to optimal forecasts, given the available information. Then use statistical techniques to gauge these optimal forecasts.
3. Use market data to infer expectations of inflation.

The main shortcoming of the first approach is that the sample may not be representative of the whole economy. Also, economists have better theories of how households take actions than of how they answer survey questions. Nevertheless, surveys can be useful, and we discuss applications to expected inflation in the next section.

The second approach, based on rational expectations, has produced both successes and failures. One challenge is to figure out what information households possess when they form expectations. Another issue is the choice among statistical models to generate forecasts of inflation.

The third approach has become especially useful since the governments of many advanced countries began in the 1980s and 1990s to issue **indexed bonds**. Unlike more familiar nominal bonds, which specify the nominal interest rate, indexed bonds prescribe the real interest rate. For example, a 10-year indexed bond adjusts nominal payouts of interest and principal in response to inflation to ensure the promised real rate of return over 10 years. We discuss later how to use these data to infer expected inflation rates, $\pi_t^e$.

**U.S. expected inflation and interest rates since World War II**    A commonly used survey measure of expected inflation is the one initiated in 1946 by Joseph Livingston, a Philadelphia journalist. The survey asks around 50 economists for their forecasts of the CPI 6 and 12 months in the future.[2] These forecasts allow us to construct expected

---

[2] For a discussion of the Livingston survey, see John Carlson (1977).

| Figure 11.2 | Actual and Expected Inflation Rates in the United States |

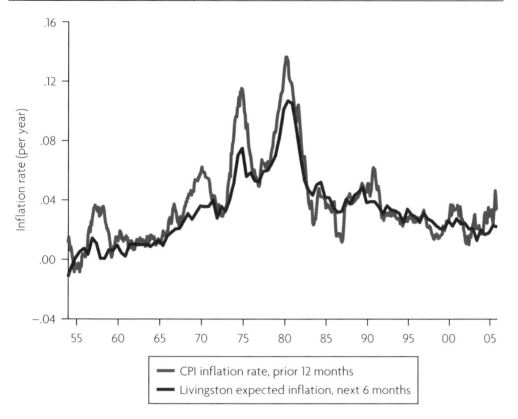

The blue graph shows the inflation rate over the prior 12 months, computed from the consumer price index (CPI). The red graph shows the expected CPI inflation rate. These expectations, formed six to eight months in advance, are from the Livingston survey, available from the Federal Reserve Bank of Philadelphia.

inflation rates. The 6-month-ahead forecasts of inflation are shown as the red graph in Figure 11.2. The figure also shows as the blue graph the actual inflation rate over the previous 12 months. These inflation rates were known to the survey respondents when they made their forecasts.

Figure 11.2 shows that actual and expected inflation rates tended to move together from 1954 to 2006. Inflation rates were low from the mid-1950s to the mid-1960s, rose until the start of the 1980s, then fell sharply in the early 1980s. Inflation rates were low and fairly stable following the mid-1980s. In June 2006, the expected inflation rate for the next six months was 2.2%.

Figure 11.3 on the next page shows as the blue graph the nominal interest rate, $i_t$, on three-month U.S. Treasury bills. The red graph is the expected real interest rate, $r_t^e$, calculated by subtracting the Livingston expected inflation rate, $\pi_t^e$, shown in Figure 11.2, from $i_t$:

(11.8)
$$r_t^e = i_t - \pi_t^e$$

The nominal interest rate, $i_t$, moved upward from the mid-1950s to the early 1980s. However, because the expected inflation rate, $\pi_t^e$, rose in a similar way, the expected real interest rate, $r_t^e$, did not have this upward trend. This tendency for $i_t$ and $\pi_t^e$ to move

b. What is the relation between $\mu$ and $\pi$ for a country in which the nominal interest rate, $i$, has increased?

c. Suppose that the expected real interest rate, $r_t^e$, is given. What is the relation between $\mu$ and $\pi$ for a country in which the expected inflation rate, $\pi_t^e$, has increased?

7. Statistical relations between money growth and inflation

Students who have studied econometrics and have access to a statistical package can do the following exercise.

a. Use the data in Table 11.1 to run a regression of the inflation rate, $\pi$, on a constant and the growth rate of money (currency), $\mu$. What is the estimated coefficient on $\mu$, and how should we interpret it? What is the meaning of the constant term?

b. Run a regression of the growth rate of real money balances, $\mu - \pi$, on the growth rate of real GDP, $\Delta Y/Y$, and a constant. What is the estimated coefficient on $\Delta Y/Y$, and how should we interpret it?

c. Suppose that we add the variable $\Delta Y/Y$ to the regression run in question a. What is the estimated coefficient on $\Delta Y/Y$, and how should we interpret it?

8. Effects on the nominal interest rate

What are the effects on the price level, $P$, and the nominal interest rate, $i$, from the following events?

a. A once-and-for-all increase in the nominal quantity of money, $M$

b. A once-and-for-all increase in the money growth rate, $\mu$

c. A credible announcement that the money growth rate, $\mu$, will rise beginning one year in the future

9. Seasonal variations in money

Suppose that the real quantity of money demanded is relatively high in the fourth quarter of each year and relatively low in the first quarter. Assume that there is no seasonal pattern in real interest rates.

a. Suppose that there were no seasonal pattern in the nominal quantity of money, $M$. What would the seasonal pattern be for the price level, $P$, the inflation rate, $\pi$, and the nominal interest rate, $i$?

b. What seasonal behavior for the nominal quantity of money, $M$, would eliminate the seasonal variations in $P$, $\pi$, and $i$?

10. Interest-rate targeting

Suppose that the monetary authority wants to keep the nominal interest rate, $i$, constant. Assume that the real interest rate, $r$, is fixed. However, the real demand for money, $M^d/P$, shifts around a great deal.

a. How should the monetary authority vary the nominal quantity of money, $M$, if the real demand for money, $M^d/P$, increases temporarily? What if the real demand increases permanently?

b. How does the price level, $P$, behave in your answers to question a.? What should the monetary authority do if it wants to dampen fluctuations of $P$, as well as maintain a constant nominal interest rate, $i$?

11. Money growth and government revenue

Can the government always increase its real revenue from printing money by raising the money growth rate, $\mu$? How does the answer depend on the responsiveness of real money demand, $M^d/P$, to the nominal interest rate, $i$?

12. Prepayment of mortgages and callability of bonds

Mortgages typically allow the borrower to make early payments ("prepayments") of principal. Sometimes the mortgage contract specifies a prepayment penalty, and sometimes there is no penalty. Similarly, long-term bonds (though typically not those issued by the U.S. government) sometimes allow the issuer to prepay the principal after a prescribed date, with a specified penalty. When the bond issuer exercises this option to prepay, he or she is said to "call" the bond. Bonds that allow this prepayment are said to be "callable" or to have a "call provision."

a. When would a borrower want to prepay (or call) his or her mortgage or bond? Would we see more prepayments when the nominal interest rate, $i$, unexpectedly increased or decreased?

b. From the late 1970s until 1982, banks and savings and loan associations were eager for customers to prepay their mortgages. Why was this the case? Later on, customers wanted to prepay. Why did they want to do so?

c. Suppose that the year-to-year fluctuations in nominal interest rates become larger. (These fluctuations—or volatility—were particularly great from the mid-1970s through the early 1980s.) From the standpoint of a borrower, how does this change affect the value of having a prepayment option—that is, callability—in his or her mortgage or bond?

13. Rational expectations and measures of expected inflation

How would the hypothesis of rational expectations help us to measure the expected inflation rate, $\pi_t^e$? What seem to be the pluses and minuses of this approach?

14. Indexed bonds

a. Consider a one-year nominal bond that costs $1,000. After one year, the bond pays the principal of $1,000 plus an interest payment of $50. What is the one-year nominal interest rate on the bond? What are the actual and expected one-year real interest rates on the bond? Why is the nominal interest rate known but the real rate uncertain?

b. Consider now a one-year indexed bond (such as the U.S. Treasury's TIPS, Treasury Inflation-Protected Securities). Suppose that the bond costs $1,000. One year later, the nominal principal of the bond is adjusted to be $1,000 \cdot (1 + \pi)$, where $\pi$ is the actual inflation rate over the year. Then the bond pays off the adjusted principal of $1,000 \cdot (1 + \pi)$ plus an interest payment of, say, 3% of the adjusted principal. What is the one-year real interest rate on the indexed bond? What are the actual and expected one-year nominal interest rates on the bond? Why is the real rate known but the nominal rate uncertain?

c. Can you think of other ways to design indexed bonds? Are the nominal and real interest rates both uncertain in some cases?

15. A case of counterfeiting

In 1925, a group of swindlers induced the Waterlow Company, a British manufacturer of bank notes, to print and deliver to them 3 million pounds' worth of Portuguese currency (escudos). Since the company also printed the legitimate notes for the Bank of Portugal, the counterfeit notes were indistinguishable from the real thing (except that the serial numbers were duplicates of those from a previous series of legitimate notes). Before the fraud was discovered, 1 million pounds' worth of the fraudulent notes had been introduced into circulation in Portugal. After the scheme unraveled (because someone noticed the duplication of serial numbers), the Bank of Portugal made good on the fraudulent notes by exchanging them for newly printed, valid notes. The Bank subsequently sued the Waterlow Company for damages. The company was found liable, but the key question was the amount of damages. The Bank argued that the damages were 1 million pounds (less funds collected from the swindlers). The other side contended that the Bank suffered only negligible real costs in having to issue an additional 1 million pounds' worth of money to redeem the fraudulent notes. (Note that the currency was purely a paper issue, with no convertibility into gold or anything else.) Thus, the argument was that the only true costs to the Bank were the expenses for paper and printing. Which side do you think was correct? (The House of Lords determined in 1932 that 1 million pounds was the correct measure. For discussions of this fascinating episode in monetary economics, see Ralph Hawtrey [1932] and Murray Bloom [1966].)

# The Government Sector

Transfer Payments for Social Security, Medicare, and Medicaid

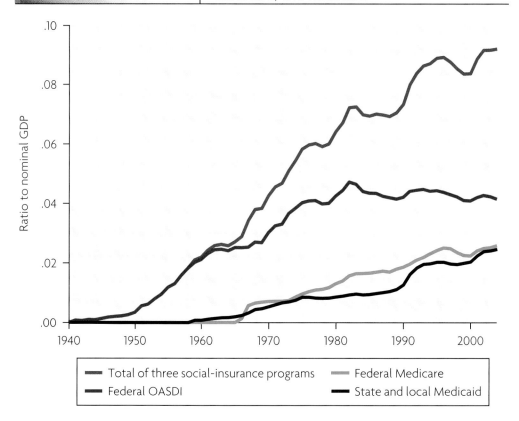

The red graph is the ratio to GDP of federal transfers for the main Social Security program, OASDI (old age, survivors, and disability insurance). The green graph is for federal transfers for Medicare, the health program for elderly people. The black graph is for state and local transfers for Medicaid, the health program for poor people. The blue graph is the ratio to GDP for the sum of the three social-insurance programs.

spending on goods and services: consumption, $C_t$, and gross investment, $I_t$. The total of the three terms, $C_t + I_t + G_t$, is the aggregate real spending on goods and services in year $t$. Let $V_t$ represent the government's real expenditure on transfers. Unlike $G_t$, real transfers, $V_t$, are not spending on goods and services. A transfer just represents the government's shuffling income around, taking from one group of people (through taxes) and giving to another (through transfers).

In Chapter 11, the government's only revenue came from printing money. The real value of this revenue for year $t$ is $(M_t - M_{t-1})/P_t$, where $M_t$ is the nominal quantity of money in year $t$, and $M_{t-1}$ is the quantity one year earlier. In the United States, the revenue from printing money accrues directly to the central bank, which is the Federal Reserve (or "Fed"). The Fed turns over most of its revenue to the U.S. Treasury. In the model, we consolidate the central bank with the government.

Now we assume that the government also levies taxes on households. These taxes might apply to businesses, but remember that the households own and run the businesses. Let $T_t$ be the total real taxes collected by the government in year $t$.

Table 12.1 | General Government Expenditure as a Ratio to GDP in a Sample of Countries, 2000–2002

| Country | Spending Ratio | Country | Spending Ratio |
|---------|---------------|---------|---------------|
| Australia | 0.33 | Latvia | 0.39 |
| Austria | 0.50 | Lithuania | 0.32 |
| Azerbaijan | 0.23 | Luxembourg | 0.41 |
| Belgium | 0.47 | Malaysia | 0.27 |
| Bolivia | 0.37 | Moldova | 0.24 |
| Botswana | 0.42 | Netherlands | 0.42 |
| Brazil | 0.37 | New Zealand | 0.38 |
| Bulgaria | 0.41 | Norway | 0.42 |
| Canada | 0.38 | Panama | 0.28 |
| Chile | 0.23 | Peru | 0.29 |
| Croatia | 0.51 | Russia | 0.16 |
| Czech Rep. | 0.32 | Singapore | 0.18 |
| Denmark | 0.52 | Slovakia | 0.39 |
| Ecuador | 0.25 | Slovenia | 0.42 |
| Egypt | 0.26 | South Korea | 0.24 |
| Estonia | 0.37 | Spain | 0.38 |
| Finland | 0.44 | Sweden | 0.53 |
| France | 0.49 | Switzerland | 0.38 |
| Germany | 0.47 | Taiwan | 0.25 |
| Greece | 0.47 | Thailand | 0.18 |
| Hong Kong | 0.13 | Trinidad | 0.32 |
| Hungary | 0.53 | Ukraine | 0.26 |
| Ireland | 0.30 | United Kingdom | 0.38 |
| Italy | 0.46 | United States | 0.32 |
| Japan | 0.37 | Venezuela | 0.23 |
| Kazakhstan | 0.22 | | |

**Note:** The table shows the ratio of general government expenditure to GDP, averaged for 2000–02. Countries are included only when data are available for general government expenditure, which includes spending at all levels of government for purchases of goods and services, transfers, and interest payments. Data for countries other than the United States are from Economist Intelligence Unit, *EIU Country Data* (http://www.eiu.com).

The **government's budget constraint** says that its total uses of funds must equal its total sources of funds. The uses are for purchases of goods and services and transfer payments. The sources are taxes and money creation. Therefore, we can write the government's budget constraint in real terms for year $t$ as

---

Key equation (government budget constraint):

total uses of funds = total sources of funds

(12.1)    $$G_t + V_t = T_t + (M_t - M_{t-1})/P_t$$

*real purchases + real transfers = real taxes + real revenue from money creation*

---

Note that we have not introduced public debt in the model. Therefore, the government's uses of funds on the left-hand side do not include interest payments, and the government's sources of funds on the right-hand side do not include the proceeds from issue of public debt. We will make the extensions to include interest payments and public-debt issue in Chapter 14.

We mentioned in Chapter 11 that the real revenue from printing money, $(M_t - M_{t-1})/P_t$, is normally a minor part of overall government revenue. We shall find it convenient to ignore the revenue from printing money, and we can do this by returning to the case in which the nominal quantity of money, $M_t$, is constant. In this case, we can substitute $M_t - M_{t-1} = 0$ in equation (12.1) to get

(12.2)    $$G_t + V_t = T_t$$

*real purchases + real transfers = real taxes*

In Chapter 11, transfer payments took the form of helicopter drops of cash that households picked up. The important assumption was that these transfers were lump sum—the amount the household received did not depend on the household's income, money holdings, and so on. We continue to assume that the real transfers, $V_t$, are lump sum. That is, the household's transfers do not depend on its decisions.

We also assume **lump-sum taxes** in this chapter. That is, the real taxes, $T_t$, that the household pays are independent of its income, consumption, and so on. This assumption is unrealistic. In the real world, elaborate tax laws specify how a household's taxes depend on its income, consumption, and so on. There are many things a household can do—including hiring accountants, working less, underreporting income, and exploiting tax loopholes—to lower its taxes. These possibilities imply substitution effects from the tax system on labor supply, consumption, and even the number of children. Although we want to study these substitution effects, we shall find it convenient to ignore them provisionally to isolate the effects from government expenditure. That is why we assume lump-sum taxes in this chapter. In Chapter 13, we will allow for substitution effects from realistic types of taxes. That analysis also brings in substitution effects from transfer programs.

## Public Production

We assume that the government uses its real purchases of goods and services, $G_t$, to provide services to households and businesses, and that the government delivers these services free of charge to the users. In most countries, public services include national defense, enforcement of laws and private contracts, police and fire protection, elementary and secondary schooling and some portions of higher education, parts of health services, highways, parks, and so on. The range of governmental activities has expanded over time, although this range varies from one country or locality to another.

We could model public services as the output from the government's production function. The inputs to this function would be the government-owned stock of capital, labor services from public employees, and materials that the government buys from the private sector. To simplify, we ignore government production and assume instead that the government buys final goods and services from private producers. That is, the government's purchases, $G_t$, add to the demand for goods and services by private consumers, $C_t$, and investors, $I_t$.

In effect, we are assuming that the government subcontracts all of its production to the private sector. In this setup, public investment, publicly owned capital, and government employment are zero. Ultimately, we would get different answers by allowing for public production only if the government's production function—that is, its technology and management capability—differed from that of the private sector. Otherwise, it would not matter whether the government buys final goods and services, as we assume, or, instead, buys capital and labor inputs to produce things itself.

## Public Services

We have to take a position on the uses of the services that the government provides. One possibility is that these services yield utility for households. Examples are parks, libraries, school lunch programs, subsidized health care and transportation, and the entertaining parts of the space program. These public services may substitute for private consumption. For example, if the government buys a student's lunch at school, the student does not have to buy his or her own lunch.

Another possibility is that public services are inputs to private production. Examples include the provision and enforcement of laws and contracts, aspects of national defense, government-sponsored research and development programs, the technologically valuable parts of the space program, fire and police services, and regulatory activities. In some cases, public services substitute for private inputs of labor and capital services. For example, the government's police services may substitute for guards hired by a private company. In other cases—including infrastructure activities such as the provision of a legal system, national defense, and perhaps transportation facilities—the public services are likely to raise the marginal products of private inputs.

We shall find it convenient to begin with the hypothetical case in which public services have zero effect on utility and production. This setup is akin to assuming that the government buys goods and services and then throws them into the ocean. We will consider later how the conclusions change if we allow public services to be useful.

## The Household's Budget Constraint

The government's taxes and transfers affect each household's budget constraint. To see how, start with the household budget constraint from Chapter 8:

(8.6)
$$C + (1/P) \cdot \Delta B + \Delta K = (w/P) \cdot L^s + i \cdot (B/P + K)$$

*consumption* + *real saving* = *real income*

The analysis in Chapter 8 neglected inflation; that is, the price level, $P_t$, was constant over time. We simplify by returning to this case. Note that our assumption of a constant $P_t$ is consistent with our assumption of a constant nominal quantity of money, $M_t$. Neither of these unrealistic assumptions affects our analysis of government purchases.

The right-hand side of equation (8.6) includes real asset income, $i \cdot (B/P + K)$, which depends on the nominal interest rate, $i$. However, since we are assuming that the inflation rate, $\pi$, is zero, the real interest rate, $r$, equals the nominal rate, $i$. We shall find it useful to replace $i$ by $r$, because then the analysis will be valid when we allow $\pi$ to be nonzero. If we apply equation (8.6) to year $t$ and replace $i$ by $r$, we get

(12.3) $$C_t + (1/P) \cdot \Delta B_t + \Delta K_t = (w/P)_t \cdot L_t^s + r_{t-1} \cdot (B_{t-1}/P + K_{t-1})$$

$$\textit{consumption} + \textit{real saving} = \textit{real income},$$

where $\Delta B_t = B_t - B_{t-1}$ and $\Delta K_t = K_t - K_{t-1}$

The existence of the government leads to two modifications of the household's budget constraint in equation (12.3). First, year $t$'s real taxes, $T_t$, subtract from real income on the right-hand side. One unit more of real taxes means one unit less of **real disposable income**, which is the real income available after taxes. Second, year $t$'s real transfers, $V_t$, add to real income on the right-hand side. Therefore, the household's budget constraint becomes

(12.4) $$C_t + (1/P) \cdot \Delta B_t + \Delta K_t = (w/P)_t \cdot L_t^s + r_{t-1} \cdot (B_{t-1}/P + K_{t-1}) + V_t - T_t$$

$$\textit{consumption} + \textit{real saving} = \textit{real disposable income}$$

The new term on the right-hand side, shaded in yellow, is the difference between real transfers and real taxes, $V_t - T_t$.

We showed in Chapters 7 and 8 how to extend the household's one-year budget constraint to many years. The result, when we modify equation (8.7) to replace the nominal interest rate, $i_t$, by the real interest rate, $r_t$, is

(12.5) $$C_1 + C_2/(1 + r_1) + C_3/[(1 + r_1) \cdot (1 + r_2)] + \cdots = (1 + r_0) \cdot (B_0/P + K_0)$$
$$+ (w/P)_1 \cdot L_1^s + (w/P)_2 \cdot L_2^s/(1 + r_1) + (w/P)_3 \cdot L_3^s/[(1 + r_1) \cdot (1 + r_2)] + \cdots$$

$$\textit{present value of consumption} = \textit{value of initial assets}$$
$$+ \textit{present value of wage incomes}$$

When we allow for taxes and transfers, as we did in going from equation (12.3) to equation (12.4), we get an extension to the multiyear budget constraint from equation (12.5). The extended version is

---

Key equation (multiyear household budget constraint with transfers and taxes):

(12.6) $$C_1 + C_2/(1 + r_1) + \cdots = (1 + r_0) \cdot (B_0/P + K_0) + (w/P)_1 \cdot L_1^s + (w/P)_2 \cdot L_2^s/(1 + r_1) + \cdots$$
$$+ (V_1 - T_1) + (V_2 - T_2)/(1 + r_1) + (V_3 - T_3)/[(1 + r_1) \cdot (1 + r_2)] + \cdots$$

$$\textit{present value of consumption} = \textit{value of initial assets} + \textit{present value of wage incomes}$$
$$+ \textit{present value of transfers net of taxes}$$

---

The new term on the right-hand side, shaded in yellow, is the present value of real transfers net of real taxes,

$$(12.7) \quad (V_1 - T_1) + (V_2 - T_2)/(1 + r_1) + (V_3 - T_3)/[(1 + r_1) \cdot (1 + r_2)] + \cdots$$

$$= \textit{present value of real transfers net of real taxes}$$

A lower present value of real transfers net of real taxes lowers the overall sources of funds for the household. Our analysis from Chapter 7 predicts that the household would react just as it would to any other loss of income. In particular, the income effects predict reductions in consumption, $C_t$, and leisure in each year. The decrease in leisure implies an increase in labor supply, $L_t^s$, in each year.

Our analysis from Chapter 7 tells us that the strength of the income effect depends on whether a change in real transfers net of real taxes is temporary or permanent. For a temporary change, we can consider a decrease in real transfers net of real taxes for year 1, $V_1 - T_1$, while holding fixed the terms $V_t - T_t$ for other years $t$. In this case, the present value of real transfers net of real taxes falls in equation (12.7), but by only a small amount. Therefore, we predict small decreases in $C_t$ and small increases in $L_t^s$ for each year. In contrast, if the decline in $V_t - T_t$ applies for all years $t$, the present value of real transfers net of real taxes falls in equation (12.7) by a large amount. Therefore, we predict large decreases in $C_t$ and large increases in $L_t^s$ for each year.

## Permanent Changes in Government Purchases

We now turn our attention to government purchases. We begin by considering the economic effects from a permanent change in government purchases. Recall that Figure 12.2 showed the U.S. data on government purchases, expressed as a ratio to GDP. The present analysis does not apply to large temporary changes, such as the surges in defense purchases during World War II and the Korean War. The analysis does apply to most other variations in government purchases; empirically, most changes in the ratio of government purchases to GDP have been long lasting.

### A Permanent Change in Government Purchases: Theory

Suppose that government purchases, $G_t$, rise by one unit each year. Since we are considering the same change each year, we can simplify by dropping the year subscript, $t$. In this case, the government's budget constraint from equation (12.2) is

$$G + V = T$$

Therefore, we can rearrange the terms to get a formula for real transfers net of real taxes:

$$(12.8) \quad V - T = -G$$

If $G$ rises by one unit each year, $V - T$ falls by one unit each year. Hence, the typical household's disposable real income falls by one unit each year. The income effects predict, accordingly, a decrease in each year's consumption, $C$, and an increase in each year's labor supply, $L^s$.

We can get the main results by ignoring for now the changes in labor supply, $L^s$. That is, we assume that each year's $L^s$ equals a constant, $L$. We reconsider this assumption in Chapter 13, where we allow also for the substitution effects from realistic forms of taxes.

Consider the income effect on consumption, $C$. Since the typical household has one less unit of real disposable income each year, we predict that the decrease in $C$ each year will be roughly by one unit. This prediction follows from the result in Chapter 7 that the propensity to consume out of a permanent change in income would be close to one.

Now let's consider how the increase in government purchases affects the demand and supply of capital services and real GDP. Recall that real GDP, $Y$, is given by the production function from Chapter 9:

(9.1) $$Y = A \cdot F(\kappa K, L)$$

This formulation allows for a variable capital utilization rate, $\kappa$, so that $\kappa K$ is the quantity of capital services. We are assuming that the capital stock, $K$, is fixed in the short run. We are also assuming that the technology level, $A$, and the quantity of labor input, $L$, are fixed.

As in Chapter 9, the quantity of capital services demanded, $(\kappa K)^d$, comes from the equation of the marginal product of capital services, MPK, to the real rental price, $R/P$. This condition determined a downward-sloping demand curve for capital services, as shown in Figure 9.5. We reproduce this demand curve as the red graph in Figure 12.4.

Since the capital stock, $K$, is given, the quantity of capital services supplied, $(\kappa K)^s$, varies only because of changes in the capital utilization rate, $\kappa$. As in Figure 9.5 in Chapter 9, the chosen $\kappa$ and, hence, the quantity of capital services supplied, $(\kappa K)^s$, is an upward-sloping function of the real rental price, $R/P$. We show this supply curve as the blue graph in Figure 12.5.

**Figure 12.5** | Clearing of the Market for Capital Services

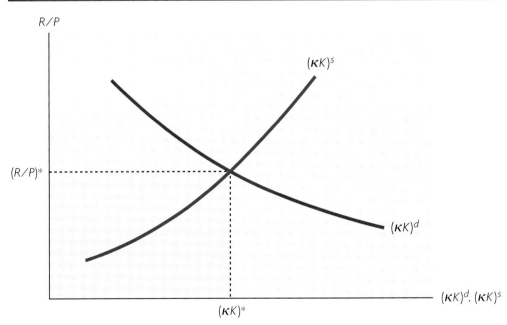

This construction comes from Figure 9.5. The demand curve for capital services, $(\kappa K)^d$, comes from the equation of the marginal product of capital services, MPK, to the real rental price, $R/P$. When $R/P$ rises, the quantity of capital services demanded falls. The supply of capital services, $(\kappa K)^s$, applies for a given capital stock, $K$. If $R/P$ rises, owners of capital raise the capital utilization rate, $\kappa$. Therefore, the quantity of capital services supplied rises. The market clears where the quantity of capital services supplied equals the quantity demanded. At this point, $R/P$ equals $(R/P)^*$ on the vertical axis, and $\kappa K$ equals $(\kappa K)^*$ on the horizontal axis.

The important observation is that an increase in government purchases, $G$, does not shift the curves for the demand or supply of capital services. The demand curve does not shift because the rise in $G$ does not affect the MPK (for a given input of capital services, $\kappa K$). The supply curve does not shift because, first, $K$ is given, and, second, the change in $G$ does not affect the choice of the capital utilization rate, $\kappa$ (as worked out in Figure 9.3 in Chapter 9). Because the demand and supply curves do not shift in Figure 12.5, we conclude that the market-clearing real rental price, $(R/P)^*$, and quantity of capital services, $(\kappa K)^*$, do not change.

Real GDP, $Y$, is given from the production function in equation (9.1) as $Y = A \cdot F(\kappa K, L)$. We found that the quantity of capital services, $\kappa K$, is unchanged, and we assumed that the technology level, $A$, and the quantity of labor input, $L$, are fixed. Therefore, $Y$ is unchanged. Thus, *we have the important conclusion that a permanent increase in government purchases does not affect real GDP.*

Consider the real interest rate, $r$. We know from Chapter 11 that $r$ is given by

(11.8)
$$r = (R/P) \cdot \kappa - \delta(\kappa)$$

*real rate of return on bonds = real rate of return from owning capital*

where $R/P$ is the real rental price and $\kappa$ is the capital utilization rate. The term $(R/P) \cdot \kappa$ is the real rental income per unit of capital. We have found that a permanent increase in government purchases, $G$, does not affect $R/P$ or $\kappa$. Therefore, equation (11.8) implies that the real interest rate, $r$, does not change. Thus, we have another important result: *a permanent increase in government purchases does not affect the real interest rate.*

Now we turn to the labor market. As in Chapters 6 and 8, the quantity of labor demanded, $L^d$, comes from the equation of the marginal product of labor, MPL, to the real wage rate, $w/P$. This condition determines a downward-sloping demand curve for labor, as shown in Figures 6.4 and 8.6. We reproduce this demand curve as the red graph in Figure 12.6 on the next page.

We discussed in Chapter 8 how an increase in the real wage rate, $w/P$, motivates households to increase the quantity of labor supplied, $L^s$. However, we are assuming for now that labor supply, $L^s$, is a constant, $L$. Therefore, Figure 12.6 shows $L^s$ as a vertical line at $L$. We assume that the increase in government purchases, $G$, does not change $L$.

The permanent increase in government purchases, $G$, does not the shift the labor-demand curve, $L^d$, in Figure 12.6. The reason is that the rise in $G$ does not affect the MPL (for given input of labor, $L$). To get this answer, we use the result from Figure 12.5 that the quantity of capital services, $\kappa K$, is unchanged. If capital services had changed, the MPL would be different (at a given $L$), and the $L^d$ curve would shift in Figure 12.6.

The increase in government purchases, $G$, does not shift labor supply, $L^s$, which is fixed at $L$, and does not shift the labor-demand curve, $L^d$. Therefore, the increase in $G$ changes nothing in Figure 12.6. Hence, the market-clearing real wage rate, $(w/P)^*$, does not change. We conclude that *a permanent increase in government purchases does not affect the real wage rate.*

Now we return to the behavior of consumption, $C$. We know from our analysis of income effects that a permanent rise in government purchases, $G$, by one unit reduces $C$ in each year by roughly one unit. To find the full effect on current consumption, we have to consider whether any substitution effects apply. The intertemporal-substitution effect depends on the real interest rate, $r$. Since $r$ does not change, the intertemporal-substitution effect does not operate. Another substitution effect involves consumption and leisure, but

| **F i g u r e   1 2 . 6** | Clearing of the Labor Market |

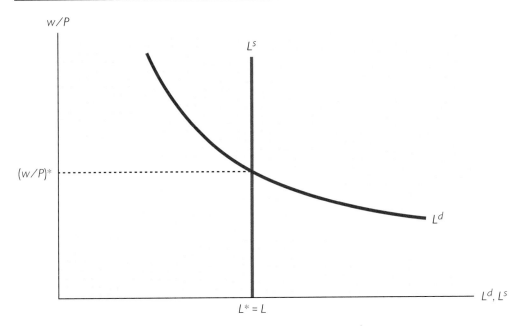

This construction comes from Figure 8.6. The demand curve for labor, $L^d$, shown in red, comes from the equation of the marginal product of labor, MPL, to the real wage rate, $w/P$. When $w/P$ rises, the quantity of labor demanded falls. We assume here that labor supply, $L^s$, shown in blue, equals the constant $L$. The market clears where $w/P = (w/P)^*$ on the vertical axis, so that the quantity of labor demanded equals $L$.

we have assumed that the quantity of labor and, hence, the quantity of leisure, is fixed. In any event, this substitution effect depends on the real wage rate, $w/P$, which does not change.

Since no substitution effects arise, we can determine the change in current consumption, $C$, solely from the income effect. As already noted, the income effect causes $C$ to decline by roughly one unit. Therefore, *our prediction is that a permanent increase in government purchases by one unit causes consumption to decrease by about one unit.*

To find the response of gross investment, $I$, recall that real GDP, $Y$, equals the sum of consumption, $C$, gross investment, $I$, and government purchases, $G$:

(12.9) $$Y = C + I + G$$

In the present case, $Y$ is unchanged, $G$ rises by one unit, and $C$ falls by one unit. Therefore, equation (12.9) tells us that the changes in $C$ and $G$ fully offset each other and, thereby, allow $I$ to remain unchanged. We conclude that *a permanent increase in government purchases does not affect gross investment.*

To sum up, we predict that a permanent increase in government purchases, $G$, reduces consumption, $C$, roughly one to one. The variables that do not change include real GDP, $Y$; gross investment, $I$; the quantity of capital services, $\kappa K$; the real rental price, $R/P$; the real interest rate, $r$; and the real wage rate, $w/P$.

9038.0
18.860
7.7577
61.851

# Extending The Model

## Useful public services

We did not consider that the government may use its purchases, $G$, to provide useful public services. We study here the case in which these services provide utility for households. As examples, the government might provide free or subsidized school lunches or transportation, or concerts in the park. We assume that these publicly provided services combine with private consumer expenditure to determine overall household utility. For example, utility depends on transportation, one part of which is provided by the government.

Suppose that each household views a unit of government purchases, $G$, as equivalent in utility to $\lambda$ units of private consumption, $C$. We assume that $\lambda \geq 0$ applies. Differences of opinion about the size of $\lambda$ are at the heart of debates about the desirable size of government. The case $\lambda = 1$ means that a unit of $G$ is equivalent in utility to a unit of $C$. The case $\lambda < 1$ means that a unit of resources that goes through the government provides less utility than a unit of private consumer spending. This case might apply because the lack of market incentives makes government operations relatively inefficient. We could instead have $\lambda > 1$ if there are scale benefits in the provision of public goods.

Recall from equation (12.4) that the household budget constraint, when written without year subscripts, is

The two new terms are shaded in yellow. This specification is useful because $C + \lambda G$ on the left-hand side can be thought of as *effective consumption*: the sum of private consumption, $C$, and the utility received from public services, $\lambda G$. The new term on the right-hand side, $\lambda G$, is the implicit value of the free or subsidized public services. Thus, we can think of the right-hand side as *effective real disposable income*, the sum of real disposable income and the implicit value of public services, $\lambda G$.

Consider the case in which government purchases, $G$, rise by one unit each year. The government's budget constraint in equation (12.8) says that the difference between real transfers and real taxes, $V - T$, falls by one unit each year. Therefore, an increase in $G$ by one unit changes the combination of the last three terms on the right-hand side of equation (12.10) by

$$\Delta(V - T + \lambda G) = \Delta(V - T) + \Delta(\lambda G)$$
$$= -1 + \lambda$$

where we used the conditions $\Delta(V - T) = -1$ and $\Delta(\lambda G) = \lambda$. Thus, the change in effective real disposable income depends on whether $\lambda$ is less than, equal to, or greater than 1. If $\lambda < 1$, effective real disposable income declines by $1 - \lambda$ units when $G$ rises by one unit, but if $\lambda > 1$, effective real disposable income rises by $\lambda - 1$ units when $G$ increases by one unit. In the main text, we assumed $\lambda = 0$, so that effective

$$C + (1/P) \cdot \Delta B + \Delta K = (w/P) \cdot L^s + r \cdot (B/P + K) + V - T$$

*consumption + real saving = real disposable income*

We can add $\lambda G$ to each side of the equation to get

(12.10)
$$(C + \lambda G) + (1/P) \cdot \Delta B + \Delta K = (w/P) \cdot L^s + r \cdot (B/P + K) + V - T + \lambda G$$

*effective consumption + real saving = effective real disposable income*

real disposable income fell by one unit when $G$ rose by one unit.

To fix ideas, consider the case in which $\lambda < 1$. (However, the analysis also applies if $\lambda = 1$ or $\lambda > 1$.) Since effective real disposable income falls by $1 - \lambda$ units each year, we predict that the household's effective consumption, $C + \lambda G$, would fall by about $1 - \lambda$ units each year. That is, the change in effective consumption will be close to the change in effective real disposable income. To determine the change in $C$, use the condition

$$\Delta(C + \lambda G) = -1 + \lambda$$

If we separate out the two changes on the left-hand side, we get

$$\Delta C + \lambda \cdot \Delta G = -1 + \lambda$$

If we substitute $\Delta G = 1$ and cancel out $\lambda$ on each side, we get

$$\Delta C = -1$$

The result $\Delta C = -1$ means that a permanent increase in $G$ by one unit crowds out private consumption, $C$, by one unit. We have found that this result holds for any value of $\lambda$. It works for the case in the main text in which public services are useless ($\lambda = 0$), when a unit of public services provides less utility than a unit of private consumption ($0 < \lambda < 1$), when public and private services are viewed equally ($\lambda = 1$), and when public services are valued more highly ($\lambda > 1$). The only difference among the cases—but an important difference—is that the higher $\lambda$, the happier households are when the government expands $G$.

### The Cyclical Behavior of Government Purchases

One prediction from the equilibrium business-cycle model is that long-lasting changes in real government purchases would not have much impact on real GDP. We mentioned that most changes in U.S. real government purchases fit the assumption of being long lasting. The main contrary examples come from military purchases during wartime. If we look at U.S. data from 1955 to 2006, after the end of the Korean War, the variations in war-related government purchases were relatively minor. Therefore, the model predicts that the fluctuations in real government purchases from 1955 to 2006 should bear little relation to the fluctuations in real GDP.

To test this proposition, Figure 12.7 uses our standard approach of comparing the cyclical part of a variable—in this case, real government purchases—with the cyclical part of real GDP. The variability of real government purchases from 1955 to 2006 is similar to that of real GDP. However, the cyclical parts of the two variables were virtually unrelated—the correlation was −0.01. This result provides support for our equilibrium business-cycle model. Note also that the pattern for government purchases is very different from the ones we found for consumer expenditure and investment (Figures 8.9 and 8.10), each of which was strongly procyclical.

## Temporary Changes in Government Purchases

Now we will analyze temporary changes in real government purchases. We begin by extending the equilibrium business-cycle model to include temporary variations in government purchases. Then we apply the extended model to wartime experiences.

### A Temporary Change in Government Purchases: Theory

Assume now that year 1's real government purchases, $G_1$, rise by one unit, while those for other years, $G_t$, do not change. That is, everyone expects that $G_t$ in future years will return

## Figure 12.7 | Cyclical Behavior of U.S. Real GDP and Government Purchases

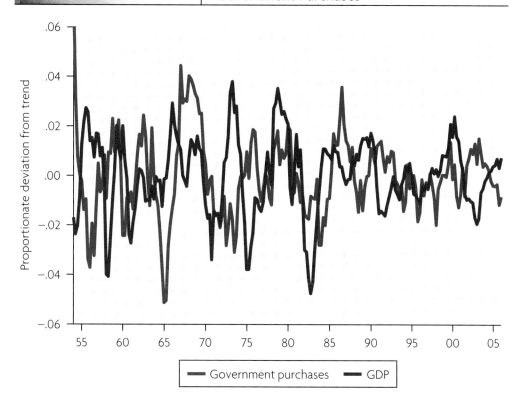

The red graph is the deviation of real GDP from its trend. The blue graph is the deviation of real government purchases from its trend. (We measure government purchases by the national-accounts data on government consumption and investment—this concept adds to government purchases the estimated depreciation of government capital stocks.) The deviations are measured in a proportionate sense. The data on GDP and government purchases are quarterly and seasonally adjusted. Government purchases are about as variable as GDP but have little cyclical pattern. The correlation of the cyclical part of real government purchases with the cyclical part of real GDP was −0.01.

to the original level. We can think of this case as representing a war that begins at the start of year 1 and is expected to last one year. Of course, this description is a simplification, intended to capture the main features of temporarily high government purchases. In reality, the durations of wars vary, and the interval of heightened government purchases might be greater or less than one year.

The government's budget constraint from equation (12.8) implies for year $t$:

(12.11)
$$V_t - T_t = -G_t$$

Therefore, in year 1, the net of real transfers over real taxes, $V_1 - T_1$, falls by one unit, and households have one unit less of real disposable income. In subsequent years, $V_t - T_t$ and, hence, real disposable incomes return to their original levels. Thus, the difference from a permanent rise in government purchases is that the expected real disposable income in future years is unchanged. Our analysis from Chapter 7 predicts that households would spread their reduced disposable income in year 1 over reduced consumption, $C_t$, in all years $t$. Therefore, the effect on year 1's consumption, $C_1$, will be relatively small. The propensity to consume out of a temporary change in income is greater than zero but much less than one.

Now, to simplify the notation, we again drop the time subscripts, with each variable implicitly applying to the current year, year 1. Much of the analysis of a temporary change in government purchases is the same as that worked out for a permanent change. As before, we ignore any changes in labor supply, so that $L^s = L$. In Figure 12.5, the change in government purchases still does not affect the MPK (for a given quantity of capital services, $\kappa K$) and, therefore, does not shift the demand curve for capital services, $(\kappa K)^d$. The change in government purchases also does not affect the way that suppliers of capital services choose their utilization rate, $\kappa$ (for a given real rental price, $R/P$). Therefore, with a fixed stock of capital, $K$, the supply curve for capital services, $(\kappa K)^s$, does not shift. Since neither curve shifts in Figure 12.5, we conclude, as before, that the real rental price, $R/P$, and the quantity of capital services, $\kappa K$, do not change.

Since capital services, $\kappa K$, do not change and labor is fixed at $L$, we know from the production function,

(9.1)  $$Y = A \cdot F(\kappa K, L)$$

that real GDP, $Y$, does not change. Since the real rental price, $R/P$, and the capital utilization rate, $\kappa$, do not change, we also have that the real interest rate, $r$, stays the same. This result follows from the formula:

(11.8)  $$r = (R/P) \cdot \kappa - \delta(\kappa)$$

*real rate of return on bonds = real rate of return from owning capital*

In Figure 12.6, the change in government purchases still does not affect the MPL (for a given labor input, $L$) and, therefore, does not shift the labor demand curve, $L^d$. Since labor supply, $L^s$, is fixed at $L$, the change in government purchases also does not shift the labor-supply curve. Since neither curve shifts, the real wage rate, $w/P$, does not change.

New results come when we consider consumption and investment. Consider again the expression for real GDP:

(12.9)  $$Y = C + I + G$$

Real GDP, $Y$, is unchanged; real government purchases, $G$, are higher in year 1 by one unit; and consumption, $C$, is lower, but by much less than one unit. Consequently, equation (12.9) implies that gross investment, $I$, must fall. In fact, since the decrease in $C$ is relatively small, the decline in $I$ is large. That is, year 1's extra $G$ comes mainly at the expense of $I$, rather than $C$. In contrast, when the change in $G$ was permanent, we predicted that most or all of the extra $G$ came at the expense of $C$.

## Government Purchases and Real GDP During Wartime: Empirical

We will now evaluate the equilibrium business-cycle model's predictions for the effects of a temporary change in real government purchases. We test the model by studying the response of the economy to the temporary changes in government purchases that have accompanied U.S. wars.

9038.0
18.860
7.7577
61.851

# Extending The Model

## Effects on the term structure of interest rates

We found that a temporary increase in government purchases, $G$, did not affect the real interest rate, $r$. We also found that investment, $I$, declined. For example, $I$ would be depressed during a war, which might last several years. Over time, the decline in investment means that the stock of capital, $K$, will be lower than it otherwise would have been—in particular, $K$ will be lower at the end of the war. The decrease in $K$ reduces the supply of capital services and leads, thereby, to an increase in the market-clearing real rental price, $R/P$. The rise in $R/P$ leads to an increase in $r$, in accordance with equation (11.8), $r = (R/P) \cdot \kappa - \delta(\kappa)$. Hence, although the current real interest rate does not change, future real interest rates rise.

In our model, the real interest rate, $r$, is a short-term real rate. In the real world, bonds are traded with varying maturities. For example, if we think about the indexed U.S. Treasury bonds that we studied in Chapter 11, a one-year bond might pay the real rate of return $r(1)$, a five-year bond the real rate of return $r(5)$, and so on. The **term structure of real interest rates** is the relation between the real rate of return, $r(j)$, and the maturity, $j$. If $r(j)$ increases with $j$, the term structure is upward sloping; otherwise, it is flat or downward sloping.

If we consider, say, a five-year horizon, an individual can hold to maturity a five-year indexed U.S. government bond or can instead hold a sequence of five one-year indexed bonds. In the first case, the real rate of return is $r(5)$. In the second, the real rate of return is an average of the five one-year returns, $r(1)$. Competition in the financial markets will work to equate the anticipated rates of return from the two options. Hence, $r(5)$ will be an average of the $r(1)s$ expected to prevail over the next five years.

In the case of a temporary increase in government purchases, short-term real interest rates, such as $r(1)$, did not change initially. However, anticipated future values of $r(1)$ increased. Therefore, the average of the $r(1)s$ expected to prevail over the next five years rose. Since $r(5)$ equals the average of the expected $r(1)s$, it follows that $r(5)$ rises immediately when government purchases increase. In other words, the model predicts an effect on the term structure of real interest rates. Short-term rates do not change immediately, but longer-term rates increase. Hence, the term structure becomes more upward sloping.

Table 12.2 on the next page covers World War I, World War II, the Korean War, and the Vietnam War. We can measure the temporary part of real defense purchases by the difference between actual purchases and an estimated trend. The trend is calculated in our usual manner by fitting a line through the historical data. We focus on the peaks of wartime purchases: 1918, 1943–44, 1952–53, and 1967–68. The values of temporary real purchases, in 1996 dollars, were $84 billion, or 16% of trend real GDP, in 1918; $537 billion, or 44% of trend real GDP, in 1943–44; $56 billion, or 3% of trend real GDP, in 1952–53; and $46 billion, or 1.4% of trend real GDP, in 1967–68. Based on these numbers, we can be confident that wartime purchases, and possibly other effects from war, were the major influences on the economy during World Wars I and II. That is, we do not have to worry about holding constant other factors. Wartime purchases would also be a major influence during the Korean War, though not necessarily the dominant force. In the Vietnam War, the temporary

# Table 12.2 | U.S. Wartime Spending, Real GDP, and Employment

**I: Real GDP and Components. Each entry is the deviation from trend in billions of 1996 dollars. Values in parentheses are percentage of own trend.**

| | Wartime Years | | | |
|---|---|---|---|---|
| | 1918 (WW I) | 1943–44 (WW II) | 1952–53 (Korea) | 1967–68 (Vietnam) |
| Category of GDP: | | | | |
| Defense purchases | 84 (679) | 537 (317) | 56 (25) | 46 (15) |
| % of trend real GDP | 16 | 44 | 3 | 1 |
| Real GDP | 42 (8) | 433 (36) | 49 (3) | 81 (2) |
| Consumption | −21 (−5) | −1 (0) | 0 (0) | 31 (1) |
| Gross investment | −21 (−28) | −58 (−51) | 0 (0) | 5 (1) |
| Nondefense government | 0 (0) | −20 (−19) | 5 (3) | 5 (1) |
| Net exports | 0 | −23 | −11 | −5 |

**II: Employment. Each entry is the deviation from trend in millions. Values in parentheses are percentage of own trend.**

| Category of employment: | | | | |
|---|---|---|---|---|
| Total employment | 3.0 (8) | 9.1 (17) | 0.9 (1) | 1.0 (1) |
| Civilian employment | 0.5 (1) | 1.5 (3) | 0.2 (0) | 0.4 (1) |
| Military personnel | 2.5 (566) | 7.7 (296) | 0.7 (24) | 0.6 (19) |

**Notes:** In part I, each cell shows the deviation of a real expenditure component from its estimated trend in billions of 1996 dollars per year. The values in parentheses express the deviations as a percentage of the trend. For example, as an average for 1943 and 1944, defense purchases were $537 billion or 317% above trend, real GDP was $433 billion or 36% above trend, and so on. Each real expenditure component is the nominal value divided by the deflator for the GDP. (The trend for real GDP was constrained to equal the sum of the trends estimated for the components of GDP.) In part II, total employment is the sum of civilian employment and military personnel. Each entry shows the deviation of a component of employment from its own trend in millions. For example, as an average for 1943 and 1944, total employment was 9.1 million or 17% above its own trend, civilian employment was 1.5 million or 3% above its own trend, and military personnel was 7.7 million or 296% above its own trend. (The trend for total employment was constrained to equal the sum of the trends estimated for its two parts, civilian employment and military personnel.) Data for the last three wars are from Bureau of Economic Analysis (http://www.bea.gov). Data for 1918 are from John Kendrick (1961), Christina Romer (1988), and U.S. Department of Commerce (1975).

military purchases of only 1.4% of real GDP were unlikely to be the overriding factor; other disturbances were likely of comparable or greater significance.

Other U.S. wartime experiences since 1869—the period with reliable national-accounts data—were of lesser magnitude, as gauged by the ratio of temporary defense purchases to GDP. The next largest ratios were 0.6% during the Spanish-American War in 1898 and 0.5% for the Afghanistan-Iraq conflicts in 2002–03. The ratio was 0.6% at the peak of the Reagan defense buildup in 1987. However, these defense purchases were not associated with a war and were probably not viewed as temporary. The ratio equaled 0.2% during the Gulf War in 1991.

Unfortunately, the lack of data prevents our studying some earlier large U.S. wars, notably the Civil War and the Revolutionary War. These wars, fought on U.S. soil, featured important negative effects on real GDP from the destruction of domestic capital stock. The loss of life was also substantial during the Civil War. Wartime destruction of domestic capital stock has not been important in the United States since the Civil War but was highly significant for many other countries during World Wars I and II.

To illustrate the main results, we focus in Table 12.2 on World War II and the Korean War. In each case, real GDP was above its trend, but by less than the excess of real defense purchases from its trend. For example, in 1943–44, the excess for real defense purchases of $537 billion was matched by an excess for real GDP of $433 billion. For 1952–53, the numbers were $56 billion and $49 billion, respectively.

Since real GDP was up by less than defense purchases, the other components of GDP had to be below trend overall. In 1943–44, the shortfalls from trend were $58 billion in gross investment and $20 billion in nondefense forms of government consumption and investment. Consumption was about equal to trend, and net exports of goods and services were $23 billion below trend. (We will study net exports in Chapter 17.) In 1952–53, gross investment and consumption were each about equal to trend, nondefense government consumption was $5 billion above trend, and net exports were $11 billion below trend.

Consider how the equilibrium business-cycle model relates to these wartime observations. The main discrepancy is that the model predicted no change in real GDP, whereas the data reveal substantial increases in real GDP. The data also show that the rises in real GDP are by less than the increases in government purchases. That is, aside from military purchases, the totals of the other components of real GDP are down during wartime. The model accords with this pattern. However, the components of real GDP other than military purchases do not fall nearly as much as predicted by the model.

## Wartime Effects on the Economy

The main failing of the model—and quite a striking one—is its prediction that real GDP would be unchanged during wartime. The source of this prediction is our assumption that labor input, $L$, is fixed. Therefore, it is worthwhile to reconsider this assumption. We begin by looking at the data on employment during wartime.

**Employment during wartime** We can illustrate the main pattern from World War II. The number of persons in the military soared—in 1943–44, military personnel reached 7.7 million persons above its estimated trend. But surprisingly, civilian employment also increased, rising by 1.5 million or 3% above its estimated trend. Putting the two parts together, total employment—civilian plus military—was 9.1 million or 17% above trend. The basic pattern is that the military took in a significant number of persons—primarily by the military draft in the wars up to Vietnam—and total employment expanded a little more. To do better with our predictions, we have to explain why the total quantity of labor supplied increased so much.

**Effects of war on labor supply** At this point, there is no settled view among economists about the best way to understand labor supply during wartime. Thus, we consider a number of possibilities and will not be able to reach a definitive explanation. Here are some ideas that have been advanced.

- A large expansion of real government purchases, $G$, means that households have less real disposable income. The negative income effect predicts reductions in consumption and leisure and, hence, an increase in labor supply, $L^s$. Several considerations influence the size of the income effect. For one thing, we have stressed that the increase in $G$ is likely to be temporary, at least if the wars are expected to last no more than a few years and if no major destruction of capital stock and population is anticipated.[3] This consideration makes the income effects on consumption and leisure relatively small. On the other hand, military outlays would not substitute for private consumption in the provision of utility—that is, the parameter $\lambda$ introduced in the box entitled "Useful Public Services" would be zero. This consideration makes the income effects large in comparison with those from nonmilitary government purchases. Overall, the income effect predicts an increase in labor supply, $L^s$. The problem, however, is that the same argument predicts a decrease in consumption, $C$. This prediction conflicts with the finding in Table 12.2 that $C$ did not decrease much during the wars.

- Casey Mulligan (1998) argues that labor supply, $L^s$, increases during wartime because of patriotism. That is, for a given real wage rate, $w/P$, and for given total real income, people are willing to work more as part of the war effort. The attraction of this argument is that it does not rely on a negative income effect and can, therefore, explain why consumption does not fall much during wartime. However, it may be that the effect of patriotism is more important during a popular war, such as World War II, than in other conflicts.

- From the standpoint of families, we want to understand how the military draft's forced removal of many men would influence the labor supply of those not drafted, especially women. One part of this analysis involves married couples, with the man drafted into the military. In these cases, the postponement of having children would be an important part of the story. Thus, women might participate more in the labor force as a temporary alternative to raising a family or having a larger family. Another consideration involves the postponement of marriage. Through this channel, the military draft would affect the labor supply of single women. That is, women who would otherwise have married and had children found market work to be an attractive, temporary alternative.

The upshot of these arguments is that wartime likely entails an increase in labor supply, $L^s$. Thus, we now assume that the occurrence of a war shifts the labor-supply curve, $L^s$, as shown in Figure 12.8. Unlike in Figure 12.6, we now allow for a positive effect of the real wage rate, $w/P$, on $L^s$. Thus, before the war, the labor-supply curve, shown in blue, slopes upward versus $w/P$. The war shifts the curve rightward to the green one, denoted $(L^s)'$. At any $w/P$, the quantity of labor supplied is larger along the green curve than along the blue one.

The labor-demand curve, denoted by $L^d$ and shown in red in Figure 12.8, slopes downward versus $w/P$. This curve is the same as the one in Figure 12.6. We still assume that the occurrence of a war does not shift the labor-demand curve (because the change in government purchases, $G$, does not affect the MPL).

Before the war, the labor-market clears at the quantity of labor, $L^*$, and real wage rate, $(w/P)^*$, shown in Figure 12.8. During the war, the quantity of labor rises to $(L^*)'$ on the horizontal axis, and the real wage rate falls to $[(w/P)^*]'$ on the vertical axis. Thus, when we allow for an increase in labor supply, the model can explain a rise in total employment, as observed in Table 12.2. A new prediction is that the occurrence of war lowers the real wage rate, $w/P$.

---

[3] In terms of destruction of human life, the highest U.S. casualty rates in relation to the population were during the Civil War, when roughly 500,000 people died. U.S. war-related deaths during World Wars I and II were 117,000 and 405,000, respectively, well below 1% of the total labor force. Casualties for the Korean and Vietnam Wars were much smaller. For many countries during World Wars I and II, casualty rates were far higher than anything ever experienced by the United States.

| **Figure 12.8** | Effect of a Wartime Increase in Labor Supply on the Labor Market |

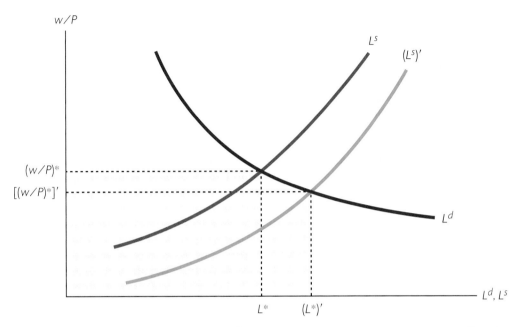

The downward-sloping labor-demand curve, $L^d$, shown in red, comes from Figure 12.6. We now allow the real wage rate, $w/P$, to have a positive effect on labor supply, $L^s$, shown by the blue curve. We assume that the occurrence of a war shifts the labor-supply curve rightward from $L^s$ to $(L^s)'$, shown in green. The quantity of labor input rises from $L^*$ to $(L^*)'$ on the horizontal axis, and the real wage rate falls from $(w/P)^*$ to $[(w/P)^*]'$ on the vertical axis.

**Effects of war on the real wage rate**  We now consider the prediction from Figure 12.8 that a war reduces the real wage rate, $w/P$. This proposition receives a mixed verdict from the main U.S. wartime experiences. If we compute the average percentage deviation of the real wage rate from its trend during the years of the main wars, we get the following:[4]

- World War I (1917–18): $-4.0\%$
- World War II (1942–45): $+3.1\%$
- Korean War (1951–53): $0.0\%$

Thus, the predicted negative effect on $w/P$ shows up only for World War I. The excess of $w/P$ from trend during World War II conflicts with our prediction. For the Korean War, $w/P$ deviates negligibly from its trend.

A further analysis suggests that the model might be doing better than these numbers indicate. Price controls and rationing of goods were imposed during World War II and, to a lesser extent, during the Korean War. Consequently, the reported price level, $P$, understated the true price level—typically, households could not buy additional goods just by

---

[4] The nominal wage rate is the average hourly earnings of production workers in manufacturing. The real wage rate is the nominal wage rate divided by the GDP deflator. The trend for the real wage rate is calculated in our usual manner. The results for the Korean War come from quarterly data since 1947. The results for World Wars I and II come from annual data since 1889.

explained by positive effects of patriotism on wartime labor supply. A promising idea is that wartime raises the perceived probability of global disaster and tends, thereby, to increase the demand for comparatively safe assets. This shift in demand may explain the low real interest rates during major wars.

## Key Terms and Concepts

government's budget constraint          Social Security
lump-sum taxes                          term structure of real interest rates
real disposable income

## Questions and Problems

**A.** Review questions

1. What are the economic differences between the government's purchases of goods and services and the government's transfer payments?

2. Derive the households' multiyear budget constraint in equation (12.6). Explain how real transfers and real taxes enter into this equation.

**B.** Problems for discussion

3. Government consumption in the national accounts

The national accounts treat all government purchases of goods and services, G, as part of real GDP. But suppose that the public services derived from government purchases are an input to private production, say

$$Y = F(\kappa K, L, G)$$

In this case, public services are an intermediate product—a good that enters into a later stage of production. Hence, we ought not to include these services twice in real GDP—once when the government buys them and again when the services contribute to private production.

a. Suppose that businesses initially hire private guards. Subsequently, the government provides free police protection, which substitutes for the private guards. Assume that the private guards and public police are equally efficient and receive the same wage rates. How does the switch from private to public protection affect measured real GDP?

b. How would you change the national accounts to get a more accurate treatment of government purchases of goods and services? Is your proposal practical? (These issued are discussed by Simon Kuznets, 1948, pp. 156–57, and Richard Musgrave, 1959, pp. 186–88.)

4. Public ownership of capital and the national accounts

Until the revision of 1996, the U.S. national accounts included in GDP the government's purchases of goods and services but took no account of the flow of services on government-owned capital. The accounts also did not subtract depreciation of this capital to calculate net domestic product.

a. In the pre-1996 system, what happened to GDP if the government gave its capital to a private business and then bought the final goods from that business?

b. In the current system of national accounts, the GDP includes an estimate of the flow of implicit rental income generated by public capital. However, this income flow is assumed to equal the estimated depreciation of the public capital. Redo question a. in the context of this system.

5. A prospective change in government purchases

Suppose that people learn in the current year that government purchases, $G_t$, will increase in some future year. Current government purchases, $G_1$, do not change.

a. What happens in the current year to real GDP, $Y$, consumption, $C$, and investment, $I$?

b. Can you think of some real-world cases to which this question applies?

6. The price level during the Korean War

In 1949, the inflation rate was negative. With the start of the Korean War, the price level (GDP deflator) rose at an annual rate of 10% from the second quarter of 1950 to the first quarter of 1951. In contrast, the inflation rate was only around 2% from the first quarter of 1951 to the first quarter of 1953. The table shows—for various periods—the inflation rate, $\pi$; the growth rates, $\mu$, of currency and the M1 monetary aggregate; and the growth rate of real government purchases, $\Delta G/G$. Can we use these data to explain the surge of the price level at the start of the Korean War, followed by a moderate inflation rate?

(This question does not have a definite answer. However, a significant fact is that price controls were stringent during World War II. People may have expected a return to these controls when the Korean War started in June 1950. The controls implemented beginning in December 1950 were more moderate than those applied during World War II.)

| Period | Inflation Rate ($\pi$) | M1 Growth Rate ($\mu$) | Currency Growth Rate ($\mu$) | Growth Rate of G |
|---|---|---|---|---|
| | (all figures in percent per year) | | | |
| 1949.1 to 1950.2 | −1.2 | 1.8 | −1.6 | 2.5 |
| | Start of War | | | |
| 1950.2 to 1951.1 | 10.2 | 4.0 | −0.5 | 19.3 |
| 1951.1 to 1952.1 | 1.7 | 5.3 | 4.7 | 32.0 |
| 1952.1 to 1953.1 | 2.2 | 3.2 | 4.5 | 9.4 |

7. The role of public services

We studied in the box entitled "Useful Public Services" the role of public services in providing utility to households. We assumed that each unit of government purchases, $G$, was equivalent to $\lambda$ units of private consumption, $C$, in terms of household utility.

a. Consider various categories of government expenditure, such as military spending, police, highways, public transit, and research and development. How do you think the coefficient $\lambda$ varies across these categories?

b. Suppose that $G$ rises permanently by one unit. What are the responses of real GDP, $Y$, consumption, $C$, and investment, $I$? How do the results depend on the size of the coefficient $\lambda$?

| Figure 13.2 | Breakdown of Federal Government Revenue |

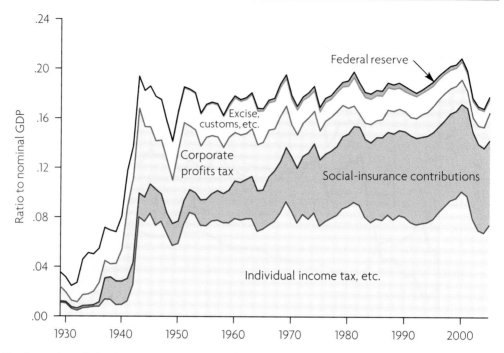

The figure shows federal government revenue, in five categories, as ratios to GDP. The categories are individual income taxes, and so forth (including estate taxes and personal nontax payments); contributions for social insurance (including payments by employers and employees for pension funds, Medicare, and unemployment insurance premiums); corporate profits taxes; excise taxes, customs duties, and so forth (including taxes on petroleum products, alcohol, and tobacco, and nontax payments, such as deposit-insurance premiums); and the Federal Reserve's transfers to the U.S. Treasury (treated in the national accounts as a part of corporate profits taxes).

1937. The ratio of federal social insurance revenue to GDP reached 7% in the late 1980s. Since then, the ratio has changed little. In 2003–05, the revenue from federal social insurance contributions nearly equaled the receipts from the federal individual income tax.

Corporate profits taxes began in 1909. The ratio of these taxes to GDP rose from 1% in 1929 to 7% during World War II. After falling to 4% in 1946, the ratio rose again, to 6%, during the Korean War in 1951. Since then, the ratio of corporate profits taxes to GDP has fluctuated around a declining trend and was only 1–2% of GDP between 1980 and 2005.

The category that includes excise taxes and customs duties was the major source of federal revenue before World War I and still comprised about 60% of federal revenue in the early 1930s. As a ratio to GDP, this category was around 3% from 1933 to 1958 but has since declined steadily, to reach only 1% in 2005.

Finally, we have the payments from the Federal Reserve to the U.S. Treasury—these payments represent the government's revenue from printing money. This component of federal revenue is relatively minor—it peaked at 0.5% of GDP in 1982 and accounted for only 0.2% of GDP in 2002–05.

| Figure 13.3 | Breakdown of State and Local Government Revenue |

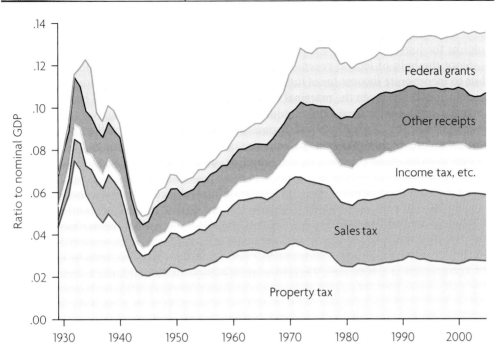

The figure shows state and local government revenue, in five categories, as ratios to nominal GDP. The categories are: property taxes; sales taxes; individual income taxes and so forth (including estate taxes and personal nontax payments); other receipts (corporate profits taxes, social insurance contributions, and miscellaneous fees and taxes); and federal grants-in-aid (transfers from the federal government to state and local governments). The black graph is for total state and local revenue exclusive of federal grants-in-aid. This graph corresponds to the green graph in Figure 13.1.

Figure 13.3 gives a breakdown of revenue for state and local governments. Property taxes were traditionally the largest component but declined in relative importance during World War II. The ratio to GDP has been close to 3% since 1949. Sales taxes rose from 1% of GDP in the early 1930s to 3% in 1970 and have since remained roughly stable. More recently, state and local governments have turned to individual income taxes. This category rose from less than 1% of GDP in 1965 to over 2% since 1987. The other form of state and local revenue that rose in relative importance is federal grants-in-aid, which are transfers from the federal government to state and local governments. These transfers go primarily for welfare, medical care, transportation, education, housing, and training programs. As a share of GDP, federal grants-in-aid climbed from less than 1% of GDP in 1964 to 3% in 2002–05.

## Types of Taxes

Some taxes fall on forms of income: individual income taxes, corporate profits taxes, and contributions for Social Security and Medicare. The social insurance contributions are collected from a payroll tax on wage earnings. Other taxes are based on expenditures: sales

The numbers in brackets in Table 13.2 show the percentages of **adjusted gross income**—a broad concept of income shown on income tax forms—reported by the corresponding tax returns. For example, in 1970, the top 1% of returns ranked by taxes paid received 7% of the adjusted gross income. However, this group paid 17% of the taxes. The excess of the share of taxes paid over the share of income received for upper-income taxpayers is a reasonable measure of the progressivity of the income tax. By 2000, the top 1% had a higher share of income, 21%—but this group paid 37% of the taxes. The table provides similar information for other taxpayer groups. For example, in 2000, the top 50% of returns ranked by taxes paid received 87% of the adjusted gross income while paying 96% of the taxes.

Another important form of income tax in the United States is the levy on wage earnings and self-employment income to finance Social Security and Medicare. Although the government calls these levies a contribution, they are more like taxes because the benefits that individuals get do not depend very much on the amount that an individual pays. In the case of Social Security, the benefits do depend somewhat on the amounts paid over one's lifetime. Hence, the payments are partly a tax and partly a contribution.

The tax for Social Security and Medicare is much simpler than the individual income tax. In 2006, covered employees paid 6.2% of earnings up to an earnings ceiling of $94,200 to finance the old age, survivors, and disability program (OASDI) and 1.45% of all earnings to finance Medicare. Employers paid an equal amount. Thus, the combined marginal income tax rate was 15.3% for labor earnings between $0 and $94,200, and 2.9% thereafter.

Notice that, for incomes between $0 and $94,200, the average tax rate equals the marginal tax rate. This property applies to a **flat-rate tax** system. However, at $94,200, the system has a single, sharp reduction in the marginal tax rate to 2.9%. As income rises above $94,200, the average tax rate falls gradually from 15.3% to 2.9%. Therefore, in this range, the marginal tax rate is *less* than the average tax rate. This pattern is the opposite of the one that applies to the individual income tax.

Empirically, it is difficult to measure marginal income tax rates, because these rates differ across persons and types of income. Some studies have, however, computed the average of marginal income tax rates across all taxpayers. The blue graph in Figure 13.4 gives an estimate of this average marginal income tax rate in the United States.[1] The measure considers the two most important forms of income taxes: the federal individual income tax and Social Security taxes. These two levies accounted for 80% of federal revenue in 2005. Because of data limitations, the measure does not include state and local income taxes.

Figure 13.4 shows that the average marginal income tax rate was very low in the pre-World War II years; individual income taxes covered a small minority of the population, and Social Security taxes were not yet significant. The tax rate rose dramatically to 26% at the end of World War II in 1945. Then the rate fell to 18% in 1949 before increasing back to 26% during the Korean War in 1952–53. From then until the early 1960s, the rate remained between 24% and 26%. Then the rate fell to 23% in 1965 because of the Kennedy-Johnson income tax cuts. The rate then rose gradually to its peak of 39% in 1981. Subsequently, the rate fell, because of the Reagan tax cuts of 1981 and 1986, to reach 30% in 1988. The rate then rose to 31% in 1990 and 32% in 1994, because of the

---

[1] The construction weights households by their adjusted gross incomes. That is, higher-income households count more in the calculation of the average.

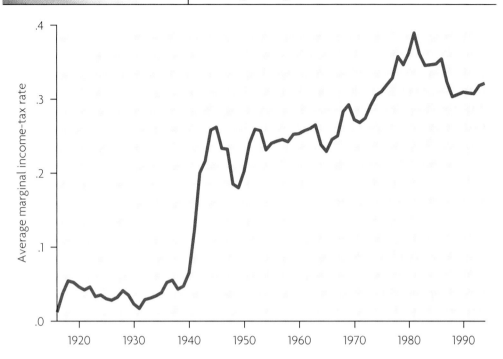

| **Figure 13.4** | Average Marginal Income Tax Rate, 1916–1994 |

The graph shows the average across taxpayers of the marginal income tax rate from the federal individual income tax and Social Security. The average weights by adjusted gross income. This variable was constructed in Robert Barro and Chaipat Sahasakul (1983, 1986) and has been updated to 1994 in unpublished research by Casey Mulligan.

tax rate increases under the first President Bush and Clinton. However, these increases in average marginal income tax rates were much smaller than those from 1965 to 1981. Unfortunately, these data have not been updated beyond 1994.

## Taxes in the Model

To incorporate tax rates into the equilibrium business-cycle model, start with the household budget constraint from equation (12.4). When written without year subscripts, the budget constraint is

(13.1)
$$C + (1/P) \cdot \Delta B + \Delta K = (w/P) \cdot L^s + r \cdot (B/P + K) + V - T$$
*consumption + real saving = real disposable income*

Up to now, we regarded real transfers, $V$, and real taxes, $T$, as lump sum. Therefore, the household's real transfers net of real taxes, $V - T$, did not depend on the household's characteristics, including its income and consumption. Now we allow a household's real taxes, $T$, to depend on some of its characteristics. Analogous considerations enter into an analysis of real transfers, $V$.

The various taxes that exist in the United States and other countries can be represented as levies on the terms that appear on the two sides of equation (13.1). Sales, excise, and value-added taxes depend on consumption, $C$. Labor-income taxes—for example, from the individual income tax and the Social Security payroll tax—depend on real labor income, $(w/P) \cdot L^s$. Taxes on asset income, a part of the individual income tax, depend on real asset income, $r \cdot (B/P + K)$.[2] In the real world, the income base for this tax includes interest, dividends, and capital gains.[3]

We will now assess the economic effects from taxation. In order to affect real GDP, a tax has to influence the quantities of one of the factors of production: labor or capital services. Therefore, the various taxes can be broken down into whether they affect labor or capital services, or both. We get the main results by considering two types of taxes—one that depends on labor income and another that depends on asset income.

## A Tax on Labor Income

We start with a tax on labor income, such as the individual income tax or the payroll tax that finances Social Security. Let $\tau_w$ be the marginal tax rate on labor income. To simplify, we do not allow for a graduated-rate structure for $\tau_w$, as in the U.S. individual income tax system. Rather, we assume that $\tau_w$ is the same at all levels of income. Our main results will apply to the real world if we think of $\tau_w$ as the average of the marginal income tax rates across households.

We assume that the marginal income-tax rate, $\tau_w$, does not change over time—at least, households do not anticipate that future tax rates will differ from the current rate. Anticipated differences between today's tax rate and future tax rates would motivate households to work more in years with relatively low tax rates and less in years with relatively high tax rates. That is, anticipated changes in $\tau_w$ over time have intertemporal-substitution effects on labor supply. Since we treat $\tau_w$ as unchanging, we are ignoring these intertemporal-substitution effects.

Households may be eligible for deductions and credits that reduce the amount of taxes paid. These deductions create a gap between the average and marginal income tax rates; the average rate is less than the marginal rate because of the deductions. If the deductions are the same for everyone, the average tax rate will be lower for low-income households than for high-income households (as in the U.S. data). (Recall our assumption that the marginal tax rate, $\tau_w$, is the same for all households.) In some cases, a household's tax payment would be negative, amounting to a transfer from the government. In the U.S. system, these negative taxes arise because of "refundable" tax credits, which are credits that not only reduce taxes but also allow for cash payments when the computed taxes are less than zero. The most important of these refundable credits is the earned-income tax credit (EITC).

The real taxes paid by a household equal the average tax rate multiplied by labor income. The average tax rate depends on the marginal income-tax rate, $\tau_w$, and on the

---

[2] U.S. taxes are levied on nominal interest payments, $i \cdot (B/P)$, which are computed from the nominal interest rate, $i$, rather than the real rate, $r$. This treatment of interest income leads to an effect of the inflation rate, $\pi$, on real taxes. Another real-world complication is that parts of household interest expenses are allowed as deductions from income for tax purposes. In the United States, the deduction applies to itemized deductions for interest on home mortgages and debt used to purchase financial assets.

[3] To consider a tax on corporate profit, we could reintroduce real business profit, $\Pi$, as a form of household income. We dropped $\Pi$ before because it equaled zero in equilibrium. However, in most tax systems, the definition of profit differs from the one in our model. The most important difference is that our definition includes the real rental payments to capital, $(R/P) \cdot K$, as a negative item. In the real world, only parts of this rental income—depreciation and interest expenses—are allowed as deductions from income in the computation of corporate profits taxes. With this real-world definition of profit, the corporate profits tax amounts to another levy on the income from capital. Since the income from capital is also taxed at the household level, the corporate profits tax is often described appropriately as **double taxation** of income from capital.

available deductions. If we hold constant the structure of deductions, a higher $\tau_w$ implies a higher average tax rate. Therefore, for given deductions, a higher $\tau_w$ will generate more tax revenue for the government unless the amount of labor income falls sharply.

To assess the economic effects from a tax on labor income, we have to extend our analysis of household labor supply. The key force is the substitution effect between leisure and consumption. Without taxation of labor income, this substitution effect depended on the real wage rate, $w/P$. If a household raised the quantity of labor supplied, $L^s$, by one unit of time, it raised real labor income, $(w/P) \cdot L^s$, by $w/P$ units. This extra income enabled the household to increase consumption by $w/P$ units. At the same time, the rise in $L^s$ by one unit of time meant that leisure time fell by one unit. Therefore, the household could substitute $w/P$ units of consumption for one unit of leisure time. If $w/P$ rose, this deal became more favorable. Hence, we predicted that the household would raise the quantity of labor supplied, enjoy less leisure time, and consume more.

The new consideration is that an extra unit of labor income is taxed at the marginal income tax rate, $\tau_w$. If the household raises the quantity of labor supplied, $L^s$, by one unit of time, it again raises pretax real labor income, $(w/P) \cdot L^s$, by $w/P$ units. This extra income enters as the yellow shaded term on the right-hand side of the budget constraint in equation (13.1):

(13.1) $$\boxed{C} + (1/P) \cdot \Delta B + \Delta K = \boxed{(w/P) \cdot L^s} + r \cdot (B/P + K) + V - \boxed{T}.$$

The additional labor income raises the household's real taxes, $T$, by $\tau_w$ units. These taxes also appear on the right-hand side of the equation—the pink shaded term—but with a negative sign. Overall, the right-hand side of the equation rises by $(1 - \tau_w) \cdot (w/P)$ units. That is, after-tax real labor income rises by this amount. We also see from the equation that the household can use this additional after-tax real income to increase consumption, $C$—the blue shaded term on the left-hand side—by $(1 - \tau_w) \cdot (w/P)$ units.

We found that, by working one more unit of time, the household can raise consumption, $C$, by $(1 - \tau_w) \cdot (w/P)$ units. The increase in work by one unit of time still means that leisure time falls by one unit. Therefore, households can substitute $(1 - \tau_w) \cdot (w/P)$ units of $C$ for one unit of leisure time. Another way to say this is that, with a labor income tax, the substitution effect on labor supply depends on the **after-tax real wage rate**, $(1 - \tau_w) \cdot (w/P)$, rather than the pretax real wage rate, $w/P$. If the marginal tax rate, $\tau_w$, rises, for a given $w/P$, $(1 - \tau_w) \cdot (w/P)$ falls. Hence, we predict that the household would reduce the quantity of labor supplied, take more leisure time, and consume less.

We stressed before that labor supply depends also on income effects. We predicted that more household income would lead to more consumption and more leisure—hence, less work. What income effects arise when the marginal income tax rate, $\tau_w$, increases? Equation (13.1) shows that a household's real income on the right-hand side depends on real transfers net of real taxes, $V - T$. Recall also from Chapter 12 that the government's budget constraint requires

(12.8) $$V - T = -G.$$

Therefore, if government purchases, $G$, are unchanged, equation (12.8) implies that real transfers net of real taxes, $V - T$, must also be unchanged. Hence, for given $G$, we do not get any changes in household real income through the term $V - T$. In other words, if $G$ is fixed, there are no income effects from a change in $\tau_w$.

We need to explore this result further, because it seems that a rise in the marginal income-tax rate, $\tau_w$, should have a negative income effect. The results depend on what else changes when the marginal income tax rate, $\tau_w$, rises. One possibility is that the government adjusts other features of the tax system to keep the total real taxes collected, $T$, unchanged. For example, marginal income tax rates, $\tau_w$, might rise in the individual income tax, but deductions also rise to keep $T$ fixed. Another possibility is that the government shifts away from collecting revenue through a tax that has a relatively low marginal income tax rate—for example, the Social Security payroll tax—toward one that has a relatively high marginal rate—such as the individual income tax. Shifts of this kind raise the marginal tax rate on labor income, $\tau_w$, for a given total of real taxes collected, $T$.

Another possibility is that real tax revenue, $T$, rises along with the increase in $\tau_w$, and all of the extra revenue pays for added real transfers, $V$. In that case, the term $V - T$ is again unchanged, and there is still no income effect.

Finally, we could have that real tax revenue, $T$, rises along with the increase in $\tau_w$, and the extra revenue pays for added government purchases, $G$. In this case, the economic effects combine two forces: the rise in $\tau_w$, which we are now studying, and the rise in $G$, which we considered in Chapter 12. Recall that the rise in $G$ did have a negative income effect. To keep things straight, it is best to analyze the effects from $\tau_w$ and $G$ separately. We are now assessing the effects from an increase in $\tau_w$ for given $G$. In this case, there are no income effects on labor supply. We can therefore be confident that, for a given real wage rate, $w/P$, a rise in $\tau_w$ reduces the quantity of labor supplied, $L^s$, through the substitution effect from a lower after-tax real wage rate, $(1 - \tau_w) \cdot (w/P)$.

Figure 13.5 shows the effects on the labor market from an increase in the marginal tax rate on labor income, $\tau_w$. We use the construction from Figure 8.15 in Chapter 8. We plot

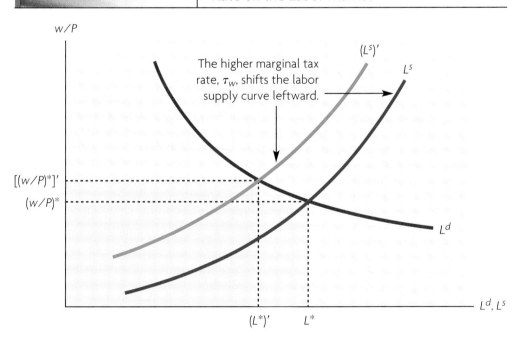

**Figure 13.5**   Effect of an Increase in the Labor-Income Tax Rate on the Labor Market

The downward-sloping labor demand curve, $L^d$, shown in red, comes from Figure 8.15. The upward-sloping labor supply curve, $L^s$, shown in blue, also comes from Figure 8.15. An increase in the marginal tax rate on labor income, $\tau_w$, shifts the labor supply curve leftward to the green one, $(L^s)'$. Consequently, the market-clearing, before-tax real wage rate rises from $(w/P)^*$ to $[(w/P)^*]'$ on the vertical axis. The market-clearing quantity of labor input falls from $L^*$ to $(L^*)'$ on the horizontal axis.

the pretax real wage rate, $w/P$, on the vertical axis. As before, a lower $w/P$ raises the quantity of labor demanded, $L^d$, along the red curve. Unlike in Chapter 12, we also allow for a positive effect of $w/P$ on the quantity of labor supplied, $L^s$, along the blue curve. This positive slope applies if the substitution effect from a higher $w/P$ dominates the income effect.

For a given pretax real wage rate, $w/P$, a higher $\tau_w$ implies a lower after-tax real wage rate, $(1 - \tau_w) \cdot (w/P)$. Therefore, in Figure 13.5, a rise in $\tau_w$ shifts the labor supply curve leftward from the blue one labeled $L^s$ to the green one labeled $(L^s)'$. This decrease in labor supply reflects the substitution effect from the higher labor-income tax rate, $\tau_w$.

The tax on labor income does not affect the labor demand curve, $L^d$, in Figure 13.5. The reason is that businesses (run by households) still maximize profit by equating the marginal product of labor, MPL, to the real wage rate, $w/P$. For a given $w/P$, the labor-income tax rate, $\tau_w$, does not affect the profit-maximizing choice of the quantity of labor input, $L^d$.

We can see from Figure 13.5 that the market-clearing real wage rate rises from $(w/P)^*$ to $[(w/P)^*]'$ on the vertical axis. The market-clearing quantity of labor declines from $L^*$ to $(L^*)'$ on the horizontal axis.

We also know that the after-tax real wage rate, $(1 - \tau_w) \cdot (w/P)$, must fall overall. That is, the rise in $w/P$ less than fully compensates for the decrease in $1 - \tau_w$ due to the rise in $\tau_w$. To see why, note from Figure 13.5 that $L$ is lower (because the labor demand curve does not shift, and the labor supply curve shifts to the left). However, for $L$ to be lower, the quantity of labor supplied, $L^s$, must be lower. The only way that $L^s$ falls is that $(1 - \tau_w) \cdot (w/P)$ declines.

We found from our analysis of the labor market that a higher marginal tax rate on labor income, $\tau_w$, lowers the quantity of labor input, $L$. This effect will spill over to the market for capital services because the reduction in $L$ tends to reduce the marginal product of capital services, MPK.

Figure 13.6 on the next page shows the effects on the market for capital services. As in Figure 12.5, we plot the real rental price, $R/P$, on the vertical axis. The reduction in labor input, $L$, reduces the MPK (at a given quantity of capital services, $\kappa K$). The demand for capital services decreases accordingly from the blue curve, labeled $(\kappa K)^d$, to the green one, labeled $[(\kappa K)^d]'$. The supply curve for capital services, $(\kappa K)^s$, shown in red, does not shift. That is, the stock of capital, $K$, is given, and, for a given real rental price, $R/P$, suppliers of capital services have no reason to change the capital utilization rate, $\kappa$.

Figure 13.6 shows that the market-clearing real rental price falls from $(R/P)^*$ to $[(R/P)^*]'$ on the vertical axis. The quantity of capital services falls, because of a decrease in the utilization rate, $\kappa$, from $(\kappa K)^*$ to $[(\kappa K)^*]'$ on the horizontal axis. Thus, although the tax rate on labor income, $\tau_w$, does not directly affect the market for capital services, it has an indirect effect on this market. By reducing labor input, $L$, and thereby decreasing the MPK, an increase in $\tau_w$ reduces the quantity of capital services, $\kappa K$.[4]

Recall that real GDP, $Y$, is given by the production function from Chapter 9:

(9.1) $$Y = A \cdot F(\kappa K, L)$$

In the present case, the technology level, $A$, does not change. However, we found that a rise in the labor-income tax rate, $\tau_w$, reduced the quantities of labor, $L$, and capital services, $\kappa K$.

---

[4] The decrease in $\kappa K$ lowers the MPL, and leads thereby to a leftward shift in the labor demand curve, $L^d$, in Figure 13.5. This shift leads to a further decrease in $L$.

Part 5

| **F i g u r e  1 3 . 6** | Effect of an Increase in the Labor-Income Tax Rate on the Market for Capital Services |
|---|---|

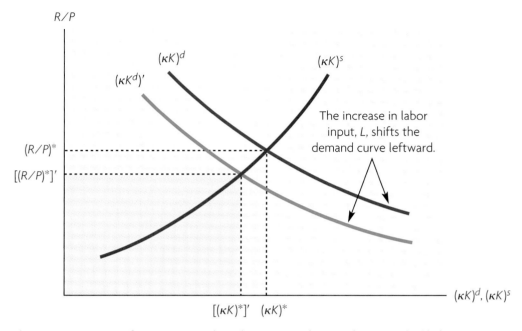

This construction comes from Figure 12.5. The reduction in employment from $L^*$ to $(L^*)'$, shown in Figure 13.5, reduces the marginal product of capital services, MPK (at a given quantity of capital services, $\kappa K$). Therefore, the demand curve for capital services shifts leftward, from $(\kappa K)^d$, shown in blue, to $[(\kappa K)d]'$, shown in green. The supply curve for capital services, $(\kappa K)^s$, shown in red, does not shift. Consequently, the market-clearing real rental price of capital falls from $(R/P)^*$ to $[(R/P)^*]'$ on the vertical axis. The quantity of capital services declines from $(\kappa K)^*$ to $[(\kappa K)^*]'$ on the horizontal axis. This decrease in capital services corresponds, for a given capital stock, $K$, to a reduction in the capital utilization rate, $\kappa$.

Therefore, $Y$ declines.[5] Thus, our conclusion is that a higher marginal tax rate on labor income, $\tau_w$, leads to a reduction in overall market activity, as gauged by real GDP, $Y$.

## A Tax on Asset Income

Now we will consider a tax on asset income. Go back to the household's budget constraint:

(13.1)    $$C + (1/P) \cdot \Delta B + \Delta K = (w/P) \cdot L^s + r \cdot (B/P + K) + V - \blacksquare$$

Suppose now that real taxes, $T$, depend on a household's real asset income, $r \cdot (B/P + K)$, the term shaded in yellow. Note that this part of income equals the real interest payments on bonds, $r \cdot (B/P)$, plus the return on ownership of capital, $rK$. The term $rK$ equals the

---

[5] We can work out how the decrease in real GDP, $Y$, divides up between consumption, $C$, and gross investment, $I$. We know from Chapter 7 that a fall in $Y$ by one unit corresponds to a decrease in real household income by one unit. Since the decrease in income is long lasting, we predict that the propensity to consume would be close to one. Hence, $C$ would fall by roughly one unit. However, the decrease in $R/P$ implies a fall in the real interest rate, $r$. This change has an intertemporal-substitution effect, which raises current consumption compared to future consumption. This effect offsets the decrease in $C$ by one unit. Hence, we find that current consumption would decrease overall by less than $Y$. Since $Y = C + I + G$ and $G$ is fixed, $I$ must decline.

# 9038.0
# 18.860
# 7.7577
# 61.851

# Extending The Model

## A consumption tax

We show here that a consumption tax has the same effects as the labor income tax that we studied in the main text. Suppose that real labor income, $(w/P) \cdot L^s$, is untaxed, but an increase in consumption, $C$, by one unit raises each household's real taxes, $T$, by $\tau_c$ units. This tax could be a sales tax, an excise tax, or a value-added tax. We assume that the consumption tax is proportional to $C$, so that the marginal tax rate, $\tau_c$, equals the average tax rate. We also assume that $\tau_c$ is the same for all households and does not vary over time.

If a household works one more unit of time, it again gets $w/P$ additional units of real labor income. Our assumption now is that this additional labor income is untaxed. Suppose that the household raises consumption by $\Delta C$ units. This change raises consumption taxes by $\tau_c \cdot \Delta C$. Therefore, the extra income of $w/P$ units must cover the added consumption, $\Delta C$, plus the added taxes, $\tau_c \cdot \Delta C$:

$$w/P = \Delta C + \tau_c \cdot \Delta C$$
$$w/P = \Delta C \cdot (1 + \tau_c)$$

If we divide through by $1 + \tau_c$, we can solve out for the additional consumption:

$$(13.2) \qquad \Delta C = (w/P)/(1 + \tau_c)$$

Hence, for each unit more of labor—and, therefore, each unit less of leisure time—a household gets $(w/P)/(1 + \tau_c)$ units more of consumption. For example, if $\tau_c = 0.10$, the household gets about $0.9 \cdot (w/P)$ extra units of consumption. The important point is that the higher the $\tau_c$, the worse the deal. Therefore, if $\tau_c$ rises, we predict that the household would work less, enjoy more leisure time, and consume less.

With a labor income tax at the marginal rate $\tau_w$, a household's labor supply, $L^s$, depended on the after-tax real wage rate, $(1 - \tau_w) \cdot (w/P)$. With a consumption tax at the marginal rate $\tau_c$, equation (13.2) shows that the after-tax real wage rate—in terms of the extra consumption that can be bought with an additional unit of labor—is $(w/P)/(1 + \tau_c)$. Therefore, $L^s$ depends on $(w/P)/(1 + \tau_c)$. Thus, increases in $\tau_w$ and $\tau_c$ have analogous negative effects on $L^s$. The conclusion is that consumption taxation has the same economic effects that we found for labor income taxation.

The results are different if tax rates vary over time. If the consumption tax rate, $\tau_c$, varies predictably, households would consume a lot in years when $\tau_c$ is relatively low. In contrast, if the labor income tax rate, $\tau_w$, varies predictably, households would work a lot when $\tau_w$ was relatively low.

net real rental payments on capital, $[(R/P) \cdot \kappa - \delta(\kappa)] \cdot K$, because of the condition from Chapter 11 that the real rates of return on bonds and capital are the same:

$$(11.8) \qquad r = (R/P) \cdot \kappa - \delta(\kappa)$$

*real rate of return on bonds* $=$ *real rate of return from owning capital*

Let $\tau_r$ be the marginal tax rate on asset income. We assume that all forms of asset income are taxed at the same rate. In reality, tax systems treat differently various forms of asset income, which include interest, dividends, capital gains, and parts of self-employment income. However, the simplifying assumption that all forms of asset income are treated the same will give us the main effects from taxation of asset income. Since the tax rate, $\tau_r$, is the same for interest income as for income on ownership of capital, the equality between the two rates of return still holds in equation (11.8).

We know that the real interest rate, $r$, has an intertemporal-substitution effect on consumption. A reduction in year 1's consumption, $C_1$, by one unit allowed the household to raise year 2's consumption, $C_2$, by $1 + r$ units. Therefore, an increase in $r$ motivated the household to lower $C_1$ compared to $C_2$. The difference now is that the additional $r$ units of asset income in year 2 are taxed at the rate $\tau_r$. This taxation means that the added $r$ units of income are offset by an added $\tau_r \cdot r$ units of taxes; that is, the pink shaded term, $T$, in equation (13.1) rises by $\tau_r \cdot r$. Thus, if the household reduces $C_1$ by one unit, it can raise $C_2$ by the amount

$$\Delta C_2 = 1 + r - \tau_r \cdot r$$
$$\Delta C_2 = 1 + (1 - \tau_r) \cdot r$$

What matters, therefore, for the choice between $C_1$ and $C_2$ is the **after-tax real interest rate**, $(1 - \tau_r) \cdot r$. If $\tau_r$ rises, for given $r$, $(1 - \tau_r) \cdot r$ declines. Therefore, the household has less incentive to defer consumption, and it reacts by increasing $C_1$ compared to $C_2$. For given real income in year 1, an increase in $\tau_r$ motivates the household to consume more and save less in year 1.

If we multiply both sides of equation (11.8) by $(1 - \tau_r)$, we can relate the after-tax real interest rate to the after-tax return on ownership of capital:

**(13.3)**     $$(1 - \tau_r) \cdot r = (1 - \tau_r) \cdot [(R/P) \cdot \kappa - \delta(\kappa)]$$

*after-tax real interest rate = after-tax rate of return on ownership of capital*

Thus, we can calculate $(1 - \tau_r) \cdot r$ if we know—on the right-hand side of equation (13.3)—the real rental price, $R/P$, and the capital utilization rate, $\kappa$. These values are determined, as before, by the clearing of the market for capital services.

Refer back to Figure 13.6, which considered the demand for and supply of capital services. The marginal tax rate on asset income, $\tau_r$, does not affect the demand curve for capital services, $(\kappa K)^d$, which is shown in blue. Since business profit, $\Pi$, is not taxed, this curve still comes from equating the MPK to $R/P$.[6] Therefore, a change in $\tau_r$ does not shift the demand curve, $(\kappa K)^d$.

In Chapter 9, we worked out the supply curve for capital services, $(\kappa K)^s$. For a given stock of capital, $K$, owners of capital chose the utilization rate, $\kappa$, to maximize the net rental income:

$$[(R/P) \cdot \kappa - \delta(\kappa)] \cdot K$$

We assumed that a higher $\kappa$ resulted in a higher depreciation rate, as represented by the function $\delta(\kappa)$. From this formulation, we found that an increase in the real rental price, $R/P$, raised the utilization rate, $\kappa$, and thereby increased the quantity of capital services supplied, $(\kappa K)^s$. That is why the curve $(\kappa K)^s$, shown in red in Figure 13.6, slopes upward.

---

[6] A tax on business profit tends to affect the demand for capital services. For example, in the system of corporate profits taxation described in fn. 3, an increase in the tax rate on corporate profits would reduce this demand.

With a tax on income from capital at the rate $\tau_r$, owners of capital would seek to maximize their after-tax net rental income, given by

$$(1 - \tau_r) \cdot [(R/P) \cdot \kappa - \delta(\kappa)] \cdot K$$

For any $\tau_r$, this maximization is equivalent to the maximization of $[(R/P) \cdot \kappa - \delta(\kappa)] \cdot K$—that is, the same expression as before. Therefore, for a given real rental price, $R/P$, the chosen utilization rate, $\kappa$, does not depend on the tax rate, $\tau_r$. Since the capital stock, $K$, is fixed, and $\tau_r$ does not affect $\kappa$, we conclude that $\tau_r$ does not affect the supply of capital services, $(\kappa K)^s$. Therefore, a change in $\tau_r$ does not shift the supply curve, $(\kappa K)^s$, in Figure 13.6.

Since a change in $\tau_r$ does not affect the demand and supply curves in Figure 13.6, it does not affect the market-clearing real rental price, $(R/P)^*$, and the quantity of capital services, $(\kappa K)^*$. That is, the capital stock, $K$, is fixed, and the capital utilization rate, $\kappa$, does not change.

Since the quantity of capital services, $\kappa K$, does not change, there is no effect on the demand curve for labor, $L^d$, shown in red in Figure 13.5. The supply curve for labor, $L^s$, shown in blue, also does not shift. Therefore, the market-clearing real wage rate, $(w/P)^*$, and the quantity of labor, $L^*$, do not change. Since $\kappa K$ and $L$ are the same, we have from the production function, $Y = A \cdot F(\kappa K, L)$, that real GDP, $Y$, does not change. Thus, our conclusion is that a change in the marginal tax rate on asset income, $\tau_r$, does not affect real GDP. We should stress, however, that this result applies in the short run, when the stock of capital, $K$, is given.

Since the real rental price, $R/P$, and the capital utilization rate, $\kappa$, are unchanged, the pretax rate of return on ownership of capital, $(R/P) \cdot \kappa - \delta(\kappa)$, does not change. But then, the increase in $\tau_r$ implies that the after-tax rate of return, $(1 - \tau_r) \cdot [(R/P) \cdot \kappa - \delta(\kappa)]$, falls. Equation (13.3) tells us that the after-tax real interest rate, $(1 - \tau_r) \cdot r$, equals the after-tax rate of return on ownership of capital:

**(13.3)**      $$(1 - \tau_r) \cdot r = (1 - \tau_r) \cdot [(R/P) \cdot \kappa - \delta(\kappa)]$$

Therefore, the increase in $\tau_r$ lowers the after-tax real interest rate, $(1 - \tau_r) \cdot r$.

We know that a decrease in $(1 - \tau_r) \cdot r$ has intertemporal-substitution effects on consumption. The household raises year 1's consumption, $C_1$, compared to year 2's, $C_2$. Hence, for given real income in year 1, the household consumes more and saves less in year 1. Recall, however, that year 1's real GDP, $Y_1$, does not change, and that $Y_1 = C_1 + I_1 + G_1$. We are assuming that government purchases, $G_1$, are unchanged. Therefore, the increase in $C_1$ must correspond to an equal-sized reduction in year 1's gross investment, $I_1$. Thus, the key result is that a higher tax rate, $\tau_r$, on asset income leads to higher $C_1$ and lower $I_1$.

In the long run, the reduction in gross investment, $I$, means that the stock of capital, $K$, is smaller than it otherwise would have been. This reduced $K$ will lead to a lower real GDP, $Y$. Therefore, although an increase in the tax rate on asset income, $\tau_r$, does not affect real GDP in the short run, it decreases real GDP in the long run.[7]

---

[7] A tax on asset income is equivalent to a consumption tax that taxes future consumption more heavily than current consumption. Most economists agree that the economy does better if the government raises a given total of revenue through a consumption tax that is uniform over time, rather than time varying. Therefore, from the standpoint of optimal taxation, a constant tax rate on consumption, $\tau_c$, tends to be preferred to a tax on asset income, $\tau_r$ (which is equivalent to a time-varying consumption tax).

- As already assumed, the money stock, $M_t$, and the price level, $P_t$, do not change over time. With a zero inflation rate, $\pi$, the real interest rate, $r$, equals the nominal rate, $i$.
- Real transfers, $V_t$, are zero each year.
- The government starts with no debt, so that $B_0^g = 0$.
- Finally, the most important assumption: *the government has a given time path of purchases*, $G_t$. We are *not* assuming here that $G_t$ is unchanging over time. Rather, we are assuming that, whatever complicated path $G_t$ takes, this whole path stays the same when we consider different choices of budget deficits or different starting levels of public debt.

Since real transfers, $V_t$, are zero each year, the government's budget constraint for year $t$ simplifies from equation (14.2) to

(14.8)
$$G_t + r \cdot \left( B_{t-1}^g / P \right) = T_t + \left( B_t^g - B_{t-1}^g \right) / P$$

Since the government starts with zero debt, we have $B_0^g / P = 0$. Therefore, in year 1, the government's real interest payments, $r \cdot (B_0^g / P)$, are zero, and the budget constraint is

(14.9)
$$G_1 = T_1 + B_1^g / P$$

*government purchases in year* 1 = *real taxes in year* 1 + *real debt at end of year* 1

Suppose, to begin, that the government balances its budget each year. Then, in year 1, real purchases, $G_1$, equal real taxes, $T_1$. In that case, equation (14.9) implies that the real public debt remains at zero at the end of year 1; that is, $B_1^g / P = 0$. Continuing on, if the government balances its budget every year, the real public debt, $B_t^g / P$, is zero in every year $t$.

What happens if, instead of balancing its budget in year 1, the government runs a real budget deficit of one unit? Since we are assuming that the path of government purchases stays the same, year 1's real purchases, $G_1$, do not change. Therefore, the deficit must come from a cut in real taxes, $T_1$, by one unit. Equation (14.9) implies that the real deficit of one unit requires the government to issue one unit of real public debt at the end of year 1, so that $B_1^g / P = 1$.

Assume that the government decides to restore the public debt to zero from year 2 onward, so that $B_2^g / P = B_3^g / P = \cdots = 0$. We have to figure out what this policy requires for year 2's real taxes, $T_2$. To calculate $T_2$, we use the government's budget constraint for year 2. This constraint is given from equation (14.8) as

(14.10)
$$G_2 + r \cdot \left( B_1^g / P \right) = T_2 + \left( B_2^g - B_1^g \right) / P$$

*government purchases in year* 2 + *real interest payments in year* 2
= *real taxes in year* 2 + *real budget deficit in year* 2

If we substitute $B_1^g / P = 1$ and $B_2^g / P = 0$ in equation (14.10), the constraint simplifies to

$$G_2 + r = T_2 - 1$$

Therefore, we can rearrange the terms to calculate real taxes for year 2:

$$T_2 = G_2 + 1 + r$$

This equation says that the government must raise real taxes in year 2, $T_2$, above year 2's government purchases, $G_2$, to pay the principal and interest, $1 + r$, on the one unit of debt, $B_1^g / P$, issued in year 1. (Recall our assumption that $G_2$ does not change.)

Putting the results together, year 1's real taxes, $T_1$, fall by one unit, and year 2's real taxes, $T_2$, rise by $1 + r$ units. How do these changes affect the total present value of real taxes paid by households? Recall the household's multiyear budget constraint:

(14.7)  $$C_1 + C_2/(1 + r_1) + \cdots = (1 + r_0) \cdot \left( B_0/P + B_0^g/P + K_0 \right)$$
$$+ (w/P)_1 \cdot L_1^s + (w/P)_2 \cdot L_2^s/(1 + r_1) + \cdots + (V_1 - T_1)$$
$$+ (V_2 - T_2)/(1 + r_1) + (V_3 - T_3)/[(1 + r_1) \cdot (1 + r_2)] + \cdots$$

According to this equation, we have to divide year 2's real taxes, $T_2$, by the discount factor, $1 + r$, to compute a present value. Therefore, the overall effect of the changes in $T_1$ and $T_2$ on the present value of real taxes is given by

*decrease in year 1's real taxes + present value of increase in year 2's taxes*
$$= -1 + (1 + r)/(1 + r)$$
$$= -1 + 1$$
$$= 0$$

Hence, households experience no net change in the present value of real taxes when the government runs a budget deficit in year 1 and pays off the debt with the necessary budget surplus in year 2.

In our simple example, the government's budget deficit does not affect the present value of real taxes. Moreover, we are assuming that real transfers, $V_t$, are zero in each period. Therefore, the budget deficit does not affect the present value of real transfers net of real taxes on the right-hand side of equation (14.7). We conclude that the budget deficit has no income effects on households.

We can interpret the result as follows. Households receive one unit extra of real disposable income in year 1 because of the cut in year 1's real taxes, $T_1$, by one unit. However, households also have $1 + r$ units less of real disposable income in year 2 because of the rise in year 2's real taxes, $T_2$, by $1 + r$ units. If households use the extra unit of real disposable income in year 1 to buy an extra unit of bonds, they will have just enough additional funds—$1 + r$ units—to pay the extra real taxes in year 2. Thus, the tax cut in year 1 provides enough resources, but no more, for households to pay the higher taxes in year 2. That is why there is no income effect. Nothing is left over to raise consumption or reduce labor supply in any year.

We can view the results as saying that households view real taxes in year 1, $T_1$, as equivalent to a real budget deficit in year 1, $(B_1^g - B_0^g)/P$. If the government replaces a unit of real taxes with a unit of real budget deficit, households know that the present value of next year's real taxes will rise by one unit. Thus, the real budget deficit is the same as a real tax in terms of the overall present value of real taxes. This finding is the simplest version of the **Ricardian equivalence theorem** on the public debt. (The theorem is named after the famous British economist David Ricardo, who first expressed the idea in the early 1800s.[5])

We can interpret the results in terms of saving. The real budget deficit of one unit in year 1 means that real government saving is minus one unit. Since households do not change consumption, they place the entire extra unit of year 1's real disposable income into bonds. Therefore, real household saving in year 1 rises by one unit. Thus, the extra

---

[5] For discussions, see David Ricardo (1846), James Buchanan (1958, pp. 43–46, 114–122), and Robert Barro (1989). Gerald O'Driscoll (1977) points out Ricardo's doubts about the empirical validity of his own theorem.

real household saving exactly offsets the government's real dissaving. The sum of household and government real saving—real national saving—does not change. Thus, another way to express the result is that a budget deficit does not affect real national saving.

## Another Case of Ricardian Equivalence

Our basic result was that a deficit-financed cut in year 1's real taxes by one unit led to an increase by one unit in the present value of future real taxes. In our simple example, all of the higher future taxes appeared in year 2. More generally, some of the increases in real taxes would show up in later years.

To get a more general result, we can drop the assumption that the government runs enough of a budget surplus in year 2 to pay off all of the bonds issued in year 1. Assume, as before, that the government issues one unit of real debt, $B_1^g/P$, at the end of year 1. Recall that the government's budget constraint for year 2 is

(14.10) $$G_2 + r \cdot \left(B_1^g/P\right) = T_2 + \left(B_2^g - B_1^g\right)/P$$

Suppose now that, in year 2, the government does not pay off the one unit of debt, $B_1^g/P$, issued in year 1. Assume instead that the government carries the principal of this debt, one unit, over to year 3, so that

$$B_2^g/P = B_1^g/P = 1$$

If we substitute $B_1^g/P = 1$ and $B_2^g/P = 1$ into equation (14.10), we get

$$G_2 + r = T_2$$

Therefore, year 2's real taxes, $T_2$, cover the interest payment, $r$, but not the principal, 1, for the real debt, $B_1^g/P$, issued in year 1. In other words, the government balances its budget in year 2: real taxes equal real purchases plus real interest payments.

If the government again balances its budget in year 3, we find by the same reasoning that year 3's real taxes, $T_3$, cover the interest payment, $r$, on the one unit of real debt. Similarly, if the government balances its budget every year, real taxes, $T_t$, cover year $t$'s interest payment, $r$. The time profile for the changes in real taxes is

- year 1: $T_1$ falls by 1
- year 2: $T_2$ rises by $r$
- year 3: $T_3$ rises by $r$

and so on. Hence, $T_t$ increases by $r$ units in each year after the first.

Think about the sequence of higher real taxes by $r$ units each year. What quantity of real bonds would households need at the end of year 1 to pay these extra taxes? If households hold one more unit of real bonds, the real interest income in year 2 would be $r$, and this income could pay year 2's additional taxes. Then, if the principal of the bond—one unit—were held over to year 3, the real interest income of $r$ could pay year 3's added taxes. Continuing this way, we find that the real interest income each year would allow households to meet their extra real taxes every year.

What, then, is the present value of the increase in real taxes by $r$ units starting in year 2? This present value must be the same as the one extra unit of real bonds in year 1 needed to pay the additional real taxes in each subsequent year. But, obviously, the present value of one unit of real bonds in year 1 is one unit. Therefore, the present value of the additional future real taxes is one.[6]

Given the results about the present value of the higher future real taxes, the overall change in the present value of real taxes comes from combining two terms:

- $-1$: real tax cut in year 1
- $+1$: present value of real tax increases in future years

Since the sum of the two terms is zero, we conclude, as in our first example, that a deficit-financed cut in year 1's real taxes, $T_1$, leads to no change in the overall present value of real taxes. Therefore, we find again that the deficit-financed tax cut in year 1 has no income effects on households.

## Ricardian Equivalence More Generally

We now have two examples in which a deficit-financed tax cut does not affect the present value of real taxes paid by households. To get this answer, we made a number of unrealistic assumptions. However, the result still holds if we relax most of these assumptions.

We can allow the initial real public debt, $B_0^g/P$, to be greater than zero. Notice that $B_0^g/P$ enters as a part of households' sources of funds on the right-hand side of the multiyear budget constraint:

$$(14.7) \quad C_1 + C_2/(1+r_1) + \cdots = (1+r_0) \cdot \left(B_0/P + B_0^g/P + K_0\right) + (w/P)_1 \cdot L_1^s$$
$$+ (w/P)_2 \cdot L_2^s/(1+r_1) + \cdots + (V_1 - T_1)$$
$$+ (V_2 - T_2)/(1+r_1) + (V_3 - T_3)/[(1+r_1) \cdot (1+r_2)] + \cdots$$

However, if the time path of government purchases, $G_t$, is given (and if real transfers, $V_t$, are zero), we can show that a higher $B_0^g/P$ requires the government to collect a correspondingly higher present value of real taxes, $T_t$, to finance the debt. This higher present value of real taxes exactly offsets the higher $B_0^g/P$ on the right-hand side of equation (14.7). Thus, we still have no income effects on households.

If we allow real transfers, $V_t$, to be greater than zero, we find that a deficit-financed tax cut does not affect the present value of real transfers net of real taxes, $V_t - T_t$, on the right-hand side of equation (14.7). Hence, there are again no income effects on households.

We can allow for variations in the money stock, $M_t$, and the price level, $P_t$. In this case, the new feature is that the revenue from money creation—often called the inflation

---

[6] We can verify this answer by summing the present values:

$$\frac{r}{1+r} + \frac{r}{(1+r)^2} + \frac{r}{(1+r)^3} + \cdots = \left(\frac{r}{1+r}\right) \cdot \left[1 + \left(\frac{1}{1+r}\right) + \left(\frac{1}{1+r}\right)^2 + \cdots\right]$$

The infinite sum inside the brackets has the form of the geometric series $1 + x + x^2 + \cdots$, which equals $1/(1-x)$ if $x$ is less than one in magnitude. In our case, $x = 1/(1+r)$. Therefore, we have

$$\frac{r}{1+r} + \frac{r}{(1+r)^2} + \frac{r}{(1+r)^3} + \cdots = \left(\frac{r}{1+r}\right) \cdot \left[\frac{1}{1 - \left(\frac{1}{1+r}\right)}\right]$$
$$= \left(\frac{r}{1+r}\right) \cdot \left(\frac{1+r}{1+r-1}\right)$$
$$= \left(\frac{r}{1+r}\right) \cdot \left(\frac{1+r}{r}\right)$$
$$= 1$$

As a concrete example, assume that a married couple plans to leave a bequest with a present value of $50,000 to their children. Then suppose that the government runs a budget deficit, which cuts the present value of the couple's taxes by $1,000 but raises the present value of their children's taxes by $1,000. Our prediction is that the parents use the tax cut to raise the present value of their intergenerational transfers to the children to $51,000. The extra $1,000 provides the children with just enough resources to pay their higher taxes. Parents and children then end up with the same amounts of consumption that they enjoyed before the government ran its budget deficit.

One concern is that these kinds of calculations assume that each person possesses a lot of information and computational ability. More realistically, we should acknowledge that budget deficits make it harder for households to figure out exactly the future taxes that they or their descendants will bear. However, it is not obvious that this uncertainty would cause households systematically to underestimate the consequences of budget deficits for future taxes. In fact, the typical response to greater income uncertainty—caused, in this case, by uncertainty about future taxes—is to raise saving. This *precautionary saving* guards against a future that might be worse than anticipated. This behavior implies that private saving may increase by more than one unit when the budget deficit increases by one unit. That is, national saving might increase in response to a budget deficit—the opposite of the standard view.

**Imperfect credit markets**   Thus far, we have assumed that the real interest rate, $r$, on private bonds equaled the rate on government bonds. Since households could issue private bonds, as well as hold them, our model assumes that households can borrow at the same real interest rate, $r$, as the government. In practice, credit markets are not this perfect. Many households that would like to borrow have to pay substantially higher real interest rates than the government. The borrowing rate is especially high if people borrow without collateral (such as a house or car).

When credit markets are imperfect, some households will calculate present values of future real taxes by using a real interest rate above the government's rate. We found before that a deficit-financed cut in year 1's real taxes by one unit led to an increase in the present value of future real taxes by one unit. However, we got this result when we calculated present values using the government's real interest rate, $r$. For households that face a higher real interest rate, the present value of the future real taxes will fall short of one unit.

To illustrate, suppose again that the government cuts year 1's real taxes by one unit and runs a budget deficit of one unit. Assume, as in one of our previous cases, that the government raises real taxes in year 2 by enough to pay the principal and interest on the one unit of new public debt. If the government's real interest rate is 2%, real taxes in year 2 rise by 1.02 units. To calculate the present value of these taxes, households would discount the 1.02 not by the government's interest rate but by the real interest rate paid by households. If households use a real interest rate of, say, 5%, the result is

$$present\ value\ of\ increase\ in\ year\ 2's\ real\ taxes = 1.02/1.05$$
$$\approx 0.97$$

Thus, the overall change in the present value of real taxes paid by households is

$$change\ in\ present\ value\ of\ real\ taxes$$
$$= tax\ cut\ in\ year\ 1 + present\ value\ of\ increase\ in\ year\ 2's\ real\ taxes$$
$$= -1 + 0.97$$
$$= -0.03$$

Hence, the tax cut by one unit in year 1 decreases the overall present value of real taxes by 0.03 units. The effect would be larger if the government delayed its repayment of public debt beyond year 2.

Suppose now that some households (or businesses) have good access to credit and therefore use a real interest rate equal to the government's rate to calculate present values of future real taxes. For these households, a deficit-financed tax cut still leaves unchanged the overall present value of real taxes. What happens if the economy consists partly of households that face the same real interest rate as the government and partly of households that face higher real interest rates? In this case, a deficit-financed tax cut leaves unchanged the present value of real taxes for the first group and reduces the present value for the second group. Thus, in the aggregate, the tax cut makes households feel wealthier.

Why does the imperfection of credit markets make households feel wealthier in the aggregate when the government runs a budget deficit? By running a deficit, the government effectively loans money to households—the loan is one unit if real taxes fall in year 1 by one unit. Then the government effectively collects on the loan in future years when it raises real taxes. The real interest rate charged on these loans is implicitly the rate paid by the government on its bonds. Households view this loan as a good deal if the government's real interest rate is less than the rate at which households can borrow directly. That is why the overall real present value of taxes falls for households that use a high real interest rate to calculate present values.

The implicit assumption is that the government's use of the tax system is an efficient way to lend money to some households. That is, the government is better than private institutions, such as banks, at lending funds (by cutting taxes) and then collecting on these loans in the future (by raising future taxes). If the government is really superior at this lending process, the economy will function more efficiently if the government provides more credit—that is, in our case, if the government runs a larger budget deficit. By operating more efficiently, we mean that the available resources will be better channeled toward higher-priority uses. These uses might be for year 1's consumption or investment by households that previously lacked good access to credit.

In the end, the imperfection of credit markets can provide a reason why budget deficits affect the economy. However, the results do not resemble those from the conventional analysis, in which a larger public debt leads in the long run to lower levels of the capital stock and real GDP. With imperfect credit markets, budget deficits matter if they improve the allocation of credit—that is, if they alleviate some of the imperfections in private credit markets. In other words, budget deficits matter, but in a desirable way. Therefore, we cannot use this reasoning to argue that budget deficits and public debt are burdens on the economy.

## Social Security

Retirement benefits paid through social security programs are substantial in the United States and most other developed countries. Some economists, such as Martin Feldstein (1974), argue that these public pension programs reduce saving and investment. We can use our equilibrium business-cycle model to examine this idea.

The argument for an effect on saving applies when social security is not a **fully funded system**. In a funded setup, workers' payments accumulate in a trust fund, which later provides for retirement benefits. The alternative is a **pay-as-you-go system**, in which benefits to elderly persons are financed by taxes on the currently young. In this setup, people who are at or near retirement age when the program begins or expands receive benefits without

9038.0
18.860
7.7577
61.851

# By The Numbers

## Empirical evidence on the macroeconomic effects of budget deficits

An important prediction from the conventional analysis is that real budget deficits raise consumption and reduce national saving and investment. Over time, the reduction in investment leads to a lower stock of capital. This smaller capital stock implies a higher marginal MPK, which leads to a higher real interest rate, $r$.

Many economists believe that budget deficits reduce national saving and investment and raise real interest rates. Nevertheless, this belief is not well supported by empirical evidence. For example, Charles Plosser (1982, 1987) and Paul Evans (1987a, 1987b) carried out statistical analyses of the effects of budget deficits on interest rates in the United States and other developed countries. Their main finding was that budget deficits had no significant effects on real or nominal interest rates.

Despite many empirical studies for the United States and other countries, it has proved difficult to reach definitive conclusions about the effects of budget deficits on consumption, national saving, and investment. One difficulty concerns the direction of causation. As discussed before, budget deficits often arise as responses to economic fluctuations and temporary government purchases, such as in wartime. Since consumption, national saving, and investment tend to vary as part of economic fluctuations and during wartime, it is hard to isolate the effects of budget deficits on these variables.

An empirical study by Chris Carroll and Lawrence Summers (1987) avoids some of these problems by comparing saving rates in the United States and Canada. The private saving rates were similar in the two countries until the early 1970s but then diverged; for 1983–85 (the final years in their study), the Canadian rate was higher by six percentage points. After holding fixed the influences of macroeconomic variables and tax systems, Carroll and Summers concluded that budget deficits did not affect national saving. That is, the higher private saving rates in Canada were just offsets to higher budget deficits. This finding is consistent with Ricardian equivalence.

The Israeli experience from 1983 to 1987 comes close to providing a natural experiment for studying the interplay between budget deficits and saving. In 1983, the national saving rate of 13% corresponded to a private saving rate of 17% and a public saving rate of −4%. (This measure of public saving includes public investment.) In 1984, a dramatic rise in the budget deficit reduced the public saving rate to −11%. The interesting observation is that the private saving rate rose to 26%, so that the national saving rate changed little, actually rising from 13% to 15%. Then a stabilization program in 1985 eliminated the budget deficit, so that the public saving rate rose to 0% in 1985–86. The private saving rate declined dramatically at the same time—to 19% in 1985 and 14% in 1986. Therefore, the national saving rate remained relatively stable, going from 15% in 1984 to 18% in 1985 and 14% in 1986. Thus, the changes in private saving roughly offset the fluctuations in public saving and led to near stability in national saving. This experience therefore accords with Ricardian equivalence.

paying a comparable present value of taxes. Correspondingly, members of later generations (including most readers of this book) pay taxes that exceed their expected benefits in present-value terms.

The U.S. system, like that of most countries, operates mainly on a pay-as-you-go basis.[13] Although the initial plan in 1935 envisioned an important role for the Social Security trust fund, the system evolved after 1939 primarily toward a pay-as-you-go operation. Retirees increasingly received benefits that exceeded their prior contributions in present-value terms.

Consider the economic effects of social security in a pay-as-you-go system. We focus here on income effects and neglect the types of substitution effects from taxes and transfers that we discussed in Chapter 13. The usual argument goes as follows. When a social security system starts or expands, elderly persons experience an increase in the present value of their social security benefits net of taxes. The increase in the present value of real transfers net of real taxes implies a positive income effect on the consumption of this group.

Young persons face higher taxes, offset by the prospect of higher retirement benefits. Thus, the present value of real transfers net of real taxes may fall for this group. However, the decline in this present value is not as large in magnitude as the increase for the currently old. Why? Because the currently young will be able to finance their future retirement benefits by levying taxes on members of yet unborn generations. Thus, the fall in consumption by the currently young tends to be smaller in size than the increase for the currently old. Hence, we predict an increase in current aggregate consumption. Or, to put it another way, total private saving declines. Since government saving does not change, national saving falls. The decline in national saving leads in the short run to a decrease in investment and, in the long run, to a reduced stock of capital.

This analysis of the economic effects of social security parallels our previous discussion of the conventional analysis of a budget deficit. In both cases, the increase in aggregate consumption arises only if people neglect the adverse effects on descendants. Specifically, an increase in the scale of a pay-as-you-go social security program means that the typical person's descendants will be born with a tax liability that exceeds their prospective retirement benefits in present-value terms. If persons currently alive took full account of these effects on descendants, the income effects from a social security program would be nil.

As in the case of a deficit-financed tax cut, more social security enables older persons to extract funds from their descendants. However, also as before, people value this change only if they give no transfers to their children and receive nothing from their children. Otherwise, people would respond to more social security by shifting private intergenerational transfers, rather than by consuming more. In the United States, for example, the growth of Social Security has strongly diminished the tendency of children to support their aged parents.

On an empirical level, there has been a great debate since the 1970s about the connection of social security to saving and investment. Martin Feldstein (1974) reported a dramatic negative effect of Social Security on capital accumulation in the United States. However, subsequent investigators argued that this conclusion was unwarranted.[14] The evidence for the United States and from a broad cross-section of countries does not yield convincing evidence that social security depresses saving and investment.

[13] Privatized arrangements, such as the main pension system in Chile, are fully funded but do not involve a government trust fund. For a discussion, see Jose Piñera (1996). The World Bank (1994) provides an overview of social security systems throughout the world.

[14] For a summary of the debate, see Louis Esposito (1978) and Dean Leimer and Selig Lesnoy (1982).

# Chapter 15

## Money and Business Cycles I: The Price-Misperceptions Model

Thus far, our macroeconomic model has stressed real factors, such as shifts in technology, as sources of business fluctuations. The government can affect real variables by changing its purchases of goods and services and its tax rates, but there is little evidence that these fiscal actions have been major sources of economic fluctuations in the United States. Many economists believe that **monetary shocks**—created mainly by the monetary authority—have been a principal cause of these fluctuations in the U.S. and other economies. In this chapter, we begin our analysis of monetary effects by studying the *price-misperceptions model*.

---

### Effects of Money in the Equilibrium Business-Cycle Model

We should start by recalling our results on the interactions between nominal and real variables in the equilibrium business-cycle model. One result from Chapter 10 is that a one-time change in the nominal quantity of money, $M$—interpreted in our model as currency—is neutral. This change leads to responses in the same proportion of nominal variables, such as the price level, $P$, and the nominal wage rate, $w$. Real variables, including real GDP, $Y$, employment, $L$, and the real interest rate, $r$, do not change.

We found in Chapter 11 that persisting changes in the nominal quantity of money affect the inflation rate, $\pi$, and thereby the nominal interest rate, $i$. A change in $i$ affects the real quantity of money demanded, $L(Y, i)$, and thereby influences the quantity of real money, $M/P$. These changes have real effects, because increases in $\pi$ and $i$ induce people to spend more time and other resources to economize on real money holdings, $M/P$. Higher inflation leads to more resources expended on transaction costs. If we broadened the model to include costs of changing prices, we would find that higher inflation raises these costs as well. However, transactions costs and costs of changing prices are not important enough in normal times to have significant effects on real GDP.

Although money is neutral, at least as an approximation, we were able to use the model in Chapter 10 to derive implications for the empirical association between real and nominal variables. In our equilibrium business-cycle model, technology shocks affect real GDP, $Y$, and the nominal interest rate, $i$, and thereby influence the real quantity of money demanded, $L(Y, i)$. Typically, this real quantity demanded will be high in booms and low in recessions (because the effect from $Y$ dominates that from $i$). If the nominal quantity of money, $M$, does not respond to changes in the real quantity demanded, the price level, $P$, will move in the direction opposite to the change in $L(Y, i)$. Therefore, the model predicts that $P$ would be countercyclical—low in booms and high in recessions. This prediction accords with U.S. data from 1954 to 2006. (See Figure 10.4 in Chapter 10.)

If the monetary authority wants to stabilize the price level, $P$, it should adjust the nominal quantity of money, $M$, to balance the changes in the real quantity demanded, $L(Y, i)$. In this case, $M$ will be procyclical. The U.S. data from 1954 to 2006 show a weak procyclical pattern in currency. However, the procyclical pattern is stronger for broader monetary aggregates, such as M1 and M2.

# The Price-Misperceptions Model

Empirical evidence suggests that money is not as neutral as predicted by our equilibrium business-cycle model. The **price-misperceptions model** provides a possible explanation for the non-neutrality of money.[1] In this model, households sometimes misinterpret changes in nominal prices and wage rates as changes in relative prices and real wage rates. Therefore, monetary shocks—which affect nominal prices and wage rates—end up affecting real variables, such as real GDP and employment.

## A Model with Non-Neutral Effects of Money

The model retains most of the features of our equilibrium business-cycle model. We still maintain the microeconomic foundations that underlie the supply and demand functions for labor and capital services. We continue to assume that prices—prices of goods, wage rates, and rental prices—adjust rapidly to clear markets. However, the important difference from before is that households have *incomplete current information* about prices in the economy. For example, a worker may know his or her current nominal wage rate and the prices of goods purchased recently. But the worker has less accurate information about wage rates available on other jobs, prices of goods encountered in the distant past or not at all, and so on.

The price-misperceptions model usually focuses on the labor market. We analyzed this market in Figure 8.15 in Chapter 8; Figure 15.1 on the next page reproduces the main parts of this analysis. Recall that an increase in the real wage rate, $w/P$, lowers the quantity of labor demanded, $L^d$. This demand comes from producers (households that own and run businesses) who pay the nominal wage rate, $w$, to workers and receive the price level, $P$, on sales of goods.

An increase in the real wage rate, $w/P$, makes work more attractive to households. Therefore, Figure 15.1 shows that a rise in $w/P$ raises the quantity of labor supplied, $L^s$. More precisely, we found in Chapter 8 that the slope of the labor supply curve depends on the balancing between a substitution effect and an income effect. The substitution effect from a higher $w/P$ motivates less leisure time—hence, more work—and more consumption. The income effect from a higher $w/P$ motivates more leisure time—hence, less work—and more consumption. Thus, the labor supply curve has a positive slope, as shown in Figure 15.1, if the substitution effect dominates the income effect.

---

[1] This model originated from Milton Friedman (1968c) and Edmund Phelps (1970). Later contributions were made by Robert Lucas—see his papers collected in Lucas (1981). For a survey of the main research through the 1970s, see Ben McCallum (1979).

### Figure 15.1 | Clearing of the Labor Market

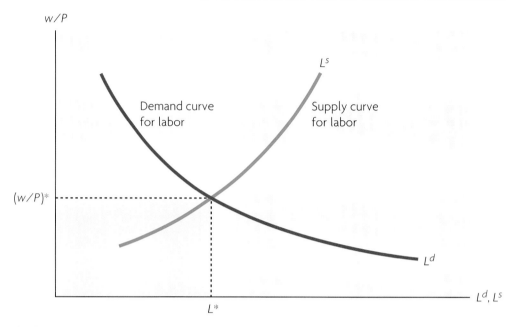

This figure reproduces our analysis of the labor market from Figure 8.15 in Chapter 8. A reduction in the real wage rate, $w/P$, raises the quantity of labor demanded, $L^d$. An increase in $w/P$ raises the quantity of labor supplied, $L^s$. The market clears when the real wage rate is $(w/P)^*$ on the vertical axis and the quantity of labor is $L^*$ on the horizontal axis.

Now we will allow for incomplete current information about prices across the economy. Consider the effect of the real wage rate, $w/P$, on the quantity of labor demanded, $L^d$. The demanders of labor are the employers. We can reasonably assume that an employer has accurate current information about the nominal wage rate, $w$, paid to his or her employees. With respect to the price level, $P$, the price that matters is the one attached to the employer's own product. That is, the employer compares the nominal cost of labor, given by $w$, with the nominal amount, $P$, received on sales of the employer's good or service.[2] We can reasonably assume that the employer has accurate current information about prices of his or her own products. Therefore, the real wage rate that determines the quantity of labor demanded, $L^d$, is the actual value, $w/P$. Hence, we do not have to modify the labor-demand curve drawn in Figure 15.1.

Consider now the real wage rate that matters for labor supply, $L^s$. The suppliers of labor are the workers. For a worker, the relevant nominal wage rate, $w$, is the amount received from the employer. We can again reasonably assume that a worker has accurate current information about his or her own $w$. However, for the price level, $P$, the relevant variable is the price of a market basket of goods. These goods will be purchased from many locations at various times. Therefore, a worker will typically lack good current information about some of these prices. To bring in this effect, we denote by $P^e$ the price that

---

[2] The employer cares also about the prices of other inputs to production, including the nominal rental price, $R$, paid for capital services. In a more general model, another important input price would be for energy. We are assuming that the employer knows the values of all these input prices.

a worker expects to pay for a market basket of goods. The real wage rate that determines the quantity of labor supplied, $L^s$, is the ratio of $w$ to this expected price—that is, $w/P^e$.

Consider again the effects from an increase in the nominal quantity of money, $M$. In Chapter 10, we found that the nominal wage rate, $w$, and the price level, $P$, rose in the same proportion as the increase in $M$. In particular, in Figure 15.1, an increase in $M$ does not change the market-clearing real wage rate, $(w/P)^*$, and the market-clearing quantity of labor input, $L^*$. The constancy of $(w/P)^*$ and $L^*$ accords with the result from Chapter 10 that a change in $M$ is neutral; that is, does not affect any real variables.

Consider, however, what happens when workers do not understand that an increase in the nominal wage rate, $w$, stems from a monetary expansion that inflates all nominal values, including the price level, $P$. Each worker may think instead that the rise in $w$ constitutes an increase in his or her real wage rate, $w/P$. The **perceived real wage rate** is the ratio of $w$ to the expected price level, $P^e$. This ratio, $w/P^e$, rises if the expected price level, $P^e$, increases proportionately by less than $w$. If $w/P^e$ increases, the worker increases the quantity of labor supplied, $L^s$.

As an example, suppose that the nominal wage rate, $w$, is initially \$10 per hour, and the price level is $P = 1$. Thus, the real wage rate, $w/P$, is initially 10 units of goods per hour worked. Assume that $w$ doubles to \$20 per hour. As a worker, how would you respond to this change? If $P$ is still 1, $w/P$ has gone up to 20 units of goods per hour worked, and it is attractive to work more hours. However, if $P$ also doubles, so that $P = 2$, the real wage rate, $w/P$, is still 10 units of goods per hour worked. In this case, you have no reason to work more.

If the worker does not immediately observe the actual price level, $P$, the assessment of the higher nominal wage rate, $w$, depends on the change in the expected price level, $P^e$. If $P^e$ starts at 1 and then rises to less than 2, the perceived real wage rate, $w/P^e$, goes up, and the worker will supply more labor. If $P^e$ rises to 2—that is, if the worker regards the higher $w$ as just a sign of general inflation—$w/P^e$ does not change, and labor supply stays the same.

To analyze the new effect graphically, we can use the revised version of Figure 15.1 shown in Figure 15.2. The labor demand curve, $L^d$, is the same as before, because employers determine their quantity of labor demanded in accordance with the actual real wage rate, $w/P$.

The labor supply curves in Figure 15.2 on the next page are different from before, because the perceived real wage rate, $w/P^e$, determines the quantity of labor supplied. To understand the new labor supply curves, we can use the condition

(15.1)  $$w/P^e = (w/P) \cdot (P/P^e)$$

This equation implies that, for a given actual real wage rate, $w/P$, an increase in $P/P^e$ raises the perceived real wage rate, $w/P^e$. In other words, if workers are underestimating the price level—so that $P^e < P$—they must be overestimating their real wage rate—that is, $w/P^e > w/P$.

To see how price misperceptions affect the labor market, assume that, initially, $P = P^e$ holds, so that $w/P^e = w/P$. The first labor supply curve, denoted by $L^s$ and shown in green in Figure 15.2, applies in this situation. As usual, along this curve, an increase in $w/P$ raises the quantity of labor supplied, $L^s$.

Suppose, as in Chapter 10, that an increase in the nominal quantity of money, $M$, raises the price level, $P$. If the rise in $P$ is only partly perceived by households, $P^e$ increases proportionately by less than $P$. Consequently, $P/P^e$ goes up, and equation (15.1) implies that $w/P^e$ rises for a given $w/P$. Therefore, at any given $w/P$, the quantity of labor supplied is greater than before. We show this result in Figure 15.2 with the new labor supply

that a monetary expansion raised real GDP, $Y$, and labor input, $L$. However, one difference between the two models concerns the real wage rate, $w/P$. In the price-misperceptions model, an expansion of $L$ had to be accompanied by a fall in $w/P$ in order to induce employers to use more labor input. Thus, that model predicted—counterfactually—that $w/P$ would be countercyclical. We now demonstrate that the new Keynesian model does not have this problem.

Figure 16.1 shows that a monetary expansion increases the market-clearing real wage rate from $(w/P)^*$ to $[(w/P)^*]'$ on the vertical axis. Therefore, the model generates a procyclical pattern for $w/P$. Thus, the new Keynesian model correctly predicts that $w/P$ will be procyclical. The reason that the model gets this result is that employers are willing to employ more labor, even though $w/P$ is higher. The key point is that, under imperfect competition, the markup ratio is greater than one. The margin provided by this markup means that—at fixed prices of goods—firms can profitably use more labor to produce and sell more goods, even though the real cost of production has gone up (because $w/P$ increased). The monetary expansion does cut into the markup ratios of firms. However, as long as the markup ratio remains above one, firms are willing to expand labor input and production.

As in the equilibrium business-cycle model studied in Chapter 8, the prediction for procyclical labor input, $L$, in the new Keynesian model depends on the upward slope of the labor supply curve, $L^s$, in Figure 16.1. That is, the analysis relies on the assumption that an increase in the real wage rate, $w/P$, motivates households to work more.

One respect in which the new Keynesian model works less well than the equilibrium business-cycle model concerns the average product of labor, $Y/L$. We found in Chapter 8 that $Y/L$ was procyclical because of the direct effect of a change in the technology level, $A$, on the production function. This prediction for procyclical labor productivity accords with the U.S. evidence, discussed in Chapter 8.

In contrast, the new Keynesian model assumes that the technology level, $A$, is fixed. Therefore, we know from the production function that an increase in $L$ tends to reduce the MPL and the average product of labor, $Y/L$. Hence, an expansion of $L$ during an economic boom goes along with a reduction in the average product of labor, $Y/L$, whereas a decrease of $L$ during a recession goes along with a rise in $Y/L$. Consequently, the new Keynesian model predicts, counterfactually, that $Y/L$ would be countercyclical.

Keynesian economists have used the idea of **labor hoarding** to improve the model's predictions about labor productivity. Because of the costs of hiring and firing workers, employers are motivated to retain workers during temporary downturns. Therefore, businesses may "hoard labor" in recessions as a cost-effective way of having labor available for the next upturn. Although labor input, $L$, still falls during a recession, it falls by less than it would if not for the hoarded labor. Moreover, during a recession, the "excess" labor may not actually produce much output. The workers may be exerting less than full effort on the job, or they may be performing maintenance tasks that do not show up in measured output.[5] In either case, measured output per worker, $Y/L$, would be relatively low in a recession. Thus, we may be able to use labor hoarding to explain why the observed average product of labor, $Y/L$, is procyclical.[6]

---

[5] Jon Fay and James Medoff (1985) found from a survey of 168 manufacturing companies that the typical firm responded to a recession by assigning an additional 5% of its work hours to maintenance, overhaul of equipment, training, and other activities that do not show up in measured output. This reallocation of labor can help to explain why measured output per worker, $Y/L$, tends to be low during a recession.

[6] A richer version of the new Keynesian model has a different way of explaining why the average product of labor, $Y/L$, is procyclical. The new feature is that goods produced by firms serve not only as final products but also as intermediate inputs for other firms. A monetary expansion lowers markup ratios and, therefore, lowers the real cost of intermediate inputs. Consequently, firms use more of these intermediate inputs, and this increased use tends to raise the MPL and the average product of labor, $Y/L$. Therefore, $Y/L$ can rise in a boom even though $L$ increases.

## Price Adjustment in the Long Run

Our analysis of the new Keynesian model applies in the short run, when we do not allow for adjustments in the prices, $P(j)$, set by each firm $j$. In the longer run, the prices adjust, and these adjustments tend to undo the real effects from a change in the nominal quantity of money, $M$.

To study the longer run dynamics, go back to the formula for firm $j$'s markup ratio:

(16.5)    *firm j's markup ratio* $= P(j)/(firm\ j's\ nominal\ marginal\ cost)$

$$= P(j)/[w/MPL(j)]$$

We assumed, thus far, that $P(j)$ was fixed for each firm $j$. Therefore, the overall price level, $P$, was also fixed. We then got the result, in Figure 16.1, that an increase in the nominal quantity of money, $M$, raised the real wage rate, $w/P$, and the quantity of labor input, $L$. Since $P$ is fixed, the increase in $w/P$ must correspond to a rise in the nominal wage rate, $w$. We can see from equation (16.5) that, for fixed $P(j)$, the increase in $w$ raises firm $j$'s nominal marginal cost and, thereby, lowers its markup ratio. Moreover, the increase in $L(j)$ reduces the marginal product of labor, $MPL(j)$. Equation (16.5) shows that the fall in $MPL(j)$ further raises firm $j$'s nominal marginal cost and, therefore, further decreases the markup ratio.

Suppose, as an example, that firm $j$'s preferred (profit-maximizing) markup ratio is 1.2; that is, the firm likes to set its price, $P(j)$, 20% above its nominal marginal cost, $w/MPL(j)$. With $P(j)$ fixed, the increase in the nominal wage rate, $w$, and the decrease in the marginal product of labor, $MPL(j)$, cut into the markup ratio and lower it to, say, 1.1. Since the markup ratio is still above one, the firm meets the extra demand for its good at the fixed price, $P(j)$. However, the firm would still like to have a markup ratio of 1.2. Therefore, at least eventually, the firm would restore this ratio by raising its price, $P(j)$.

When each firm $j$ raises its price, $P(j)$, the overall price level, $P$, increases. Therefore, for a given nominal quantity of money, $M$, real money balances, $M/P$, decrease. This change reverses the initial effect, whereby $M$ rose for fixed $P$, and, therefore, $M/P$ increased. In Figure 16.1, the rightward shift in the labor demand curve came from the effect of the higher $M/P$ on the demand for each firm's good, $Y^d(j)$. As $P$ rises and $M/P$ declines, the demand for each firm's good, $Y^d(j)$, comes back down. Hence, the labor demand curve shifts leftward, back toward its initial position. In the long run, $P$ rises in the same proportion as $M$, and the labor demand curve is back where it started. Thus, in the long run, we get back to our familiar conclusion that a change in the nominal quantity of money, $M$, is neutral: there are no effects on real variables, including the real wage rate, $w/P$, labor input, $L$, and real GDP, $Y$.

Our conclusion is that the real effect of a monetary shock in the new Keynesian model is a short-run result that applies only as long as prices fail to adjust to their equilibrium levels. In this respect, the results are analogous to those from the price-misperceptions model from Chapter 15. In that context, the real effect of a monetary shock applied only in the short run as long as households failed to perceive fully the economy-wide changes in prices. Thus, a key issue for the price-misperceptions model was whether the slow adjustment of price expectations was quantitatively significant. In the new Keynesian model, the parallel issue is whether the slow adjustment of prices is quantitatively significant.

Recently available data, discussed in the box entitled "Evidence on the stickiness of prices," give us a lot of information about the frequency of price adjustment at the microeconomic level. These data do reveal stickiness of some prices; that is, prices for some types of products often do not change for several months. However, a tentative conclusion from empirical research with these new data is that price stickiness is insufficient to explain a

9038.0
18.860
7.7577
61.851

# By The Numbers

## Empirical evidence on the contracting approach

A number of empirical studies provide evidence about the macroeconomic implications of the contracting approach. Shaghil Ahmed (1987) used a data set for 19 industries in Canada over the period 1961–74. He used these data because an earlier study by David Card (1980) calculated the extent of **indexation**—automatic adjustment of nominal wage rates for changes in the price level—in each industry's labor contracts. Indexation ranged from zero to nearly 100%. According to theories in which labor contracts are the basis for the Keynesian model, industries with little indexation should show substantial responses of real wage rates and, hence, of employment and output, to nominal shocks. Industries with a lot of indexation would be affected little by nominal disturbances.

Ahmed found that monetary shocks had positive effects on hours worked in most of the 19 industries. The important point for present purposes, however, is that the extent of an industry's response to these shocks bore no relation to the amount of indexation in the industry. Those with a lot of indexation were as likely as those with little indexation to respond to monetary shocks. This finding is damaging to theories that use long-term contracts as the basis for the Keynesian sticky-wage model.

Mark Bils (1989) studied labor contracts for 12 manufacturing industries in the United States. He reasoned that, if the signing of new contracts was important, we should observe unusual behavior of employment and real wage rates just after these signings. His results were mixed. Some industries, notably motor vehicles, showed substantial changes in employment just after the implementation of new labor agreements. Prior changes in employment tended to be reversed just after a new contract came into effect. These results, although applying only to a few industries, support the contracting approach. However, Bils did not find any corresponding changes in real wage rates after the new labor contracts were implemented. Since these changes in real wage rates are central to the contracting approach, it is difficult to reconcile this part of Bils's findings with that approach.

A study by Giovanni Olivei and Silvana Tenreyro (2007) suggests that the contracting approach may be important for understanding the real effects of monetary policy. They first observed that a preponderance of firms set wage rates toward the end of each calendar year, with the changes taking effect in January of the next year. In the contracting approach, this timing means that monetary disturbances that occur toward the end of the calendar year would be undone within a few months by the changes of wage rates in the next annual adjustment. In contrast, monetary disturbances early in the calendar year would take up to 12 months to be undone by the next adjustment.

Using this conceptual framework, Olivei and Tenreyro investigate whether the response of real GDP to monetary shocks looks different depending on the quarter of the year in which the shock occurs. They measure the shocks by unusual movements in the Federal Funds rate. The unusual movements are those that cannot be explained by prior variations in real GDP, the GDP deflator, and commodity prices. The main finding, for the period 1966 to 2002, was that the response of real GDP to a Funds-rate shock is substantial when the shock takes place in the first or second quarter of the year. A decline in the interest rate by one-quarter of a percentage point is estimated to raise real GDP by 0.2% over the following two years. However, the response is smaller if the shock to the Funds rate occurs in the third or fourth quarter of the year. In that case, a decrease in the funds rate by one-quarter of a percentage point is estimated to raise real

GDP by less than 0.1% over the following two years. Olivei and Tenreyro suggest that the difference in response arises because nominal wage rates tend to be sticky during the calendar year but flexible from the end of one calendar year to the beginning of the next.

harder when there is more work to do—that is, when the demand for a firm's product is high—and work less hard when there is little work. Unlike in an impersonal auction market, these efficient adjustments in work and production can occur even if wage rates do not change from day to day.[14] The important point is that, in the context of labor contracts, stickiness of nominal wage rates does not necessarily cause errors in the determination of labor input and production.

To take a concrete example, suppose that inflation is sometimes lower than expected and sometimes higher. Rational firms and workers know that inflation—if not accompanied by real changes in the economy—does not alter the efficient levels of labor input and production. Therefore, it makes sense to agree on a contract that insulates the choices of labor input and production from the inflation rate. Over many years, when the effects of unanticipated inflation on real wage rates tend to average out, both parties to the contract would benefit from this provision. However, in an economic climate where inflation is high and unpredictable, firms and workers prefer either to index nominal wage rates to the price level or to renegotiate contracts more frequently.

An important lesson from the contracting approach is that stickiness of the nominal wage rate, $w$, need not lead to the unemployment and underproduction that appears in the Keynesian model. Within a long-term agreement, it is unnecessary for $w$ to move all the time in order for the economy to approximate the market-clearing quantity of labor, $L^*$. Thus, instead of supporting the Keynesian perspective, the contracting analysis demonstrates that observed stickiness of nominal wage rates may not matter very much for the workings of the macroeconomy. This reasoning applies also to the sticky prices in the new Keynesian model if we try to explain this price stickiness not from literal menu costs but instead from contractual agreements—for example, between producers and their suppliers.

## Summing Up

In Chapter 15, we began our study of the non-neutrality of money by focusing on price misperceptions. In this chapter, we considered another source of monetary non-neutrality: the stickiness of nominal prices and wage rates. This stickiness reflects costs of changing prices and wages.

The new Keynesian model features stickiness in prices of goods. In a setting of imperfect competition, individual firms set prices as markups over nominal marginal costs of production. If prices are fixed in the short run, firms meet expansions of demand—over some range—by raising production and labor input. Therefore, a monetary expansion increases the economy-wide quantity of labor demanded. The boost to labor demand raises the real wage rate and, if the labor supply curve slopes upward, the quantity of labor

---

[14] However, for large short-term increases in labor input, contracts often prescribe overtime premiums or other types of bonuses.

input. This expansion of labor allows for an increase in real GDP. The model thereby predicts that nominal money, labor, and the real wage rate will be procyclical. The prediction for procyclical real wage rates—which is consistent with the data—distinguishes this model from the price-misperceptions model. However, the new Keynesian model has the counterfactual prediction that the average product of labor will be countercyclical. The idea of labor hoarding has been offered to eliminate this error.

An older-style Keynesian model relied on sticky nominal wage rates. If the nominal wage rate is typically too high, the quantity of labor supplied tends to exceed the quantity demanded. Employment equals the quantity demanded, and the shortfall from the quantity supplied equals the amount of involuntary unemployment. In this setting, a monetary expansion lowers the real wage rate, thereby raising the quantity of labor demanded and, hence, the level of employment. However, this model predicts, counterfactually, that the real wage rate will be countercyclical.

## Key Terms and Concepts

| | |
|---|---|
| aggregate demand | marginal cost of production |
| constant-growth-rate rule | markup ratio |
| Federal Funds market | menu cost |
| Federal Funds rate | multiplier |
| imperfect competition | sticky nominal wage rates |
| indexation | sticky prices |
| involuntary unemployment | voluntary exchange |
| labor hoarding | |

## Questions and Problems

A. Review questions
   1. What is involuntary unemployment?

   2. Explain how an increase in the nominal quantity of money, $M$, reduces the nominal interest rate, $i$, in the new Keynesian model. Why does this effect not arise in the market-clearing model?

B. Problems for discussion
   3. The new Keynesian model

   a. What are the main differences between the new Keynesian model and the equilibrium business-cycle model?
   b. Does a change in the nominal quantity of money, $M$, have real effects in the new Keynesian model? Is imperfect competition among producers sufficient to generate non-neutrality of money in this model?
   c. How does the new Keynesian model explain sticky prices?
   d. What does the new Keynesian model predict for the cyclical behavior of the real wage rate and the average product of labor? Are the results consistent with the data?
   e. Are money-supply shocks the only kinds of shocks that have real effects in the new Keynesian model? What other shocks have real effects in this model?
   f. What are the relative strengths of the new Keynesian and equilibrium business-cycle models?

4. The paradox of thrift

Suppose that households become thriftier in the sense that they decide to raise current saving and reduce current consumer demand.

a. In the new Keynesian model, what happens to real GDP, $Y$, and labor, $L$?
b. What happens to the amount of saving? If it decreases, there is said to be a *paradox of thrift*.
c. Can there be a paradox of thrift in the equilibrium business-cycle model?

5. The Keynesian multiplier

Explain why there can be a multiplier in the new Keynesian model. How is the size of the multiplier affected by the following:

a. adjustments of the price level, $P$?
b. the extent to which markup ratios exceed one?
c. reactions of the nominal quantity of money demanded, $M^d$, to real GDP, $Y$?

Can there be a multiplier in the equilibrium business-cycle model?

6. Perceived wealth in the new Keynesian model

Suppose that the U.S. president makes a speech and announces that we are all wealthier than we thought. If we all believe the president, what does the new Keynesian model predict for changes in real GDP, $Y$, and labor, $L$? Do we actually end up being "wealthier"? Contrast these predictions with those from the equilibrium business-cycle model.

7. Sticky-wage models

How does the model with sticky nominal wage rates differ from the new Keynesian model? What are the relative strengths of the two kinds of models? Why do you think that Keynes emphasized sticky nominal wages, rather than sticky prices?

# International Macroeconomics Part 7

# C h a p t e r  1 7
## World Markets in Goods and Credit

Thus far, we have carried out our analysis for a single, closed economy. Therefore, we have neglected the interactions among countries on international markets. Many macroeconomists, especially those in the United States, focus on a closed-economy framework. One justification is that the U.S. economy represents a large share of the world economy, which really is a closed economy (if we neglect trade with Mars). Another rationale for the neglect of world markets, applicable particularly to the 1950s and 1960s, was that various restrictions inhibited the flows of goods and credit from one country to another. In particular, for the United States, the share of gross domestic product (GDP) that entered into international trade was not large.

With the opening up of international markets—often termed **globalization**—over the last 50 years, the practice of ignoring the rest of the world became increasingly unsatisfactory, even for the U.S. economy. The ratio of U.S. imports to GDP rose from 4% in 1950 to 17% in 2006, while the ratio of exports to GDP increased from 4% to 11%. The years from the mid-1980s through 2006 also featured large U.S. borrowing from foreigners.

To study international trade, we have to extend our model to the world economy, which comprises many countries. We carry out the analysis from the perspective of a *home country*. To simplify, we think of the rest of the world as a single entity, which we call the *foreign country*. (The existence of many foreign countries will not affect our main results.) Residents of the home country buy goods and services from foreigners (imports) and sell goods and services to foreigners (exports). Residents of the home country also borrow from and lend to foreigners.

Sometimes we assume that the home country has a negligible effect on the equilibrium in the rest of the world. This assumption is satisfactory if the home country is a minor part of the world economy. The United States is an intermediate case between a small open economy and the world economy, which is a closed economy. That is, the United States is large enough to have a noticeable effect on the equilibrium of world markets.

We begin with a number of unrealistic assumptions, which we can later relax. Assume first that the goods produced in each country are physically identical. In addition, suppose that transport costs and barriers to trade across national borders are small enough to neglect. Finally, pretend that, instead of using their own money, all countries use a common currency, such as the U.S. dollar or the euro. The idea of a common currency is that the households and businesses in each country use a single type of money and measure all prices in terms of this money. To be specific, we assume that the residents of each country hold money as U.S. dollars and quote prices in units of U.S. dollars.

Given these assumptions, goods in all countries must sell at the same dollar price, $P$. If prices differed, households would want to buy all goods at the lowest price and sell all goods at the highest price. Thus, in an equilibrium where goods are bought and sold in all locations, all prices must be the same. This result is the simplest version of the **law of one price**. The idea of this law is that markets work to ensure that the same good sells at the same price for all buyers and sellers in all locations. We also simplify by ignoring inflation, so that the price level, $P$, is constant over time.

Suppose that the nominal interest rate for year $t$ in the home country is $i_t$. Since we neglect inflation, the real interest rate, $r_t$, equals $i_t$. Suppose that the nominal interest rate in the rest of the world is $i_t^f$. Since we also neglect inflation in the rest of the world, the foreign real rate, $r_t^f$, equals $i_t^f$. In our previous analysis, we neglected differences among borrowers in creditworthiness. Now we will go further, to neglect differences in creditworthiness between households in the home country and households in the foreign country. Furthermore, we assume that no transaction costs exist for carrying out financial exchanges across international borders. Given these assumptions, world credit markets would have to function effectively as a single market with a single nominal interest rate. That is, we have

$$i_t = i_t^f$$

*home nominal interest rate = foreign nominal interest rate*

and

$$r_t = r_t^f$$

*home real interest rate = foreign real interest rate*

The nominal and real interest rates are the same for lenders and borrowers in the home and foreign country.

| | Ratio of U.S. Net Factor Income from Abroad |
|---|---|
| **F i g u r e   1 7 . 4** | to GDP, 1929–2005 |

Net factor income payments are income paid by foreigners to domestic capital and labor, less income paid by domestic residents to foreign capital and labor. For the United States, most of the net factor income from abroad reflects net asset income from abroad, which enters into our model. The graph shows the ratio of the net factor income from abroad to nominal GDP. The data are from the Bureau of Economic Analysis (http://www.bea.gov).

To get a baseline for comparison, suppose first that the home economy is closed to the rest of the world. Since the economy is closed, we can use our previous analysis of the equilibrium business-cycle model to determine real GDP, $Y_t$, consumption, $C_t$, and gross domestic investment, $I_t$. Real GDP, $Y_t$, has to equal the total real expenditure on goods and services, as in equation (17.1):

(17.1) $$Y_t = C_t + I_t + G_t$$

Since the market for capital services clears, the real rental price, $(R/P)_t$, equals the marginal product of capital, MPK (evaluated at the given capital stock, $K$). The real rate of return on capital equals $(R/P)_t$ minus the depreciation rate, $\delta$. Since the real interest rate on bonds, $r_t$, has to equal the real rate of return on capital, we have

(17.9) $$r_t = MPK - \delta$$

*real rate of return on bonds = real rate of return from owning capital*

What happens if this closed economy gets access to the world credit market? We assumed earlier that the world credit market operates effectively as a single market. Consequently, the real interest rate in the home country has to be brought into equality with the real interest rate in the rest of the world.

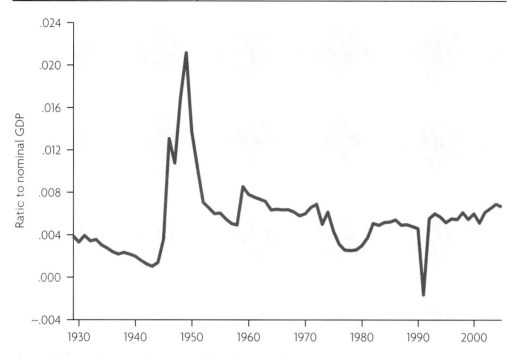

**Figure 17.5** | Ratio of Net U.S. Transfers Abroad to GDP, 1929–2005

The graph shows the ratio of net nominal transfers abroad to nominal GDP. The positive spike in the late 1940s represents the large transfers to U.S. World War II allies. The downward spike in 1991 reflects transfers to the United States from Saudi Arabia and other Gulf War allies. The data are from the Bureau of Economic Analysis (http://www.bea.gov).

Suppose, to begin, that the real interest rate in the rest of the world, $r^f$, is constant and happens to equal the real interest, $r_t$, determined in equation (17.9). That is, the home country would, if closed to the rest of the world, have the real interest rate $r_t = r^f$. In this case, the opening up to the world credit market would not change the real interest rate available to the home country's households. Therefore, decisions about consumption, saving, labor supply, and so on would not change. Consequently, the home country would end up with the same real GDP, $Y_t$, consumption, $C_t$, gross domestic investment, $I_t$, and so on. Therefore, the condition $Y_t = C_t + I_t + G_t$ would continue to hold in equation (17.1). We see, accordingly, that the trade balance would be zero:

(17.6) $$trade\ balance = Y_t - (C_t + I_t + G_t)$$
$$trade\ balance = 0$$

Recall that we add the net real asset income from abroad to the trade balance to get the real current-account balance:

(17.7) $$\left(B_t^f - B_{t-1}^f\right)/P = Y_t - (C_t + I_t + G_t) + r_{t-1} \cdot \left(B_{t-1}^f/P\right)$$

$$real\ current\text{-}account\ balance = trade\ balance + net\ real\ asset\ income\ from\ abroad$$

Since the home country had initially been closed, it must have started with a zero net international investment position, $B_{t-1}^f = 0$. Therefore, the net real asset income from abroad is zero. Since the trade balance is also zero, we have that the current-account balance is zero. Therefore, although the home country has the opportunity to borrow and lend on the world credit market, this option is not exercised in equilibrium. However, this conclusion depends on our assumption that $r_t$, the real interest rate that the home country would have if it were closed, equals $r^f$.

To see how the world credit market can be important, start from the situation we just described. Then assume that the technology level, $A$, in the home country rises, while the technology level in the rest of the world does not change. The increase in $A$ raises the home MPK, evaluated at the given capital stock, $K$. Therefore, if the home country were a closed economy, the real interest rate, $r_t$, would rise, as indicated by equation (17.9).[6] If the home economy is a negligible part of the world economy, the foreign real interest rate, $r^f$, would not change.[7] Hence, the real interest rate, $r_t$, that the home country would have if it were closed is now greater than $r^f$.

What happens if the home country's real interest rate, $r_t$, rises above the foreign rate, $r^f$? Since we assumed that households and governments view all asset claims as equivalent, foreigners would want to do all of their lending in the home country, whereas domestic residents would want to do all of their borrowing abroad. Clearly, this response would not be an equilibrium. To see how markets come into equilibrium, we have to add something to our model.

Equation (17.9) says that the home country's real interest rate, $r_t$, must equal the rate of return on capital in the home country, MPK $- \delta$. The rise in the home country's technology level, $A$, raises the MPK and, therefore, tends to raise $r_t$ above the foreign rate, $r^f$ (since $r_t = r^f$ applied initially). Since this divergence cannot apply in equilibrium, something has to give. Specifically, if $r^f$ does not change (because the home country is small) and $r_t = r^f$ still holds, the rate of return on capital at home, MPK $- \delta$, has to come back down to its initial value. The problem is that, if we treat the stock of capital at home, $K$, as fixed in the short run—that is, if we neglect the contribution of the current flow of net domestic investment to the stock of capital—there is no way for a rise in $A$ not to increase the MPK.

One way that economists resolve this problem is to bring in **adjustment costs for investment**. The flow of net domestic investment—equal to gross investment, $I_t$, less depreciation, $\delta K_{t-1}$—leads over time to increases in the stock of capital, $K_t$, which appears as new plant and equipment. Businesses incur costs—called adjustment costs—for expanding the plant and equipment used in production. These costs effectively subtract from the rate of return on investment. Therefore, a large enough flow of gross investment, $I_t$, brings the rate of return on investment in the home country down to equal the given foreign real interest rate, $r^f$. Through this mechanism, an increase in the home country's technology level, $A$, motivates the home country to borrow a finite amount from foreigners to finance a high, but finite, flow of gross investment, $I_t$. To study the main effects on the current-account balance, we do not have to go through the details of this analysis. The main point is that an increase in the home MPK leads to a high, but finite, flow of gross domestic investment, $I_t$.

To see the effects of an increase in the technology level, $A$, on the current-account balance, go back to the definition:

**(17.7)** $$\left(B_t^f - B_{t-1}^f\right)/P = Y_t - (C_t + I_t + G_t) + r_{t-1} \cdot \left(B_{t-1}^f/P\right)$$

*real current-account balance = trade balance + net real asset income from abroad*

---

[6] The full increase in $r_t$ includes a positive effect from higher labor input, $L_t$, on the MPK. If we allowed for an increase in the capital utilization rate, $\kappa_t$, as in Chapter 9, we would get a further boost to $r_t$.

[7] If the home country is the United States, its economy would be large enough to have a noticeable impact on worldwide real interest rates. We could modify our analysis accordingly, but the same basic ideas still apply.

On the right-hand side, the net real asset income, $r_{t-1} \cdot (B^f_{t-1}/P)$, is given—for example, at zero if the home country starts with a zero net international investment position, $B^f_{t-1}/P$. Real government purchases, $G_t$, are also given. The higher $A$ raises the MPK and thereby increases gross domestic investment, $I_t$. This change reduces the current-account balance; that is, it moves it toward deficit. The question is, what happens to the difference between real GDP and consumption, $Y_t - C_t$?

We know that the increase in the technology level, $A$, raises real GDP, $Y_t$. This change reflects partly the direct impact of $A$ on the production function and partly an effect from increased labor input, $L_t$. We know from Chapter 7 that the response of $C_t$ depends on the strength of the income effect. If the change in $A$ is permanent, $C_t$ will rise by roughly as much as $Y_t$, so that $Y_t - C_t$ does not change.[8] In this case, we see from equation (17.7) that the current-account balance falls overall because of the increase in $I_t$.

We can gain insight on this result by considering real national saving. The total real income of the home country is real GNP, $Y_t + r_{t-1} \cdot (B^f_{t-1}/P)$, less depreciation of capital, $\delta K_{t-1}$. That is, real income equals real net national product (real NNP). Real national saving equals real NNP less real expenditure on consumption and government purchases, $C_t + G_t$:

**(17.10)**
$$real\ national\ saving = Y_t + r_{t-1} \cdot \left(B^f_{t-1}/P\right) - \delta K_{t-1} - (C_t + G_t)$$

*real national saving = real NNP − real expenditure on consumption and government purchases*

We can rearrange the right-hand side of equation (17.7) to get that the real current-account balance is

$$\left(B^f_t - B^f_{t-1}\right)/P = Y_t + r_{t-1} \cdot \left(B^f_{t-1}/P\right) - (C_t + G_t) - I_t$$

Then, if we add and subtract depreciation, $\delta K_{t-1}$, we get yet another way to express the current-account balance:

---

Key equation (current-account balance, saving, and investment):

**(17.11)**     $\left(B^f_t - B^f_{t-1}\right)/P = Y_t + r_{t-1} \cdot \left(B^f_{t-1}/P\right) - \delta K_{t-1} - (C_t + G_t) - (I_t - \delta K_{t-1})$

*real current-account = real national saving − net domestic investment*
*balance*

---

Note from equation (17.10) that the yellow shaded term in equation (17.11) equals real national saving. Thus, we have shown that the real current-account balance is the difference between real national saving and net domestic investment.

In the case of a permanent increase in the technology level, $A$, we found that real GDP, $Y_t$, and consumption, $C_t$, rose by the same amount. Therefore, real national saving does not change in equation (17.10). Equation (17.11) shows, accordingly, that the rise in net domestic investment, $I_t - \delta K_{t-1}$, leads to a decline in the real current-account balance.

To summarize, we have the following results concerning the opening up of the home country to the world credit market.

- Suppose that the real interest rate, $r_t$, that would prevail in the home country if it were closed is greater than the rate in the rest of the world, $r^f$. In this case, the opening up

---

[8] The home real interest rate is fixed at the foreign value, $r^f$. Therefore, we do not get an intertemporal-substitution effect from a change in the real interest rate.

of the home country to the world credit market results in a current-account deficit. The home country borrows from the rest of the world to pay for higher net domestic investment, $I_t - \delta K_{t-1}$.

- If the real interest rate, $r_t$, that would prevail in the home country if it were closed is less than the rate in the rest of the world, $r^f$, the results are the opposite. The home country has a current-account surplus—it lends to the rest of the world and has lower net domestic investment, $I_t - \delta K_{t-1}$.

- The final possibility—the first one we considered—is that the real interest rate, $r_t$, that would prevail in the home country if it were closed happens to equal the rate in the rest of the world, $r^f$. In this case, the current account is balanced, and the opening to the rest of the world does not affect $I_t - \delta K_{t-1}$.

These results may be surprising because the general view in popular commentary is that current-account deficits are a symptom of bad economic conditions. A better way to look at the current-account balance is to recall from equation (17.11) that it equals the difference between real national saving and net domestic investment. Thus, for given national saving, higher net domestic investment—often viewed as a good thing—goes along with a lower current-account balance, perhaps a current-account deficit. On the other hand, for given net domestic investment, greater national saving—also often viewed as a good thing—goes along with a higher current-account balance, possibly a current-account surplus. More generally, we cannot say that current-account deficits are necessarily a bad sign or that current-account surpluses are necessarily a good sign. As we show in the following sections, we need more information about what is happening in the economy to make these kinds of judgments.

## Economic Fluctuations

In this section, we use our open-economy version of the equilibrium business-cycle model to predict how the current-account balance varies with economic fluctuations. We assume that the home country is open to world credit markets and is small enough to have a negligible effect on the real interest rate, $r^f$, in the rest of the world. We treat $r^f$ as constant, and we assume that the home country's economic fluctuations come from shocks to the technology level, $A$. Based on our analysis of the equilibrium business-cycle model in Chapters 8 and 9, we assume that the shocks to $A$ are persistent over time but less than fully permanent.

Recall that the real current-account balance is given by

(17.11) $$\left(B_t^f - B_{t-1}^f\right)/P = Y_t + r_{t-1} \cdot \left(B_{t-1}^f/P\right) - \delta K_{t-1} - (C_t + G_t) - (I_t - \delta K_{t-1})$$

*real current-account balance = real national saving − net domestic investment*

We know that an increase in $A$ raises net domestic investment, $I_t - \delta K_{t-1}$. We also have that consumption, $C_t$, rises, but by less than the increase in real GDP, $Y_t$ (because the increase in $A$ is less than fully permanent). Therefore, real national saving increases. The overall change in the real current-account balance in equation (17.11) depends on whether $I_t - \delta K_{t-1}$ rises by more or less than real national saving. In general, the overall effect on the real current-account balance is ambiguous. However, in usual empirical implementations of equilibrium business-cycle models, net domestic investment, $I_t - \delta K_{t-1}$, is highly sensitive to the rate of return on capital, MPK $- \delta$. In this case, the increase in net domestic investment dominates the rise in real national saving, and the real current-account balance falls. Thus, *the equilibrium business-cycle model predicts that the real current-account balance will be countercyclical—low in booms and high in recessions.*

| Figure 17.6 | Cyclical Behavior of U.S. Real GDP and the Current-Account Balance |

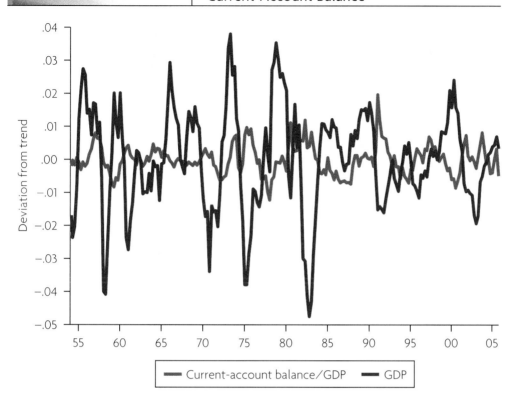

The red graph is the deviation of real GDP from its trend. This deviation is measured in proportionate terms. The blue graph is the deviation from trend of the ratio of the nominal current-account balance to nominal GDP. The data on GDP and the current-account balance are quarterly and seasonally adjusted. The ratio of the current-account balance to GDP is weakly countercyclical—it tends to fluctuate in the direction opposite to real GDP.

To check out this prediction, Figure 17.6 uses U.S. data to compare the cyclical behavior of the ratio of the current-account balance to GDP with the cyclical behavior of real GDP. The ratio of the current-account balance to GDP is weakly countercyclical—from 1954 to 2005, the correlation with the cyclical part of real GDP was −0.32. Thus, as predicted, the current account tends to move toward deficit during a boom and toward surplus during a recession.[9]

As an example, consider the boom of the late 1990s. While real GDP rose above trend from 1996 to 2000 (the red graph in Figure 17.6), the current-account deficit widened (the blue graph). From the standpoint of equation (17.11), we have that the boom in net domestic investment, $I_t - \delta K_{t-1}$, dominated the rise in real national saving. Thus, much of the investment boom of the late 1990s was paid for by borrowing from the rest of the world, as reflected in the increasing current-account deficit. This result is an example of a current-account deficit reflecting good times—in this case, surging investment at home.

[9] The cyclical behavior of the current-account balance reflects mainly the cyclical behavior of the trade balance, which equals net exports of goods and services. Thus, the model also predicts that net exports are countercyclical. This proposition accords with the U.S. data: exports and imports are both procyclical, but imports are more procyclical than exports.

22% of GDP. For an earlier example of a promising developing country that borrowed heavily from abroad, consider the United States. In 1890, the U.S. foreign debt reached $2.9 billion, or 21% of GNP. Recall from Figure 17.1 that the United States ran a current-account deficit for most of the 19th century.

## The Current-Account Deficit and the Budget Deficit

In Chapter 14, we studied how budget deficits affect the economy. Think about a cut in year $t$'s real taxes, $T_t$, corresponding to an increase in the real public debt, $(B_t^g - B_{t-1}^g)/P$. We assume that taxes are lump sum, although we could also consider distorting taxes, as we did in Chapter 13. Most importantly, we assume that the time path of government purchases, $G_t$, does not change.

In the Ricardian approach, discussed in Chapter 14, a deficit-financed cut in year $t$'s real taxes, $T_t$, did not affect the present value of real taxes paid by households. Therefore, households did not change consumption, $C_t$. Since the cut in $T_t$ raised real disposable income and $C_t$ did not change, real private saving in year $t$ went up by the full amount of the tax cut. Hence, the increase in real private saving completely offset the reduction in real public saving, and real national saving did not change.

If we allow for an open economy, the important issue is still whether a budget deficit affects real national saving. The real current-account balance is again given by

(17.11) $$(B_t^f - B_{t-1}^f)/P = Y_t + r_{t-1} \cdot (B_{t-1}^f/P) - \delta K_{t-1} - (C_t + G_t) - (I_t - \delta K_{t-1})$$

*real current-account balance = real national saving − net domestic investment*

In the Ricardian case, a budget deficit does not change real national saving. Therefore, equation (17.11) implies that the real current-account balance would not change. The reason is that the home country's households save the full amount of a tax cut and, therefore, willingly absorb all of the additional government bonds issued by the home government. Consequently, the home country does not borrow from the rest of the world to finance its budget deficit, and the real current-account balance does not change. Thus, *in the Ricardian case, a budget deficit does not create a current-account deficit.*

The conclusions are different if households do not save the full amount of the tax cut—that is, if a budget deficit reduces real national saving. For example, we mentioned in Chapter 14 that finite-lived households might feel wealthier when the government cuts taxes and runs a budget deficit. In this case, consumption, $C_t$, rises, and real national saving declines. Equation (17.11) shows that the real current-account balance moves toward deficit. That is, the home country borrows from foreigners to pay for the rise in consumption. Hence, in this case, a budget deficit leads to a current-account deficit.

When budget and current-account deficits occur at the same time, an economy is said to be suffering from **twin deficits**. Economists applied this label to the U.S. economy in the mid-1980s, when budget deficits were large and the ratio of the current-account deficit to GDP gradually widened (see Figure 17.1). However, the current-account deficit disappeared at the beginning of the 1990s, despite the continued presence of budget deficits. Moreover, the current-account deficit rose again late in the 1990s, even though the budget shifted toward surplus. Later still, in 2002–06, twin deficits reappeared. Thus, the empirical observation is that twin deficits sometimes occur, but the pairing of current-account deficits with budget deficits is not a regular feature of the U.S. economy or, it turns out, of other economies.

Even if budget deficits do not cause current-account deficits, twin deficits can arise as responses to other events. Consider, for example, a temporary expansion of government purchases, $G_t$, as in wartime. We found before that a temporary rise in $G_t$ tends to move

# Back To Reality

**Why was the U.S. current-account deficit so large in 2000–06?**

We see from Figure 17.1 that the U.S. current-account deficit of 4–5% of GDP in 2000–06 was unusual compared to the U.S. history since 1820. The $64,000 question (or, maybe, $64 million question) is: why did the current-account deficit become so large? We cannot be sure of the answer, but we can offer suggestions. For further discussion of this important puzzle, see Maurice Obstfeld and Kenneth Rogoff (2004).

We can start with 1991, when the United States ran a small current-account surplus. The ratio of the U.S. current-account deficit to GDP rose during the 1990s, especially in the latter half, with the ratio reaching 4% in 2000. A key underlying factor was the strength of the economy, notably the rise in the ratio of gross domestic investment to GDP by four percentage points (from 13.4% in 1991 to a peak of 17.7% in 2000). Much of the investment boom reflected the growth of high-tech sectors, notably telecommunications and the Internet. Since the increase in investment exceeded the normal boom-time increase of real national saving, much of the added investment had to be financed by borrowing from foreigners. Hence, the rise in investment explains a good deal of the current-account deficit of 4% of GDP in 2000.

The economy went into a recession in 2001–02, partly because of the end of the technology boom in mid-2000 and partly because of the terrorist attacks of September 11, 2001. The ratio of gross investment to GDP declined to 15% in 2002, and this change would, by itself, have reduced the ratio of the current-account deficit to GDP. However, the U.S. federal government substantially expanded its purchases, partly for defense and other aspects of national security and partly for other programs (see Figure 12.2 in Chapter 12). This increase in government purchases helps to explain why the current-account ratio stayed relatively steady in 2001–02 and then increased to 5% in 2003–06.

Some economists argue that the persisting budget deficits in 2003–06 (Figure 14.3 in Chapter 14) made a major contribution to the current-account deficit. This argument is not compelling, because the ratios of the real budget deficit to real GDP were smaller in 2003–06 than they were in the mid-1980s and early 1990s. In those earlier periods, the ratio of the current-account deficit to GDP was much smaller than in 2003–06. Thus, budget deficits cannot be the main story.

The return to a strong economy, with the ratio of gross investment to GDP rising from 15% in 2003 to 17% in 2006, contributed to the current-account deficit, and some special factors mattered as well. One factor was the sharp rise in oil prices, which financial markets viewed as partly temporary. Another unusual force, mentioned near the beginning of this chapter, is that the rate of return on U.S. holdings of foreign assets was much higher than the rate of return on foreign holdings of U.S. assets. Therefore, although the estimated net international investment position of the United States became substantially negative (Figure 17.3), the net flow of payments to the United States remained positive (Figure 17.4). Through 2006, the United States effectively did not have to pay for its indebtedness to the rest of the world. This foreign generosity may have prevented the normal adjustment of the U.S. economy toward a balanced current account.

the real current-account balance toward deficit. We also know from Chapter 14 that a temporary increase in $G_t$ motivates the government to run a budget deficit to avoid a large temporary increase in taxes. Therefore, the current-account deficit and budget deficit rise together in this case. However, we would not say that the budget deficit caused the current-account deficit. Rather, the two deficits moved in the same direction in response to a common shock—the temporary increase in government purchases because of the war.

| Figure 18.1 | Nominal Exchange Rates for U.K., Canada, and Japan |

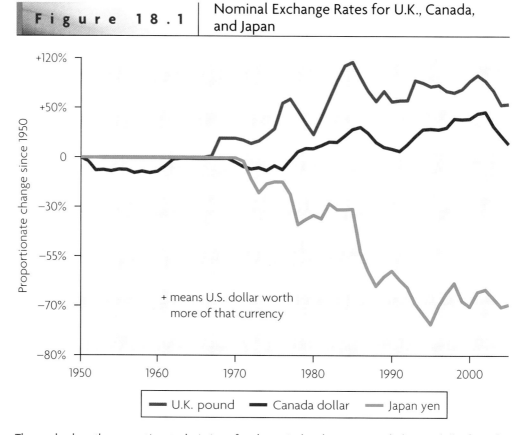

The graphs show the proportionate deviation of each nominal exchange rate with the U.S. dollar from the value that prevailed in 1950. In 1950, the nominal exchange rates were United Kingdom: 0.357 pounds per U.S. dollar; Canada: 1.09 Canadian dollars per U.S. dollar; Japan: 361.1 yen per U.S. dollar. Data are from International Monetary Fund, *International Financial Statistics*.

currencies were replaced by a common currency, the euro.[2] Therefore, the U.S. dollar nominal exchange rates with the currency of each of these countries have moved together since 1999.

## Purchasing-Power Parity

Sometimes countries allow their nominal exchange rates to move freely in response to market forces. These systems are called **flexible exchange rates**. In other circumstances, countries try to maintain a constant nominal exchange rate with respect to another currency, often the U.S. dollar. These systems are called **fixed exchange rates**. We will begin with basic theoretical propositions about international finance that hold whether nominal exchange rates are flexible or fixed. The first of these propositions connects the nominal exchange rate between two currencies to the price levels prevailing in the two countries. In our model, we consider the nominal exchange rate between U.S. dollars and U.K. pounds and the price levels in the United States and the United Kingdom.

---

[2] The conversion rates with the euro were set in 1999 at 6.56 francs, 1.96 marks, and 1936 lira. The three currencies retained separate physical presences until 2001, after which only euro notes circulated.

### Figure 18.2 | Nominal Exchange Rates for France, Germany, and Italy

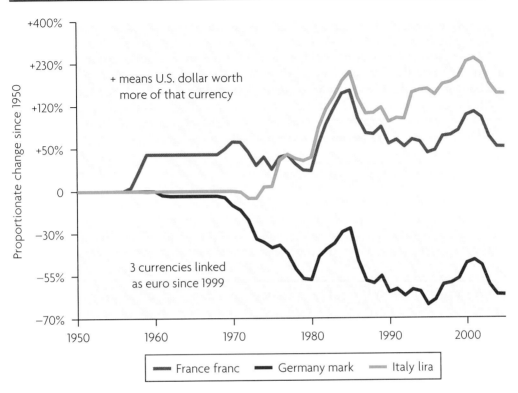

The graphs show the proportionate deviation of each nominal exchange rate with the U.S. dollar from the value that prevailed in 1950. In 1950, the nominal exchange rates were France: 3.5 francs per U.S. dollar; Germany: 4.2 marks per U.S. dollar; Italy: 625 lira per U.S. dollar. In 1999–2001, the separate currencies disappeared and were replaced by the euro. The conversion rates with the euro were fixed at the start of 1999 at 6.56 French francs, 1.96 German marks, and 1936.3 Italian lira. Data are from International Monetary Fund, *International Financial Statistics*.

## The PPP Condition and the Real Exchange Rate

The U.S. price level, $P$, is measured in dollars per unit of goods. We denote the U.K. price level (or foreign price level) by $P^f$, measured in pounds per unit of goods. To start, assume that the goods produced and used in both countries are physically identical. We also ignore any transportation or other transaction costs for buying and selling goods in the two countries. Then the central idea is that buying and selling goods has to look equally attractive in both countries for the households of both countries.

To see how this works, consider a household that has $1 of U.S. currency. (The household could reside in either country.) The household can buy goods in the United States at the price $\$P$ per unit of good. Therefore, with $1, the household gets $1/P$ units of goods. Suppose, instead, that the household uses the exchange market to get $\varepsilon$ pounds for the $1. Then, with $\varepsilon$ pounds, the household can buy $\varepsilon \cdot (1/P^f)$ units of goods in the United Kingdom. If this amount, $\varepsilon \cdot (1/P^f)$, is greater than $1/P$, the household would buy all goods in the United Kingdom. Conversely, if $\varepsilon \cdot (1/P^f)$ were less than $1/P$, the household would buy all goods in the United States. For the household to be indifferent about where

Table 18.2 | Real Exchange Rates for Selected Countries in 2004

| Country | Real Exchange Rate | Country | Real Exchange Rate |
|---|---|---|---|
| United States | 1.00 | Hungary | 1.68 |
| Canada | 1.01 | Chile | 1.95 |
| Hong Kong | 1.29 | Poland | 2.04 |
| Denmark | 0.71 | Mexico | 1.50 |
| Australia | 0.96 | Russia | 2.42 |
| Switzerland | 0.69 | South Africa | 2.40 |
| Ireland | 0.88 | Brazil | 2.45 |
| Singapore | 1.11 | Thailand | 3.12 |
| Japan | 0.82 | Turkey | 1.83 |
| Netherlands | 0.90 | Iran | 3.11 |
| Belgium | 0.92 | Costa Rica | 2.16 |
| Sweden | 0.77 | Colombia | 3.31 |
| Germany | 0.86 | Ukraine | 4.67 |
| France | 0.87 | Egypt | 3.77 |
| United Kingdom | 0.86 | Guatemala | 1.93 |
| Italy | 0.97 | China | 4.31 |
| Spain | 1.05 | Indonesia | 3.03 |
| Israel | 1.39 | India | 4.90 |
| South Korea | 1.44 | Pakistan | 3.53 |
| Greece | 1.19 | Vietnam* | 5.18 |
| Czech Republic | 1.85 | Bangladesh | 4.69 |
| Argentina | 3.17 | Nigeria | 2.16 |

**Note:** Starting with the left column, countries are listed in descending order of real per capita GDP in 2000 (Heston, Summers, and Aten [2002]). These real GDP numbers adjust for cross-country differences in the costs of the market basket of goods included in the GDP. The real exchange rate, based on the prices of goods contained in the GDP, corresponds to the concept in equation (18.3). All exchange rates use the United States as the base country. A value near 1.0 means that the market basket of goods costs about the same number of dollars in the indicated country as in the United States. Higher values mean that the market basket of goods is less expensive than in the United States. The data are from World Bank, *World Development Indicators* 2006.

* Value is for 2003.

Mark Taylor [2004].) That is, there is a long-run tendency for real exchange rates among the rich countries to approach values not too far from 1.0. This result means that we can use the configuration of real exchange rates at a point in time—such as the year 2004 in Table 18.2—to forecast long-term changes in real exchange rates. Consider a country, such as Switzerland or Sweden, that was expensive relative to the United States in 2004; their real exchange rates were 0.69 and 0.77, respectively. The prediction is that these real exchange rates would increase in the long run to approach a value closer to 1.0. From the formula for the real exchange rate in equation (18.3), this prediction means that either the nominal exchange rate, $\varepsilon$, would rise, or the ratio of foreign to home prices, $P^f/P$, would fall. That is, for a given $\varepsilon$, the inflation rate, $\pi^f$, in Switzerland and Sweden should be lower than the inflation rate, $\pi$, in the United States.

We can be bolder and apply this reasoning to a comparison between the United States and China. In 2004, when China was still a relatively poor country, it was not surprising that the real exchange rate was high—4.3 in Table 18.2. However, as discussed in Chapter 3, China has been growing rapidly for some time. If this rapid growth is sustained, China would be a rich country in 30–40 years. In that case, we would predict that the real exchange rate would fall from 4.3 in 2004 to a value much closer to 1.0. The formula for the real exchange rate in equation (18.3) tells us that either the nominal exchange rate, $\varepsilon$, has to fall a great deal, or else the ratio of Chinese to U.S. prices, $P^f/P$, has to rise a great deal. To be concrete, suppose that $\varepsilon$ did not change, and the real exchange rate between China and the United States reached 1.0 in 30 years. In that case, $P^f/P$ would have to rise by a factor of 4.3 over 30 years. For that to happen, the average inflation rate, $\pi^f$, in China would have to exceed the average U.S. inflation rate, $\pi$, by about 5% per year. To put it another way, if China does not want to have this high inflation, it has to allow the nominal exchange rate, $\varepsilon$, to fall substantially over the 30 years. That is, the value of the Chinese currency (renminbi) in terms of the U.S. dollar—$1/\varepsilon$ dollars per renminbi—would have to rise a good deal.

## The Relative PPP Condition

Now we will consider changes, rather than levels, of the real exchange rate. The PPP condition says that the nominal exchange rate, $\varepsilon$, equals the price ratio, $P^f/P$:

(18.2) $$\varepsilon = P^f/P$$

We mentioned that this condition is equivalent to saying that the real exchange rate, given by

(18.3) $$real\ exchange\ rate = \frac{\varepsilon}{P^f/P}$$

equals one.

Equation (18.3) implies that the growth rate of the real exchange rate equals the growth rate of the nominal exchange rate, which we denote by $\Delta\varepsilon/\varepsilon$, less the growth rate of the ratio of foreign to home prices, $P^f/P$. The growth rate of $P^f/P$ is the difference between the inflation rates of the two countries:

$$growth\ rate\ of\ P^f/P = \Delta P^f/P^f - \Delta P/P$$
$$growth\ rate\ of\ P^f/P = \pi^f - \pi$$

Therefore, we have

(18.4) $$growth\ rate\ of\ real\ exchange\ rate = \Delta\varepsilon/\varepsilon - (\pi^f - \pi)$$

When the PPP condition in equation (18.2) holds, so that the real exchange rate equals one, the growth rate of the real exchange rate equals zero. Therefore, the right-hand side

to exchange U.S. dollars for gold (on the request of foreign official institutions) at a fixed price, which happened to be $35 per ounce. Thus, by maintaining a fixed nominal exchange rate with the U.S. dollar, each country indirectly pegged its currency to gold.

Another historical example of a system of fixed exchange rates is the classical gold standard. In this setup, each central bank directly pegged its currency to gold at a fixed rate of exchange. The United Kingdom was effectively on the gold standard from the early eighteenth century until World War I, except for a period of suspension from 1797 to 1821 because of the Napoleonic Wars. After departing from the gold standard during World War I, the United Kingdom returned to this system in 1926 but departed again during the Great Depression in 1931. The United States was on the gold standard from 1879 until the trough of the Great Depression in 1933, when the dollar price of gold was raised from $20.67 to $35 per ounce. Earlier periods involved a greater role for silver in the United States. From an international perspective, the high point of the gold standard was from 1890 to 1914.

Under a gold standard (or other commodity standard), each central bank pegs the value of its currency in terms of gold (or other commodities). An ounce of gold might, for example, be set at $20 in New York and £4 in London (roughly the values prevailing in 1914). In this environment, the nominal exchange rate between U.K. pounds and U.S. dollars had to be close to 0.2 pounds per dollar. Otherwise (subject to the costs of shipping gold), it would be profitable to buy gold in one country and sell it in the other. As with the Bretton Woods System, the classical gold standard would—if adhered to by the participants—maintain fixed nominal exchange rates among the various currencies.

It is possible for countries to maintain fixed nominal exchange rates in a regime that has no role for gold or other commodities. For example, from 1979 to 1992, several Western European countries kept the nominal exchange rates among their currencies fixed within fairly narrow bands. This arrangement, called the European Monetary System (EMS), effectively evolved into the euro, which became the common currency of 12 Western European countries over a transition period from 1999 to 2001. Although most countries in Western Europe use the euro, some important exceptions are the United Kingdom, Sweden, Denmark, and Switzerland.

## Purchasing Power Parity Under Fixed Exchange Rates

To see the workings of a system with fixed nominal exchange rates, consider again the setting where the United States is the home country. We can still think of the United Kingdom as the foreign country, but we have to consider the pre-1971 environment in which the pound-dollar exchange rate was fixed in most years.

Suppose that the absolute PPP condition holds, so that the nominal exchange rate, $\varepsilon$, equals the ratio of the U.K. price level, $P^f$, to the U.S. price level, $P$:

(18.2)
$$\varepsilon = P^f / P$$

Rearranging the terms, we get that the U.K. price level is given by

(18.16)
$$P^f = \varepsilon P$$

Therefore, if the nominal exchange rate, $\varepsilon$, is fixed, $P^f$ must move in lockstep with $P$. This condition means that the U.K. inflation rate, $\pi^f$, equals the U.S. inflation rate, $\pi$:

*Under fixed exchange rates:*

(18.17)
$$\pi^f = \pi$$

The equality between the two inflation rates would not hold if we introduced deviations from the PPP conditions. However, we know that the PPP conditions work fairly well in the long run. Therefore, *if a country fixes its nominal exchange rate with the U.S. dollar, the country must, in the long run, experience roughly the same inflation rate as the United States.*

The interest-rate parity condition is

(18.10) $$i^f - i = (\Delta \varepsilon_t / \varepsilon_t)^e$$

With a fixed nominal exchange rate, the expected growth rate of the nominal exchange rate, $(\Delta \varepsilon_t / \varepsilon_t)^e$, equals zero. Therefore, equation (18.10) implies that the U.K. nominal interest rate, $i^f$, equals the U.S. rate:

*Under fixed exchange rates:*

(18.18) $$i^f = i$$

The equality between nominal interest rates would not hold if we introduced deviations from the interest-rate parity condition. However, we know that this condition works fairly well, at least for advanced economies. Therefore, if a country—particularly an advanced economy—fixes its nominal exchange rate with the U.S. dollar, the country must have roughly the same nominal interest rate as the United States.

## The Nominal Quantity of Money Under Fixed Exchange Rates

We will now study the determinants of the nominal quantity of money under fixed exchange rates. In working out these results, we think of the foreign country as economically small in relation to the United States. In particular, we assume that economic changes in the foreign country have negligible effects on U.S. economic variables. Thus, our conclusions will fit better if the foreign country is economically smaller than the United Kingdom.

For a closed economy in Chapter 10, we stressed the relationship between a country's nominal quantity of money, $M$, and its price level, $P$. As before, we think of money as currency in circulation or, more broadly, as high-powered money, which includes deposits held by financial institutions at the central bank. The question is, how does our present analysis of fixed exchange rates relate to our discussion from Chapter 10? Somehow we determined the U.K. price level, $P^f$, in equation (18.16) without saying anything about the U.K. nominal quantity of money, $M^f$.

As in Chapter 10, U.K. households demand a quantity of real money, $M^f / P^f$, that depends on U.K. real GDP, $Y^f$, and the nominal interest rate, $i^f$. We also have, from equation (18.18), that the U.K. nominal interest rate, $i^f$, equals the U.S. rate, $i$. Therefore, the condition that $M^f$ equal the nominal quantity demanded is

(18.19) $$M^f = P^f \cdot L(Y^f, i)$$

As in Chapter 10, the function $L(\cdot)$ determines the real demand for money in the United Kingdom. This real demand rises with real GDP, $Y^f$, and falls with the nominal interest rate, $i$.

If the absolute PPP condition holds, the U.K. price level is given by

(18.16) $$P^f = \varepsilon P.$$

Table 18.5 | Simplified Balance Sheet of Central Bank (Bank of England)

| Assets | Liabilities |
|---|---|
| International reserves (U.S. dollar currency and Treasury bills, other foreign currency, gold) | U.K. currency, $M^f$ |
| U.K. bonds | |

If we substitute for $P^f$ from equation (18.16) into equation (18.19), we get

(18.20)
$$M^f = \varepsilon P \cdot L(Y^f, i)$$

The nominal exchange rate, $\varepsilon$, is a fixed number. We are assuming that the U.S. price level, $P$, and nominal interest rate, $i$, are determined independently of conditions in the United Kingdom. Therefore, for a given U.K. real GDP, $Y^f$, equation (18.20) prescribes the nominal quantity of money, $M^f$, that must be circulating within the U.K. Hence, $M^f$ cannot be freely chosen by the Bank of England, the U.K. central bank.

To understand these results, assume that the U.K. price level, $P^f$, accorded initially with the absolute PPP condition in equation (18.16). Assume further that the U.K. nominal quantity of money, $M^f$, equaled the amount given in equation (18.20) and, therefore, equaled the nominal quantity demanded.

Suppose that the Bank of England increases the nominal quantity of money, $M^f$, by an open-market purchase of U.K. government bonds, a form of open-market operation considered in Chapter 14. Table 18.5 shows a simplified balance sheet for the Bank. For the open-market operation that we are considering, the quantity of Bank assets in the form of U.K. bonds rises on the left-hand side of the balance sheet. Correspondingly, Bank liabilities in the form of U.K. currency, $M^f$, in circulation increase on the right-hand side of the balance sheet.

Our analysis of a closed economy in Chapter 10 suggests that the increase in $M^f$ would raise the U.K. price level, $P^f$. However, if $P^f$ rose, it would exceed the PPP level dictated by equation (18.16). Hence, for a given nominal exchange rate, $\varepsilon$, goods bought in the United Kingdom would become more expensive compared to goods bought in the United States. In response, households from both countries move away from buying goods in the United Kingdom and toward buying them in the United States. To facilitate this changed pattern of expenditure, households—or, more realistically, financial institutions—take their excess U.K. money to the Bank of England to exchange for U.S. money. Note that, if the Bank is fixing the nominal exchange rate, it stands ready to exchange dollars for pounds at the rate of $1/\varepsilon$ dollars per pound. But then the U.K. nominal quantity of money, $M^f$, falls back toward its initial level. In Table 18.5, $M^f$ declines on the right-hand side of the balance sheet. On the left-hand side, the Bank of England loses assets in the form of U.S. dollar currency or, more likely, U.S. Treasury bills. These assets, along with other foreign currencies and gold, are called **international reserves** because they can be used readily to make payments with financial institutions, including other central banks.

The ultimate effect, on the left-hand side of the balance sheet in Table 18.5, is that the Bank has more assets in the form of U.K. bonds (bought in the initial open-market operation) and less international reserves. On the right-hand side, the nominal quantity of money, $M^f$, is unchanged on net. The initial increase is fully offset by the return of money to the Bank. Only then does the U.K. nominal quantity of money, $M^f$, equal the nominal quantity demanded, as prescribed by equation (18.20). This unchanged $M^f$ is consistent with an unchanged U.K. price level, $P^f$. That is, $P^f$ accords with the PPP condition given in equation (18.16).

To complete the story, we have to assess the Bank of England's reaction to its loss of international reserves. One possibility is that the Bank allows the nominal quantity of money, $M^f$, to decline back to the level consistent with equation (18.20). In that case, the Bank ends up holding more U.K. government bonds and less international reserves, but the nominal quantity of money, $M^f$, is unchanged overall. This automatic response of the nominal quantity of money is a key element of the gold standard and other systems of fixed exchange rates. The mechanism means that, as long as the central bank fixes the nominal exchange rate, $\varepsilon$, it lacks control over the nominal quantity of money, $M^f$.

As another possibility, when the automatic mechanism tends to reduce the nominal quantity of money, $M^f$, the Bank of England might resist this tendency by initiating another open-market purchase of U.K. bonds. This process is called **sterilization**, because the Bank is attempting to sterilize or insulate the outstanding nominal quantity of money, $M^f$, from the losses of international reserves. In the present case, the Bank wants to engineer a monetary expansion even though this expansion is inconsistent with the fixed nominal exchange rate. Eventually, a policy of sterilization leads to a sufficient drain on reserves so that the Bank becomes unwilling or unable to maintain the nominal exchange rate. In other words, with a shortage of reserves, the Bank of England may no longer be willing or able to provide U.S. dollars at the fixed rate of $1/\varepsilon$ dollars per pound. Instead, there may be a **devaluation**, which is a reduction in the value of the pound compared to the dollar. In the present case, a U.K. devaluation is a decrease in the exchange rate below $1/\varepsilon$ dollars per pound—so that $\varepsilon$, the number of pounds obtained for each dollar, increases. The important point is that the tendency of central banks to sterilize the flows of international reserves threatens the viability of fixed exchange rates.[6]

We should mention another possible reaction of U.K. policy to the loss of international reserves. Recall that this drain resulted from the Bank of England's excessive monetary creation. This policy tended to raise the U.K. price level, $P^f$, above the absolute PPP value given in equation (18.16). To counter the drain of international reserves, the U.K. government might impose trade restrictions, which artificially raise the cost of U.S. goods for U.K. households. The more general point is that the U.K. government might interfere with free international trade to prevent the absolute PPP condition from holding. Thus, there are two types of ill effects from excessive monetary expansion in a regime of fixed exchange rates. One is the loss of international reserves, an outcome that tends, eventually, to cause a devaluation. Second, to avoid either devaluation or monetary contraction, the government may interfere with free trade. The frequency of these interferences during the post-World War II period was a major argument used by opponents of fixed exchange rates (see Milton Friedman [1968a, Chapter 9]).

## Devaluation and Revaluation

We discussed a situation in which the United Kingdom loses international reserves and is thereby pressured to devalue its currency. In other circumstances, the U.K. gains international reserves and is pressured to raise the value of its currency. An appreciation of the U.K. currency—an increase in $1/\varepsilon$, the number of dollars that exchange for each pound—is called a **revaluation**.

The pressures for devaluation and revaluation in systems of fixed nominal exchange rates are not symmetric. Devaluations typically result from losses of international reserves. The threat of running out of reserves provides direct pressure for devaluation—for

---

[6] This discussion uses a framework called the **monetary approach to the balance of payments**. This approach was developed by Robert Mundell (1968, part 2; 1971, part 2). The early origins of this theory are found in the 18th-century writings of David Hume; see Eugene Rotwein (1970).

example, the Bank of England may no longer have the ability to exchange dollars for pounds at the rate of $1/\varepsilon$ dollars per pound. In the reverse situation, the Bank of England accumulates international reserves. In this case, the pressure to revalue is less direct. Mostly, the Bank has to decide that holding large quantities of international reserves is undesirable. An example in 2006 was the vast amounts of U.S. Treasury bonds amassed by central banks in Japan, China, and other Asian countries. Revaluation is a way to counter this buildup of international reserves.

Figures 18.1 and 18.2 provide examples of devaluations and revaluations during the mainly fixed-exchange-rate period before the early 1970s. France devalued the franc by a total of 40% in 1957–58, Germany revalued the mark by 5% in 1961 and 7% in 1969, and the United Kingdom devalued the pound by 14% in 1967. In addition, several revaluations occurred in 1971–72, just as the Bretton Woods System was passing into history: Japan revalued the yen by 16%, Germany revalued the mark by 13%, and Switzerland revalued the franc by 13%.

World history shows many examples of fixed-exchange-rate systems that ended with substantial devaluations. However, aside from the cases already mentioned up to the early 1970s, it is hard to find fixed-rate regimes that ended with substantial revaluations. In 2005–06, China revalued its currency—the renminbi—but by only 3%, when it ended its fixed-rate system with the U.S. dollar. In recent times, fixed-exchange-rate systems that culminated in large devaluations included the United Kingdom (32% devaluation in 1992, following a period of fixed exchange rates with major European currencies under the European Monetary System), Mexico (97% in 1994–95), South Korea (91% in 1997–98), Malaysia (67% in 1997–98), Thailand (109% in 1997–98), Indonesia (495% in 1997–98), Russia (266% in 1998), Brazil (71% in 1999), and Argentina (280% in 2002).

We will now consider the effects from an exogenous devaluation. Suppose that the Bank of England normally maintains a fixed nominal exchange rate with the U.S. dollar (as it did before 1971). Then, for no particular reason, the Bank decides to lower the number of dollars, $1/\varepsilon$, paid out for each pound. That is, it increases the number of pounds, $\varepsilon$, paid out for each dollar.

Consider again the real exchange rate:

(18.3)
$$real\ exchange\ rate = \frac{\varepsilon}{P^f/P}$$

which gives the number of goods that can be bought (with one U.S. dollar) in the United Kingdom compared to the number that can be bought in the United States. If the United Kingdom devalues its currency—raises the nominal exchange rate, $\varepsilon$—the real exchange rate increases for a given ratio of U.K. to U.S. prices, $P^f/P$. Therefore, the demand for U.K. goods rises. This increase in demand tends to raise the U.K. price level, $P^f$. Ultimately, $P^f$ would rise by enough to restore the real exchange rate to its equilibrium level, something close to 1.0. The main point is that the U.K. devaluation creates inflationary pressure in the United Kingdom.[7]

Notice the two-way direction of causation between devaluation and inflation. We found before that expansionary monetary policy—increases in $M^f$ and $P^f$—created pressure for devaluation. In this sense, domestic inflation tends to cause devaluation. Now we see that an exogenous devaluation tends to raise $P^f$. In this sense, devaluation is itself inflationary.

---

[7] As in our previous analysis of the Bank of England and its balance sheet in Table 18.4, we can show that the process of raising $P^f$ entails an increase in the U.K. nominal quantity of money, $M^f$. This analysis works for a one-time devaluation. Additional effects arise if households expect future devaluations. This expectation raises the U.K. expected rate of inflation, $(\pi^f)^e$, which increases the U.K. nominal interest rate, $i^f$, in equation (18.10).

# Back To Reality

## The Asian financial crisis

As discussed in Chapter 3, many of the fastest growing countries in the world since the 1960s are in East Asia. However, many of these countries experienced a setback in 1997–98, during the Asian financial crisis. The crisis began in July 1997 with the floating of Thailand's currency, the baht, which had been fixed to the U.S. dollar since the early 1980s. The crisis spread rapidly to the Philippine peso (fairly stable against the dollar since 1990), Malaysian ringgit (nearly fixed against the dollar since the mid-1980s), Indonesian rupiah (which had been devaluing gradually against the dollar since the late 1980s), and South Korean won (fairly stable against the dollar since the mid-1980s). From summer 1997 to the worst point in 1998 (between January and September, depending on the country), the currency devaluations were between 60 and 110% for Thailand, the Philippines, Malaysia, and South Korea, and around 400% for Indonesia. Since the changes in price levels were small in comparison, these steep devaluations of nominal exchange rates also represented sharp devaluations of real exchange rates. Other East Asian economies experienced much milder devaluation (Singapore and Taiwan) or no devaluation (China and Hong Kong).

What caused the Asian financial crisis? At the time, many observers thought that these star growth performers in Asia were being unfairly punished by irrational world currency markets. However, subsequent analyses found problems in government policies and incentive structures, especially in domestic financial systems. The setups encouraged excessive borrowing on world markets, especially by banks and finance companies, to invest in construction and other projects. Although many investments were highly speculative, the limited risks borne by key decision makers—financiers and entrepreneurs—led to excessive borrowing and investing. In addition, many loans were influenced by government pressure and were directed to politically favored companies, which were often unprofitable.

Increased knowledge about the investment and lending structure in some East Asian countries led to the marking down of asset values on stock, bond, and real estate markets. These adjustments and cutbacks in investments contributed to the financial crisis and led to widespread bankruptcies, especially of banks and construction companies. The financial distress led to broad contractions of real economic activity—for example, Thailand's fall of real GDP in 1998 was its first decrease since the 1950s.

By 1999, the East Asian countries that suffered from the financial crisis had rebounded to positive economic growth, though at rates below pre-crisis levels. Some domestic financial regulations and government policies had been improved to promote lending based on sound commercial principles, rather than weak individual incentives or government pressure. Thus, despite the pain of the Asian financial crisis, some useful long-term lessons were learned.

## Flexible Exchange Rates

The international system of fixed nominal exchange rates anchored on the U.S. dollar broke down in the early 1970s. One reason was the excessive creation of U.S. dollars and the consequent rise in the U.S. price level after the mid-1960s. This inflation made it increasingly difficult for the United States to maintain convertibility of the dollar into gold at the set rate of $35 per ounce. President Nixon decided in 1971 to raise the dollar price of gold and to curb flows of gold from the United States to foreign central banks. These actions signaled the end of the Bretton Woods System, whereby currencies were linked to gold through the U.S. dollar.

Since the early 1970s, most advanced countries have allowed their currencies to vary more or less freely to clear the markets for foreign exchange. We see from Figures 18.1 and 18.2 that the nominal exchange rates of six major currencies with the U.S. dollar have fluctuated substantially since the early 1970s. Many middle- and lower-income countries, especially the high-inflation countries covered in Table 18.4, have also maintained flexible exchange rates. The table shows that the nominal exchange rates rose sharply over time for these high-inflation countries.

Groups of countries, such as the members of the European Monetary System from 1979 to 1992 and the euro countries since 1999, have maintained fixed exchange rates among their currencies. Argentina maintained a fixed exchange rate with the U.S. dollar from 1991 to 2001, China maintained a fixed exchange rate with the U.S. dollar from 1994 to 2005, and other Asian countries maintained fixed exchange rates with the U.S. dollar over various periods. Nevertheless, the most important development since the early 1970s has been the increased reliance on flexible exchange rates. To study this system, we have to extend the model to consider the determination of exchange rates in a flexible-rate system.

We again think of the United Kingdom as the foreign country and the United States as the home country. The absolute PPP condition still gives a relation between the U.K. price level, $P^f$, and the U.S. price level, $P$:

$$(18.16) \qquad\qquad P^f = \varepsilon P$$

The difference from the fixed-exchange-rate setup is that the nominal exchange rate, $\varepsilon$, is not a fixed number. Because of adjustments of $\varepsilon$ in a flexible-rate regime, $P^f$ need not move in lockstep with $P$ even if the absolute PPP condition always holds.

The Bank of England can now use its policy tools to achieve a desired path of the price level, $P^f$. As in our analysis of a closed economy in Chapters 10 and 11, this process involves adjustments of the U.K. nominal quantity of money, $M^f$, and the U.K. nominal interest rate, $i^f$. Given the path of $P^f$, the United Kingdom can allow the nominal exchange rate, $\varepsilon$, to adjust (or float) freely to satisfy the absolute PPP condition in equation (18.16). Thus, the important point is that the United Kingdom can choose a monetary policy that is independent of that chosen by the United States.

## Fixed and Flexible Exchange Rates: A Comparison

Every country has a choice about whether to have a flexible exchange rate or a fixed exchange rate, tied, for example, to the U.S. dollar (or the euro or a basket of currencies). Each system has pluses and minuses, and we cannot say that one system is superior at all times for all countries. However, we can list the pluses and minuses in the two setups.

- An extreme form of fixed nominal exchange rate is a common currency. This arrangement applies within countries; for example, California and Massachusetts use the same money, the U.S. dollar. This setup is enormously convenient; it greatly facilitates trade in goods and assets across state borders. The same kind of convenience applies to the use of a common currency across national borders. Thus, the decision to adopt a common currency, the euro, by 12 Western European countries in 1999–2001 encouraged trade in goods and assets among these countries. Fixed nominal exchange rates between different currencies are less convenient for transactions than a common currency, but a fixed exchange rate is more convenient than a flexible exchange rate. One way to make this point is to observe that choices of fixed exchange rates are not about whether to have them at all but, rather, to decide over what range of economic activity, legal jurisdiction, and physical territory they should apply. Should fixed nominal exchange rates apply only within each independent country and not across any international borders? From an economic standpoint, the identification of independent moneys with independent countries is unlikely to be optimal.

- One advantage of a flexible nominal exchange rate is that it introduces an additional way to satisfy the PPP condition, $P^f = \varepsilon P$, in equation (18.16). For a given U.S. price level, $P$, fixity of the nominal exchange rate, $\varepsilon$, means that the foreign price level, $P^f$, has to adjust on its own to satisfy the PPP condition. This adjustment might be difficult if some prices adjust slowly, as in the new Keynesian model developed in Chapter 16. Then, in the transition to a new equilibrium value of $P^f$, the economy might suffer from reduced output and higher unemployment. Some of this difficult transition might be avoided by the rapid adjustment of the nominal exchange rate, $\varepsilon$, in a flexible-rate system. Economists believe that this sticky-price argument is more important for countries that are very different from one another, that trade little with one another, and that have little mobility of labor and capital between them. Thus, this argument suggests that fixed nominal exchange rates— including common currencies—work better between economies that are basically similar, have a lot of trade, and have considerable mobility of labor and capital between them.

- Related to the previous point, a fixed-exchange rate system precludes an independent monetary policy, at least in the long run. To put it the opposite way, a flexible-rate system allows for an independent monetary policy at every point in time. This independence might be useful if the monetary authority uses its policy instruments wisely to improve the functioning of the economy. For example, with the kinds of sticky prices assumed in Chapter 16, monetary policy can be used to avoid periods of depressed output and high unemployment. Fixed nominal exchange rates preclude this kind of helpful monetary policy.

- The independence of monetary policy under flexible exchange rates is not always desirable. For example, in the price-misperceptions model developed in Chapter 15, output and employment respond to unexpected movements in the price level and monetary aggregates. Under these conditions, the monetary authority may want to surprise households with unexpected inflation, and this temptation tends to generate an equilibrium with high and variable inflation. An advantage of a fixed nominal exchange rate is that it commits the monetary authority not to pursue this kind of monetary policy. That is, if the central bank is committed to maintaining the nominal exchange rate, it cannot simultaneously create major surprise movements in the price level and monetary aggregates. From this standpoint, a fixed-rate system might produce better outcomes than a flexible-rate system. However, this conclusion is tempered by the realization that governments and central banks can renege on promises to maintain a fixed nominal exchange rate. As an example, Argentina adopted a strong form of fixed exchange rate with the U.S. dollar in 1991. This commitment was part of a broader program of economic reform, and the fixed exchange rate worked well through 1998 to improve the workings of the Argentine economy. However, after an economic crisis in 1999–2001, the Argentine government and central bank went back on their promise that 1 peso was worth 1 U.S. dollar. A sharp devaluation made the nominal exchange rate about 3 pesos per dollar. The economy suffered dramatically in 2002 from the change in regime, essentially going through an economic depression.

## Summing Up

In the previous chapter, all countries used a common currency. In this chapter, we allowed for different currencies and, therefore, for exchange rates between the currencies. The nominal exchange rate specifies the amount of foreign currency, such as U.K. pounds, that trades for each U.S. dollar. In contrast, the real exchange rate specifies the number of U.K. (or foreign) *goods* that exchanges for each unit of U.S. (or home) *goods*.

The condition for absolute PPP says that the nominal exchange rate—say, pounds per dollar—equals the ratio of the U.K. (or foreign) price level to the U.S. (or home) price level. Equivalently, the real exchange rate equals one. This condition does not hold exactly, because economies specialize in the production of different goods, and the costs of non-traded goods and services depend on where one buys them. For advanced economies, real exchange rates deviate from one, but not by too much. For middle- and lower-income countries, real exchange rates are far above one; that is, market baskets of goods and services are cheaper than in the United States.

The relative form of the PPP condition says that the growth rate of the nominal exchange rate equals the difference between the inflation rates of the U.K. (foreign) and U.S. (home) countries. Equivalently, this condition says that the growth rate of the real exchange rate equals zero. This condition does not work so well in the short run for advanced economies but does much better in the long run. It also works well for middle-income countries with high inflation.

The interest-rate parity condition says that the difference between the U.K. (foreign) and U.S. (home) nominal interest rates equals the expected growth rate of the nominal exchange rate. When combined with the relative form of the PPP condition, the interest-rate parity condition implies that expected real interest rates are the same in the two countries. The interest-rate parity condition explains a lot about cross-country behavior of interest rates, especially for rich countries. However, this condition need not hold exactly if we allow for differences across countries in tax systems, uncertainties about asset returns and exchange-rate movements, and governmental restrictions on currency exchanges and cross-border asset flows.

Fixed exchange rates applied to the advanced countries under the Bretton Woods System, which prevailed from the end of World War II until the early 1970s. Fixed rates also apply to common-currency systems, such as the euro regime adopted in 1999–2001 by 12 Western European countries. With a fixed nominal exchange rate, the U.K. (foreign) inflation rate has to be similar to that in the United States. Therefore, a country with a fixed nominal exchange rate cannot carry out an independent monetary policy. An attempt to have an independent monetary policy in a fixed-rate system can lead to losses of international reserves and, consequently, devaluation of the currency.

Under flexible exchange rates, a country can have an independent monetary policy. This policy can be managed to achieve a desired price level. The nominal exchange rate then adjusts to be consistent with this price level.

The choice between fixed and flexible exchange rates depends on a number of factors. Fixed exchange rates, especially a common currency, reduce the transaction costs for trades in goods and assets. Flexible exchange rates allow for an independent monetary policy, which can sometimes be managed wisely to avoid depressed output and high unemployment. Fixed exchange rates can usefully commit the central bank to low and stable inflation. However, by devaluing, governments and central banks can break the promise to maintain a fixed exchange rate.

# Key Terms and Concepts

| | |
|---|---|
| absolute form of PPP | monetary approach to the balance of |
| Balassa-Samuelson hypothesis | payments |
| Bretton Woods System | nominal exchange rate |
| devaluation | non-tradable goods |
| exchange market | purchasing-power parity |
| exchange rate | real exchange rate |
| fixed exchange rates | PPP |
| flexible exchange rates | relative form of PPP |
| interest-rate parity | revaluation |
| international reserves | sterilization |

# Questions and Problems

**A.** Review questions

1. Explain how the nominal exchange rate differs from the real exchange rate. Which rate is pegged in a system of fixed exchange rates?

2. Explain the conditions for absolute and relative purchasing-power parity in equations (18.2) and (18.5).

3. Explain the condition for interest-rate parity in equation (18.11). Explain how this condition leads to the equality for expected real interest rates across countries in equation (18.14).

4. Does the central bank have discretion over the quantity of domestic money in a fixed-exchange-rate system? Show how an attempt to carry out an independent monetary policy can lead to devaluation or revaluation. Why might the attempt lead to trade restrictions?

5. In a flexible-exchange-rate system, a country such as Brazil that has a persistently high inflation rate, $\pi$, will experience regular depreciation of its nominal exchange rate with the U.S. dollar. Explain why this happens. Why might the Brazilian government like this system?

6. We mentioned as examples of fixed-exchange-rate systems the classical gold standard, the Bretton Woods System, and a setup with a common currency. Explain how each of these systems operates to maintain a fixed nominal exchange rate.

**B.** Problems for discussion

7. A shift in the demand for money

Consider an increase in the real demand for money, $M^d/P$, in China.

   a. Under a fixed exchange rate with the United States, what happens to China's price level, $P$, and nominal quantity of money, $M$?
   b. Under a flexible exchange rate, with a fixed $M$, what happens to China's price level, $P$, and exchange rate, $\varepsilon$?

8. Flexible exchange rates and inflation rates

Equation (18.5) relates the growth rate of the exchange rate between the foreign and home currency to the difference in inflation rates for the two countries. Use the International Monetary Fund's *International Financial Statistics* to calculate growth rates of exchange rates and inflation rates for some countries. (Use countries other than those shown in Tables 18.2 and 18.3.) Do the results accord with equation (18.5)?

9. President Nixon's departure from the gold standard in 1971
Under the Bretton Woods System, the United States pegged the price of gold at $35 per ounce.

a. Why did trouble about the gold price arise in 1971?
b. Was President Nixon right in eliminating the U.S. commitment to buy and sell gold from foreign official institutions at a fixed price? What other alternatives were available? For example, what was the classical prescription of the gold standard? The French suggested a doubling in the price of gold. Would that change have helped?

10. Shipping gold under the gold standard
Suppose (using unrealistic numbers) that the price of gold is $5 per ounce in New York and £1 per ounce in London. Assume, initially, that gold can be shipped between New York and London at zero cost.

a. Assume that the dollar-pound exchange rate is $6 per pound. If a person starts with $1,000 in New York, what can the person do to make a profit? If the cost of shipping gold between New York and London is 1% of the amount shipped, how high does the exchange rate have to rise above $5 per pound to make this action profitable?
b. Go through the same exercise when the exchange rate is $4 per pound, from the perspective of someone who starts with £200 in London.
c. The results determine a range of exchange rates around $5 per pound for which it is unprofitable to ship gold in either direction between New York and London. The upper and lower limits of this range are called *gold points*. If the exchange rate goes beyond these points, it becomes profitable to ship an unlimited amount of gold. Can you show that the potential to ship gold guarantees that the exchange rate will remain within the gold points?

11. Futures contracts on foreign exchange
If a person buys a one-month futures contract on the euro, he or she agrees to purchase euros next month at a dollar exchange rate set today. The buyer of this contract goes long on the euro and does well if the euro appreciates (more than the amount expected) over the month. Similarly, the seller of a futures contract agrees to sell euros next month at a dollar exchange rate set today. The seller goes short on the euro and does well if the euro depreciates (more than expected) over the month.

Consider a euro bond with a maturity of one month. This bond sells for a specific number of euros today and will pay out a stated number of euros in one month. How can a person use the currency futures market to guarantee the dollar rate of return from buying the euro bond and holding it for one month?

# Bibliography

Abraham, Katharine. 1987. "Help-Wanted Advertising, Job Vacancies, and Unemployment." *Brookings Papers on Economic Activity*, 1, 207–243.

Ahmed, Shaghil. 1987. "Wage Stickiness and the Nonneutrality of Money: A Cross-Industry Analysis." *Journal of Monetary Economics* 20 (July): 25–50.

Alesina, Alberto, and Guido Tabellini. 1990. "A Positive Theory of Fiscal Deficits and Government Debt." *Review of Economic Studies* 57 (July): 403–414.

Alogoskoufis, George S. 1987a. "Aggregate Employment and Intertemporal Substitution in the U.K." *Economic Journal* 97 (June): 403–415.

Alogoskoufis, George S. 1987b. "On Intertemporal Substitution and Aggregate Labor Supply." *Journal of Political Economy* 95 (October): 938–960.

Ando, Albert, and Franco Modigliani. 1963. "The 'Life-Cycle' Hypothesis of Saving: Aggregate Implications and Tests." *American Economic Review* 53 (March): 55–84.

Attfield, Cliff, and Nigel Duck. 1983. "The Influence of Unanticipated Money Growth on Real Output: Some Cross-Country Estimates." *Journal of Money, Credit, and Banking* 15 (November): 442–454.

Azariadis, Costas. 1975. "Implicit Contracts and Underemployment Equilibria." *Journal of Political Economy* 83 (December): 1183–1202.

Baily, Martin N. 1974. "Wages and Employment under Uncertain Demand." *Review of Economic Studies* 33 (January): 37–50.

Balassa, Bela. 1964. "The Purchasing Power Parity Doctrine: A Reappraisal." *Journal of Political Economy*, 72 (December): 584–596.

Barro, Robert J. 1974. "Are Government Bonds Net Wealth?" *Journal of Political Economy* 82 (November/December): 1095–1118.

Barro, Robert J. 1978. "Comment from an Unreconstructed Ricardian." *Journal of Monetary Economics* 4 (August): 569–581.

Barro, Robert J. 1981. "Unanticipated Money Growth and Economic Activity in the United States." In *Money, Expectations, and Business Cycles,* edited by R. Barro. New York: Academic Press.

Barro, Robert J. 1987. "Government Spending, Interest Rates, Prices and Budget Deficits in the United Kingdom, 1730–1918." *Journal of Monetary Economics* 20 (September): 221–247.

Barro, Robert J. 1989. "The Ricardian Approach to Budget Deficits." *Journal of Economic Perspectives* 3 (Spring): 37–54.

Barro, Robert J., and David B. Gordon. 1983a. "A Positive Theory of Monetary Policy in a Natural Rate Model." *Journal of Political Economy* 91 (August): 589–610.

Barro, Robert J., and David B. Gordon. 1983b. "Rules, Discretion and Reputation in a Model of Monetary Policy." *Journal of Monetary Economics* 91 (August): 101–121.

Barro, Robert J., and Chaipat Sahasakul. 1983. "Measuring the Average Marginal Tax Rate from the Individual Income Tax." *Journal of Business* 56 (October): 419–452.

Barro, Robert J., and Chaipat Sahasakul. 1986. "Average Marginal Tax Rates from Social Security and the Individual Income Tax." *Journal of Business* 59 (October): 555–566.

Barro, Robert J., and Xavier Sala-i-Martin. 1990. "World Real Interest Rates." In *NBER Macroeconomics Annual 1990*. Cambridge, MA: MIT Press.

Barsky, Robert B., and Jeffrey A. Miron. 1989. "The Seasonal Cycle and the Business Cycle." *Journal of Political Economy* 97 (June): 503–534.

Beaulieu, Joseph J., and Jeffrey A. Miron. 1992. "A Cross-Country Comparison of Seasonal Cycles and Business Cycles." *Economic Journal* 102 (July): 772–788.

Bernanke, Ben S. 1983. "Nonmonetary Effects of the Financial Crisis in the Propagation of the Great Depression." *American Economic Review* 73 (June): 257–276.

Bernheim, B. Douglas, Andrei Shleifer, and Lawrence H. Summers. 1985. "The Strategic Bequest Motive." *Journal of Political Economy* 93 (December): 1045–1076.

Bils, Mark. 1989. "Testing for Contracting Effects on Employment." Working paper no. 174, Rochester Center for Economic Research, January.

Bils, Mark, and Peter Klenow. 2004. "Some Evidence on the Importance of Sticky Prices." *Journal of Political Economy* 112 (October): 947–985.

Bird, Roger C., and Ronald G. Bodkin. 1965. "The National Service Life Insurance Dividend of 1950 and Consumption: A Further Test of the 'Strict' Permanent Income Hypothesis." *Journal of Political Economy* 73 (October): 499–515.

Blinder, Alan S., Elie R. D. Canetti, David E. Lebow, and Jeremy B. Rudd. 1998. *Asking About Prices: A New Approach to Understanding Price Stickiness.* New York: Russell Sage Foundation.

Bloom, Murray T. 1966. *The Man Who Stole Portugal.* New York: Charles Scribner's Sons.

Board of Governors of the Federal Reserve System. 2003. *The Use and Counterfeiting of United States Currency Abroad,* part II. Washington, DC: U.S. Government Printing Office.

Bomberger, William A., and Gail E. Makinen. 1983. "The Hungarian Hyperinflation and Stabilization of 1945–1946." *Journal of Political Economy* 91 (October): 801–824.

Boskin, Michael J., with Ellen R. Dulberger, Zvi Griliches, Robert J. Gordon, and Dale Jorgenson. 1996. *Toward a More Accurate Measure of the Cost of Living,* Advisory Commission to Study the Consumer Price Index. Washington, DC: U.S. Government Printing Office.

Bresciani-Turroni, Costantino. 1937. *The Economics of Inflation.* London: Allen & Unwin.

Broadbent, Ben. 1996. "Monetary Policy Regimes and the Costs of Discretion." Unpublished Ph.D. dissertation, Harvard University.

Brown, E. Cary. 1956. "Fiscal Policy in the Thirties: A Reappraisal." *American Economic Review* 46 (December): 857–879.

Buchanan, James M. 1958. *Public Principles of Public Debt.* Homewood, IL: Irwin.

Cagan, Phillip D. 1956. "The Monetary Dynamics of Hyperinflation." In *Studies in the Quantity Theory of Money,* edited by Milton Friedman. Chicago: University of Chicago Press.

Carare, Alina, and Mark R. Stone. 2003. "Inflation Targeting Regimes." Working paper, International Monetary Fund, January.

Card, David. 1980. "Determinants of the Form of Long-Term Contracts." Working paper no. 135, Princeton University, June.

Carlson, John A. 1977. "A Study of Price Forecasts." *Annals of Economic and Social Measurement* 6 (Winter): 27–56.

Carlton, Dennis. 1986. "The Rigidity of Prices." *American Economic Review* 76 (September): 637–658.

Carroll, Chris, and Lawrence H. Summers. 1987. "Why Have Private Savings Rates in the United States and Canada Diverged?" *Journal of Monetary Economics* 20 (September): 249–279.

Caselli, Francesco, and Wilbur John Coleman. 2001. "Cross-Country Technology Diffusion: The Case of Computers." *American Economic Review* 91 (May): 328–335.

Cass, David. 1965. "Optimum Growth in an Aggregative Model of Capital Accumulation." *Review of Economic Studies* 32 (July): 233–240.

Cecchetti, Stephen G. (1986). "The Frequency of Price Adjustment: A Study of the Newsstand Prices of Magazines." *Journal of Econometrics* 31 (April): 255–274.

Central Statistical Office. *Annual Abstract of Statistics.* London, various issues.

Clark, Truman A. 1986. "Interest Rate Seasonals and the Federal Reserve." *Journal of Political Economy* 94 (February): 76–125.

Coe, David T., and Elhanan Helpman. 1995. "International R&D Spillovers." *European Economic Review* 39: 859–887.

Cole, Harold L., and Lee E. Ohanian. 2004. "New Deal Policies and the Persistence of the Great Depression: A General Equilibrium Analysis." *Journal of Political Economy* 112 (August): 779–816.

Cumby, Robert, and Maurice Obstfeld. 1984. "International Interest Rate and Price Level Linkages Under Flexible Exchange Rates: A Review of Recent Evidence." In *Exchange Rate Theory and Practice,* edited by John F. O. Bilson and Richard C. Marston. Chicago: University of Chicago Press.

Darby, Michael R. 1976. "Three-and-a-Half Million U.S. Employees Have Been Mislaid: Or an Explanation of Unemployment, 1934–1941." *Journal of Political Economy* 84 (February): 1–16.

Darby, Michael R., John C. Haltiwanger, Jr., and Mark W. Plant. 1985. "Unemployment Rate Dynamics and Persistent Unemployment under Rational Expectations." *American Economic Review* 75 (September): 614–637.

Deane, Phyllis, and W. A. Cole. 1969. *British Economic Growth, 1688–1959*. 2nd ed. Cambridge: Cambridge University Press.

Dotsey, Michael. 1985. "The Use of Electronic Funds Transfers to Capture the Effect of Cash Management Practices on the Demand for Demand Deposits." *Journal of Finance* 40 (December): 1493–1503.

Easterly, William M. 2001. *The Elusive Quest for Growth: Economists' Adventures and Misadventures in the Tropics*. Cambridge, MA: MIT Press.

Esposito, Louis. 1978. "Effect of Social Security on Saving: Review of Studies Using U.S. Time Series Data." *Social Security Bulletin* 41 (May): 9–17.

Evans, Paul. 1987a. "Interest Rates and Expected Future Budget Deficits in the United States." *Journal of Political Economy* 95 (February): 34–58.

Evans, Paul. 1987b. "Do Budget Deficits Raise Nominal Interest Rates? Evidence from Six Industrial Countries." *Journal of Monetary Economics* 20 (September): 281–300.

Fair, Ray C. 1979. "An Analysis of the Accuracy of Four Macroeconometric Models." *Journal of Political Economy* 87 (August): 701–718.

Fair, Ray C. 1987. "International Evidence on the Demand for Money." *Review of Economics and Statistics* 69 (August): 473–480.

Fay, Jon A., and James L. Medoff. 1985. "Labor and Output over the Business Cycle: Some Direct Evidence." *American Economic Review* 75 (September): 638–655.

Feinstein, C. H. 1972. *National Income, Expenditures, and Output of the United Kingdom, 1855–1965*. Cambridge: Cambridge University Press.

Feldstein, Martin S. 1974. "Social Security, Induced Retirement, and Aggregate Capital Accumulation." *Journal of Political Economy* 82 (September/October): 905–928.

Ferguson, James M., ed. 1964. *Public Debt and Future Generations*. Chapel Hill: University of North Carolina Press.

Fischer, Stanley. 1977. "Long-Term Contracts, Rational Expectations, and the Optimal Money Supply Rule." *Journal of Political Economy* 85 (February): 191–206.

Fisher, Irving. 1926. *The Purchasing Power of Money*. 2nd ed. New York: Macmillan.

Fleisher, Belton M., and Thomas J. Kniesner. 1984. *Labor Economics: Theory, Evidence, and Policy*. 3rd ed. Englewood Cliffs, NJ: Prentice-Hall.

Flood, Robert P., and Peter M. Garber. 1980. "An Economic Theory of Monetary Reform." *Journal of Political Economy* 88 (February): 24–58.

Friedman, Milton. 1956. "The Quantity of Money—A Restatement." In *Studies in the Quantity Theory of Money,* edited by Milton Friedman. Chicago: University of Chicago Press.

Friedman, Milton. 1957. *A Theory of the Consumption Function*. Princeton, NJ: Princeton University Press.

Friedman, Milton. 1960. *A Program for Monetary Stability*. New York: Fordham University Press.

Friedman, Milton. 1968a. "Free Exchange Rates." In *Dollars and Deficits*. Englewood Cliffs, NJ: Prentice-Hall.

Friedman, Milton. 1968b. "Inflation: Causes and Consequences." In *Dollars and Deficits*. Englewood Cliffs, NJ: Prentice-Hall.

Friedman, Milton. 1968c. "The Role of Monetary Policy." *American Economic Review* 58 (March): 1–17.

Friedman, Milton. 1969. *The Optimum Quantity of Money and Other Essays*. Chicago: Aldine.

Friedman, Milton, and Anna J. Schwartz. 1963. *A Monetary History of the United States, 1867–1960*. Princeton, NJ: Princeton University Press.

Fullerton, Don. 1982. "On the Possibility of an Inverse Relationship Between Tax Rates and Government Revenues." *Journal of Public Economics* 19 (October): 3–22.

Garber, Peter M. 1982. "Transition from Inflation to Price Stability." *Carnegie-Rochester Conference Series on Public Policy* 16 (Spring): 11–42.

Goldfeld, Steven M. 1973. "The Demand for Money Revisited." Brookings Papers on Economic Activity, no. 3, 577–638.

Goldfeld, Steven M. 1976. "The Case of the Missing Money." Brookings Papers on Economic Activity, no. 3, 683–730.

Goldfeld, Steven M., and Daniel E. Sichel. 1990. "The Demand for Money." In *Handbook of Monetary Economics*, vol. 1, edited by Benjamin M. Friedman and Frank H. Hahn. Amsterdam: North Holland.

Golosov, Mikhail, and Robert E. Lucas, Jr. 2006. "Menu Costs and Phillips Curves." unpublished, MIT, March, National Bureau of Economic Research, December.

Gordon, Donald F. 1974. "A Neo-Classical Theory of Keynesian Unemployment." *Economic Inquiry* 12 (December): 431–459.

Gort, Michael, and Steven Klepper (1982). "Time Paths in the Diffusion of Product Innovations." *Economic Journal* 92 (September): 630–653.

Gray, Jo Anna. 1976. "Wage Indexation: A Macroeconomic Approach." *Journal of Monetary Economics* 2 (April): 221–236.

Greenwood, Jeremy, Zvi Hercowitz, and Gregory Huffman. 1988. "Investment, Capacity Utilization, and the Real Business Cycle." *American Economic Review* 78 (June): 402–417.

Griliches, Zvi. 1957. "Hybrid Corn—An Exploration in the Economics of Technological Change." *Econometrica* 25 (October): 501–522.

Griliches, Zvi. 1998. *R&D and Productivity: The Econometric Evidence*. Chicago: University of Chicago Press.

Hahm, Joon-Ho. 1998. "Consumption Adjustments to Real Interest Rates: Intertemporal Substitution Revisited." *Journal of Economic Dynamics & Control* 22 (February): 293–320.

Hall, Robert E. 1979. "A Theory of the Natural Unemployment Rate and the Duration of Unemployment." *Journal of Monetary Economics* 5 (April): 153–170.

Hall, Robert E. 1989. "Consumption." In *Modern Business Cycle Theory*, edited by Robert J. Barro. Cambridge, MA: Harvard University Press.

Hall, Robert E. 2005. "Employment Efficiency and Sticky Wages: Evidence from Flows in Labor Market." Working paper no. 11183, National Bureau of Economic Research, March.

Hawtrey, Ralph G. 1932. "The Portuguese Bank Notes Case." *Economic Journal* 42 (September): 391–398.

Heckscher, Eli. 1919. "The Effect of Foreign Trade on the Distribution of Income." *Ekonomisk Tidskrift*.

Helpman, Elhanan, and Paul R. Krugman. 1985. *Market Structure and Foreign Trade*. Cambridge MA: MIT Press.

Hercowitz, Zvi. 1981. "Money and the Dispersion of Relative Prices." *Journal of Political Economy* 89 (April): 328–356.

Heston, Alan, Robert Summers, and Bettina Aten. 2002. *Penn World Table Version 6.1*. Center for International Comparisons at the University of Pennsylvania (CICUP), October.

Hsieh, Chang-Tai. 2003. "Do Consumers React to Anticipated Income Changes? Evidence from the Alaska Permanent Fund." *American Economic Review* 93 (March): 397–405.

Hubbard, R. Glenn. 2002. "Tax Notes 30th Anniversary." Unpublished working paper, Columbia University, December.

International Monetary Fund. *International Financial Statistics*, various issues.

Jaumotte, Florence. 2000. "Technological Catch-up and the Growth Process." Unpublished Ph.D. dissertation. Harvard University, November.

Jones, Charles I. 2005. "Growth and Ideas." In *Handbook of Economic Growth*, edited by Philippe Aghion and Steven Durlauf. Amsterdam: Elsevier.

Jovanovic, Boyan, and Saul Lach (1997). "Product Innovation and the Business Cycle." *International Economic Review* 38 (February): 3–22.

Kashyap, Anil K. 1995. "Sticky Prices: New Evidence from Retail Catalogs." *Quarterly Journal of Economics*, 110, 245–274.

Kendrick, John W. 1961. *Productivity Trends in the United States*. Princeton, NJ: Princeton University Press.

Kenny, Lawrence W. 1991. "Cross-Country Estimates of the Demand for Money and Its Components." *Economic Inquiry* 29 (October), 696–705.

Keynes, John Maynard. 1923. *A Tract on Monetary Reform*. Macmillan: London.

Keynes, John Maynard. 1936. The *General Theory of Employment, Interest, and Money*. New York: Harcourt Brace.

Koopmans, Tjalling C. 1965. "On the Concept of Optimal Growth." In *The Economic Approach to Development Planning*. Amsterdam: North Holland.

Kormendi, Roger C., and Phillip G. Meguire. 1984. "Cross-Regime Evidence of Macroeconomic Rationality." *Journal of Political Economy* 92 (October): 875–908.

Kreinin, Mordechai E. 1961. "Windfall Income and Consumption—Additional Evidence." *American Economic Review* 51 (June): 388–390.

Kuznets, Simon. 1948. "Discussion of the New Department of Commerce Income Series." *Review of Economics and Statistics* 30 (August): 151–179.

Kydland, Finn E., and Edward C. Prescott. 1977. "Rules Rather than Discretion: The Inconsistency of Optimal Plans." *Journal of Political Economy* 85 (June): 473–491.

Kydland, Finn E., and Edward C. Prescott. 1982. "Time to Build and Aggregate Fluctuations." *Econometrica* 51 (November): 1345–1370.

Kydland, Finn E., and Edward C. Prescott. 1990. "Business Cycles: Real Facts and a Monetary Myth." *Federal Reserve Bank of Minneapolis, Quarterly Review* (Spring): 3–18.

Lahaye, Laura. 1985. "Inflation and Currency Reform." *Journal of Political Economy* 93 (June): 537–560.

Landsberger, Michael. 1970. "Restitution Receipts, Household Savings, and Consumption Behavior in Israel." Unpublished working paper, Research Department, Bank of Israel.

Leimer, Dean, and Selig Lesnoy. 1982. "Social Security and Private Saving: New Time Series Evidence." *Journal of Political Economy* 90 (June): 606–629.

Lindsey, Lawrence B. 1987. "Individual Taxpayer Response to Tax Cuts, 1982–1984." *Journal of Public Economics* 33 (July): 173–206.

Lucas, Robert E., Jr. 1973. "Some International Evidence on Output-Inflation Trade-offs." *American Economic Review* 63 (June): 326–334.

Lucas, Robert E., Jr. 1977. "Understanding Business Cycles." *Carnegie-Rochester Conference on Public Policy* 5: 7–29.

Lucas, Robert E., Jr. 1981. *Studies in Business-Cycle Theory*. Cambridge, MA: MIT Press.

Lucas, Robert E., Jr. 1988. "On the Mechanics of Economic Development." *Journal of Monetary Economics* 22 (July): 3–42.

Maddison, Angus. 2003. *The World Economy: Historical Statistics*. Paris: OECD.

Malthus, Thomas R. 1798. *An Essay on the Principal of Population*. London: W. Pickering, 1986.

McCallum, Ben T. 1979. "The Current State of the Policy Ineffectiveness Debate." *American Economic Review* 69 (proceedings, May): 240–245.

McClure, Alexander K. 1901. *Abe Lincoln's Yarns and Stories*. New York: W. W. Wilson.

Miron, Jeffrey A. 1986. "Financial Panics, the Seasonality of the Nominal Interest Rate, and the Founding of the Fed." *American Economic Review* 76 (March): 125–140.

Mishkin, Frederic S. 1984. "Are Real Interest Rates Equal Across Countries? An Empirical Investigation of International Parity Conditions." *Journal of Finance* 39 (December): 1345–1357.

Mishkin, Frederic S., and Klaus Schmidt-Hebbel. 2001. "One Decade of Inflation Targeting in the World: What Do We Know and What Do We Need to Know?" Working paper no. 8397, National Bureau of Economic Research, July.

Mitchell, B. R., and Phyllis Deane. 1962. *Abstract of British Historical Statistics*. Cambridge: Cambridge University Press.

Mitchell, B. R., and H. G. Jones. 1971. *Second Abstract of British Historical Statistics*. Cambridge: Cambridge University Press.

Modigliani, Franco, and Richard Brumberg. 1954. "Utility Analysis and the Consumption Function: An Interpretation of Cross-Section Data." In *Post-Keynesian Economics*, edited by Kenneth Kurihara. New Brunswick, NJ: Rutgers University Press.

Morgan Guaranty Trust. 1983. *World Financial Markets*. New York, February.

Mulligan, Casey B. 1995. "The Intertemporal Substitution of Work—What Does the Evidence Say?" Population Research Center Discussion Paper Series #95-11, July.

Mulligan, Casey B. 1998. "Pecuniary and Nonpecuniary Incentives to Work in the United States during World War II." *Journal of Political Economy* 106 (October): 1033–1077.

Mulligan, Casey B. 2001. "Capital, Interest, and Aggregate Intertemporal Substitution." Unpublished working paper, University of Chicago.

Mulligan, Casey B., and Xavier Sala-i-Martin. 2000. "Extensive Margins and the Demand for Money at Low Interest Rates." *Journal of Political Economy* 108 (October): 961–991.

Mundell, Robert A. 1968. *International Economics.* New York: Macmillan.

Mundell, Robert A. 1971. *Monetary Theory.* Pacific Palisades, CA: Goodyear.

Musgrave, Richard. 1959. *Theory of Public Finance.* New York: McGraw-Hill.

Muth, John F. 1961. "Rational Expectations and the Theory of Price Movements." *Econometrica* 29 (July): 315–335.

Nakamura, Emi and Jon Steinsson. 2006. "Five Facts about Prices: A Reevaluation of Menu Cost Models." Unpublished, Harvard University, August.

North, Douglas, and Barry Weingast. 1989. "Constitutions and Commitment: The Evolution of Institutions Governing Public Choice in Seventeenth Century England." *Journal of Economic History* (December): 803–832.

Obstfeld, Maurice, and Kenneth Rogoff. 2004. "The Unsustainable U.S. Current Account Position Revisited." Unpublished working paper, Harvard University, October.

Ochs, Jack, and Mark Rush. 1983. "The Persistence of Interest Rate Effects on the Demand for Currency." *Journal of Money, Credit, and Banking* 15 (November): 499–505.

O'Driscoll, Gerald P., Jr. 1977. "The Ricardian Nonequivalence Theorem." *Journal of Political Economy* 85 (February): 207–210.

Ohlin, Bertil. 1933. *Interregional and International Trade.* Cambridge MA: Harvard University Press.

Olivei, Giovanni, and Silvana Tenreyro. 2007. "The Timing of Monetary Policy Shocks." *American Economic Review* (forthcoming).

Organization of American States. *Statistical Bulletin of the OAS,* various issues.

Parker, Jonathan A. 1999. "The Reaction of Household Consumption to Predictable Changes in Social Security Taxes." *American Economic Review* 89 (September): 959–973.

Persson, Torsten, and Lars E. O. Svensson. 1989. "Why a Stubborn Conservative Would Run a Deficit: Policy with Time-Inconsistent Preferences." *Quarterly Journal of Economics* 104 (May): 325–345.

Phelps, Edmund S. 1970. "The New Microeconomics in Employment and Inflation Theory." In *Microeconomic Foundations of Employment and Inflation Theory,* edited by Edmund S. Phelps. New York: Norton.

Pinera, Jose. 1996. *Empowering Workers: The Privatization of Social Security in Chile.* Washington, DC: Cato Institute.

Plosser, Charles I. 1982. "The Effects of Government Financing Decisions on Asset Returns." *Journal of Monetary Economics* 9 (May): 325–352.

Plosser, Charles I. 1987. "Fiscal Policy and the Term Structure." *Journal of Monetary Economics* 20 (September): 343–367.

Porter, Richard D., and Ruth A. Judson. 2001. "Overseas Dollar Holdings: What Do We Know?" *Wirtschaftspolitische Blatter* 48: 431–440.

Radford, R.A. 1945. "The Economic Organisation of a P.O.W. Camp." *Economica* 12 (November): 189–201.

Ramaswami, Chitra. 1983. "Equilibrium Unemployment and the Efficient Job-Finding Rate." *Journal of Labor Economics* 1 (April): 171–196.

Ricardo, David. 1819. *Principles of Political Economy and Taxation.* 2nd ed. London: John Murray.

Ricardo, David. 1846. "Funding System." In *The Works of David Ricardo,* edited by J. Ramsey McCulloch. London: John Murray.

Rogoff, Kenneth S. 1989. "Reputation, Coordination, and Monetary Policy." In *Modern Business Cycle Theory,* edited by Robert J. Barro. Cambridge, MA: Harvard University Press.

Romer, Christina D. 1986. "Spurious Volatility in Historical Unemployment Data." *Journal of Political Economy* 94 (February): 1–37.

Romer, Christina D. 1988. "World War I and the Postwar Depression: A Reinterpretation Based on Alternative Estimates of GNP." Journal of Monetary Economics 22 (July): 91–115.

Romer, Christina D. 1989. "The Prewar Business Cycle Reconsidered: New Estimates of Gross National Product, 1869–1908." *Journal of Political Economy* 97 (February): 1–37.

Romer, Christina D., and David H. Romer. 2003. "A New Measure of Monetary Shocks: Derivation and Implications." Working paper no. 9866, National Bureau of Economic Research, July.

Romer, Paul M. 1990. "Endogenous Technological Change." *Journal of Political Economy* 98 (October): S71–S102.

Rotwein, Eugene, ed. 1970. *David Hume—Writings on Economics*. Madison: University of Wisconsin Press.

Runkle, David E. 1991. "Liquidity Constraints and the Permanent Income Hypothesis: Evidence from Panel Data." *Journal of Monetary Economics* 27: 73–98.

Sala-i-Martin, Xavier. 2006. "The World Distribution of Income: Falling Poverty and . . . Convergence, Period." *Quarterly Journal of Economics* 121 (May): 351–397.

Samuelson, Paul A. 1964. "Theoretical Notes on Trade Problems." *Review of Economics and Statistics* 46 (May): 145–154.

Samuelson, Paul A., and Wolfgang F. Stolper. 1941. "Protection and Real Wages." *Review of Economic Studies* 9 (November): 58–73.

Sargent, Thomas J. 1982. "The Ends of Four Big Inflations." In *Inflation: Causes and Effects*, edited by Robert E. Hall. Chicago: University of Chicago Press.

Sargent, Thomas J., and Francois R. Velde. 1995. "Macroeconomic Features of the French Revolution." *Journal of Political Economy* 103, no. 3 (June): 474–518.

Sargent, Thomas J., and Neil Wallace. 1975. "Rational Expectations, the Optimal Monetary Instrument, and the Optimal Money Supply Rule." *Journal of Political Economy* 83 (April): 241–254.

Sargent, Thomas J., and Neil Wallace. 1981. "Some Unpleasant Monetarist Arithmetic." *Federal Reserve Bank of Minneapolis, Quarterly Review* (Fall): 1–17.

Scoggins, John F. 1990. "Supply Shocks and Net Exports." Unpublished working paper, University of Alabama at Birmingham.

Shimer, Robert. 2003. "The Cyclical Behavior of Equilibrium Unemployment and Vacancies: Evidence and Theory." Working paper no. 9536, National Bureau of Economic Research, February.

Solow, Robert M. 1956. "A Contribution to the Theory of Economic Growth." *Quarterly Journal of Economics* 70 (February): 65–94.

Solow, Robert M. 1957. "Technical Change and the Aggregate Production Function." *Review of Economics and Statistics* 39 (August): 312–320.

*Sonderhefte zur Wirtschaft und Statistik*. 1929. Berlin: R. Hobbing.

Souleles, Nicholas S. 1999. "The Response of Household Consumption to Income Tax Refunds." *American Economic Review* 89 (September): 947–958.

Stuart, Charles E. 1981. "Swedish Tax Rates, Labor Supply, and Tax Revenues." *Journal of Political Economy* 89 (October): 1020–1038.

Taylor, Alan M., and Mark P. Taylor. 2004. "The Purchasing Power Parity Debate." *Journal of Economic Perspectives* 18 (Fall): 135–158.

Taylor, John B. 1980. "Aggregate Dynamics and Staggered Contracts." *Journal of Political Economy* 88 (February): 1–23.

Thornton, Henry. 1802. *An Enquiry into the Nature and Effects of the Paper Credit of Great Britain*. London: J. Hatchard.

U.S. Department of Commerce. 1975. *Historical Statistics of the U.S., Colonial Times to 1970*. Washington, DC: U.S. Government Printing Office.

U.S. President. 1962. *Economic Report of the President*. Washington, DC: U.S. Government Printing Office.

Van Ravestein, A., and H. Vijlbrief. 1988. "Welfare Cost of Higher Tax Rates: An Empirical Laffer Curve for the Netherlands." *De Economist* 136: 205–219.

Walre de Bordes, J. van. 1927. *The Austrian Crown*. London: King.

Warren, George F., and Frank A. Pearson. 1933. *Prices*. New York: Wiley.

World Bank. 1994. *Averting the Old Age Crisis*. Oxford: Oxford University Press.

World Bank. 2006. *World Development Indicators*. Washington, DC: IBRD, World Bank.

# Glossary

**absolute convergence**   The tendency of real per capita GDP in poor economies to grow faster than in rich ones, so that poor economies catch up over time to rich ones. The term "absolute" means that the convergence is not conditioned on other economic variables.

**absolute form of PPP**   The version of purchasing-power parity that involves levels of exchange rates and prices.

**acyclical**   Having no regular relation with the business cycle; that is, with detrended real GDP.

**adjusted gross income**   Gross income less adjustments for tax purposes, such as business and moving expenses and deferred compensation through pension plans.

**adjustment costs for investment**   Costs that have to be paid to change the quantity of capital (plant and equipment) used in production.

**after-tax real interest rate**   The real interest rate calculated after netting out the real income tax paid on the interest earnings.

**after-tax real wage rate**   The real wage rate calculated after netting out the real income tax paid on the wage income.

**aggregate demand**   The total demand for goods and services in the forms of consumption, gross investment, and government purchases.

**Ak model**   A growth model in which the production function is linear in capital; that is, $y = Ak$, where $y$ is output per worker and $k$ is capital per worker.

**average product of capital**   The ratio of output (real GDP) to the capital stock.

**average tax rate**   The ratio of taxes to a measure of income. See *marginal tax rate*.

**balance of international payments**   The summary statement of a country's international trade in commodities, bonds, and international reserves.

**balance on current account**   A zero current-account balance.

**balanced budget**   Equality between the government's purchases, transfers, and interest payments and the government's tax revenue.

**Balassa-Samuelson hypothesis**   Theory that, in poor countries, the prices of non-traded goods and services are low compared to prices of traded goods. Therefore, a market basket of goods and services tends to be less expensive in poor countries than in rich ones.

**barter**   Direct exchange of one good for another, without the use of money. See *medium of exchange*.

**bond**   A contract that gives the holder (lender) a claim to a specified stream of payments from the issuer (borrower).

**bond market**   Market on which bonds are traded.

**boom**   A period in which real GDP is high and rising.

**Bretton Woods System**   A system of international payments established after World War II in which each country pegged the exchange rate between its own currency and the U.S. dollar. The United States exchanged dollars for gold at a fixed price ($35 per ounce), thus pegging the value of each country's currency to gold.

**budget constraint**   An equation relating the sources of funds in a period, such as wage and asset income and initial assets, to the uses of funds in that period, such as consumption and end-of-period assets.

**budget deficit**   Excess of the government's purchases, transfers, and interest payments over the government's tax revenue.

**budget line**   A graph of the combinations of consumptions over two periods that satisfy the household's two-period budget constraint.

**budget surplus**   Excess of the government's tax revenue over the government's purchases, transfers, and interest payments.

**burden of the public debt**   The possible negative effect of the public debt on saving and investment and, hence, on the stock of capital available later.

**business cycle**   Pattern of real GDP rising during a boom and falling during a recession.

**capital levy**   Tax rate on capital when levied after investments have been made.

**capital stock**   Stock of goods in the forms of plant and equipment, used as input to production.

**capital utilization rate**   Rate at which stock of capital is used in production.

**chain-weighted real GDP**   A method for constructing real GDP in which the relative-price weights continually adjust for the changing composition of production.

**checkable deposits**   Deposits, issued by financial institutions, against which account holders can write checks.

**closed economy**   An economy isolated from the rest of the world.

**commodity money**   Money that takes a physical form, such as gold and silver coins.

**common currency**   A regime in which all countries use the same currency and quote prices in units of this currency.

**conditional convergence**   The idea that real per capita GDP in poor countries grows faster than in rich countries, for given values of government policies, propensities to save money and have children, and other variables.

**constant-growth-rate rule**   A rule for monetary policy in which a specified monetary aggregate grows at a constant rate.

**constant returns to scale**   The property of a production function that a proportionate increase in all inputs results in an equiproportionate increase in output.

**consumer durables**   Consumable commodities purchased by households that last for a long time. Examples are automobiles, furniture, and appliances.

**consumer nondurables and services**   Consumable commodities purchased by households that last for a short time.

**consumer price index (CPI)**   A weighted average of prices of consumer goods, measured relative to a base year.

**convergence**   The tendency of real per capita GDP in a poor economy to grow faster than in a rich one. Therefore, the poor economy's real per capita GDP tends to catch up over time to that in the rich economy.

**copyright**   Property right over the use of a book, trademark, or similar object.

**countercyclical**   Moving in the direction opposite to the business cycle; that is, to detrended real GDP.

**CPI**   Consumer price index.

**currency**   Non-interest-bearing paper money issued by the government.

**currency union**   A group of countries that use a common currency.

**current-account balance**   The value of goods and services produced by domestic residents (including the net factor income from abroad) plus net transfers from abroad, less the expenditure by domestic residents on goods and services. If the current-account balance is positive (negative), the current account is in surplus (deficit).

**current-account deficit**   A negative current-account balance.

**current-account surplus**   A positive current-account balance.

**cyclical part of real GDP**   The difference between real GDP and its trend.

**deflation**   A sustained decrease in the general price level over time. See *inflation*.

**demand curve**   A curve expressing the relation between the quantity demanded and the price of a good or service.

**demand for money**   The amount of money that households desire to hold, expressed as a function of real GDP, the nominal interest rate, transaction costs, and other variables.

**depreciation**   The wearing out of capital goods over time.

**devaluation**   An action by the central bank that raises the number of units of a country's currency that exchange for other currencies.

**diffusion of technology**   Spread of technology from one country or region to another.

**diminishing average product of capital**   Tendency for the average product of capital to fall as capital per worker rises.

**diminishing marginal product of capital**   Tendency for the marginal product of capital to fall as capital per worker rises.

**diminishing marginal product of labor**   Tendency for the marginal product of labor to fall as the quantity of labor rises, for given capital input.

**discount factor**   The relative value of a dollar in different periods of time; for example, between one year and the next. The nominal discount factor is one plus the nominal interest rate.

**discounted**   Use of the discount factor to express future income or expenditure in units comparable to current income or expenditure.

**discouraged workers**   Workers who leave the labor force following a period of unemployment.

**discretionary policy**   A setup in which government policy is not restricted by prior commitments.

**disequilibrium**   Absence of equilibrium in a market; lack of market clearing.

**disposable personal income**   Personal income less taxes.

**double taxation**   Taxation of something twice. For example, corporate profits are taxed at the corporate level and then taxed again at the household level when paid out as dividends.

**duration of unemployment**   The length of time that a spell of unemployment is expected to last. The duration of unemployment is inversely related to the job-finding rate.

**economic fluctuations**    Variations in real GDP during a business cycle.

**economies of scale in cash management**    The property of the demand for money that the desired average real money-holding increases less than proportionately with a rise in real GDP.

**employment**    The number of persons working at jobs in the market sector.

**employment rate**    The ratio of employment to the labor force.

**endogenous growth theory**    Long-run economic growth that is explained by the interactions within a model.

**endogenous money**    The automatic response of the quantity of money to changes in the economy. Money is endogenous under the gold standard and in regimes in which the monetary authority targets nominal interest rates or the price level.

**endogenous variables**    Variables determined by the model.

**equilibrium**    Condition that determines quantities and prices in a market. *Quantity supplied equals quantity demanded* is an example of an equilibrium condition.

**equilibrium business-cycle model**    A model of economic fluctuations that uses equilibrium conditions to determine how shocks affect real GDP and other macroeconomic variables. In our model, supply and demand functions accord with microeconomic foundations. Given these functions, the key equilibrium conditions are that markets have to clear.

**exchange market**    Market in which the currency of one country is traded for that of another country.

**exchange rate**    The number of units of a country's currency that trades for one unit of another currency, such as the U.S. dollar. See *nominal exchange rate*.

**exogenous technological progress**    Improvements of technology that are not explained within the model.

**exogenous variables**    Variables that are not explained within the model.

**expectation of inflation**    Forecast of the inflation rate.

**expected real interest rate**    The real interest rate that is expected to be earned (or paid) after adjusting the nominal interest rate by the expectation of inflation.

**exports**    Goods and services produced by the residents of the home country that are sold to foreigners.

**Federal Funds market**    The market for very short-term borrowing and lending between financial institutions, such as commercial banks.

**Federal Funds rate**    The interest rate on loans made in the Federal Funds market.

**Federal Open-Market Committee (FOMC)**    A committee of the Federal Reserve that has responsibility for open-market operations.

**fiat money**    Money, such as paper currency, that has value due to government fiat, rather than intrinsic value, such as gold.

**finite horizon**    Finite planning period used by households in determining consumption, saving, and labor supply. See *infinite horizon*.

**fiscal policy**    The choice of government spending, taxes, and borrowing to influence the level of aggregate economic activity.

**fixed exchange rates**    Systems in which countries peg the exchange rate between their currency and other currencies, such as the U.S. dollar. Examples of fixed-exchange rate regimes are the gold standard, the Bretton Woods System, and a currency union.

**flat-rate tax**    A kind of income tax in which the amount of tax is a constant fraction of taxable income. See *graduated-rate tax*.

**flexible exchange rates**    Systems of international payments, prevalent since the early 1970s, in which countries allow the exchange rates for their currencies to fluctuate so as to clear the exchange market.

**flow variable**    A variable, such as real GDP or consumption, expressed per unit of time, such as a year.

**foreign direct investment**    Purchases of capital goods by home-country residents in foreign countries.

**fully funded system (for Social Security)**    A system in which each individual's payments accumulate in a trust fund, and retirement benefits are paid out of the accumulated funds. See *Social Security; pay-as-you-go system*.

**GDP**    Gross domestic product.

**GDP in constant dollars**    Gross domestic product expressed in terms of dollars from a base year. See real GDP.

**GDP in current dollars**    Gross domestic product expressed in current dollars. See nominal GDP.

**general equilibrium**    Clearing of all markets at the same time.

**general price level**    The dollar price per unit of goods and services. The average price of all goods and services.

**globalization**    The increased tendency for production and other economic activities to be carried out on a worldwide basis.

**GNP**  Gross national product.

**gold standard**  A system of international payments under which countries agree to buy or sell gold for a fixed amount of their currencies. The high point of this system was from 1890 to 1914.

**goods market**  A market in which goods and services are exchanged for money.

**governmental budget constraint**  The equation showing the balance between the government's sources and uses of funds.

**graduated-rate tax**  A kind of income tax in which the marginal tax rate rises with taxable income. See *flat-rate tax*.

**Great Depression**  The worldwide decline in aggregate economic activity in the United States and many other countries from 1929 to 1933.

**gross domestic product (GDP)**  The market value of an economy's domestically produced goods and services over a specified period of time, such as a year.

**gross investment**  Purchases of capital goods with no adjustment for the depreciation of the existing capital goods.

**gross national product (GNP)**  The total market value of the goods and services produced by the residents of a country over a specified period of time; GNP equals gross domestic product plus the net factor income from abroad.

**gross private domestic investment**  Total private expenditure on capital goods, including business spending on plant and equipment, the net change in business inventories, and residential construction. This total contains no adjustment for depreciation.

**gross state product (GSP)**  Gross domestic product for an individual state.

**growth accounting**  A formula that relates growth of real GDP to the growth of inputs, capital and labor, and to technological change.

**GSP**  Gross state product.

**help-wanted advertising**  Media advertising for job openings; used as a proxy for job vacancies.

**high-powered money**  The total amount of Federal Reserve notes (currency) and non-interest-bearing deposits (reserves) held at the Fed by depository institutions; the monetary base.

**household budget constraint in nominal terms**  The equation showing the balance between a household's sources and uses of funds. In this case, the equation is in nominal terms.

**household budget constraint in real terms**  The equation showing the balance between a household's sources and uses of funds. In this case, the equation is in real terms.

**human capital**  Skills and training that are embodied in workers and add to productivity.

**hyperinflation**  A sustained period with an extraordinarily high inflation rate, such as in Germany after World War I.

**imperfect competition**  A competitive environment in which each business has some pricing power. See *perfect competition*.

**implicit GDP deflator**  The price index that relates the gross domestic product, measured in nominal terms, to real GDP.

**imports**  Goods and services produced in foreign countries that are purchased by the residents of the home country.

**imputed rental income**  Rental income on capital, such as owner-occupied housing, that is not explicitly paid and received.

**income effect**  The effect of higher income on choices such as consumption and labor supply.

**indexation**  A system of contracts, such as for labor, in which payments are revised upward or downward automatically for increases or decreases in the general price level, so as to keep the real value of payments independent of inflation.

**indexed bonds**  Bonds on which the nominal payments of interest and principal are automatically adjusted for inflation to ensure a contracted real interest rate.

**inequality**  Differences in levels of real income across persons in an economy or across economies.

**infinite horizon**  Planning period of indefinite (infinite) length used by households in determining consumption, saving, and labor supply. See *finite horizon*.

**infinite-horizon budget constraint**  Budget constraint for a household over an infinite horizon.

**inflation rate**  The percentage change in a price index between two periods of time, such as from one year to the next.

**inflation targeting**  A regime for monetary policy in which the central bank adjusts nominal interest rates to achieve a target inflation rate.

**infrastructure capital**  Capital, often publicly owned, in the form of transportation, communications, energy and water provision, and so on.

**intellectual property rights**  Ownership rights in discoveries and ideas.

**interest rate**  The ratio of the interest payment to the amount borrowed; the return to lending or the cost of borrowing.

**interest-bearing assets**    Assets, such as bonds, that pay interest.

**interest-rate parity**    Equalization of interest rates across countries, adjusting for prospective changes in exchange rates.

**international reserves**    Assets, such as U.S. dollars and gold, that are commonly used for international transactions and as stores of value by central banks and other financial institutions.

**intertemporal-substitution effect**    The effect on current consumption (leisure) when the cost of future consumption (leisure) changes relative to that of current consumption (leisure).

**inventories**    Stores of commodities held by businesses either for sale or for use in production.

**involuntary unemployment**    The inability of workers to obtain employment at the prevailing market wage; a feature of Keynesian models.

**irrelevance result for systematic monetary policy**    The theoretical finding that a systematic policy of changing the quantity of money in response to the state of the economy is predictable and therefore powerless to affect real variables.

**job-finding rate**    The rate at which workers move from unemployment or outside of the labor force to employment.

**job-separation rate**    The rate at which workers move from employment to unemployment or outside of the labor force.

**labor force**    The total number of employed workers plus the number of unemployed.

**labor hoarding**    The tendency of firms to retain their workers during a recession. Labor hoarding may explain the tendency for measured labor productivity to fall during recessions and rise during booms.

**labor market**    The market on which workers sell, and producers buy, labor services.

**labor-force participation rate**    The fraction of the population (sometimes the noninstitutional population) that participates in the labor market.

**Laffer curve**    A graph showing that tax revenues initially rise as the marginal income tax rate rises, but eventually reach a maximum and subsequently decline with further increases in the marginal tax rate.

**law of one price**    The condition that identical goods in different places must sell at the same dollar price.

**legal tender**    A characteristic of money, whereby its use as a medium of exchange is reinforced by government statute.

**life-cycle model**    The theory of the choices of consumption and leisure that are made when the planning horizon equals an individual's expected remaining lifetime. The theory predicts that an individual will build up savings during working years and exhaust them during retirement years.

**Lucas hypothesis on monetary shocks**    The hypothesis that the effect of a given-size money shock on real GDP is larger, the less volatile money growth is historically.

**lump-sum tax**    A tax paid by an individual to the government in which the amount paid does not depend on any characteristic of the individual, such as income or wealth.

**lump-sum transfer**    A transfer payment from the government to an individual in which the amount paid does not depend on any characteristic of the recipient, such as income or wealth.

**M1**    The monetary aggregate that comprises currency held by the public, checkable deposits, and travelers' checks. M1 comprises the assets that serve regularly as media of exchange.

**M2**    M1 plus household holdings of savings deposits, small time deposits, and retail money-market mutual funds.

**marginal cost of production**    The added nominal cost to a producer from raising output by one unit.

**marginal product of capital (MPK)**    The increase in output from an increase in capital services by one unit, while holding fixed the technology and the quantity of labor.

**marginal product of labor (MPL)**    The increase in output from an increase in labor by one unit, while holding fixed the technology and the quantity of capital services.

**marginal tax rate**    The fraction of an additional dollar of income that must be paid as tax. In a graduated-rate system, this tax rate rises with the level of income. See *average tax rate*.

**market-clearing approach**    The viewpoint that prices, such as the wage rate, rental price, and general price level, are determined to clear markets.

**market-clearing condition**    Conditions that quantity supplied equal quantity demanded in a market.

**markup ratio**    In imperfect competition, the ratio of the price charged to the marginal cost of production.

**maturity**    The date at which a bond expires and its principal is repaid.

**medium of exchange**    A commodity or other item used as a means of payment; money.

**menu cost**   Cost that must be paid to adjust a nominal price or wage. New Keynesian models rely on these costs to rationalize the sluggish adjustment of prices.

**microeconomic foundations**   The microeconomic analysis of individual choices that underlies the macroeconomic model of the economy.

**monetary aggregate**   Total nominal quantity of a concept of money, such as the monetary base, M1, or M2.

**monetary approach to the balance of payments** Analyses of the balance of international payments and exchange rates that stress the nominal quantity of money and the demand for money in each country.

**monetary base**   Another name for high-powered money.

**monetary rule**   A regular procedure for altering the nominal quantity of money in response to developments in the macro economy.

**monetary shocks**   Unanticipated changes in the nominal quantity of money.

**money**   The usual means of payment or medium of exchange in an economy. Money also serves as a store of value. Money may take the form of paper currency, commodities, or deposits at financial institutions.

**money growth rate**   The proportionate change per year in the nominal quantity of money.

**MPK**   The marginal product of capital.

**MPL**   The marginal product of labor.

**multiplier**   The change in aggregate output per unit of increase in real aggregate demand. In Keynesian models, the multiplier can be greater than one.

**multi-year budget constraint**   The budget constraint for a household over more than one year.

**national income**   The income earned from aggregate production. National income equals gross domestic product less depreciation, which equals net domestic product.

**national-income accounting**   The summary statement of gross domestic product and its components during a year.

**national saving**   Total saving carried out by the residents of a country; the sum of private and public saving.

**natural unemployment rate**   The average unemployment rate that prevails in an economy in the long run. The unemployment rate tends to adjust over time toward the natural unemployment rate.

**NDP**   Net domestic product.

**neoclassical growth model**   A model of economic growth that extended the Solow growth model to allow for household choices of saving rates.

**net domestic product (NDP)**   Gross domestic product less depreciation.

**net exports**   The difference between the value of exports and the value of imports.

**net factor income from abroad**   Net income earned by the residents of a country from claims on foreign assets and from labor supplied to foreign countries.

**net foreign investment**   The change in a country's net holdings of foreign assets.

**net international investment position**   The stock of foreign claims held by home residents (including the home government) net of the stock of home claims held by foreign residents (including foreign governments).

**net investment**   The change in the capital stock; gross investment less depreciation.

**net private domestic investment**   Gross private domestic investment less depreciation.

**neutrality of money**   The theoretical finding that once-and-for-all changes in the nominal quantity of money affect nominal variables, such as the general price level, but do not affect real variables, such as real GDP.

**new Keynesian model**   Models that attempt to explain the role of sticky prices and aggregate demand in the Keynesian framework. These models incorporate imperfect competition and allow for menu costs of changing prices.

**nominal**   Measured in current dollar magnitudes; valued at current dollar prices; unadjusted for changes in the general price level.

**nominal exchange rate**   The exchange rate between one currency and another. See *real exchange rate*.

**nominal GDP**   Gross domestic product expressed in current dollars.

**nominal interest rate**   The amount paid as interest per dollar borrowed for each period; the rate at which nominal assets held as bonds grow over time.

**nominal rental price**   The nominal amount paid per year for each unit of capital used in production.

**nominal saving**   The current dollar value of real saving, calculated by multiplying real saving by a price index.

**nominal wage rate**   The nominal amount paid per year for each unit of labor used in production.

**non-rival good**   A good used by one household that does not reduce the quantity available for other households. An idea is an example of a non-rival good.

**non-tradable goods**   Goods and services, such as labor services and real estate, that do not enter readily into international trade.

**open economy**   An economy that conducts trade with the rest of the world.

**open-market operations**   The purchase or sale of government securities by the central bank in exchange for high-powered money.

**patent**   Property right over the use of an invention.

**pay-as-you-go system (for Social Security)**   A system in which benefits to retired persons are financed by taxes on the current working generation.

**perceived real wage rate**   The real wage rate as perceived by workers. In the price-misperceptions model, the perceived real wage rate is the ratio of the nominal wage rate to the expected price level.

**perfect competition**   Market setting in which each participant is sufficiently small to neglect any influence on the market price. A perfect competitor assumes that he or she can buy or sell any quantity desired at the market price.

**perfect foresight**   A situation in which expectations of inflation or of other variables are accurate, so that there are no forecast errors.

**permanent income**   Long-run average real income. The hypothetical amount of real income that, when received constantly throughout a household's planning horizon, has the same real present value as the actual flow of income.

**personal consumption expenditure**   Purchases of goods and services by households for use in consumption.

**personal income**   Income received directly by persons; national income adjusted for undistributed corporate profits, Social Security contributions, transfer payments, and some other items.

**planning horizon**   The number of years that enter into the household's plan for choosing consumption, saving, and labor supply.

**policy rule**   A rule or commitment for governmental actions with regard to money or other variables.

**population growth**   Increase over time in population.

**poverty**   An estimated level of real income required to pay for basic necessities of life.

**PPI**   Producer price index.

**PPP**   Purchasing-power parity

**present value**   The value of future dollar expenses or receipts, expressed in terms of current-dollar equivalents.

**price level**   Dollar price of a market basket of goods and services.

**price stability**   Rough constancy over time in the price level.

**price taker**   A participant in a market who regards the market price as given. See *perfect competition*.

**price-level targeting**   A rule for monetary policy that dictates maintenance of price stability.

**price-misperceptions model**   A model of economic fluctuations in which some participants incorrectly perceive the general price level. Money is not neutral in this model.

**principal of bond**   The dollar amount borrowed, to be repaid at maturity.

**procyclical**   Moving in the same direction as the business cycle; that is, with detrended real GDP.

**producer price index (PPI)**   A weighted average of prices of raw materials and semi-finished goods, measured relative to base-year prices.

**production function**   The relationship between the quantity of output and the quantities of inputs to production, such as labor and capital.

**productivity**   Output measured relative to quantities of inputs, such as labor.

**productivity slowdown**   A reduction in the rate of growth of output per worker, thought to have occurred in OECD countries after the early 1970s.

**profit**   The difference between revenue and costs for a firm.

**propensity to consume**   The response of real consumer expenditure to a rise in real income.

**propensity to save**   The response of real saving to a rise in real income.

**public debt**   The dollar stock of interest-bearing government bonds.

**public investment**   Investment by government in plant and equipment or in public infrastructure.

**purchasing-power parity (PPP)**   The condition that the exchange rate between the foreign and home currencies equals the ratio of prices of foreign goods to prices of home goods.

**quantity theory of money**   The theory that changes in the nominal quantity of money account for the bulk of long-run movements in the general price level. This theory usually assumes that money is neutral in the long run.

**quota**   A limitation on the quantity of goods that can be imported or exported.

**Ramsey model**   A form of the neoclassical growth model due to the economist Frank Ramsey.

**rate of economic growth**   Proportionate change per year in real GDP.

**rational expectations** The viewpoint that individuals make forecasts or estimates of unknown variables, such as the general price level, in the best possible manner, utilizing all information currently available.

**real business-cycle (RBC) model** A theory of economic fluctuations that relies on real disturbances rather than monetary shocks. The RBC model is a type of equilibrium business-cycle model.

**real demand for money** A function that determines the quantity of real money demanded.

**real disposable income** Income measured after taxes and in real terms.

**real exchange rate** The exchange rate between the foreign and home currencies divided by the ratio of the foreign price level to the home price level.

**real GDP** Real gross domestic product.

**real GNP** Real gross national product.

**real gross domestic product** The real value of the nominal gross domestic product.

**real gross national product** The real value of the gross national product.

**real interest rate** The nominal interest rate on a bond less the inflation rate. The rate at which the real value of dollar assets held as bonds grows over time.

**real rental price** The real value of the nominal rental price.

**real saving** The change in the real value of assets held by households or by the economy as a whole. The real value of nominal saving.

**real terms** Measured in units of goods; valued at base-year prices; dollar magnitudes adjusted for inflation by deflating by a price index.

**real wage rate** The real value of the nominal wage rate.

**recession** A period of decline in real GDP. A shortfall of real GDP from trend.

**relative form of PPP** The version of purchasing-power parity that involves changes in exchange rates and in the ratio of foreign to home prices.

**rental market** A market in which capital services are bought and sold at the rental price.

**rental price** The price charged per year for using a unit of capital.

**research and development (R&D)** Expenditure dedicated to discovery of new goods and improved methods of production.

**reservation real wage** The real wage rate that is just high enough to induce someone to accept a job.

**revaluation** An increase in the value of a country's currency in terms of another currency, such as the U.S. dollar.

**revenue from printing money** Revenue that the government obtains by printing paper currency.

**Ricardian equivalence theorem** The theoretical finding that, for given government purchases, an increase in current taxes has the same effect on the economy as an equal increase in the government budget deficit.

**risk premium** The higher rate of return required on risky assets, such as corporate stock, compared to safe assets.

**rival good** A good that, if used by one person, cannot be used by another person.

**saving** The change in a household's assets over a year. The difference between total income and consumption.

**seasonally adjusted data** Adjustment of economic variables, such as real GDP, for normal seasonal variations.

**shocks** Exogenous disturbances that affect the macro economy. A shift to the technology level is an example of a shock.

**Social Security** Transfer payments made by the government to households to cover old age pensions, survivors' benefits, and disability insurance.

**Solow growth model** A model of economic growth. Key elements are a production function with capital and labor inputs, the saving rate, the population growth rate, and the rate of technological progress.

**sources of funds** In a budget constraint for households or government, the sources of funds are initial assets and various types of income.

**standard deviation** A measure of the variability of a variable. The standard deviation is the square root of the variance. The variance is the average squared deviation from the mean.

**standard of living** Level of consumption that can be sustained, given a household's long-run income.

**steady state** A long-run situation in which variables such as capital per worker and real GDP per worker are not changing.

**steady-state growth** A long-run situation in which variables such as capital per worker and real GDP per worker are growing at a constant rate.

**sterilization** An action by the central bank that prevents increases (decreases) in the amount of international reserves from increasing (decreasing) the nominal quantity of money in the country.

**sticky nominal wage rates**   Sluggish adjustment of the nominal wage rate to changed conditions in the labor market. A characteristic of the Keynesian model.

**sticky prices**   Sluggish adjustment of goods prices to changed conditions in the goods market. A characteristic of the new Keynesian model.

**stock market**   A market on which households trade shares of ownership in firms. The owners of stock receive the dividends paid out by firms.

**stock variable**   A variable, such as capital or money, expressed in units of goods or dollar value. Stock variables do not have a dimension per unit of time. See *flow variable*.

**stores of value**   Forms of holding assets, such as bonds, money, and ownership of capital.

**strategic budget deficits**   Manipulation of budget deficits to influence choices made by future governmental regimes.

**subsistence level**   Standard of living regarded as the minimal requirement for sustaining life.

**supply curve**   A curve expressing the relation between the quantity supplied and the price of a good or service.

**surplus (deficit) on current account**   A positive (negative) current-account balance.

**tariff**   Tax levied on international trade, usually on imports.

**tax-rate smoothing**   Fiscal policy aimed at maintaining stable tax rates over time.

**technological progress**   Inventions and improved knowledge about methods of production that generate continuing upward shifts of the production function.

**technology level**   The level of the production function. A higher technology level means that real GDP is higher for given inputs of capital and labor.

**term structure of real interest rates**   The relation of real interest rates to the maturity of bonds.

**terms of trade**   The price of a country's produced tradable goods expressed relative to the price of the world's produced tradable goods.

**total hours worked**   Total worker-hours per year; the product of employment and average hours worked per year for each worker.

**trade balance**   The difference between the value of exports of goods and services and the value of imports of goods and services.

**transaction costs**   Costs incurred in the process of making sales or purchases, such as brokerage fees or the value of the time required.

**transfer payment**   Transfers of funds from government to individuals, such as welfare payments.

**transition path**   In a growth model, such as the Solow model, the path from the initial position to the steady-state position.

**trend real GDP**   The smooth part of the time series on real GDP. We view this trend as reflecting long-run economic growth, rather than economic fluctuations.

**twin deficits**   Simultaneous appearance of budget and current-account deficits.

**two-year budget constraint**   The budget constraint for a household over two years.

**unanticipated money growth**   The difference between actual money growth and anticipated money growth.

**unemployment**   The number of persons in the labor force (and, therefore, classified as seeking work) without a job.

**unemployment insurance**   The government program of providing temporary benefits to workers who have lost their jobs and are currently unemployed.

**unemployment rate**   The ratio of unemployment to the labor force.

**unexpected inflation**   The difference between the actual inflation rate and the expected inflation rate; the forecast error made in predicting inflation.

**user costs**   Additional costs incurred while using capital goods; for example, the costs of electric power, security services, and so on.

**uses of funds**   In a budget constraint for households or government, the uses of funds are expenditures on goods and services and final values of assets.

**utility**   The level of happiness of a household, measured in units called utils. Utility increases with increases in either consumption or leisure. See *utility function*.

**utility function**   The relationship between the amount of utility obtained and the amounts of consumption and labor chosen by the household.

**vacancies**   The difference between the number of job openings at firms and the level of employment.

**vacancy rate**   The ratio of vacancies to the total number of jobs that firms want occupied.

**value added**   The increase in value of a product at various stages of production.

**voluntary exchange**   Voluntary sales and purchases made at going prices.

**wage rate**   The dollar amount paid and received on the labor market for each hour of labor services.

**wholesale price index**   Another name for the producer price index.